D1447459

NEW ENGLAND'S MORAL LEGISLATOR

RELIGION IN NORTH AMERICA
Catherine L. Albanese and Stephen J. Stein,
EDITORS

New England's Moral Legislator

Timothy Dwight, 1752–1817

JOHN R. FITZMIER

Indiana University Press

BLOOMINGTON AND INDIANAPOLIS

This book is a publication of

Indiana University Press
601 North Morton Street
Bloomington, Indiana 47404-3797 USA

www.indiana.edu/~iupress

Telephone orders 800-842-6796
Fax orders 812-855-7931
Orders by email iuporder@indiana.edu

© 1998 by John R. Fitzmier

The paper used in this publication meets the minimum
requirements of American National Standard for Information
Sciences—Permanence of Paper for Printed Library
Materials, ANSI Z39.48-1984.

Manufactured in the United States of America

Library of Congress Cataloging-in-Publication Data

Fitzmier, John R.
  New England's moral legislator : Timothy Dwight
1752–1817 / John R. Fitzmier.
      p.   cm. — (Religion in North America)
  Includes bibliographical references (p.   ) and index.
  ISBN 0-253-33433-0 (cl : alk. paper)
  1. Dwight, Timothy, 1752–1817. 2. Congregational churches—United
States—Clergy—Biography. 3. Theologians—United States—Biography
  I. Title. II. Series.
BX7260.D84F57   1998
285.8'092—dc21
[B]   98-22498

1 2 3 4 5 03 02 01 00 99 98

To M.M.F.

Contents

Foreword

Timothy Dwight—grandson of Jonathan Edwards, Congregational minister, literary figure, president of Yale College—was in the public eye much of his adult life. Therefore it is not surprising that scholars continue to find him a key figure as they seek the pulse of elite New England Anglo-American culture in the post-Revolutionary and early national eras. John R. Fitzmier joins others engaged with that effort in this perceptive and wide-ranging analysis of Dwight's life and religious system. Fitzmier's research exploits the full range of Dwight's written corpus, including his strictly theological writings as well as his sermons, poetry, and occasional literature. In addition, he adds significantly to our understanding of Dwight as a person—in particular, Dwight as a visually impaired individual.

This volume is intellectual biography and more. Fitzmier examines the major contributions for which Dwight was hailed as a religious leader of New England society through a focused investigation of his roles as preacher, theologian, and historian. In each of these areas of endeavor Dwight managed to provoke responses from his contemporaries, and in doing so to achieve considerable reputation among both admirers and opponents. But Fitzmier's insights carry beyond a functional analysis of these multiple areas of activity, for he recognizes that it was Dwight's religious system that served as the integrator of his life, a system aptly called by Fitzmier "Godly Federalism." Dwight's sermons, warm and extemporaneous, sounded the theme of Christian duty. His theological writings, systematized from his preaching, stressed the importance of moral action and engagement in activity as the means to grace. His writings concerned with "holy history," or what his grandfather Edwards called the "work of redemption," repeatedly focused on the place of practical moralism in the life of the young American nation.

For Fitzmier, therefore, Dwight was New England's consummate moralist, both with respect to individual morality and to the public concerns of church and state. Much of his moralism was responsive to the shaping forces of his day. The democratic thrust in the young nation moved Dwight toward an ever more rigid political Federalism. The threat, real or imagined, of infidelity in the form of deism and Enlightenment rationalism moved him into the camp of Scottish Common Sense philosophy. The military conflicts during his lifetime confirmed his confidence in a patriotic Americanism. Yet none of these elements in Dwight's "Godly Federalism" changed the fact that his old-fashioned moralism was out of step with his times; culturally speaking, his cultural conservatism was a failed project.

Fitzmier's portrait will do little to endear Dwight as an individual to the reader, for this major figure in New England's history was often aloof, complex, and opportunistic. We do learn, however, important new information about his personal circumstances that may produce a kind of grudging admiration for someone who managed to achieve so much despite a serious visual handicap. Throughout his adult life Dwight's eyesight was badly impaired, and it appears that he was functionally blind. As a result, he took certain compensatory steps to deal with the wide range of his responsibilities. Fitzmier is the first historian to recognize the severity of this problem and to recast the story of Dwight's accomplishments in this context. This biographical insight does not change the outcome of the story, but it does cast Dwight's achievements in a different light. It assists, for example, in understanding the reasons for his distinctive homiletical patterns, the oral character of his systematic theological writings, and his characteristic way of handling sources in his publications. Reconstructing Dwight's private or intimate history throughout his long career has always been especially difficult because of the lack of personal materials dealing with his life. For that reason Fitzmier's careful and creative reading of Dwight's published writings—all of those writings—is the more important. He has been highly successful in that task.

One of Fitzmier's specific achievements in this volume is his careful positioning of Dwight in the world of the Edwardsians, that theological tradition constructed by the disciples of his grandfather Jonathan Edwards and their nineteenth-century successors. From early childhood on, Dwight was deeply influenced by the shadow of his grandfather, and yet he moved away from Edwards in significant ways. He took his place alongside other nineteenth-century evangelicals who were shifting the theological focus of evangelicalism. He patterned his life and work after Edwards, but the circumstances of the Second Great Awakening, to which Dwight was a major contributor in its New England manifestations, were different from those of the 1740s and 1750s.

In this volume Fitzmier rises above the partisan views of earlier interpreters of Dwight. He presents a sympathetic, yet critical, analysis of one of the most conspicuous New Englanders in the early nineteenth century. And he shows how Dwight's essentially conservative "Godly Federalism" distanced him from the new spirit of his times and his culture. In sum, this study of a leading religious and cultural figure, who was equally at home speculating on America's millennial role and commenting on the New England countryside, has value for more than simply historians of American religion. For Fitzmier's analysis sheds light on the development of ethics, rhetoric, belles-lettres, and theology in early America.

Catherine L. Albanese
Stephen J. Stein, Series Editors

ACKNOWLEDGMENTS

This project began as a doctoral dissertation and took an unusually long time to mature into a book. At the dissertation stage a number of my teachers offered patient and sagacious guidance: Albert Raboteau, the late Paul Ramsey, John Murrin, and Henry Bowden. I am also grateful to Jeffrey Stout who, in a wonderful teaching moment, suggested I do more with my nascent notion of "Godly Federalism." John Wilson asked me the most probing and troubling question at the defense: "Jack, what do you make of Dwight's eyesight?" John has been a model dissertation adviser, a fine professional mentor, and a faithful friend. Hopefully, this book testifies to his unique capacity to inspire his students.

Colleagues at the Vanderbilt University Divinity School have also been supportive, especially Howard Harrod, Doug Knight, and Dale Johnson (fond of asking "What is the problem?"). Another group of professional associates, friends, and family members deserve special thanks as well: Stephen Crocco, Fitz Conner, Carol Fitzmier, Donald Lankiewicz, Susie and Chap Hutcheson, Randall Balmer, Mark Noll, Anne Horan, Stephen Stein, Catherine Albanese, Roberta Diehl, and Robert Sloan. When my enthusiasm flagged, they cheerfully provided the sorts of challenges and encouragement, in conversation and in writing, that buoyed my confidence.

The staffs of the Connecticut Historical Society and the Yale University Art Gallery were very helpful in my search for extant portraits of Dwight. Librarians at Princeton University and Yale University offered access to their rich resources, as did William Hook, Anne Womack, and the staffs at the Divinity and Heard Libraries at Vanderbilt University. During my summer retreats from administrative duties at Vanderbilt, the staffs of Louisville Presbyterian Theological Seminary and Columbia Theological Seminary, especially Joe Coalter and James Hudnut-Beumler, were perfectly hospitable and gracious. Most helpful of all were my research assistants, Douglas Sweeney, Suzette Lemrow, and Gary Reyes. Blessed with keen eyes, solid editorial skills, wonderful patience, and plenty of good will, they have become valued interlocutors and friends.

Over the years, and especially in recent months, my family has often asked me how "T.D." was coming along. Sometimes their question was met with something less than they had hoped to hear—sighs and grumbles. At other times they got more more than they bargained for—long soliloquies about some new puzzle, discovery, or insight. Though they tolerated my grousing and listened patiently to my explanations, what they really wanted to hear was that "T.D." was finally finished. Now it is. Dan and Kate are relieved. So am I. And so is Martha, to whom this book is dedicated.

New England's Moral Legislator

A Problem of Lights and Shades

> Was not this greatness?—not the greatness of
> genius, for after all Dr. Dwight was only a man
> of large common sense and a large heart,
> inspired by high moral principles. He was, in
> fact, a Yankee, Christian gentleman—nothing
> more, nothing less. Where could such a
> character—with such lights and shades—be
> produced, except here in our stern, yet kindly
> climate of New England?
>
> —S. G. Goodrich

One of my colleagues is fond of pressing his neophyte students with a series of rapid-fire queries: "What is the problem? What is the matter? What is the issue?" His auditors are often at first repelled by these questions because they know so little about the activity in which they are engaged. Inevitably, they take the questions personally, but in the wrong way: "Does this professor think that *I* have a problem? That something is the matter with *me?*" What their history professor wants of them is personal but has little to do with character, vice, or virtue. He is asking them to engage in personal intellectual reflection. He is urging them to formulate and articulate the problems that attend their ventures into historical interpretation. He is requiring, even demanding, that they explain what they want to do, why it is worth doing, and how they plan to do it.

For several years now, "What is the problem?" has plagued my work with Timothy Dwight. This project began as a doctoral dissertation—a discrete assignment that stood at the end of a clearly defined graduate curriculum in American religious history. The dissertation met the requirements for that assignment, but like most newly completed dissertations, it was not yet a book. Although it argued that some interpretations of certain elements of Dwight's life were inadequate, it struggled—with only modest success—to provide a comprehensive, alternate interpretation of his life and his meaning to America. It was, I realized, a prolegomenon to a more thorough treatment. Happily employed at an institution that valued scholarship, I began what I took to be the straightforward process of revision and expansion. To my dismay, every effort suggested that some larger and more comprehensive transformation of the project was necessary. So I began additional research. I did more careful investigation into the details of Timothy Dwight's life; I re-read major sections of his works; I scoured the secondary literature in search of hints, traces, or ideas that might move the project and my thinking forward. Notwithstanding all these efforts, larger interpretive patterns remained elusive.

This reengagement of the material proved both frustrating and revelatory: frustrating, because there is a cacophany of voices speaking about the several aspects of Dwight's life and writings; revelatory, because amid the clamor of secondary interpretations of Dwight, the central problem of this study finally manifested itself. In short, while we know a good deal about each of Dwight's several professional interests and activities, we know precious little about him. For a historian, then, the problem (the matter, the issue) becomes the attempt to discover the single person, the individual human being, who did all these things. It is the challenge of providing a biography of a complex and busy person whose various activities have been examined but whose life has been largely ignored. This Introduction sets the stage for my attempt to provide students of American history with that sort of wholistic biography. It begins with a brief introduction of Timothy Dwight and a statement about his prominence in the affairs of his day. It then develops five critical interpretive problems to which any Dwight biographer must attend. The Introduction concludes with a preview of and rationale for the following chapters.

Samuel Griswold Goodrich, better known to the nineteenth century as the creator of the enormously successful Peter Parley children's tales, published the details of his life in a rambling, two-volume autobiography entitled *Recollections of a Lifetime*. He tells the story of a visit to New Haven in 1809, when he was fifteen years old. It was "a sort of Jerusalem in my imagination—a holy place, containing Yale College, of which Dr. Dwight was president." Dwight "was then at the zenith of his fame—a popular poet, an eloquent divine, a learned author, and, crowning all, president of the college." Happily, young Goodrich's pilgrimage fulfilled his expectations. He heard Dwight, "second only to St. Paul" among preachers, deliver a sermon in the college chapel and later met him at a social gathering where, to Goodrich's delight, he discovered the great man "even more distinguished in conversation than in the pulpit." Little wonder that Goodrich would conclude that Dwight "was unquestionably, at that time, the most conspicuous man in New England, filling a larger space in the public eye and exerting a greater influence than any other individual."[1] Although Goodrich's assessment may seem partisan, hyperbolic, even hagiographic in retrospect, his appreciation of Dwight is based on a fairly accurate interpretation of the data. Despite different, even contrary judgments about Dwight's significance (many of which will be examined in the course of this volume), the present study is grounded on the belief that Dwight did stand as one of the most "conspicuous" New Englanders of the early national era. Two bodies of evidence help to establish this claim at the outset: Dwight's prominence in the institutions and affairs of his era and Dwight's remarkable literary corpus.

Dwight was one of the colonies' most promising young men. He was the grandson of Jonathan Edwards, the scion of the Dwight clan of the Connecticut Valley, and the youngest member of Yale's class of 1769. At age 18 he was appointed a Yale tutor, and soon helped to begin the Connecticut Wits, a group of prominent colonial poets including Joel Barlow and John Trumbull. He left Yale to become a military chaplain during the Revolution, spent five years as a gentleman farmer in Northampton, began publishing poetry, was twice elected to the Massachusetts Assembly, and in 1783 was ordained and installed as the pastor of the church at Greenfield, Connecticut. From there his regional prominence grew even further. He began a highly successful grammar school in Greenfield, continued writing religious and patriotic verse, and began preaching what would later become a massive, popular systematic theology. In 1795 Dwight was elected president of Yale. Already an accomplished poet, educator, minister, and keen observer of the American scene, Dwight began a presidential tenure that would extend for over two decades, during which he would train an army of young professionals whose service to the nation would continue until well after the Civil War. His vocational accomplishments alone, then, establish Dwight as a major figure in early national America.

Dwight's writings, both published and in manuscript, are further verification of his status as a leading American. Though it would be difficult to make a determinative judgment, Dwight likely published a larger and more diverse body of writings than any other New England religious figure of his generation. His major poems, *America: or, A Poem on the Settlement of the British Colonies*, *The Conquest of Canaan*, *The Triumph of Infidelity*, and *Greenfield Hill*, fill a one-volume modern facsimile edition. His minor poems, though never collected, would also fill a sizable volume.[2] Though many Americans first learned of Dwight through his poetry, especially during the first half of his public career, his national reputation was more firmly established by his endeavors as a Congregational clergyman and teacher. The corpus of his theological work, comprised almost entirely of sermons, is quite large. *Theology, Explained and Defended*, a four-volume collection of one hundred and seventy-three sermons, functioned as a systematic theology and went through twelve editions in the United States alone. Scores of other pulpit addresses on topics as diverse as foreign missions, the French Revolution, the character of George Washington, and the evils of duelling were published separately. Sixty-one of these occasional addresses made their way into a two-volume set entitled *Sermons by Timothy Dwight*.[3]

Dwight had a keen eye for politics. Though he never ran for office after he left the Massachusetts Assembly, he was active behind the scenes in Connecticut affairs, advising and scheming with his political friends. He was as loyal and outspoken a Federalist as Connecticut could ever claim, and several of his publications reveal a good deal about his political convictions: "Farmer Johnson's Political Catechism," a newspaper series published in the *Mercury and New-England Palladium, Remarks on the Review of Inchiquin's Letters*, a response to an English attack on American culture, and *Decisions of Questions Discussed by the Senior Class in Yale College, in 1813 and 1814*, which contains Dwight's comments to his senior class on a host of important questions, ranging from "Ought Representatives to be bound by the will of their Constituents?" to "Which have the greatest influence in forming a National Character: Moral or Physical Causes?"[4] In addition to these collections of verse, sermons, and political commentary, Dwight also published one of the nation's earliest travelogues. An inveterate peripatetic, Dwight took extended tours throughout the Northeast. He compiled notes about local history and customs, described scenic vistas, and made extended comments on religion and morals in both settled and frontier areas. The resultant four-volume collection of observations appeared posthumously in 1822 as *Travels in New England and New York*. In addition to being a useful source of information about early national New England, *Travels* serves as a treasure trove of Dwight's historical reflections, political commitments, and cultural attitudes.[5]

Given his professional accomplishments and the visibility of his literary efforts in New England, Dwight should be acknowledged as one of the most important men of his day. Yet interpretations of his life and work—be they sympathetic, indifferent, or hostile—often leave the reader with a sense of incompleteness or ambiguity, as if there existed some fundamental lack of vocational integrity in Dwight. We see pieces of the man, but not a person; activities, but not a life. Although a number of factors account for this apparent inability to imagine a single life of Dwight, the difficulties can be organized under five rubrics or interpretive problems.

A Dearth of Personal Sources

First among the difficulties one faces in attempting to reconstruct Dwight's life is the absence of personal sources of information. Although his literary corpus is quite large, few of the materials in that corpus address Dwight's personal situation. It is rather easy to construct the chronological narrative of Dwight's career, but more difficult to discover what sort of a person he was. He left no diary, compiled no set of private notes on his studies, and the few manuscript letters that survive give only scant hints about his private life. Most often, we experience Dwight through the eyes of others—opponents, colleagues, and students—few of whom can be classed as unbiased or objective onlookers. These sources, while not abundant, are sufficient to allow for the construction of the basic outlines of Dwight's biography. The composite image that emerges reveals Dwight as an intelligent, aggressive, and ambitious man of intense feeling. Plagued by ill health and depression during a critical period of his adolescence, he determined to become an accomplished scholar, a great man, and nearly ruined his eyes in the process. During the remainder of his life he struggled with eyesight so poor that at points he was functionally blind.

Nor were his family circumstances easy. His distant relationship with his father ended after the senior Dwight, a quiet but determined loyalist, fled Northampton and the Revolution and died while seeking refuge on the banks of the Mississippi near Natchez. Dwight's relationship with his mother was more important and intimate, but it too was complicated by strong conviction and calamity. Dwight's mother was the fourth daughter of Jonathan and Sarah Edwards and the only member of the Edwards family to remain in Northampton after Edwards's dismissal in 1750. Forever bitter over that event, Mary Edwards Dwight taught young Timothy to view her father as a worthy exemplar, a martyr to the forces of congregational polity and democracy run amok. Although one student admirer claimed that Dwight was "by nature a proud and ambitious man, loving greatly distinction and influence, and claiming superiority above others," he had to compete for recognition in a family full of famous figures, both dead and living.[6] In addition to the ghost of grandfather Edwards, Dwight had to contend with an impressive and contentious group of living relatives. Three of his uncles were prominent in public affairs: Jonathan Edwards, Jr., was a distinguished pastor and theologian; Aaron Burr, Sr. was president of Princeton; and Pierpont Edwards was an active leader of Connecticut's Republican party. Family members of his own generation—his brother Theodore, of Hartford Convention fame, and his cousin, the enigmatic Aaron Burr, Jr., Vice President of the United States—were also notable public figures. That Dwight excelled in a family rife with achievers bespeaks of his strong ego, his native intelligence, and his diligence. Nonetheless, though we can recite his impressive achievements—Yale tutor, Connecticut Wit, Revolutionary chaplain, Greenfield pastor, Yale president, evangelist, social reformer, nemesis of infidelity—the narrative remains impersonal. We can guess what Dwight thought about his vocation and his role in New England, but our guessing must remain just that—speculative, conjectural, and, ultimately, tentative.

Change over Time

The problem of time and, specifically, the ways in which Dwight changed over time, poses a second interpretive problem. Dwight's public career can be said to have begun in 1772 with his first publication, *A Dissertation on the History, Eloquence, and Poetry of the Bible,* and continued until his death as president of Yale in 1817. This forty-five year period was one of the most critical in American history. Years of contention with England culminated in the Declaration of Independence, the Revolutionary war was fought and won, the Constitution was conceived and ratified, western migration began, the Jeffersonians triumphed over the Federalists, and in the New England states, established religions met their demise. Although Dwight has often been typecast as an intractable, conservative zealot, his views developed over time. Perhaps the best illustration of this can be seen in his emerging understanding of the Revolution and democracy. In this connection, Dwight's poetry can be read as an American variant of British Opposition verse, which had its roots in British Country ideology. Echoing Country thinkers, young Dwight mistrusted powerful central governments and instead preferred political authority to be local and regional. But like many of the Revolutionary generation, Dwight became suspicious of democracy. In mid-career, he fled to the Federalists, a collection of early national aristocrats that looked more like an elite Court alliance of central government advocates than it did a collection of Country ideologues.

Given these shifts over time, in which published tracts does one begin searching for Dwight? In his *America: or a Poem on the Settlement of the British Colonies* (1780), which exults in the millennial prospects of the new nation? In his *The Duty of Americans at the Present Crisis* (1798), which represents his most shrill warning about the contagion of French infidelity? Or in his *Sermon Delivered in Boston . . . before the American Board of Commissioners of Foreign Missions* (1813), in which the commonsensical, reserved, evangelistic Dwight seems to be dominant? Does one think of Dwight as a progressive *belles lettrist,* Yale's young tutor seeking to establish Lord Kames's *Elements of Style* in Yale's curriculum? Or as a defender of all things American in his 1813 tract *Remarks on the Review of Inchiquin's Letters*? Do we begin with Dwight the Revolutionary chaplain whose dread of warfare was finally overcome by his sense of British injustice? Or with Dwight the Old-School Federalist who managed Yale

College as if he owned it? Born in an era of change, Timothy Dwight was a man of change, and that change makes an appraisal of his life so much the more difficult.

A History of Partisan Interpretation

A third problem plagues the interpretive literature on Dwight. Despite the fact that little is known about his personal life and about how he developed and changed over time, few people, either in his day or since, have been dispassionate about him. Somehow, Timothy Dwight has managed to become one of the most loved and most loathed characters of the American past. So many are the interpreters who either praise or disdain Dwight, in fact, that a truly even-handed treatment is both rare and refreshing.

Ezra Stiles, Dwight's predecessor in the presidency of Yale College, believed that Dwight was "certainly an honor to Yale College," despite his "disposition . . . to struggle for preheminence [sic]."[7] Stiles had the grace to make such a charge privately, but other men opposed Dwight more openly. When Dwight became president of Yale he was already known as a vocal apologist for Connecticut's Federalist Standing Order. His new prominence made him an easy target, prompting his political opponents to turn satire and invective against him. John C. Ogden claimed that Dwight was "constitutionally zealous, obstinate, busy, ready at inventing, unalterable—a divine, a poet, eloquent, talkative, and undaunted, he wants all meekness, patience, vigilance." With other antagonists he feared that Dwight's political leverage extended beyond Yale students to elected officials, all of whom apparently believed that Dwight held "the keys which command their political damnation or salvation."[8] Indeed, it is Ogden who used, perhaps for the first time, the oft-cited allusion to Dwight's influence in Connecticut being as extensive as the Pope's was in Rome.[9] Dwight's allies, however, were as free with commendation as were his enemies with denunciation. Yale graduates published a plethora of eulogies in the months following his death, all of which, not surprisingly, are full of the highest praise.[10] Dwight's sons, who published a memoir in *Theology, Explained and Defended,* there proclaimed him a "father of New England— her moral legislator."[11] More prominent New Englanders shared these sentiments. Two of the most important to Yale and New Haven, Lyman Beecher and Nathaniel W. Taylor, were profuse in their affection and praise of their beloved teacher. Upon hearing of Dwight's death in 1817, Beecher exclaimed from his pulpit, "Dr. Dwight is gone! . . . My father! My father!" Taylor, ever more reserved and coolly intellectual, wrote a eulogy in which he claimed that Dwight held "a place scarcely second to any of his contemporaries" in "original powers, mental acquisitions and especially elegant literature."[12]

Dwight's contemporaries were polarized in their assessments of him, and twentieth-century historians have continued this pattern of partisan reaction. Vernon Louis Parrington, for example, viewed Dwight with open disdain. Dwight's mind, he quipped, was "closed as tight as his study windows in January." Dwight and his Federalist allies "would not open the door to the nineteenth century." The notion that Dwight was an interesting anachronism—Clinton Rossiter claimed that he "should have been born in 1652 rather than 1752"—perhaps led to Richard Hofstadter's belief that Dwight typified the "paranoid style in American politics." Other historians have attempted to polish Dwight's tarnished image. Charles Cuningham, author of the most complete twentieth-century biography of Dwight, insisted that his stature equaled, if not surpassed, that of Jonathan Edwards. Stephen Berk, who was particularly interested in Dwight's religious thought, claimed that by 1817 Dwight was the "foremost advocate of New England orthodoxy," whose theological system "set the standard for nineteenth-century Protestant Evangelicalism." It seems that historians of every stripe have found in Dwight a convenient primary source. He has become a whipping boy for progressives and a folk hero for American conservatives.[13]

Visual Impairment

To the problems of sources, historical context, and partisan interpretation, we must add a fourth difficulty that faces students of Dwight's life, namely, his poor eyesight or, more accurately, his periods of functional blindness. Nearly every account of Dwight notes in passing that he suffered from a "weakness of the eyes." Although no one has ever proposed a technical medical diagnosis of Dwight's condition, the most authoritative source of biographical information suggests that his vision permanently deteriorated after he received a smallpox inoculation. As one of Dwight's admirers noted, "Before he was entirely recovered from the effects of that disease, he injured his eyes in some degree, by too early and too great use of them, though not very seriously."[14] This sympathetic contemporary is guilty of two errors—one of omission, another of commission. He omits to mention that the "too early and too great use" of Dwight's eyes occurred during a phase of his life when he was contending with deep religious anxiety, severe asceticism, and resultant ill health. Something like a nervous breakdown, not merely a bout with the smallpox, occasioned Dwight's loss of sight. The admirer's error of commission lies in his careful discounting of the loss—Dwight injured his eyes "though not very seriously." While our author would have us believe that Dwight's vision was only slightly affected during this episode, the fact is that soon after his twentieth year, his eyes were permanently impaired.

The extent of his visual disability seems to have varied considerably. At the time of the initial trauma, he was said to have gone days at a time without any sight whatever. Although he was able to navigate his Yale environs without help, could apparently recognize people with no difficulty, and was able to enjoy scenic views on his journeys, Dwight experienced episodes of near blindness throughout his life. By his own account, his condition hindered his ability to read for any length of time, it made writing difficult, and at times these problems combined to make his responses to letters embarrassingly slow.[15] After his death Dwight's sons spoke freely about the physical pain that accompanied his temporary bouts of blindness and also his fear that his condition would grow progressively worse and eventually leave him totally blind. During his periodic seasons of limited vision, Dwight would become "greatly alarmed, with the symptom of an approaching *gutta serena*. Repeatedly the pressure on the brain was so great as to produce momentary blindness, and obviously to threaten apoplexy. Occurring for weeks together the anguish of his eyes was so intense, that it required powerful exertion to draw off his mind to any other object."[16]

Dwight's only extended public description of his visual disability appears in an article he wrote near the end of his life. Entitled "Observations on Light" and published in the *Memoirs of the Connecticut Academy of Arts and Sciences*, the essay offers Dwight's rather fanciful analysis of how light enters the eye and is processed by the brain.[17] Notwithstanding its pseudoscientific, amateurish character, the essay yields several interesting insights into the ways in which Dwight experienced and compensated for his problem.

Dr. Anne Horan, Instructor in Ophthalmology at Vanderbilt University School of Medicine, based on my description of Dwight's condition and on her reading of Dwight's "Observations," speculates that Dwight probably suffered from moderate to high myopia, that he most likely experienced severe ocular migraine headaches, and that his condition might have been considerably helped by the use of eyeglasses. Dr. Horan also described some of the psychological patterns and coping strategies that are not uncommon among adolescents who lose partial or total vision. Some young people in these circumstances use their eye problems to excuse their failure to perform well. Others develop what is called "functional blindness"—a condition that occurs when a person has the physical ability to see (i.e., their eyes function properly) but report that they are blind. Still others allow their condition to develop into unhealthy social patterns—petulance, manipulation of others, and an unusually high need to control their circumstances. Finally, it is interesting to note that Dwight described perfectly what modern physicians call "ocular digital reflex," which both seeing and blind persons experience. He reported that when he pressed on his closed eyes with his fingers, "the whole field of vision becomes instantaneously luminous and bright; resembling in appearance a circular, polished plate of silver; covered with small drops of water, glittering with its lustre."[18] Some visually impaired individuals use this technique to meet their need for visual stimulation, and Dwight seems to have done so regularly. While it would be incorrect to say that Dwight perfectly conformed to the problematic psychological patterns Dr. Horan described, these attitudes and behaviors appear throughout the materials that treat his life.

The first significant consequence of Dwight's disability has to do with his reading habits. At a number of places in the secondary literature one can find a commentator expressing dissatisfaction with Dwight's work: he failed to give a careful, detailed, and accurate description of a theological or philosophical position he criticized; he was apparently unaware of important developments in a discipline about which he spoke; he insisted that things were simpler than they really were; his ideas were not creative but borrowed and derivative. As Noah Porter summarized it, Dwight was "far more distinguished for clearness of method in presenting the thoughts of others than for any special subtlety of analysis or profoundness of principles of his own."[19] These observations, while certainly plausible, might lead to the conclusion that Dwight was intellectually simplistic, careless, or even arrogant. The facts, however, lead to another conclusion altogether. Because he could not read Dwight was prevented from learning the nuances and subtleties that could only come from carefully studying a text. He did not treat complex philosophical or theological arguments in depth because he rarely studied with care the work of the authors he cited, approved, or rejected. Making the best of a bad situation, Dwight relied on brief summaries of texts that he could read, or on amanuenses who undoubtedly read materials to him.[20] Although he compensated for his disability in a number of ways (he wore eyeglasses, for instance), the use of personal secretaries had an enormous impact on Dwight's writings and must be taken into account in any consideration of his work.

Dwight's first experiments with amanuenses were apparently so successful that he increasingly came to rely on their services. Prior to the start of his presidency and in the first decade of his presidential tenure, he used friends and volunteers in this role. But in 1805 the Yale Corporation granted him a stipend to hire students to serve in this capacity and the arrangement suited him perfectly. It allowed him to work closely with some of Yale's best students (to be chosen Dr. Dwight's personal secretary was a distinct honor) and his productivity soared.[21] Indeed, Dwight became so accomplished at dictation that, according to one of his young protégés, he could simultaneously keep two amanuenses busy on two different projects.[22] Although Dwight's use of secretaries afforded him a number of professional benefits, its chief significance lies elsewhere. The amanuenses left their tracks throughout the Dwight literary corpus and their trail cannot be overlooked. Here, two antebellum writers are instructive.

The first is Abel Stevens, who wrote an effusive commemoration of Dwight's character—a full thirty years after Dwight's demise—under the guise of a "review" of *Theology* for the *Methodist Quarterly Review* in 1847. Stevens noted that while the author of *Theology* displayed "high powers of discrimination" and "bold and powerful reasoning," his style was "sometimes rather diffuse." The second writer is Rufus Griswold, who edited *The Prose Writers of America* in 1851. In a brief literary biography that introduces a collection of Dwight's prose works, Griswold claimed that "the style of Dr. Dwight is fluent, graceful, picturesque and glowing; but diffuse. The erasure of redundancies would render it much more vigorous and attractive. . .[H]ardly a discourse, or essay or letter can be pointed to in all his works the effect of which is not injured by superfluous epithets."[23] Though these citations may seem rather curious at first blush, a modern reader of Dwight's prose will concur almost immediately with these assessments. Dwight's prose does have a curious character. It is overpunctuated, repetitive, diffuse, and moves with a cadence that seems almost mechanical. The reason for this odd effect is simple: Dwight's major works—certainly *Theology, Sermons,* and perhaps even the *Travels*—were not originally put forth in written form. Rather, they were oral productions designed specifically for aural reception. Indeed, some of Dwight's most famous sermons were dictated to an amanuensis either prior to or after they were preached. Benja-min Silliman, Dwight protégé and Yale faculty member, recalls that because of "the weakness of his eyes, [Dwight] was compelled to dictate most of his writings. Even his great theological work was put on paper by the hand of an amanuensis."[24]

The oral character of Dwight's "writings" and the circumstances of their production imply several pertinent points. First, Dwight's preaching really was extempore. Though this style certainly made positive impressions on his student auditors—who greatly preferred his discursive, fluid manner to "metaphysical" lectures that would have to be read—Dwight's adoption of extempore address was something of a marriage of convenience. His Scottish homiletic mentors, George Campbell and Hugh Blair, taught him to eschew "read sermons" on theological grounds. But Dwight was also incapable of reading for any extended period of time. Hence, for both philosophical and physical reasons, Dwight adopted the extempore style. Although Dwight may have deserved his reputation as one of the nineteenth century's greatest pulpit orators, his success resulted in part from his capacity to overcome a strictly physical limitation.

Second, any study of Dwight's prose must operate with an understanding of its oral/aural character. A sermon included in *Theology* or a letter in *Travels* was originally a spoken production and is best understood when heard rather than read. This feature helps to explain the overuse of commas, for instance, which most probably served as the functional equivalent of "breath marks." Moreover, in the case of sermons that were given on several different occasions, as was the case with the addresses in *Theology,* it is certain that the addresses changed over time. Dwight probably used the same scripture text, doctrine, and central points each time he preached a particular sermon (indeed, he may have taken a brief outline into the pulpit with him), but he likely changed his illustrations and applications to fit the occasion. Doubtless he had the overall structure of *Theology* in mind from the Greenfield days, but each sermon in the series, to some extent, had a life of its own. This feature of *Theology* gives rise to a third point, namely, the problem of dating some of Dwight's materials. Many of Dwight's sermons were delivered on specific public occasions that are noted in the titles of published versions of the sermons. Moreover, dates are written on the covers of manuscript sermons that remain unpublished, as well as on the booklets that contain the records of his *Travels* journeys. The important theological sermons contained in *Theology,* however, are impossible to date with any accuracy. These sermons may or may not be a verbatim report of what Dwight said in the pulpit, and they may or may not be the same sermons he preached when he began the series during his Greenfield pastorate. Dwight, with the help of his student secretaries, may have edited or redictated the sermons that comprise *Theology.* Hence, Dwight may have undergone substantive theological changes between the 1780s and the 1810s that are difficult or impossible to discern by use of *Theology* alone.

Disciplinary Boundaries of the Modern Academy

The foregoing interpretive difficulties concern Dwight and his circumstances—his biography, his development, his friends and enemies, his periods of sightlessness. As one contemplates constructing a life of Dwight, an additional interpretive challenge lies in the manner in which modern historians have approached him as a subject of scholarly interest. Although scholars have done a good deal of work on individual aspects and themes of Dwight's career, their research has been limited and circumscribed by the disciplinary boundaries that exist in the academic world. Hence, we know something of Dwight as poet, as author of *Travels,* as theologian, or as pedagogue, but precious little about how these discrete roles interacted within this single individual's life. A brief outline of the contours of the secondary literature will help to clarify the problems that hinder efforts to craft a holistic and critical life of Timothy Dwight. Readers may wish to consult the Bibliographic Essay that appears near the end of the present volume. It provides full bibliographic details of the secondary literature on Dwight, groups that literature into several categories, and provides brief assessments of the more important entries.

Timothy Dwight (1935), by Deane Keller, based on the 1817 portrait by Trumbull. Yale University Art Gallery. Commissioned by the University. Used by permission.

Despite the fact that Dwight is a well-known figure in the early national era, only one full biography has been written, Charles Cuningham's *Timothy Dwight, 1752–1817, A Biography*. Cuningham portrays a renaissance man of Revolutionary and early national America, the quintessential great man of Yale. Dwight's professional activities as poet, educator, theologian, and political pundit are treated at length, but Cuningham tends to overlook or obscure interesting and problematic elements of his subject's life. One of the book's virtues lies in the way it compiles the ninteenth-century literature about Dwight. Yet this very contribution leads to the book's central weaknesses: Cuningham uncritically echoes the hagiographic tone that characterizes Dwight's nineteenth-century admirers. The portrait of Dwight by John Trumbull, used as the frontispiece of Cuningham's work, perfectly captures this image of Dwight. Designed to flatter, Trumbull's painting and Cuningham's biography reveal a one-dimensional, learned man of the nineteenth century.[25]

Scholarly treatments of Dwight's literary efforts abound. The four most sustained assessments view Dwight from decidedly different perspectives. Leon Howard's *The Connecticut Wits* provides invaluable background information on the British poets and literary critics on whom Dwight relied. From Howard's perspective, although Dwight's struggles to create a distinctly American *belles lettres* were largely unsuccessful, he did manage to provide a degree of literary stability in an era of rapid and disconcerting change. Kenneth Silverman's *Timothy Dwight* is less appreciative. Silverman argues that Dwight used poetry as a means of expressing his views of America's changing fortunes. According to Silverman, Dwight's views of Amercia fall into a fourfold taxonomy—Ideal America, Possible America, Probable America, and Real America. While each of these images of America might have developed into imaginative and useful assessments of the nation's situation, Silverman's Dwight was stifled by a manichean mentality that allowed him to see only dreadful doomsdays or cheery birthdays. In the end, Dwight was little more than a seventeenth-century Puritan stranded in late eighteenth-century America—unimaginative, droll, and reactionary. Emory Elliott's *Revolutionary Writers* examines Dwight in context of his literary contemporaries: Joel Barlow, Philip Freneau, Hugh Henry Brackenbridge, and Charles Brockden Brown. He argues that Dwight and his Revolutionary colleagues attempted to repristinate the values of New England Puritanism. Whereas Silverman offered a largely negative portrait of Dwight, Elliot paints a more positive picture; his Dwight looks into the future with confidence and hope.

William Dowling's *Poetry and Ideology in Revolutionary Connecticut*, the most recent addition to these four literary studies, represents a distinct departure from Howard, Silverman, and Elliott. Dowling's interest is in ideology, particularly the manner in which Dwight and his fellow Wits used prevailing

British ideologies as tools of social criticism. Whereas Howard and Silverman viewed Dwight's use of social commentary as a failure, Dowling, like Elliot, discerned in Dwight the capacity for progressive social criticism. In Dowling, however, we find high irony. As a young man, Dwight effectively used his poetry to promote civic humanism and oppose tyranny. As a member of the revolutionary generation, he led numerous literary assaults on the privileges of powerful and unjust, centralized authority. As his career developed and he embraced the tenets of Federalism, Dwight appears to have affirmed the very thing he had previously attacked.

These four major literary studies yield vastly different views of Dwight, and so do a host of shorter treatments of individual elements within his literary corpus. Using Dwight's *Travels in New England and New York* as a starting place, a variety of scholars have analyzed the way in which he described scenes in a structured, often oversimplified, or even monolithic manner. In *Travels,* for instance, he used the established village to offset the wilderness and used regions of economic prosperity as counterpoints to impoverished townships. Dwight used his literary landscapes as opportunities to raise larger questions: he participated in the quasi-millennial "environmental reform" movement of the period; he used his art to inculcate a distinctly Protestant point of view; he dealt with timely moral questions such as slavery, race, sexuality, and gender; he used descriptive prose as a teaching device, touching on scientifical and ethical subjects. Each of these interpretations provides puzzling and tantalizing clues to Dwight and his personality.

Literary scholars have comprehended Dwight in different, even contrary, ways. Students of American religious history have generated an even wider array of interpretations of Dwight's religious beliefs and activities. Most often these scholars begin their treatment of Dwight by citing the now famous comments of his student, Lyman Beecher:

> Before [President Dwight] came college was in a most ungodly state. The college church was almost extinct. Most of the students were skeptical, and . . . intemperance, profanity, gambling, and licentiousness were common. That was the day of the infidelity of the Tom Paine school. . . . [M]ost of the class before me were infidels and called each other Voltaire, Rousseau, D'Alembert, etc., etc. They thought the faculty were afraid of free discussion. But when they handed Dr. Dwight a list of subjects for class disputation, to their surprise he selected this one: "Is the Bible the word of God?" and told them to do their best. He heard all they had to say, answered them, and there was an end. He preached incessantly for six months on the subject, and all infidelity skulked and hid its head.[26]

Working from this classic text, over the last half century scholars have issued increasingly grand interpretations of Dwight's importance in American religion. In 1942, Charles Roy Keller claimed that Dwight's Yale revival began a new religious movement in Connecticut. In 1968, William Clebsch argued that Dwight's work at the college inaugurated changes in the evangelical climate of the Eastern Seaboard. In 1977, Sidney Mead went further: he argued that Dwight's defeat of infidelity marked the beginning of a national event—the Second Great Awakening. By 1989, the stage was set for an even more remarkable claim: Annabelle Wenzke attempted to persuade readers that Dwight's theology served as the foundation of a genuinely international religious movement—Evangelical Protestantism. According to these interpretations, Dwight left his mark on religion from New Haven to the larger Anglo-American community. These sorts of expanding claims suggest comparisons between Dwight and Jonathan Edwards. While it may be clever to suggest that Dwight was an *Edwards redivivus,* that he led the Second Awakening as his grandfather had led the First Awakening, this proves to be a convenient but facile interpretive move.

Problems with this alleged national and international character of Dwight's campaign against infidelity emerge when his political views undergo scrutiny. A number of scholars have observed, quite rightly, that because Dwight's religious commitments and political commitments were intertwined, one cannot be viewed apart from the other. Sidney Mead was the first to insist on this, in his *Nathaniel William Taylor, 1786–1858: A Connecticut Liberal.* For Mead, Dwight's sermons and literary work provide further evidence of his manichaen, polar view of the world. Dwight pitted the forces of goodness—Christianity, the Standing Order, and New England Federalism—against a trinity of opposites—Infidelity, Jacobinism, and Jeffersonian Republicanism. Mead's interpretation was taken a step further by one of his students. Stephen Berk, in *Calvinism Versus Democracy: Timothy Dwight and the Origins of American Evangelical Orthodoxy,* forwarded the idea that Dwight and his Standing Order allies purposely contrived the Awakening for political purposes. By filling the churches with converts, the Federalist clergy hoped to enervate the Republican threat to the status quo.

Both the Keller-to-Wenzke trajectory of interpretation regarding Dwight's expanding influence and the correlative Mead-Berk line of interpretation about Dwight's nefarious religio-political plans have been challenged. In an essay entitled "Ezra Stiles and Timothy Dwight," Edmund S. Morgan established this revisionist agenda by challenging the accuracy of Beecher's account of Dwight's Yale revival. According to Morgan, the religious events at Yale *followed* similar revivals in surrounding churches in Connecticut. Dwight did not lead a regional event and the membership of the college church, long thought to be the chief beneficiary of the college revival, did not begin to grow until seven years after Dwight chased off infidelity. Moreover, Beecher's belief that Dwight had set a new standard in collegiate pedagogy by publicly debating the question of biblical authority was incorrect. Previous Yale presidents had used the same tactic.

Two other scholars took Morgan's lead and helped to provide a different and more detailed picture of how New England's religious landscape changed in the early national era. Richard Birdsall offered convincing data that showed that the New England theater of the larger Second Awakening began at the popular level, and not as a result of the machinations of Federalist clerical elites. Richard Shiels extended Birdsall's critique by overturning three additional standard elements of the traditional interpretation. First, New England's tall steeple preachers did not begin the Awakening by developing a new, warmer, popular style of homiletics. Second, it was not the preaching efforts of ecclesiastical statesmen like Dwight who triggered the revival, but an increase in religious activity—notably missions and religious journalism—that prompted the genesis of the Awakening in New England. Third, the leaders of the Awakening were not high-profile Federalist clergy, such as Dwight, but local pastors whose visibility was confined to more circumscribed locales. In sum, while it is true that President Dwight somehow amalgamated Reformed theology and American Federalism, observers in his day and ours have puzzled over the meaning of the mix.

If historians have been divided in their assessments of Dwight's role in the Second Great Awakening, they have been even further puzzled as to his overall theological identity. Several schools of theology competed for the hearts, minds, and souls of New England's citizens—Old Lights, New Lights, Unitarians, Trinitarians, Universalists, Congregationalists, Presbyterians, Methodists, Episcopalians, Old Calvinists, Arminians, Edwardseans, and New Divinity theologians. The list of rival groups is long and differentiating one camp from another can prove a mind-numbing exercise. At first glance, it seems a rather easy task to locate Dwight theologically. He was a Calvinist, a Trinitarian, and a paedo-baptist. He affirmed Congregational polity, he believed that church membership ought to be restricted to converted persons only, and he held a high view of the authority of the scriptures.

Careful inquiries into the more subtle aspects of Dwight's theology complicate this matter. Determining Dwight's relationship to his grandfather's theological legacy, for instance, proves a vexing problem. To put the question sharply, did Dwight affirm the broader categories of Edwards's thought, or did he belong to one of the narrower, more carefully nuanced "New Divinity," "Hopkinsian, " or "Consistent Calvinist" camps within the larger Edwardsean milieu? Some scholars place Dwight squarely in the New Divinity camp; others argue that Dwight is best described as a member of the broad Edwardsean camp and that he was opposed to New Divinity innovations; still others eqivocate on the distinction. Here again, however, the devil is in the details. Dwight's family connections and educational background, as well as his easy adoption of themes found in Edwards's major treatises and his views on the Halfway Covenant, place him squarely in the broader Edwardsean camp. Distinguishing his thought from that of the more ardent and rigorous among the Edwardseans, however, remains a challenge.

Dwight's role in the Second Awakening is ambiguous, his participation in the Edwardsean movement is anomalous, and, not surprisingly, his views on millennial theology—the branch of doctrine that treats "end times" and its accompanying divine culmination of the created order—is similarly enigmatic. That Dwight affirmed the canons of postmillennial theology (in which one believes that the millennium, a thousand-year era of peace and prosperity, would precede the return of Christ) is certain. His understanding of the relationship between the divine intrusions necessary to the establishment of the millennium (e.g., the second coming, the appearance of the Antichrist) and mundane events (e.g., the efforts of believers, the exercise of political power, and force of social mores and cultural attitudes) is less clear. In addition to his study of the mysterious promises of the biblical books of Daniel and Revelation, Dwight looked to contemporary events for signs of God's culminating activity in the world. The pool of data from which he drew, then, was both historical and contemporary and the tools he used to read the signs of the times were highly subjective.

Ernest Tuveson in his book *Redeemer Nation* was the first scholar to treat Dwight's postmillennial theology at length. Operating within an interpretive structure akin to Silverman's "doomsday" or "birthday" scenario, and offering careful readings of several of Dwight's poems, Tuveson concluded that Dwight's enthusiasm for American exceptionalism stood at the heart of what would later become the religio-political doctrine of manifest destiny. Although other scholars would later challenge this particular claim when they discovered earlier sources of this distinctly American habit of mind, none have denied Tuveson's observation that Dwight played a very important role in the history of millennial thought in America. Indeed, other historians, working from Tuveson's research, have provided a host of additional insights into Dwight's millennial rhetoric.

James West Davidson in *The Logic of Millennial Thought* explored the intellectual and theological contexts on which Dwight drew. Using Dwight's sermons, Davidson paid particular attention to Dwight's belief that the millennium would not commence by miracles but by the faithful efforts of everyday Christians. Though millennialism may appear a rather odd place to find Dwight inculcating duty—he urged believers to be faithful in evangelism, missions, and social reform precisely because such efforts would help inaugurate the millennium—this is perfectly consistent with his inclinations toward the moralism and ethics-of-duty outlook visible in other areas of his thought. Mason Lowance in *The Language of Canaan* described the cultural productions Dwight identified as harbingers of the millennium. Lowance argued that Dwight's image of the Kingdom of God on earth could be found in the ideal worlds he described in *Conquest of Canaan* and *Greenfield Hill*. In so doing, Dwight managed to secularize millennialism; the eschaton was not to be found in a miraculous divine intrusion but in the gradual progress of human beings working in the world.

Finally, in what is surely the most detailed, subtle, and helpful study treating Dwight's millennial thinking, Ruth Bloch in her *Visionary Republic: Millennial Themes in American Thought, 1756–1800* explored the ways in which millennial theology, the ideology of civic republicanism, and the secular utopianism of the Enlightenment interacted during the Revolutionary era. She observes that the focus of millennial rhetoric changed with the vicissitudes of political events in the young nation. While a type of eschatological biblicism dominated preaching during the 1750s, during the Revolution secular political thought combined with traditional millennial doctrines to produce Tuveson's "Redeemer Nation" ideology. Later, when the young nation was faced with the challenges, both internal and external, of becoming a genuine participant in international affairs, preachers' sentiments swung back to more traditional and steady biblical interpretations of eschatology. Instead of seeing the nation as a critical participant in the great cosmic drama, the clergy invested missions and social reform with millennial significance. In some respects, Dwight's career as a millennial interpreter fits the shifting patterns Bloch discerns. His earliest poems, for instance, fit the millennialism of the revolutionary period rather neatly. His later millennial work, found in his *Nature and Danger of Infidel Philosophy, Duty of Americans at the Present Crisis* and *Sermon Delivered . . . before the American Board of Commissioners for Foreign Missions*, also conforms to her pattern. What remains to be seen is exactly how Dwight mixed "political" and "biblical" categories during the crucial middle period of his life.

* * *

Having surveyed the interpretive problems and complex literatures surrounding Timothy Dwight, we may ask again: What is the problem? The matter? The issue? Quite simply, we know too much about Dwight and also too little. In the face of a plethora of contrary and partial interpretations, a wholistic and plausible portrait of Dwight remains elusive. He left few personal documents; he changed dramatically over time; he is judged a hero or a villain but rarely without ulterior motives. Scholarly assessments of Dwight vary in significant ways, both within and between the academic disciplines. At one moment, Dwight—nearly blind yet nearly prescient—appears forward looking. He was committed to moving American *belles lettres* and Yale College into the modern world; he expressed a remarkably optimistic view of the prospects of the American nation; he championed the transformative power of missions work, revivals, and social reform; he affirmed the outlines of the "didactic" Enlightenment. At other times Dwight looms as a backward-looking, even reactionary figure. He celebrated the halcyon days of the Puritan era and yearned for its reestablishment; he resisted the disestablishment of Connecticut Congregationalism; he identified religious innovation, be it from skeptics or uneducated western revivalists, as demonic; Quixote-like, he tilted against the progressive forces of the radical Enlightenment. Some hail him as the dreadnought of infidelity and the creative genius of America's Second Great Awakening; others find his writings and sermons dull, his theological contributions derivative, and his religious legacy provincial and ambiguous. Pedagogue, poet, politician, preacher, pundit, and president, each role reveals something about Dwight, but none by itself can explain him. He was, in the words of the same admirer who dubbed him "the most conspicuous man in New England," an individual of "lights and shades" who lived in the shadowy interstices between rapidly changing events, ideas, and cultures.[27]

Constructing the major outlines of that unique life is the task to which we now turn. This book presents a carefully circumscribed life of Timothy Dwight. The thesis of the volume is quite simple: Dwight's religious system served a powerful, integrative function among what might otherwise appear to be a disparate set of professional activities. That system is "Godly Federalism," and can best be seen when Dwight functions as a "moralist." In order to provide the reader with sufficient background to understand Dwight and his role in Revolutionary and early national America, the project begins with a biographical chapter that outlines the dynamics of Dwight's family background, his education at Yale, his work on behalf of the Revolution, his Greenfield pastorate, his ascent to the Yale presidency, his ministerial and educational endeavors at Yale, the political debates into which he became entangled, and his ongoing development as a major religious figure of the day. Where possible, this chapter is based on manuscript sources and the observations of contemporaries. Given the dearth of personal information about Dwight this chronology of his life relies heavily on textual evidence drawn from Dwight's literary corpus.

Whereas the first chapter functions biographically and chronologically, chapters 2, 3, and 4 operate on a modal or functional basis, treating Dwight as preacher, theologian, and historian, respectively. These professional activities are understood loosely in ways that overlap. Dwight's preaching was dependent on his theological views, his theology was powerfully shaped by his historical consciousness, and his understanding of America undergirded many a sermon and theological treatise. Dwight's activities as poet, pastor, politician, or educator also suggested themselves as possible routes to a fuller picture. Notwithstanding the value of viewing Dwight through such roles they have proved incapable of providing interpretive avenues broad enough to sustain new insights. All things considered, Dwight's roles as preacher, theologian, and historian comprehend and include these other activities yet remain sufficiently distinct to justify separate treatment. They are fundamental roles by which Dwight identified himself.

Chapter 2 examines what is arguably Dwight's most important role, that of preacher. It begins with a description of Dwight's sermon corpus and gives particular attention to the ways that a partially sighted Dwight developed his extempore homiletic style. The chapter procedes to an analysis of the ways that Scottish Common Sense thinking, then only a thin shadow of what it would become for later generations of American theologians, shaped Dwight's views on skepticism, rhetoric, criticism, biblical authority, and the art of homiletics. With these foundational issues in place, the chapter will examine two distinct subjects within Dwight's sermon corpus—his campaign against infidelity and his understanding of the evangelistic enterprise. This larger perspective on Dwight the preacher will move discussion well beyond the Beecher myth and the few Dwight sermons that have attracted attention— notably *The Nature and Danger of Infidel Philosophy* and *The Duty of Americans at the Present Crisis.*

Chapter 3 examines Dwight's theology with particular reference to the Edwardsean tradition. It describes the peculiarities of Edwardsean theology and practice and argues that far from being a devotee of Consistent Calvinism Timothy Dwight was deeply suspicious of both the method and the conclusions of the more radical theologians among the Edwardseans. The chapter seeks to provide a more detailed and accurate description of Dwight's systematic theology and the compromises he made to establish his place within the New England theological tradition.

Chapter 4 reconstructs Dwight's historical consciousness in order to understand his world view. Dwight used historical "facts" to construct fairly straightforward, "objective" narratives of the American past. He also employed biblical millennialism and Revolutionary nationalism to formulate "subjective," highly imaginative interpretations of the cosmic significance of the nation. Hence, both the stories he retells in *Travels* and the sermons he delivers on the Revelation of St. John become important sources for understanding Dwight's beloved America. When viewed in a comprehensive manner Dwight's eschatological speeches and writings operate on a grand, cyclic plan. At high points in the national story, he invokes language that is progressive and millennial in character. When he discerns threats to American piety and virtue, he turns to foreboding, apocalyptic language. Not surprisingly, his eschatological diagnoses run parallel to his personal experience. Dwight's political perceptions, cultural discernments, fears, and personal mood swings serve as indicators of his highly subjective eschatological reflections.

In chapter 5 Dwight's professional activities as preacher, theologian, and historian became constituents of a larger role—that of moralist. The chapter begins with an assessment of the ways in which Dwight's professional roles combined and helped him to become an American moralist. His prescriptions for the systematic maintenance of American piety and his understanding of the character of the good ruler provide the outlines of his ideal vision of the American nation. Understanding the ways in which his moralism shaped his vision leads to a fuller appreciation of the "Godly Federalism" that Dwight created and promulgated from the moral high ground of the Yale presidency.

The book closes with a brief Afterword. It begins by noting the remarkable cultural power of the notion that Christians should expect the establishment of the Kingdom of God. It concludes by suggesting that Dwight's lasting legacy can be found in a diverse group of American religious visionaries who in their own ways have promoted that idea.

I

The Light of Yale

Dwight is gone! The Light of Yale is extinguished. The vital fire is fled. Like some clear
planet, it has left behind its lucid track, and
darted to eternity.

—Gardiner Spring

Northampton in the Shadow of Edwards

For nearly three centuries the Dwight family played an auspicious role in the
culture and politics of New England. The family's colonial patriarch John
Dwight emigrated from England and helped settle the town of Dedham,
Massachusetts, under the guidance of the Puritan nonconformist, John
Rogers. Known to history as "John Dwight, yeoman," this Puritan layman
founded an American family whose major interests were political and religious. By 1700, the Dwights were established members of the Massachusetts
Bay gentry. Nathaniel Dwight (1666–1711), grandson of John, led his family
west, first to Hatfield and finally to Northampton, the subsequent center of the
family holdings. The Dwight men proved themselves able citizens of western
Massachusetts, serving in the militia and the provincial courts. Indeed, by
mid-century, "the county judiciary was almost completely a family affair." In
1758, three Dwights (Timothy, Josiah, and Joseph) sat on the Inferior Court of
Common Pleas, and generations of Dwights ascended through the hierarchy of
the Probate Court system with remarkable consistency.[1]

In Colonel Timothy Dwight (1693–1771) the family reached the zenith of
its colonial power. Though rarely identified as one of the Connecticut Valley's
elite and powerful "river gods" (the term used by historians to describe the
Hampshire County patriarchs who monopolized lands and political offices),
the colonel's large estate and social and business relationships indicate that he
was a contender for a position within that influential group.[2] Colonel John
Stoddard, who "managed Massachusetts nearly as a man manages his walking
stick," was among Dwight's closest friends, as was the "monarch of Hampshire," Israel Williams.[3] By his death in 1771, Colonel Dwight had managed to
amass an estate twice the size of Stoddard's. Though historians reckoned him
neither god nor monarch, Colonel Timothy Dwight was very near the top of
Northampton society.

Colonel Dwight's position in the upper stratum of his social world assured him a good deal of deference from those below him on the social scale, as well as competition—sometimes rather fierce—from people alongside or above him. He thought of himself as an irenic, benevolent public servant who could solve problems long before they ripened into disruptive conflicts that might jeopardize him or his family's social status. Like many other eighteenth-century judges, he encouraged disputants to settle their differences outside the courts. Indeed, he boasted that during eighteen years of practice none of Northampton's inhabitants had brought a civil suit to the bar.[4] Notwithstanding his real or imagined abilities to circumvent conflict, Colonel Dwight himself failed to dodge public controversy in at least one conspicuous instance. Certainly, the most celebrated case of a colonial New England minister's dismissal at the hands of his congregation is that of Jonathan Edwards. Traditionally, interpreters have viewed the separation as the result of a theological dispute. More recent studies, however, have concluded that more than Edwards's ecclesiology and sacramental theology were at issue. Social change, shifting political power, and family rivalries also contributed to the crisis.[5] Edwards was not insensitive to the familial aspects of the controversy, nor did he fail to assess the political character of the situation. In a rare allusion to contemporary English politics, he described Northampton society:

> It has been a very great wound to the church at Northampton, that there has been for forty or fifty years a sort of settled division of the people into two parties somewhat like the Court and Country party in England (if I may compare small things with great.) There have been some of the chief men in the town, of chief authority and wealth, that have been great proprietors of their lands, who have had one party with them. And the other party, which has commonly been the greatest, have been of those, who have been jealous of them, apt to envy them, and afraid of their having too much power and influence in town and church.[6]

The Northampton church crisis of 1750 was not simply a contest between the town's elites and middling sorts. Nor was it confined to Northampton proper. Jonathan Edwards, progressive Calvinist theologian, grandson of the celebrated Solomon Stoddard, and recognized leader of the colonial New Lights, had succeeded in dividing the Hampshire county elites.

Two of these worthies, Israel Williams and Joseph Hawley (neither of whom lived in Northampton), devised one stratagem after another to remove Edwards from his pulpit.[7] Among the river gods only Colonel John Stoddard, believed by Edwards to be "probably one of the ablest politicians that ever New England bred," stood at Edwards's side. Stoddard's untimely death in 1748 left Edwards with few allies among the river gods, the region's most powerful citizens. Thereafter, most of Edwards's support came from common folk, and the leadership of these partisans fell to Colonel Timothy Dwight. Despite all Edwards's hopes, notwithstanding the machinations of his allies, efforts to save his beloved pulpit were doomed. Early in June 1750 the Northampton congregation voted 230 to 23 to dismiss Edwards. On 22 June a special Council of ministers confirmed the action of the congregation by a narrow margin.[8]

Edwards felt keenly the sting of the dismissal, as did both his immediate family and his other allies in Northampton. Their pain and embarrassment did not escape his attention. In a letter written five months after his "Farewell Address," Edwards described the emotional damage that the conflict created:

> There is a number whose hearts are broken at what has come to pass, and I believe are more deeply affected than even they were at any temporal bereavement. It is thus with one of the principal men of the parish, Colonel Dwight. Such is the state of things among us, that a person can not appear on my side without greatly exposing himself to the resentment of his friends and neighbors, and becoming the object of much odium.[9]

Though he may well have become the object of odium, Colonel Dwight continued to work for Edwards's vindication. Both men entertained the lingering hope that published accounts of the manner in which the Northampton dismissal had been handled might justify Edwards in the public eye. With the hope of vindication uppermost in his mind, Edwards asked Dwight to discuss the aftermath of the dismissal with the Reverend Foxcroft of the First Church in Boston. In a letter on Edwards's behalf dated 13 October 1750, Dwight told Foxcroft that Edwards believed "there are some great misrepresentations in a pamphlet lately printed here by the Hampshire Ministers in vindication of their conduct respecting [Edwards'] dismission which will evidently appear by sundry things well attested." Dwight went on to ask that Foxcroft arrange for Mr. Hobby, the Congregational minister at Reading, Massachusetts, to "publish some thing in answer" to the damaging accusations that were circulating.[10] In addition to his efforts to exonerate Edwards from any guilt that might have accrued from the events leading to the dismissal, Dwight also offered financial support in connection with a proposal that Edwards and his supporters form a second congregation in Northampton.[11] That plan never came to fruition. Edwards secured a ministry among Housatunnock and Mohawk natives in Stockbridge and soon abandoned Northampton, leaving behind a discouraged and embittered Dwight.

It took several years for the Northampton Church to secure another pastor, a task made considerably more difficult given the stature of the most recent incumbent of the pulpit and the circumstances of his removal. The search for a new minister only served to exacerbate Colonel Dwight's bitterness. In June

1753 he complained to Foxcroft that "we are governed by the old spirit of anarchy still." The church had in view a candidate named John Hooker and, though Dwight believed him the best of the nominees the church had yet heard preach, he considered it imprudent to call a new minister "till Providence has taken us in hand and given us a new apprehension of our state, and the means of our being brought unto it. . . . At this time our case appears awfull [sic] to me being as I esteem it in a state of ruin and no proper sense of it."[12] Despite Dwight's misgivings, Hooker was elected in September 1753 and ordained in December of the same year. Not unexpectedly, the controversy surrounding Edwards's dismissal lingered in the town, and Dwight seems to have borne its full weight. Just days after Hooker's ordination, Dwight reported that Hooker "has been here a considerable time, but never been at my house. I suppose he is convinced by his friends and my enemies that it's dangerous for him to visit me." Even worse, fears about Hooker's theological views were circulating, and though Dwight inclined to the charitable view that "allowance must be made for false reports in these awful times," he confided in Foxcroft his private fear that Hooker had been "drawn aside from the Gospell [sic] salvation."[13] Within a year Dwight confirmed his suspicions and dissatisfaction with Hooker. "I can't be satisfied with his preaching, no experimental religion, no rules of examination, a constant dwelling on works. And am really afraid he lurches toward an Arminian [doctrine of] justification." Though some in the church apparently shared Dwight's discontent, he continued to believe that the church had yet to assuage the guilt it had incurred in dismissing Edwards.

> I can't but think that this people have something to suffer for their abominable tretment [sic] of that faithful messenger of Christ. And I have thought it likely they may be punished as multitudes of others have been, by being permitted to go on in that idolatrous sin of ecclesiastical contention till they are a byword, a hissing and gazing stock of others. However, God's ways are not ours and I verily believe our people are endeavoring to find a broader way to heaven than heretofore we have been taught. They are not endeavoring to enter by the door but climbing up some other way.[14]

As late as 1754, Dwight still maintained the hope that the church would ask Edwards to return. In a detailed letter to Foxcroft, Dwight spoke of an unnamed person in Stockbridge—the context suggests that the subject was Edwards—who was in some difficulty and might find attractive the prospect of a return to Northampton. Such a move could occur, said Dwight,

> if the people, enough of them, will unite to call him, and provide him a comfortable support. He is at present, and I don't see but his is like to abide so, (viz.) as a sheep, etc. He has a very considerable number of

friends here that I hope if he comes will rejoyce [sic] in his light, but there
he is like a candle set under a bushel. . . . I esteem him a gentleman of
great powers and I verily believe he suffers from many on that very
account. They can't endure he should so much exceed them that in the
real tho' very unjust foundations of the Wmss [sic] hatred of him.[15]

Although Colonel Dwight had himself become a casualty of the ecclesiastical warfare in Northampton, he could take solace in at least one venture with
the Edwards family that gave him great satisfaction. On 8 November 1750,
some five months after his dismissal from the Northampton pulpit, Edwards's
fourth daughter, Mary, and Colonel Dwight's eldest son, Timothy, Jr., were
married. As the Reverend Mr. Edwards watched, Dwight himself performed the
ceremony. For Edwards and Dwight, the marriage held deep personal meaning
because it forever sealed their important friendship. In a larger context the
marriage held other significance. Edwards had been defeated—from Dwight's
perspective even martyred—and would move to Stockbridge and later to the
presidency of the College of New Jersey at Princeton. As titular leader of the
pro-Edwards faction, Dwight had suffered public defeat as well. A man of
strong convictions and known for his ardor in debate, he "never recovered his
former spirits" after Edwards's defeat.[16] In the marriage of their children these
two friends established an abiding legacy in Northampton. Mary and Timothy,
Jr. (who would later become a major in the local militia and is herein referred
to by his military title) would live for twenty-five years in the town. Long after
their fathers had died, these children of Northampton's leading citizens would,
in turn, gain reputations as people of strong conviction. In the tradition of the
great New England families, their marriage represented a significant genealogical alliance. The Dwights were a wealthy and powerful presence in western
Massachusetts. Although Edwards struggled financially all of his life, he
represented both intellectual brilliance and the finest Puritan pedigree. Timothy and Mary stood at the confluence of two of New England's great families.
They had every reason to believe that their own children would inherit both
wealth and intellectual prowess.[17] Their part in passing down the traditions of
their elders began 14 May 1752 with the birth of their first child and the third
in a five-generation line of prominent Timothy Dwights.[18] Though few details
of young Timothy's childhood survive, a good deal is known about the town
and the home in which he spent his formative years.

Northampton, like many of its Hampshire County neighbors, experienced
rapid social and political changes in the latter half of the eighteenth century.
The population grew continually, and until 1749 the town repeatedly divided
large tracts of land in order to open new areas for settlement. Thenceforth,
choice lands near the Connecticut River were occupied, forcing newcomers to
settle the hilly country some distance from the river. In later years, young

Timothy Dwight would remark on the inferior quality of the soil in these "hilltown" areas. The relative scarcity of prime lands, however, did not slow the increase in population. Between 1765 and 1776 the county's population doubled. Northampton grew by thirty-eight percent, second only to Springfield among the older towns of the county. This rapid expansion was not due to natural generation only. Migration accounted for the bulk of the growth. By the mid 1760s, little arable land was available and immigrants to the town soon found their hopes of obtaining good land at a reasonable price disappointed. Northampton's oldest families—the Dwights among them—controlled the town and were unwilling to divide their family holdings among newcomers. The lack of suitable land for sale did not immediately stem the tide of immigration, and transiency emerged as a vexing social and legal problem. The "strolling poor" were visible throughout the region, and Northampton was especially plagued by the problem of indigence.[19]

As newcomers settled inferior farms, they found themselves with a correspondingly small voice in town politics. In this regard, Northampton's political history paralleled that of most other towns in the county. The small number of families who owned the best lands virtually controlled the board of selectmen. By 1750, more than half of all selectmen bore the name of one of Northampton's leading families. These same people served repeatedly, averaging five terms each, and this pattern would not change until the Revolution.[20] In short, a stratified system of deference was woven through the social, economic, and political fabric of the town.

Major Timothy Dwight, after the manner of the Dwight men, was an active leader in community affairs. According to Governor Caleb Strong's recollection, he "possessed the good qualities of his father, with a milder disposition and more engaging qualities."[21] In local politics he followed in his father's footsteps. In addition to serving as register of probate, he served terms as delegate to the Massachusetts General Court (1758–1766), judge of common pleas (1758–1774), town selectman (1760–1774), and town recorder (1760–1774). Though Major Dwight's primary activity centered on his mercantile interests, his sizable land holdings (approximately three thousand acres at his death) undoubtedly provided other income.[22] Soon after his marriage, he built a fine house located in the center of Northampton. Mary Edwards Dwight found herself little removed from the home of her childhood; her new house was erected on a lot adjacent to what had been the Edwards manse.

Young Timothy was afforded opportunities beyond those of the eldest son of a local judge. After all, he was the grandson of two of Northampton's most notable citizens. Though many of Northampton's citizens were anxious to let Edwards fade from memory, in the Dwight household he was enshrined as a champion of orthodoxy, a martyr to the insidious forces of Arminianism. The few reliable biographical accounts of Mary Edwards Dwight suggest that she inherited many of her father's intellectual gifts. Although scant data survive to test this claim, clearly Mary Edwards Dwight reared her children much as Jonathan and Sarah Edwards had raised her. Study of the Bible began as soon as young Timothy could speak. Shortly after he mastered the alphabet, he began a lifelong interest in Latin. At age six, he was enrolled at the local grammar school where, over the initial objections of his father, he began the formal study of Latin. By the age of eight Timothy knew enough Latin to pass Yale's entrance examination. Because his father insisted that he was too young for collegiate training, Timothy's studies continued at home. Young Dwight honed his academic skills under the direction of his mother, with the encouragement of his paternal grandfather, Colonel Dwight, and within the bounds of his father's substantial library. At age eleven, his parents arranged for him to begin formal preparation for college with the Reverend Enoch Huntingdon of Middletown. Two years later Timothy traveled to New Haven, met the entrance requirements, and was admitted to Yale College, becoming the youngest member of the class of 1769.[23]

Dwight's first two years at Yale were relatively uneventful. Bright and academically well prepared, he found the introductory material repetitive and tedious. Apparently, Dwight took advantage of the lax discipline that prevailed during the administration of the College's president, Thomas Clap. His discipline flagged and he became particularly fond of card playing, a vice he later reckoned a positive evil. His failure to address his studies with the proper energy did not go unnoticed. Stephen Mix Mitchell, Dwight's cousin, and later Chief Justice of the Connecticut Supreme Court, was a tutor at Yale in those years.[24] He took his young kinsman aside with a paternal discipline that would later characterize Dwight himself and admonished the sophomore to reform. Dwight took the advice to heart. Indeed, he may have taken it too seriously. In order to compensate for what he now believed to be lost opportunities, Dwight embarked on an intensive course of independent study. He rose earlier than necessary and parsed one hundred lines of Homer before chapel or breakfast. Although this supererogatory behavior paid handsome academic benefits at the time, Dwight's sophomoric asceticism represented the first steps along a dangerous path.

Dwight completed his course of study in 1769. In order to show their support for the colonial resistance against the restrictive Townshend Acts, Dwight and his fellow graduates appeared at commencement dressed in homespun. Although Dwight's father was unhappy with this overtly political gesture, he also had reason to be proud. Dwight and classmate Nathan Strong fought to a virtual tie for the highest honors at commencement. Timothy barely missed valedictorian honors. The honor of delivering the Valedictory Address finally went to Strong, he being the older of the two scholars.[25] Dwight's early success indicated his potential for a career that would require additional study. Accordingly, he arranged to spend two more years at Yale, supporting himself by teaching grammar school. The recipient of a Yale master's degree was especially well suited for two careers, the law and the ministry. At commencement in 1771, Dwight took his master's and delivered a public address. Its title indicates Dwight's vocational direction: *A Dissertation on the History, Eloquence, and Poetry of the Bible*. The central thesis of the essay was that the scriptures, though recorded by simple, barely literate people, were vastly superior to the recognized classics of history, eloquence, and poetry. A "peculiar simplicity" characterized the Bible. This simplicity was, indeed, the key to the literary power of the scriptures. Eschewing "art" and avoiding the overuse of metaphor and comparison, the biblical authors relied on "nothing but the natural, unstudied language of affection."[26] In his first address-turned-publication, one can discern hints and shadowy outlines of what would later characterize Dwight's major intellectual commitments. For Dwight, the scriptures were the source of religious authority; the most effective religious language was straightforward and devoid of the niceties of style and metaphysics; the target of religious language was the heart; and the heart could only be reached through the exercise of the mind. Though it would be nearly a full generation until these sorts of commitments would be commonly gathered under the banner of Scottish "Common Sense" thought, there can be little doubt that Dwight was already operating within a similar intellectual environment.

Immediately after taking his master's degree, Dwight was asked by the Yale Corporation to serve as College tutor, a position he gladly accepted. Subscribing with "free and hearty assent to the doctrines contained in the Assembly's Catechism and the Confession of Faith" and consenting "to the rules of church discipline agreed upon and established in this colony," he began his formal educational career in the fall of 1771.[27] Even in this early period, Dwight's career as an educator is noteworthy. Historians have often slighted Dwight's educational achievements, assuming that his traditionalism in other areas extended into every aspect of his career. However, Dwight was a progressive educator. As tutor, he began experiments in Yale's curriculum that later characterized his presidency. The development of *belles lettres* along contemporary British lines was of particular interest to him. Readings in Milton, Pope, and Dryden supplemented his students' more traditional exercises in the classics. With fellow tutors Joseph Howe and John Trumbull, and with Yale undergraduates Joel Barlow and David Humphreys, Dwight founded the "Connecticut Wits." Following literary paths suggested in Lord Kames's *Elements of Criticism*, the authors sought to grapple with aesthetic and sociopolitical problems in colonial America. Although the Wits' poetry has sometimes been considered mere mimicry of prevailing British style (despite their desires to avoid both provincialism and literary Anglophilia), most regard them as the first genuinely American school of literary criticism to emerge in the Revolutionary period.

Dwight had begun a career as a man of letters, and although his decision to pursue this afforded him some security, it did not lead him to complacency. Having triumphed over the problem of lax discipline, he accelerated even further along an already hazardous course. All indications confirm that at age twenty Dwight was a compulsive, driven young man. In a letter to his son, Major Dwight indicated his concern for the lad, hoping that he would enjoy "external as well as internal peace."[28] But Timothy was anxious about success and was anything but serene. Believing that overeating was causing an annoying sluggishness that interfered with his studies, Dwight restricted his daily intake of food. Combined with overwork and youthful zeal, the meager twelve mouthfuls of vegetables he allowed himself at each meal quickly took a heavy toll on Dwight's health. His most troubling affliction involved his eyesight—a condition erroneously believed to have been brought on during a bout with smallpox. After reading for long periods of time, he was overtaken by severe headaches that forced him to rest. Though he tried several popular remedies, nothing seemed to alleviate the discomfort. The attacks became more frequent and began to render his eyes useless for days at a time. Fits of nausea began to accompany the eye problem, and these more severe physical attacks drew the attention of his colleagues. Alarmed at what they considered Dwight's hastening demise, they persuaded Dwight's father to come to New Haven and take charge of the situation.

Forced to cease his academic endeavors, Dwight spent months recuperating in the relative quiet of Northampton. He regained his vigor, but slowly; the illness did have lasting effects. Dwight's eyes were permanently damaged. He lost the capacity to read for any significant length of time, a handicap that also affected his ability to write. As early as 1772, Dwight began a letter to his cousin, Aaron Burr, Jr.: "By a poor candle, with poor eyes, and a poorer brain, I sit down to introduce a long wished for correspondence."[29] Indeed, Dwight's eyes grew worse over the course of his life. As late as 1805, he wrote a brief note to his friend Jedidiah Morse in which he complained, "My eyes are materially worse than ever; and not improbably hopeless of even continuing where they are. I do almost nothing with them but read a little in the Bible, or at solitary seasons in a newspaper; and once in a great while I answer a letter."[30] Although his impaired vision was "a source of serious embarrassment through his whole subsequent life," Dwight turned his handicap to good advantage.[31] Because he could not rely upon pulpit notes, he developed an extempore preaching style for which he became famous. After Dwight became president of Yale, its Corporation recognized that Dwight's handicap might impair his effectiveness. Beginning in 1805, they allowed him to employ student amanuenses to assist with his correspondence and writing. Yale undergraduates coveted this extracurricular job and from among these young secretaries Dwight chose and trained his most trusted disciples, Lyman Beecher and Nathaniel W. Taylor.[32] Dwight's illness can be considered an indirect cause of another of his achievements. On his doctor's advice, Dwight began to take long walks and, later, extended trips on horseback. These developed into yearly tours during which he compiled the notes for his *Travels in New England and New York*.

Despite the good Dwight may have salvaged from his physical ailments, they cannot be dismissed as unimportant. Clearly, they transcended a simple illness—something that proper medication might have arrested. Judging from his self-conscious asceticism, the sudden alarm of his Yale companions, and the months of recuperation his illness required, Dwight appears to have experienced a major physical and emotional breakdown. The scion of a clan in which success in education and vocation was taken for granted, Dwight had stumbled in the moral realm. The result was that his first two years at Yale were nearly a total loss. Having suffered this defeat, he came to believe that nothing short of superhuman effort would redeem him. Though few documents survive to describe Dwight's motivation, little imagination is needed to reconstruct his image of success—Jonathan Edwards. His paternal grandfather, Colonel Timothy Dwight, had suffered under the pain of the Northampton church convulsions until his death in 1771. Although Dwight's father, Major Timothy Dwight, appears to have been a private man when it came to religious affairs, he also had supported Edwards. Perhaps more than any other person who witnessed the separation, Dwight's mother, herself an Edwards, bore resentment over her father's dismissal. Mary Edwards Dwight was the only member of the Edwards household to remain in Northampton after Edwards's removal to Stockbridge. Though she joined the Northampton church in 1771 and lived in the town until her death in 1807, she refused to sit with her neighbors in the meetinghouse during Sunday services, choosing instead a lone chair set aside for her in the vestibule of the church. Nor would she celebrate communion with the townsfolk, preferring on communion days to ride to the church at Norwich, twelve miles distant. Given her evident animosity against her neighbors and the fact that she raised her eldest son "in the Edwards manner," it is entirely plausible to think that the spectre of the martyred Edwards dwelt in the Dwight household.

As Timothy began to focus on things academic and religious, he had not far to look for a heroic model. Indeed, as a young child he often heard visitors to his home speak of "the distinguished characters then acting in the theatre of life. Among these President Edwards and Lord Chatham were considered as standing at the head, as being the two preeminently great men of the age." Doubtless the exploits and accomplishments of prominent citizens were often discussed in the Dwight household, but young Dwight made object lessons of these routine social conventions: "He determined in his own mind that he would be as great as either of them."[33] Confirming what must have been Mary's hopes, direct parallels existed between Dwight's early life and that of his esteemed grandfather.[34] Precocious, both entered Yale at thirteen. Asceticism in food, drink, and worldly pleasure characterized their early lives. Both were Yale graduates, took master's degrees, and were elected tutors. A tragic parallel existed between the two; both were victims of smallpox despite the requisite innoculations. These similarities could not have escaped Dwight or his family, and there is little question as to who his model must have been. He determined to become another Edwards although the effort nearly proved fatal.

Dwight himself was cognizant and concerned about his personal situation. In January 1774, just two months before his health forced his return to Northampton, Dwight joined Yale's College Church. Two observations, one about his ecclesiology and a second about the congregation he joined, shed light on this decision. Throughout his life Dwight held a view of church membership that was strictly Edwardsean—membership in the church rested on a full, public profession of faith. Neither theologian recognized membership on the Halfway Covenant model. Hence, Dwight's decision to join a church marked nothing less than his full conversion to Christianity. Though no record of the particulars of this experience has survived—it is never mentioned in any detail by Dwight or his biographers—one may surmise that Dwight's personal difficulties led him to take this critically important step on the journey of faith. Moreover, Dwight's choice of congregations—Yale's College Church, not his contentious and waffling "home church" in Northampton— owed its very existence to a New Light, Edwardsean theological rationale. When President Thomas Clap defected from his Old Light, anti-Awakening position in 1753, the New Light, pro-Awakening camp, which understood the Awakening as a genuine work of God, gained more than a prestigious new proselyte. As a New Light, Clap successfully argued that Yale's chapel constituted a particular congregation. Thus, in Thomas Clap the New Lights gained an influential man, a fine apologist, and a new congregation comprised of some of the finest young minds in New England. Ezra Stiles would seek to undo some of these New Light gains, but this attempt to reclaim Yale for the traditionalists would not begin until 1778. The College Church that Dwight joined in 1774 was essentially a New Light institution. In sum, by 1774 Dwight had resolved questions he recognized as bearing eternal significance. His prodigious efforts at virtue had only brought him closer to his demise; he acknowledged his helplessness, confessed his sins, and made a public profession of faith. The New Light crisis of conscience—whatever particular forms it may have taken—had done its work.[35]

At the dawn of the American Revolution, Dwight had completed what may be considered a rocky period of adolescence. Reared in a family of gifted and contentious adults, living in tumultuous times, graced with a degree of genteel prodigy, he had set his sights on personal greatness. His path to success was beset with physical, emotional, and spiritual obstacles, and over it hovered the shadow of Edwards. As he prepared to enter public life, Dwight bore peculiar stigmata: functional blindness, bouts of ill-health, periods of moody and fearful introspection, powerful religious stirrings, and a New Light conversion experience. Eager to make his mark but hindered by his own limitations, he entered the age of revolution.

Revolution

In the months prior to the onset of the Revolution, Dwight found his attention riveted on the brewing conflict with the British. As political temperatures rose, the heady rhetoric of independence was frequently heard in the College. Not surprisingly, Dwight was soon marching lockstep with his Yale colleagues into the patriot cause. Indeed, if loyalist Thomas Jones of the class of 1750 was correct, the Yale community was totally committed to American independence. He called it a "nursery of sedition, of factions, and republicanism."[36] Although every British citizen in the colonies would experience the effects of the rapidly changing political scene, Dwight's experience of the Revolution became the occasion for another intensely personal crisis. Dwight's religious crisis had pitted him against a wrathful yet loving heavenly father figure. That dilemma had been ritually resolved within the New Light conversion paradigm. But at a personal level, the crisis of the Revolution pitted Dwight against his strong-willed, fallible, earthly father, Major Timothy Dwight. Unlike his religious quest, the crisis with his father would elude satisfactory resolution. Just as Dwight defended the patriot cause more publicly at Yale, so his father increasingly evinced loyalist sympathies in Northampton.

As a local judge, the elder Dwight had taken the prescribed oath of fealty to the king. As the crisis of the Revolutionary era mounted and as patriotic sentiment arose in Northampton, the major struggled with his conscience but could not find it in himself to recant his sworn allegiance to his monarch. Nor was the major silent about his opinions. His loyalism was public knowledge, and he paid dearly for his political convictions. As early as April 1766, *The Boston Evening Post* published the names of representatives to the General Court whose patriotism in its opinion was suspect. The paper declared: If these individuals have been "hearty friends to their country and zealous asserters of the just rights and liberties of the people," let them be reelected. "But if they have acted a part the reverse of this, and in particular, if they have in any shape discovered an approbation of the Stamp Act . . . then they ought to be justly accounted enemies to their country."[37] Major Timothy Dwight's name was on the list.

A decade later, with the Revolution afoot, Northampton built a new jail. The military needs of the moment occasioned this decision. Many British prisoners of war were held throughout western Massachusetts, and North-ampton housed a large share of the inmates. Ironically, the jail's first occupants were the men who oversaw its construction. Major Dwight, Solomon Stoddard, Gideon Clark, and Haines Kingsley—all men who were influential in town politics—were imprisoned on suspicion of being loyalists. Their captivity, doubtless intended by overzealous patriots as a symbolic gesture, lasted only a few hours. Though Dwight made the best of a humiliating situation (he and his friends had liquor smuggled into the jail and, as one observer noted, had a "merry time"), this was but the first of many trials Major Dwight would suffer for the king he could not deny. Citizens of Northampton suspected of loyalism were hounded by mobs, put to hastily organized trials, and forced to sign confessions.[38] New forms of social egalitarianism were taking Northampton by storm: deference to the gentry waned, and social elites, be they river gods or lesser worthies, patriot or loyalist, began to lose control of the society they had dominated for generations.

Major Dwight understood that his future in Northampton and perhaps anywhere else in the colonies was uncertain, so he began to explore the idea of moving to another location. His sister Eleanor had married General Phineas Lyman, a hero of the French and Indian War. At the request of some of his impoverished soldiers, Lyman had attempted to negotiate a land grant in West Florida. During a trip to London, he secured a large tract on the Mississippi River near Natchez. Lyman then traveled to the area and made preparations for its settlement. In the spring of 1776, Lyman's wife prepared to resettle. Before she left, she tendered an offer to her brother for a share in the venture. The offer seemed reasonable, if somewhat risky. Unlike others of loyalist senti-ment, Dwight had neither family nor patrons in England, making flight across the Atlantic problematic. Nonetheless, his unyielding allegiance to the crown, given the prevailing political climate of the colonies, made his continuance in Northampton tenuous. Although his loyalist friends Solomon Stoddard and Gideon Clark signed affidavits declaring their support of the patriot cause, Dwight refused to countenance the Revolution with his signature. He decided to leave his ancestral home and abandon economic success for the frontier.

Believing that the venture promised him freedom of conscience, Dwight purchased a twenty-square-mile section of the Lyman grant. On 1 May 1776, Dwight set out from Middletown. Other travelers included his sons, Sereno and Jonathan, Mrs. Lyman, her five children, and several other families. After nearly six months, the party reached the mouth of the Mississippi. They traveled upstream to the grant. By the following spring, however, the venture was undone. Mrs. Lyman died 10 June 1777. Her brother, Major Timothy Dwight, contracted a fever and died soon thereafter. The Spanish, who were seeking to control the Mississippi Valley, forced the remaining members of the party from their new home. In what seemed a hopeless attempt to return to civilization, the party trekked eastward on foot. All five of the Lyman children died during the journey and only after a wretched year did young Timothy's brothers reach Savannah.[39]

Major Dwight's life was filled with anomalies. Son-in-law of Jonathan Edwards, the major stood firmly in the New Light religious tradition. He was a respected Northampton citizen, deferentially hailed in public as "Esquire" even as late as 1776. Moreover, Northampton's citizens repeatedly elected and appointed him to prestigious posts. A full decade after he was warned about his support of the Stamp Act, the major continued to serve as selectman, town recorder, and judge of common pleas.[40] Because he was a New Light, especially one so close to Edwards and the Northampton church experience, Major Dwight's loyalism was unusual. As a group, New Lights were overwhelmingly patriotic in their political sentiments. Few of their number sought asylum from Revolutionary New England. Dwight was the only Northampton resident, New Light or otherwise, to do so.[41]

Whatever deference and respect young Timothy may have had for his father was apparently spoiled by Major Timothy's loyalism and the ensuing debacle at Natchez. Timothy recounted the Lyman adventure in his *Travels* but, in an otherwise detailed account, he gave scant attention to his father. General and Mrs. Lyman were described in detail, but Dwight made only the following cryptic comment about his father: "Within a few months after their arrival she [Mrs. Lyman] died, and was followed by her brother the succeeding summer."[42] Indeed, though he discusses numbers of his other relatives in his writings, this is the sole mention of his father in the entire corpus. Taken by itself, this omission indicates Dwight's embarrassment over his father's loyalism, but additional data suggest that Dwight's relationship with his father was difficult in other ways as well. In literature about these two members of the Dwight family, the major is nearly always portrayed as resisting Timothy's deepest hopes. Whatever the cause of the tensions between Timothy and his father—politics, vocational choices, routine father / son authority clashes—Mary Edwards Dwight emerges in this period as the single most powerful influence on Timothy.

Dwight himself had some revolutionary adventures during these years. As was the custom for young ministerial candidates, he began the study of theology under the guidance of an established pastor. For an undetermined number of months in 1776 and 1777, Dwight studied with his uncle, Jonathan Edwards, Jr., minister of the White Haven Church in New Haven, Connecticut. Dwight's familiarity with Edwardsean theology was undoubtedly shaped in those months. Armed with two academic degrees and a course of theological study, Dwight ignored his father's previous objections and sought ecclesiastical recognition.[43] In June 1777, the Northern Association of Ministers in Hampshire County licensed him to preach.

Dwight also found time for less academic pursuits. He began to court Mary Woolsey, daughter of his father's Yale classmate Benjamin Woolsey of Long Island. They were married 7 March 1777. Once again, the Edwards family played an important part in a Dwight wedding. Jonathan Edwards, Jr., performed the ceremony, which was held in the New Haven home of another of Dwight's maternal uncles, Pierpont Edwards. In these early years, Timothy's relationship with his uncle Pierpont was apparently cordial. But later, in another ironic twist in the Edwards family history, these two descendants of Edwards would find themselves in opposing political camps. Dwight became one of the clerical champions of the Federalists, and Pierpont Edwards emerged as an important leader of Connecticut's Republican party.[44]

Though there is not abundant reason to think that Dwight's marriage was particularly unusual—he and Mary Woolsey Dwight raised a large family and were always held in the highest esteem among their social circle—the record contains hints that their relationship was formal and perhaps even distant. Mary Woolsey Dwight is virtually invisible in Dwight's story. Although the outlines of her story parallel his, we know few other details about her contributions to his development. Few data survive that indicate how frequently she traveled with him, if she took any interest in his affairs, or if she provided him the sort of solace and encouragement that was so freely offered by his mother. Though Dwight frequently appended his wife's regards in his personal letters we can only speculate on her role in his professional friendships.

About Mary Woolsey Dwight's religious life, however, we can be more certain. She outlived her husband by twenty-eight years. In her funeral sermon, preached by Leonard Bacon and entitled "The Old Age of Piety," she is lauded as a virtuous woman who was "never found wandering from her proper sphere." Bacon went on to report that "she was never able to refer to any precise period as to the date of her renewal by the Holy Spirit. . . . . [S]he was prevented from making a public declaration of her trust in the Savior till after the death of her husband, when, in the year 1819, she was received into covenant with this church [First Church, New Haven] on the profession of her faith."[45] Wife of the man who many identified as an inspired American preacher and evangelist, Mary Woolsey Dwight remained unconverted throughout her married life. What Dwight would do so effectively for his Yale students and for a generation of New England's citizens—lead them into saving relationships with Christ—he apparently failed to do with his wife of forty years. In this respect, Dwight's family biography veers away from that of his grandfather Edwards. Edwards's wife, Sarah Pierpont Edwards, weaves her way in and out of her husband's biography with remarkable regularity. He wrote about his deep love for her, she played a large role in his pastoral ministry, and she also became the subject of his own intense theological reflection. When Edwards penned his several *apologia* for the Awakening, he relied on the testimonies of converted persons—especially females—to illustrate his discoveries. Though she was not identified by name, Sarah played a prominent role in Edwards's *Some Thoughts Concerning the Present Revival of Religion in New England* (1742). By contrast, Dwight had a different sort of marriage—less open to public scrutiny and less mutual in its religious dimensions.

However formal or fulfilling Dwight's marriage may have been, it was begun in a tumultuous era. During his courtship with Mary, the war erupted. In December 1776, Yale was forced to suspend classes. The following spring Dwight moved with the senior class to Wethersfield for safety. He saw that class through commencement, and just four months after he was married he obtained a chaplain's commission through the efforts of his fellow "Wit," David Humphreys, on 6 October 1777.[46] Military activity stirred the poet in Dwight. During these months, he produced some of his best verse. He wrote several patriotic hymns, of which *Columbia* is best known, and completed his massive *Conquest of Canaan*. By means of a letter of recommendation, General Samuel Parsons, commander of the First Connecticut Brigade, introduced Dwight to George Washington. The recommendation was occasioned by Dwight's desire to dedicate *The Conquest* to Washington. He wrote to Washington on 8 March 1778 requesting permission. Therein Dwight described himself as "so independent a republican, and so honest a man, as to be incapable of a wish to palm myself upon the world under the patronage of another."[47]

Notwithstanding his protestations, Dwight's letter to Washington appears self-serving and disingenuous. Though he shamelessly flattered the most prominent man in the colonies, his desire to dedicate the work to Washington is apt given the imagery of the poem. Filled with unabashed patriotic sentiment, the epic functioned as an *apologia* for the establishment of God's eighteenth-century Israel in the new American Canaan. As the biblical hero Joshua had led the Israelites into their promised land, so America's divinely appointed Washington would free his people from oppression and deliver them to a new age. Long after the poem was published, however, Dwight engaged in some quibbling about the allegorical character of *The Conquest.* In response to a critique of the poem published in the *European Magazine* in February, March, and April of 1788, Dwight claimed that the idea that the

> poem is allegorical is so far from having a foundation, that . . . it never entered my mind that such an apprehension could be entertained by a man of Common Sense. . . . I confess a considerable resemblance between the case of the Israelites and that of the Americans. . . . That General Washington should resemble Joshua is not strange. . . . Between such men, in such circumstances, a resemblance is almost necessary. The truth is, the poem was begun in 1771 and written out several times before the year 1775, all the essential parts were finished before the war was begun.[48]

Whatever his motivation in writing the poem and whatever his own view of its several allegorical identifications, *The Conquest* described warfare in the strongest romantic and millennial terms. Although Dwight would always view the larger significance of the Revolution from this perspective, he found himself horrified by the conduct of the war itself. The unhappy duty of ministering to condemned prisoners and shocking carnage of several campaigns—described in grisly detail in his *Travels*—was sobering. Nearly four decades later he would reflect philosophically with his students on the problem of war, declaring it sometimes necessary but always productive of great physical and moral evils.[49]

Dwight served less than two years in the military. In March 1779, news of his father's death reached him, and he immediately returned home to aid his mother. Mary Edwards Dwight found herself in an exceedingly difficult position. Suddenly widowed, she was forced to take charge of her husband's business affairs, a task complicated by her large family. At the time of Major Dwight's departure, the youngest of their thirteen children was only seven months old. Dwight faced immediate challenges back in Northampton. Given the major's political sentiments, the stigma of loyalism had attached itself to the Dwight household and was exacerbated by Mary Dwight's existing hostilities toward the townsfolk. The future of the family was uncertain. Mrs. Dwight's farms had been ravaged by mobs and, because her husband's fortune had been depleted during the Lyman venture, her ability to recover was limited. Taxes rose, making the burden even greater.[50] Other family problems increased the difficulties. Dwight's younger brother Erastus had been jailed and by all accounts had suffered an emotional breakdown during some gunplay in the prison. Never fully stable, he required special care the rest of his life. In many cases the local authorities confiscated the property of loyalists but, perhaps due to Timothy's patriotic sentiments, the Dwight family home was never encumbered.[51] After two years of efforts to stabilize the situation at home, Dwight said of himself, "I remain as I was, only grown twenty years older. . . . Toil and anxiety bring a man down faster than his proportion."[52]

Toil and anxiety, however, would most often pay Dwight handsome dividends. His reputation as a learned man and published author, as well as his affection for the patriot cause, slowly rehabilitated the family name. Evidence of this shift in attitude is found in the public role that Dwight assumed after his arrival in Northampton. His neighbors twice elected him to the Massachusetts Assembly, first in 1781 and again in 1782, and the townspeople pressed him to serve in the Continental Congress, an opportunity he declined. Dwight also was permitted to open a grammar school in the town, and its great popularity reflected the town's approval.[53]

With the Revolution drawing to a close and the prospects of a new nation shaping the popular mind, Dwight's days of vocational preparation ended. The time had arrived for him to make a decision about the direction of his life's work, and as he contemplated his situation, he seems to have had only two realistic courses from which to choose. Not surprisingly, each of these alternatives focused on one of his parents. Having rescued the family's reputation and saved it from imminent economic disaster, Dwight could anticipate the acquisition of land, power, and prestige in western Massachusetts. Following in his father's footsteps, he could become the patriarch of the truly Americanized Dwights. Whatever the allure this sort of life had for Dwight, he resisted it. Though one can imagine that Dwight's father would have urged his son to remain in Northampton as head of the Dwight clan, the major himself had given Dwight ample reason to view such a course with suspicion. At crucial junctures, the major had put obstacles in his son's path. He objected to Timothy's earliest academic experiments by denying him the appropriate Latin grammars, found offensive the political statement of the class of 1769, and advised his son against entering the ministry. Finally, the major's loyalism and its deadly consequences forced Timothy to withdraw from the war and come to the defense of his mother. In each of these instances, Dwight overcame his father's objections, supplanting them with one success after another. At age twenty-seven, Dwight's self-image rested upon these victories. To conform to the wishes of his dead father would mean denying the talents and convictions he had worked so hard to cultivate in himself.

The influence of Dwight's mother and her clerical heritage presented Dwight with an alternate course. This path would lead Dwight to pulpits and podiums far from Northampton. Any prestige won in those places would not rest on his name but on the power of his mind and his voice. Whereas his father's path might have led to prominence in local civic life, his mother's line connected Dwight with the heritage of two of New England's most prestigious and influential divines—Solomon Stoddard and Jonathan Edwards. Given the choice between leadership in the state (his father's line) and leadership in the church (his mother's heritage), Dwight chose the latter. Little wonder that years later, on the occasion of Mary Edwards Dwight's death in 1807, Dwight would remark to his sister, "All that I am and all that I shall be, I owe to my mother."[54]

The Greenfield Interlude

During his stay in Northampton Dwight preached in various pulpits in western Massachusetts.[55] Within months he began entertaining the idea of permanently settling into the ministry. Several parishes extended offers to Dwight including the church in Charlestown, Massachusetts. One reaction to this invitation is particularly enlightening. In a letter to Jeremy Belknap dated 13 March 1783, John Eliot discussed Dwight's candidacy at Charlestown. He noted with approbation Dwight's service in the Massachusetts Assembly, his oratorical skills, and his enthusiasm for the natural sciences. Eliot considered Dwight a man of "liberal mind"—at least in the realm of politics. The letter continued:

> To recur to Mr. Dwight, I have given you his political character. As a divine, he is a compleat [sic] bigot on the plan of his grandfather, Mr. Edwards. He has studied little else in divinity but that scheme. He thunders out his anathemas against all who stir the pudding. He hath said (I know he hath the vanity to think so) that he hath supposed himself raised up in Providence to overset this system of errors.

Eliot's comment reveals at least two things about Dwight's theological convictions in this period. First and foremost, he was a partisan in the Edwardsean theological camp. Though this identification was multivalent and depending on which variety of Edwardseanism was affirmed could lead him to one of several quite different theological postures, clearly Dwight was viewed as both a genealogical and theological descendant of his maternal grandfather. Second, Dwight was vocally opposed to at least one liberal encroachment on orthodoxy, Universalism. Eliot's cryptic "stir the pudding" comment makes this evident. During his course of theological study Dwight learned about a group of progressive New England theologians working quietly on the margins of theological orthodoxy who had developed a rather vigorous doctrine of universal salvation. One of these progressives, Charles Chauncy (Edwards's nemesis during the Old Light / New Light controversy of the 1740s), circulated a manuscript defense of this doctrine among his friends. Unwilling to publish his essay, knowing that it would raise a storm of protest from the orthodox, Chauncy and his friends began referring to their secret conviction as "the pudding." For instance, one universalist might ask another if a third acquaintance "relishes the pudding?" In decoded form, the actual query meant "Is so-and-so a universalist?" Dwight was decidedly not sympathtic to the universalist doctrine. Not only did he "thunder anathemas" against all who "stir the pudding," but he believed that he did so with divine approbation.[56]

Though Dwight elected to decline the offer to serve the Charlestown church, other invitations followed. Several months later he accepted a call to lead the church at Greenfield, Connecticut. He was ordained on 5 November 1783. His mentor, Edwards the Younger, preached the ordination sermon, entitled "The Faithful Manifestation of the Truth, the Proper and Immediate End of Preaching the Gospel." Though Greenfield was a rural church, the parish offered Dwight a generous settlement. To the liberal salary of five hundred dollars per year was added the use of a six-acre tract of land and one thousand dollars to resettle his growing family. The church knew that it had secured the services of a pious and learned patriot. For such a leader they were willing to pay handsomely.[57]

Not surprisingly, Dwight's theological inclinations soon began to make themselves felt. Though the Edwardsean movement was quite differentiated, most of Edwards's followers agreed with their mentor on the issue of church membership. Unlike the majority of their contemporaries, they eschewed the Halfway Covenant and demanded that believers be admitted to membership and the sacraments only after a full profession of faith. Given his own pulpit, Dwight propounded these views unceasingly despite the fact that not everyone in the parish accepted his ideas. Some members questioned Dwight's orthodoxy, and they unsuccessfully sought to block his installation. Though the details of their objections are unknown, it is likely that Dwight's Edwardsean views on church membership and baptism were the object of their complaints. This is suggested by Dwight's letter of acceptance in which he reminded the congregation that in his trial sermons he had candidly explained his theology to them. The sermons were based on biblical texts from 1 Corinthians 7:14 and Acts 20:26 and concerned preaching "the whole counsel of God" and baptism respectively. In Dwight's mind, his conservative New Light theology should not have surprised any of Greenfield's members for he believed himself to have been candid from the start of their negotiations. Despite the objections Dwight had his way: Greenfield became a church that eschewed Halfway Covenant practice.[58] Throughout the Greenfield period Dwight's theological work further establishes his familiarity with Edwardsean theology. He began preaching the sermons—using only brief notes because his eyes prevented him using a manuscript—that would later be transcribed and arranged for publication after his death as *Theology, Explained and Defended*.[59] At numerous points the work affirms the broad outlines of Edwardsean teaching. All things considered, Dwight's early ministerial career suggests that he had become an Edwardsean.

Although his pastoral duties were demanding, Dwight found time to pursue other interests. *The Conquest of Canaan* (finished as early as 1775 but not published until 1785) had functioned as a postmillennial *apologia* for the establishment of the people of God in America. *Greenfield Hill* (1788), believed by some to be Dwight's best poetic accomplishment, can be seen as a pastoral description of the godly community within a divinely blessed republic.[60] Dedicated to John Adams, *Greenfield Hill* describes beautiful pastoral scenes through New England's seasons and makes clear Dwight's belief that life in a New England village—where virtuous citizens live in harmony, simplicity, and genuine faith—was perhaps the ideal existence. Dwight ended the poem with a millennial paean on the glories of America:

> One blood, one kindred, reach from sea to sea;
> One language spread, one tide of manners run;
> One scheme of science, and of morals one;
> And, God's own Word the structure, and the base,
> One faith extend, one worship, and one praise.[61]

Greenfield Hill did more than parade its author's glassy-eyed, otherworldly idealism. Sections of the poem treat controversial social problems, not least among them slavery. Here and elsewhere during his career Dwight proved himself a vocal opponent of the slave trade and slaveholding. These commitments are evident in his published works and in his teaching but can also be seen in his personal affairs. In March 1888, Dwight bought an African American named Naomi to serve as a housekeeper. In a surviving document entitled "Naomi's Bond," he laid out the conditions on which Naomi could release herself from her obligations to the Dwight family:

> This certifies that the conditions on which I bought Naomi, a negro woman, formerly belonging to Deacon Daniel Andrews ... are, that she shall work for me and mine until she shall have refunded the money which I am to pay for her, at the rate of seven pounds, sixteen shillings per year. ... [She shall] live with me and mine, until she shall, at the same rate of hire, have discharged the expense arising from the same. In which case I voluntarily bind myself, my heirs, my executors and administrators, and release her from all obligations to serve me (as I never intended her for a slave) any further time.

The record does not indicate how much Dwight initially paid for Naomi, how long she worked for the Dwight family, or when she was released from her obligation to Dwight. Whatever the details, during his sojourn in Greenfield Dwight's fortunes prospered, and though he needed a servant, he was unwilling—at least technically—to own a slave.[62]

In his writing of the period Dwight discovered that verse could serve as an aggressive weapon in ideological skirmishes with critics of the republic, or with those whose political or religious views Dwight found unacceptable. Perhaps the best example of this is his *Triumph of Infidelity* (1788). Dwight had dedicated *Greenfield Hill,* his tribute to American culture at its finest, to a man worthy of praise and emulation, Vice President John Adams. In similar fashion he dedicated *The Triumph,* his first blast against the heterodox, to Voltaire, a man he thought to be worthy of the title "infidel." Lest his readers fail to appreciate the differences between these two exemplars, Dwight drew a sharp a contrast as he could. He wrote *Greenfield Hill* for Adams "with sentiments of the highest respect for his Private Character, and for the important services he has rendered his Country." Alternately, in his facetious dedicatory epistle at the opening of *The Triumph,* he declared that Voltaire had devoted his talents "to a single purpose, the elevation of your [i.e., Voltaire's] character above [God's]" and that he taught "that the chief end of man was, to slander his god, and abuse him forever."[63] *The Triumph* is something of an upside-down ecclesiastical history. Instead of tracing the progress of the God's heavenly reign, it chronicles the great victories of Satan and his minions from hell. With a heavy poetic hand, Dwight has Satan himself serve as the narrator and grants the devil full license to glory in his many victories over the godly. Satan rehearses his artful challenges to biblical characters, his skillful manipulation of the Roman pontiffs, his temptations of Luther and Calvin (all rebuffed, of course), and his eventual triumph in eighteenth-century Europe. Only in New England under the providential leadership of remarkable divines like Edwards is Satan's advance halted.[64]

Although Deism and Enlightenment skepticism were *The Triumph's* most obvious targets, Dwight was concerned with more than theological heterodoxy in these years. Infidelity may have been conceived among intellectuals, but Dwight was troubled by its larger cultural implications and especially by the manner in which it sapped the virtues of the common citizen. Infidelity had taken on a dangerous social cast: Deism and skepticism were leading to the evils of egalitarian democracy. This was not simply an occasional political observation on Dwight's part. Rather this conviction formed the very core of his social ethics. Throughout his career Dwight insisted that orthodoxy was nothing if it was upheld merely for its own sake. Orthodoxy's real importance rested not in itself but in its social and political ramifications.

Notwithstanding the shrill denunciations evident in *The Triumph,* Dwight was no obscurantist. Indeed, he encouraged theological debate and fostered discussion of new ideas. As he would later tell his students, he believed that true religion was to be found in the scriptures but only if the Bible were allowed to speak for itself. "Preconceived schemes" and theological controversies were inevitable but should be judged critically and not adopted prior to careful scrutiny.[65] The academic freedom that such an outlook required, he believed, demanded responsibility. Scholars were free to discuss such matters, but their conversations were to be governed by the sober acknowledgment that the virtue of America's citizens was at stake. This concern with the social and moral implications of religion was the guiding principle of Dwight's *Theology,* and it explains the energy behind *The Triumph's* vehemence. Dwight's art served several purposes. Through it he engaged both offensively and defensively the disciplines of religion, politics, and ethics. He understood these areas of endeavor (which contemporary intellectuals have viewed as distinct and often unrelated aspects of culture) as a unified whole that required the scrutiny of right-thinking Christian disciples. Therefore, Dwight the champion of fidelity cannot be separated from the Dwight who would later be known as the champion of Federalism.

Educational endeavors also marked the Greenfield years. Just one month after his ordination, the *Connecticut Journal* ran the following advertisement:

> Several gentlemen having applied to the subscriber to provide for their children, in various branches of knowledge; they and others are informed that so soon as twenty scholars shall apply, a school will commence at Greenfield, where the Languages, Geography, English Grammar, Reading, Writing, Speaking, and the practical branches of Mathematics will be taught under the instruction of Timothy Dwight.

If a subsequent newspaper description of the school is to be believed, Dwight's Greenfield academy was very successful. During his tenure as the school's headmaster he directed the studies of over one thousand students, both young men and women, many of whom he prepared for collegiate work. Dwight was gaining an international reputation as an educator and leading families from Maine to the West Indies sent their children to him for training.[66] Dwight's literary and educational accomplishments were doubtless the reason that the College of New Jersey (later Princeton University) granted Dwight an honorary doctorate in 1787.[67]

Not everyone was happy with Dwight's success as a pedagogue. Chief among his critics was the president of Yale, Ezra Stiles. Both men were of New England stock, both were Congregational clergymen, and both held Yale College dear. Such parallels suggest common interests and, given Stiles's initial respect for Dwight (in 1773 Stiles remarked that "Mr. Dwight is certainly an honor to Yale College"), a lively friendship.[68] But in this instance outward appearances are deceptive. Stiles and Dwight were men of "strong likes and dislikes." Stiles "disliked Baptists, Quakers, Anglicans, and Timothy Dwight," while Dwight "disliked deists, democrats, and—apparently—Ezra Stiles."[69] Stiles was suspicious of Edwardseanism in general and of its narrower New Divinity variant which disposed him to distrust Dwight. More important, Stiles believed that Dwight coveted Yale's presidency.

This conviction was not wholly unjustified, for Dwight and Stiles had already competed for the presidency of Yale. In 1777, when President Naphtali Daggett resigned, Dwight's Yale students sought his election to the post. Dwight withdrew his name because he knew that his age (he was only twenty-five at the time) would disqualify him, and the position went to Stiles. After frictions with Britain ignited the Revolution, Dwight left Yale for the chaplaincy. Later he returned to Northampton and opened his first academy. Although a good deal of the academy's success rested on Dwight's gifts as a teacher, it was also true that he had fashioned his school's course of study on a proven model, Yale's curriculum. The parallels were so clear, in fact, that some Yale undergraduates actually transferred to Dwight's Northampton academy. Quite understandably, Stiles began to fear that Dwight was presiding over what might become a rival institution. To exacerbate Stiles's fears, rumors circulated that some of Dwight's friends were gathering funds to endow for him a chair at Yale. Stiles's reaction to such news is predictable. Of Dwight Stiles confided to his diary: "[He] meditates great things and nothing but great things will serve him—and everything that comes in the way of his preferment must fall before him. Aut Caesar, aut nullus."[70]

There exists one other perplexing element in the Dwight/Stiles story. Stiles's personal papers, one of the greatest sources of Yale's early internal history, contain an odd gap in the years 1780 to 1795. Though there is no reason to assume that Stiles wrote fewer letters during his presidential years—indeed, just the opposite is typical—virtually no correspondence survives. In addition, Stiles's *Literary Diary* has been tampered with, perhaps by family members desirous of mementos but more likely by someone who found these records damaging. Franklin B. Dexter, editor of Stiles's *Literary Diary*, believed that Stiles was responsible for the gaps because he feared that his candid comments about Dwight would be made public. Edmund S. Morgan suggests that Dwight himself may have destroyed the documents after he assumed the Yale presidency.[71] Evidence of a strained relationship with his predecessor and suggestions that he hungered for the office himself before he was actually appointed would not have served Dwight well.

The tensions that existed between Dwight and Stiles must be viewed in a larger context. In the 1780s and early 1790s, Yale College was under pressure from several quarters to reorganize itself. As stipulated in the original College charter, the Yale Corporation was made up entirely of clergymen from Connecticut parishes. After the Revolution, a spirit of anticlericalism arose in the state, and many of Connecticut's leaders began to question the wisdom of allowing the state's only college to be controlled by the clergy. As president of Yale, Ezra Stiles feared the effects that might be produced by the presence of laypeople ("civilians" as he called them) in the Corporation. He also knew that Yale's financial well-being depended upon improved relations with the state's General Assembly. Most objections could be met by expanding the Corporation to include laypeople. More vehement critics intimated that unless Yale made more significant adjustments, the Assembly would create a rival state college—a move that would ruin Yale's favored position.[72] As the political controversy became more heated, it was apparent to Stiles and others that if Yale was to survive some share in the control of the college had to be offered to the legislature.

To exacerbate these tensions further, the *Connecticut Courant* published a series of broadsides that articulated the complaints against Yale and publicly called for reform of the charter. Written under the pseudonym "Parnassus," the twelve articles were published from 4 February through 27 May 1783. Considered as political rhetoric, the essays are relatively tame. What is striking is the nature of the information revealed in the articles. Somehow Parnassus had become privy to the inner workings and private deliberations of the Yale Corporation. His 18 March column dealt with the Corporation's unfair treatment of its faculty and tutors. To the horror of Stiles and his colleagues, Parnassus gave accurate, verbatim accounts of conversations held during the Corporation's closed meetings. Armed with such privileged information, Parnassus challenged the clerical makeup of the Corporation, asking "whether it is fit that a public seminary should be under the direction of one of the learned professions to the exclusion of other learned men." Of course, in subsequent issues of the *Courant* Parnassus went on to answer his own rhetorical question. "A better acquaintance with human nature and the world, than the Corporation collectively taken, appear to possess, is required for the government of an University." Therefore, he concluded Yale's program of "education should not be be trusted to them exclusively."[73]

One aspect of the clergy's domination of Yale particularly interested Parnassus. The whole of his 22 April column was given to an attack on Yale's College Church. Speaking on behalf of Connecticut's Baptist and Anglican dissenters, Parnassus charged that the presence of a Congregational church within Yale's walls "savors of bigotry dishonorable to a literary institution."[74] Such bigotry was best illustrated by Yale's divinity professorship. Traditionally, its incumbents were prominent Congregational clergymen. How, asked Parnassus, could the professor of divinity lead Yale's president in the spiritual affairs of the college church while simultaneously submitting himself to the president's authority in the general governance of the college? Similarly, how could student members of the church be subject to the professor of divinity in the classroom and yet remain free to approach him candidly as a Christian pastor in personal, spiritual matters? These conflicts of interests, Parnassus argued, pointed to the need for the reform of Yale's power structure.

Who was this anonymous critic of the Corporation and its policies? The strongest evidence points to Timothy Dwight. Given his role as tutor, and from intelligence he was able to gather from friends who remained at Yale after he had settled in Greenfield, Dwight had the information necessary to play the part. Wounded pride may also have motivated him to launch an assault on the justice of the Corporation. According to Parnassus, the Corporation had a history of dealing unfairly with its tutors. Indeed, Parnassus claimed that in an effort to quell the call for curricular reform of the College, the Corporation had unjustly punished the chief reformer among the tutors, Dwight himself.[75] Dwight may also have had reason to hope that Yale's educational lustre could be sullied. By the time the essays appeared in the *Courant,* Dwight had demonstrated that he was a successful educator. Ezra Stiles and others feared that he would begin an institution in Greenfield that might rival Yale. Like Parnassus, Dwight knew and used the *Courant* for his own purposes. Though the Parnassus articles ran almost weekly in the *Courant,* one gap occurs on February 25. Coincidentally, that very issue contains an advertisement for Dwight's *Conquest of Canaan.*

Though Stiles himself never claimed that Dwight was Parnassus (Stiles suspected that a committee of Yale malcontents were responsible for the articles), at two places in his *Literary Diary* he recorded his suspicions of Dwight's motives. First, Stiles noted that the Corporation received a petition from a group of students to publish its financial records. Apparently, their intent was to force Yale to reveal how tuition fees were being spent. Stiles referred to this petition as "Dwight's Memorial." Second, he noted that the Assembly was petitioned to reform Yale by adding laypeople to the Corporation. Stiles believed that the petition was "draughted by Mr. Dwight praying for a Board of civilians to correct and otherwise to build a new college; this said to be genuinely rejected as abounding with Accusation and Aspersions and injurious Reflexions on the college."[76] Unfortunately, neither "Dwight's Memorial" nor his alleged petition has survived. Here one wonders with Stiles's biographer Edmund Morgan if the missing documents and perhaps more substantial proof of Dwight's complicity in the affair were contained in the missing sections of the *Literary Diary.*[77]

At least one other piece of evidence supports the claim that Dwight wrote the Parnassus articles. Fifteen years after the Parnassus affair, this clue emerged in *The American Mercury,* a Republican newspaper that delighted in regularly lampooning Federalist foibles. In a 30 April 1803 column, an anonymous pundit writing under the pseudonym "ESCHINES" published a curious and ambiguous article on Dwight's involvement in Connecticut politics. At first blush, the essay is nothing more than a Republican attack on the Standing Order clergy, cleverly put forth as a tongue-in-cheek defense of Dwight. An alternative interpretation is that the column represents a genuine Federalist defense of Dwight that calls for Republicans to repent of their unfair treatment of Yale's president. Under either reading the author's identification of Dwight as Parnassus is undeniable. ESCHINES describes Dwight as "fountain head of political and religious orthodoxy" and then launches a curious lament. Dwight, he complains, has descended from the "lofty summit of Parnassus, where he has so long held a sublime seat," has exchanged his mighty steed Pegasus for a common horse, and has ridden it to Boston, where he sojourned with Federalist partisans Morse, Tappan, and Pierson. This fateful trip seems to have silenced the "orphean harmony of Canaan's lyre." Regardless of the political persuasion of the author, the imagery is clear. Once an agent for change (who wrote under the name Parnassus), Dwight now defended the status quo; once a poet of national stature, he was now a provincial political partisan.[78]

If we conclude that Dwight wrote the Parnassus articles, some fascinating conclusions emerge as to his views and his character in the 1780s. Parnassus was, if nothing else, opposed to the privileged position of Connecticut's Congregational clergy. He attacked their control of the Yale Corporation and, more important, their domination of Yale's College Church. But Parnassus's assaults represented more than the polemic of an educational reformer. His was the literary expression of the restless mood of Connecticut's anti-establishment political faction. Privilege, elitism, and aristocracy—the Standing Order itself—was under attack from more democratic forces. Although the full-scale political war that would eventuate in the demise of the Federalists had not yet begun, the Parnassus affair was an early incident that led to that larger conflict.

The Parnassus affair demonstrates Dwight's capacity to play both sides of a controversy to his best advantage. With the leadership of Yale in the balance, Dwight assaulted the Corporation under the cover of a pseudonym, while simultaneously working hard to establish himself as a defender of Connecticut's venerable status quo. In the very months in which Parnassus wrote, Dwight began his career as a Congregational clergyman trumpeting traditional theological views. Before accepting the Greenfield call, Dwight made it clear that any church he served must be run on the traditional pre–Halfway Covenant scheme. While Parnassus was hounding his establishment foes, Dwight was busy composing his vehement poetic attack on American free-thinking, *The Triumph of Infidelity*. Ironically, after he became Yale's president and had been flayed by countless anonymous assailants in the press, Dwight (with dubious integrity) told his Yale seniors that anonymous publications should be suppressed by law. "A man who wishes to slander another," he claimed during the 1813–1814 academic year, "would not commonly do it if he were obliged to accompany the slander with his own name."[79]

Though his intent was hardly slanderous, Dwight played the role of Parnassus with premeditated guile. Parnassus' anti-establishment posturing was, in this interpretation, a daring ruse that both hid Dwight's identity and allowed him to air his real complaint, the state of the current leadership of the Yale Corporation. (Who would have imagined that Parnassus also wrote *The Triumph?*) Stiles's brief comments regarding "Dwight's Memorial," as well as other data, go far toward establishing the fact that Dwight did lobby for a realignment of power within the Corporation. Although Parnassus and his fellow reformers sought immediate change, it did not come for nearly a decade. In May 1791, the General Assembly appointed a committee to study and report on the state of Yale College. Finding the College in need of financial assistance, the committee recommended that the Assembly and the college join in a partnership to ensure Yale's well-being. Under the proposed agreement, the Assembly would grant the College financial incentives if the Yale Corporation would yield some of its seats to members of the Assembly. The agreement stipulated that Connecticut's governor, lieutenant governor, and six senior state councilors be added to the Corporation. From Stiles's perspective, this "liberal Donation, and noble Condescension" was "beyond all Expectation." One aspect of the compromise especially pleased Stiles: "that the civilians should acquiesce in being a minority in the Corporation."[80]

Even though he was settled at a distance from Yale, Dwight played a hand in the changing situation of the Corporation. After the agreement between Yale and the Assembly was finalized, the College suddenly found itself in need of a new professor of divinity. By 1793, Dwight's reputation as a Yale tutor, theologian, and preacher made him a prime candidate for the position. Accordingly, he was nominated for the post with three other clergymen, Jonathan Edwards, Jr., Joseph Lathrop, and Nathan Williams. After three ballots, Lathrop was elected to the post. Dwight was runner-up, having received six votes to Lathrop's ten. Fortunately, Stiles recorded the exact details of the voting in his *Literary Diary*. Dwight's supporters fell into two categories. Timothy Pitkin and Levi Hart, the Corporation's New Divinity clergy contingent, voted for Dwight, as did four of the six "civilian" members of the Corporation. These were John Treadwell, James Davenport, William Hillhouse, and Roger Newburg. This information is enlightening for several reasons. First, it shows that Dwight managed to garner support from the Corporation's New Divinity minority. During these years, Stiles had received several complaints from

Edwardsean partisans who felt that Yale was unsympathetic to their views and that the institution was not giving them a voice in its deliberations. Hart and Pitkin's support of Dwight shows that he was favored by New Divinity members at a time when the New Divinity felt their position was particularly insecure. Second, Dwight had the support of two-thirds of the unordained "civilians" on the Corporation, some of whom may have viewed him as a potential political ally. Moreover, each of Dwight's supporters owed his presence on the Corporation to the reforms advocated by Parnassus and, therefore, to Timothy Dwight. Indeed, it was Hillhouse and Davenport who negotiated the legislation that brought Yale and the Assembly together. It is not unreasonable to assume that in an act of political patronage these men sought to elect a qualified partisan to a prestigious post at Yale.

If this was the case, one wonders why the other two Corporation civilians, William Williams and Joseph Platt Cook, voted against Dwight. In Cook's case, there is little evidence to suggest a motive for his support of Lathrop. Williams's motives for voting against Dwight, however, were more obvious. Williams's father had led the opposition to Jonathan Edwards during the Northampton awakenings. An extant letter from Stiles to the younger Williams indicates that the son shared his father's theological convictions.[81] Given his religious outlook it is likely that young Williams would have opposed any New Light candidate for the post in Divinity. The fact that the leading New Light candidate was a friend of the Corporation's New Divinity men and the grandson of his father's archrival would only have hardened Williams's opposition to Dwight.

Although the Parnassus intrigue played but a small part in the history of Yale, it does offer some interesting insights into Dwight's relationship with Yale College during the Greenfield era. Contrary to his image as an aggressive defender of the status quo, Timothy Dwight played the role of reformer. Moreover, the Parnassus affair indicates that Dwight took more than passing interest in Yale; clearly, he wanted to return to a leading role in the college and was willing to work in public or private, forthrightly or anonymously, to obtain his ends. Although his attempts to return to his alma mater failed in the 1780s, Dwight was in his early thirties, and he hoped that another opportunity to return would soon present itself.

Meanwhile, Dwight's more public work in Greenfield was progressing well. The church was pleased with his work, his grammar school continued, and as more of his prose and poetry was published, his reputation as a clerical and civic leader grew considerably.[82] In 1788, he published "An Address to Ministers of Every Denomination," a remarkably enlightened document in which he urged American ministers to adopt a broad and catholic attitude toward one another (an echo of Parnassus?). He suggested that each of the nation's

Protestant sects appoint a representative to a federal, ecumenical convention that would eschew denominational differences ("Let no matters of faith or opinion ever be introduced into this convention, but let them be considered as badges of sovereignty of each particular sect.")[83] He also published several poems during the Greenfield era, including *The Seasons Moralized, Song Written in 1771, Epistle to Colonel Humphreys,* and several poems that appeared in *The Beauties of Poetry, British and American* (1791). This latter collection contained Dwight's optimistic, unabashedly millennial *Prospect of America.* [84] Nor did the national political issues of the day escape Dwight's attention. In May 1791, he preached an election sermon, *Virtuous Rulers a National Blessing,* a strongly millennial treatise in which he detailed his understanding of the manner in which virtue chastened self-interest and worked for the public good.[85]

As Dwight's prominence grew, other churches became interested in his pastoral skills. In 1794, he declined a generous offer from the Reformed Dutch Church in Albany, New York, an event that reveals his theological sensitivities at the time. In a letter to Philip van Rensselaer of the Albany church Dwight explained that despite his general affirmation of the Dutch Confession of Faith and Catechism he was unable to affirm the more detailed statement of faith proposed by the congregation itself. Their confession, Dwight said, was "too absolute and strict for the prosperity of their church."[86] Though Dwight was known as "a strenuous stickler for what he esteems to be the truth," he was shrewd enough to avoid the effects of what he took to be ultra-precisionism.[87]

Whatever theological scruples led Dwight to decline the Albany church's offer, another possibility engaged his attention. He knew that in the event of Stiles's retirement or death Yale would begin searching for a replacement. He had written his sister-in-law, asking her opinion about the possible move to Albany. Her reply, clever though perhaps apocryphal, could only have affirmed Dwight's most ardent hopes.

> Let marriage rites and funeral fee
> To you no object be,
> The living for a trifle join
> And let the dead go free.
>
> Have you not heard that Dr. Stiles
> Totters on his last legs,
> And to New Haven you'll be call'd
> Sure as eggs is eggs?[88]

Dwight's tenure at Greenfield was a grand success. He was recognized as a "useful and honourable" man in his community, his region, and his nation. But at forty-three Dwight had reached the "meridian of his life."[89] Despite his fame and success Dwight was getting restless. Yale College was on his mind.

The Light of Yale

For nearly twenty years Dwight had desired the presidency of Yale. In the spring of 1795, his hopes were fulfilled. On 20 May, Ezra Stiles contracted a fever, and four days later the "Gentle Puritan" died. The Yale Corporation immediately began searching for a new president, and Dwight was surely near the top of their list of candidates. As one sympathetic observer later remarked of Dwight, "the extensiveness of his acquisitions, the weight of his character, his well known talents for educating youth, and the celebrity of his name" combined to make him the obvious successor to Stiles.[90] The Corporation did have some concerns about Dwight's penchant for Edwardsean theology. Stiles himself had recorded at least two occasions when Dwight had publicly revealed his affinity to Edwardsean theology. Both of these concerned Halfway Covenant baptismal practice. Moreover, Dwight's animosity toward the Northampton church must have been particularly alarming to the Corporation. Aware of the damage the church had done to the great Edwards and keeping his own mother's vindictive spirit alive, Dwight refused to commune in the Northampton parish. On one occasion, when asked to justify this action, Dwight was said to have replied that "he would lieve [sic] commune with all the devils in hell as with that corrupt church."[91] Jonathan Ingersoll, at the request of the Corporation, queried Dwight about his theological views. When asked about the Halfway Covenant, Dwight responded:

> The admission of children to baptism on what is commonly called the half-way plan, has never appeared to me sufficient reason to refuse communing with a church; nor indeed, do I consider it as having anything to do with the subject of communing. I have repeatedly administered the Lord's Supper to the church at Stamford, in which that practice has always existed. You will make the necessary connection.[92]

With the presidency of Yale at stake, Dwight was anxious to present himself as a moderate Edwardsean who eschewed the more radical notions of the New Divinity theologians.

Dwight did not make his great desire for the post immediately evident, at least not publicly. He allowed Yale to solicit his services. Indeed, he went so far as to deny that he was interested in the position. "I do not court the appointment. . . . [T]o build up a ruined college is a difficult task. It is a pity the man who wishes for it should not be gratified. I am not the man."[93] Despite Dwight's feigned disinterest and coy remonstrations, the Corporation met on 24 June and elected him president.[94] If there were other candidates for the position, their names have not survived. Not surprisingly, Dwight immediately accepted the post though it took some time for him to free himself from his obligations in Greenfield. The Greenfield church opposed the move until the local Consociation persuaded the church to grant Dwight leave to move to New Haven. Greenfield's loss was to be Yale's gain.[95] Dwight and his family moved to New Haven during the summer, and his inauguration was scheduled to take place at Commencement in September. An eyewitness to the event indicated that the new president was less than impressive at his first commencement: "in giving the degrees, [Dwight] was obviously embarrassed; and as he had not perfectly committed the Latin form to memory, he made frequent blunders in reciting it."[96] Even though the "blunders" were likely the result of his inability to read the unmemorized text on the podium before him, such gaffes were out of character for Dwight, who later appeared to enjoy much of the pomp associated with his position at the college.

Dwight's dislike of Stiles may have been part of the motivation behind his judgment that Yale was a "ruined college," but his choice of words was not entirely unjustified. In 1795, Yale found itself plagued by a variety of difficulties. The faculty was small, the college buildings were dilapidated, and the student population had ceased growing. Fortunately, Stiles had bequeathed Yale a vision; he believed that Yale, then only a regional college, could become a university of national stature.[97] Dwight shared this vision, and with characteristic energy began working to achieve Stiles's dream. With the backing of the Corporation, he courted the favor of the General Assembly, which made funds available for the improvement of the campus. The college made progress in academic affairs as well. The library grew as did the collection of laboratory equipment. More important, a genuine liberal arts faculty developed under Dwight's leadership. On his arrival in 1795, Dwight performed the duties of the divinity professor, and Josiah Meigs remained as the chair of Mathematics and Natural Philosophy.[98] To these posts were added professorships of Law (Elizur Goodrich, 1801), Chemistry and Natural History (Benjamin Silliman, 1805), Language and Ecclesiastical History (James Kingsley, 1805), and Medicine (Nathan Smith, 1813). Though Yale College was not to become Yale University until later in the nineteenth century, Dwight made enormous strides toward the realization of Stiles's vision.[99]

The challenges of Dwight's presidency went well beyond administrative tasks, however. Stiles had begun to modernize the college laws, and Dwight made further revisions. Although his chief concern was the religious development and moral rectitude of his pupils, he was forced to deal with a host of other issues not least of which was violence among the students. Hazing, coarse language, pranks, and scuffles between students were routine events in college life. Although tutors and professors expected this sort of behavior of the adolescents in their care, sometimes more violent eruptions occurred. The first years of Dwight's presidency were relatively peaceful, but in February 1799 student unrest culminated in a brawl on the campus. According to one student participant, a group of sailors visited the campus looking for a fight, and the students gladly obliged them. The altercation lasted an hour and resulted in three wounded scholars and the arrest of several bystanders. No one recorded how the sailors fared in the brawl. Nothing short of full-scale riots broke out on campus in 1806, a town-gown affair, and again in 1812, when upwards of 800 combatants joined forces.[100] Yale College, however, was hardly an exception among colleges of the period. Student dissatisfaction at Harvard, Brown, Dartmouth, William and Mary, and Hampden-Sydney exploded into disorder and tumults. Administrators at Princeton endured all manner of criminal behavior—students fired guns, beat tutors, and in 1807 set Nassau Hall ablaze. Several features of this period of student unrest are interesting. The most rebellious and recalcitrant students, for instance, were sons of the nation's Revolutionary founders and tended to display their most aggressive behavior toward authority figures during periods of national political anxiety. For the present purpose it is instructive to note the strategies developed by college administrators to deal with the problem. Schools that did not have codes of conduct quickly published them, and schools that did have laws quickly moved to enforce both spirit and letter. Princeton and Harvard expelled student rowdies but suffered the collateral consequences of huge declines in student enrollment. As a result of disciplinary actions in 1807, fifty Princeton students withdrew from school in support of their classmates who had been disciplined, and Harvard lost forty students in a similar mass resignation.[101]

By all accounts Yale escaped the worst of the negative repercussions of student unrest. This was likely due to Dwight's approach to student life and his understanding of the relationship between students and faculty members. In a disquisition session with his Yale seniors many years later Dwight reminisced on these matters during debate on the question "Would a National University be Beneficial?"

> It was formerly the practice to govern the students of this college by a kind of municipal law . . . but I introduced the system of parental government. The importance of this change presented itself to my mind while I was a tutor, and I made an experiment at that time which satisfied me that it might be easily accomplished. Neither I nor my fellow tutors ever fined a student. . . . My three first classes I governed by the eye and by the tongue. I have made it my plan to have no point to carry, and to have no favorites.[102]

Dwight's governance by "eye and tongue" had the expected effect on his students. In the classroom he could inspire awe and even fear with a mere glance. As an undergraduate Benjamin Silliman (whom Dwight later added to Yale's faculty) confessed, "When I hear [Dwight] speak, it makes me feel a very insignificant being, and also prompts me to despair."[103] Denison Olmstead concurred with Silliman's appraisal. Olmstead observed that Dwight expected, even demanded, deference from his students. In returning student salutations, Dwight "had more the air of condescension than a reciprocation of kind and respectful feelings." Even the seniors with whom he worked so closely "could hardly feel at ease in his presence." "His person was . . . large and commanding, his manners refined and courtly, his voice deep and melodious;—authority, as one born to command, seemed to invest his entire character." Doubtless Olmstead intended this description as a compliment. It is not difficult to understand how easily Dwight's critics could have turned this sort of description against him. Olmstead's authoritative and condescending president became in Republican hands the epitome of elitism, arrogance, and undeserved privilege.[104]

Notwithstanding his formality and authoratative air, Dwight could be warm and caring. He offered his students individual counsel and attention and in times of crisis visited them in their quarters for conversation and prayer. If he knew a student's parents, he routinely offered reports on a child's progress at college and used his considerable influence with a wide range of professional acquaintances to secure good positions for college graduates.[105] Dwight's own difficulties at college remained a vivid memory, as did the humane and personal manner in which he had been helped by his tutor, Stephen Mix Mitchell.

Dwight's relationships with students were not forged occasionally, as troubles or crises arose, but regularly in chapel and the classroom. Yale's curriculum was rigorous. On application for admission students were examined in Virgil, Cicero, the Greek New Testament, and arithmetic. If they were admitted, they spent three years of intensive work in the classics, mathematics, natural philosophy, geography, astronomy, and chemistry. In their senior year, they studied with Dwight. Lyman Beecher recorded the seniors' academic regimen as follows:

> We began with Blair's Rhetoric, half an hour's recitation, and an hour or hour and a half of extempore lecture. . . . [Dwight] showed a thoroughgoing mastery of the subject. Then we took up logic and metaphysics—Duncan and Locke were our authors. In ethics we studied Paley. . . . This took up three days of each week. On two other days we had written or extempore debates before Dr. Dwight, he summing up at the close. On Saturday we had the Catechism, Vincent's Exposition, followed by a theological lecture. You see it was more than a college—it was partly a divinity school.[106]

Dwight's most celebrated classroom work took place in the debates that occupied two days of the seniors' weekly schedule. He would publish a list of questions for discussion and select students to argue for or against the question. At the close of student presentations, Dwight would assess the students' efforts and offer his opinion of the question. The exercise served several purposes. Students learned public address and were given the chance to polish their skills in argumentation, and Dwight raised a wide range of moral, political, and cultural questions that might otherwise have escaped treatment in the curriculum. Long after his father's death Dwight's son Theodore published Dwight's responses to forty-one questions that were debated by Yale seniors during the 1813–14 academic year. That year the list of topics for disputation varied widely and included the justice of capital punishment, the liberty of the press, the abilities of the sexes, public support of the clergy, the extension and division of the federal union, the Crusades, the justification of resistance to the government, the reality of spectres, the justification of duelling, the morality of war, and the immortality of the soul. Although Dwight commanded a good deal of respect from his students, the recitation room was not always placid. In 1803, in a tense class debate on the question "Would it be politic to encourage the immigration of foreigners into the United States?" young John C. Calhoun, then a Jeffersonian and later Vice President of the United States under John Quincy Adams and Andrew Jackson, crossed verbal sabers with Dwight. Calhoun argued the affirmative, but Dwight decided in the negative, noting in the process that his poem *Columbia*, which arose "from the pleasing idea of having this country become the refuge of the oppressed," was a youthful bit of "enthusiasm."[107] Notwithstanding his differences with Calhoun, Dwight held him in quite high regard. After another classroom encounter (in which they debated about the source of political power— Calhoun said it lay in the people, Dwight disagreed), Dwight is reported to have said that Calhoun "had talent enough to be the President of the United States."[108] Student notes of the debates from other years indicate that Dwight had developed a list of questions that he used repeatedly after 1800. Dwight's memory for detail and rigorous logic is what most impressed his students especially given the fact that his classroom work was performed extempore.[109]

Yale students knew Dwight before they entered his senior seminar. The College chapel was also his domain, and every student regularly heard him preach there. Lyman Beecher, one of Dwight's favorite students and one of the nineteenth century's most prominent religious promoters, created an account of Dwight's religious work that has had a lasting effect. In 1850, at age seventy-five and after fifty years of controversial ministry, Beecher deemed it important to add an autobiography to his already long list of publications. Instead of putting pen to paper, however, Beecher reminisced aloud about his life and asked his children, then fully grown and famous in their own right, to prepare stenographic notes of his personal recollections. The younger Beechers willingly obliged. They collected letters and other personal papers of their father, and one year after Lyman Beecher's death in 1863 Charles Beecher prepared the final manuscript for publication. The two-volume published text is a unique piece of American literature. Folksy, conversational in tone, extremely partisan, the *Autobiography* is filled with the selective memories of a controversial old man in his twilight years.

Dwight, whom Beecher proudly claimed as his "theological instructor and father, most beloved and revered of all the men to whom this heart of mine was ever drawn," steps in and out of the narrative.[110] He is most prominent in the early chapters, which relate to Beecher's student days at Yale. Bright, naive, and impressionable, Beecher commenced his studies with a good deal of anxiety about his religious condition. He felt particularly guilty about personal infractions of the divine law and about his ignorance of Christian doctrine. Over a period that apparently continued well into his junior year, and after strong doses of the Bible and Edwards's works, he heard Dwight's famous evangelistic address, *The Harvest Past,* and salvific light began to dawn. As Beecher would later testify in his *Autobiography,* Dwight's presence at the College was nothing short of providential.[111] Stiles (for whom Beecher had little respect) had been lax, but Dwight brought discipline; infidelity had dominated the campus, but Dwight sent it packing; and most important, the adolescent Beecher had been groping in the dark, but Dwight had turned up the light. Other students concurred with Beecher's assessment of the changes in the school. Benjamin Silliman, another Dwight protégé who returned to the school in 1805 as Professor of Chemistry and Natural Science and attended Dwight's deathbed, wrote his mother that Yale had been transformed into a "little temple" where "prayer and praise seem to be the delight of the greater part of the students."[112] No records of the reactions of skeptical students to the great transformation of Yale survive. According to Beecher's legend they were all converted and happily stayed at school. But a few young Paines and Rousseaus were probably expelled along with infidelity.

Dwight's earliest student victories at Yale prove two things: something occurred in the Yale student body soon after Dwight's arrival, and Beecher and Silliman allowed their youthful religious zeal and their undying devotion to Dwight to color their accounts of the event. Surprisingly, most American religious historians have acknowledged the former point, but fewer have considered the latter. Indeed, some of the commentators who credit Dwight with the 1796–97 Yale triumph interpret his purge of infidelity as the inauguration of America's Second Great Awakening and consider it intimately related to his campaign to bolster Federalism. Fortunately, there have been more critical treatments of the Beecher vignette and of the larger importance of the Yale revival in the history of American religion. Although these matters will be examined and assessed below, for the present note that from the start of his presidency Dwight defended the claims of traditional orthodoxy against the incursion of skeptical thought, showed interest in the moral reformation of students, and preached sermons aimed at their conversion.

Dwight's orthodox Congregationalist allies made him famous for the transformation of religion at Yale, but his Republican opponents made him infamous for his political commitments. By 1795, Dwight had already established himself as a leader among Connecticut Federalists. Few Federalists were as committed to the defense of Congregational orthodoxy, the legal establishment of Congregationalism, or the rights and privileges of the ministry. During the first years of his presidency Dwight's political activities were largely a private affair. He met with like-minded friends to discuss national events and local politics but rarely spoke publicly about these matters.

During 1797 Dwight was forced from the privacy and security of Federalist drawing rooms into the glaring light of public scrutiny. Rumors of French intrigues against the United States were circulating, and Dwight and his Standing Order allies led by a frantic Jedidiah Morse reacted with greater vigor than any segment of the community.[113] Two events transformed their fears of conspiracies into outright paranoia. The first was the XYZ affair, which seemed to offer incontrovertible proof that the French were preparing subversive plans to overthrow the United States. The second was the 1798 publication of John Robison's *Proofs of a Conspiracy against All the Governments and Religions of Europe,* which described a secret religious sect called the Bavarian Illuminati, allegedly connected to the Masonic movement, that sought the overthrow of all governmental authority.[114] In response to the crisis, Dwight preached two of his most aggressive sermons against infidelity: *The Nature and Danger of Infidel Philosophy,* which dealt with the philosophical aspect of infidelity, on 9 September 1797, and *The Duty of Americans at the Present Crisis,* which treated its political ramifications, on 4 July 1798. *Nature and Danger* was Dwight's most concerted attempt to overturn the claims of the philosophers whose skepticism gnawed at the fabric of traditional Christianity. Taking Colossians 2:8 as his text, "Beware, lest any man spoil you through philosophy and vain deceit, after the tradition of men, after the rudiments of the world, and not after Christ," he set out to accomplish three tasks: "I shall endeavor, in the First place, to prove to you that this Philosophy is vain and deceitful; Secondly, to show you that you are in danger of becoming prey to it; and Thirdly, to dissuade you by several arguments from thus yielding yourselves a prey."[115] He then compiled a long list of the philosophers and their claims, laying them before his auditors in pithy summaries. The list seems to include nearly every prominent figure whom Dwight imagined had ever opposed traditional theism or the Judeo-Christian tradition. Older infidels include Aristotle, the Stoics, Socrates, Plato, Cicero, Plutarch; modern skeptics are represented by Lord Herbert, Blount, Collins, Wollaston, Tindal, Chubb, Bolingbroke, and Hume.

Despite Dwight's effort to dispose of the complete canon of infidelity in one

grand sweep, modern readers of *Nature and Danger* will find the text unsatis-
factory. Dwight's pastiche of quotations from the philosophers is hackneyed.
Even if one grants the inherent limitations of the homiletic genre of the text—
a sermon aimed at a popular audience, not a closely argued academic treatise—the reader will find reason to question the depth of Dwight's knowledge
of the philosophers he attempts to discredit. Dwight was familiar with the
writers he cited, but evidence within the sermon itself indicates that he relied
quite heavily on secondary summaries and accounts of their work. Here
perhaps is the most pointed example of Dwight's inability to read for long
periods of time.[116] A prominent element of Dwight's argument against Hume's
view of the miraculous, for instance, is borrowed wholesale and without
attribution from the Scottish writer George Campbell.[117] Although Dwight
fails to convince the reader that he fully comprehended the nature of infidel
philosophy, he does manage to give a credible account of the threats it posed to
society, provided that one accepts his belief in the natural interdependency
that existed between religion and culture.

In this text and in many others Dwight declined the opportunity to judge
philosophy from within. His was not a careful examination of the presuppositions, definitions, and arguments of his opponents in the hope of revealing the
faultiness of their conclusions. Instead, he reversed the process. Offering only
a cursory glance at the philosophy itself, he moved immediately to an examination of its effects. Not surprisingly, Dwight's standard of judgment at this
critical juncture rested on several related propositions. First, the chief end of
religion, at least in this world if not in the next, was morality. Second, the only
true religion was Protestant Christianity, preferably enculturated in its New
England variant. Third, the truth of Christianity rested on the special revelation of the Bible and could be easily discerned by the application of unvar-
nished—even untutored—human reason. In short, Dwight functioned as a
Protestant moralist. Unlike Edwards, who grounded virtue in the benevolence
to Being in General, Dwight believed that the heart of virtue lay in an acknowledgment of the authority of God's law and in obedience to its precepts. He
rejected the philosophers because in denying the authority of the Bible they
had rejected the only legitimate system of morality and would inevitably lead
their disciples down the fast track to cultural and perhaps eternal damnation.
Where *Nature and Danger* refuted skepticism on moral grounds, *Duty of
Americans* sounded shrill warnings that revealed Dwight's deepseated fears
about the cultural ramifications of infidelity. In what would become one of the
most frequently cited passages from his sermon corpus, Dwight suggested that
infidelity inevitably led to a series of transformations: faithful churches would
become "temples of reason," ordered worship would become a "Jacobin
phrenzy," and virtuous young men and women would be polluted and debauched.[118] These addresses were ritual occasions that gave Dwight the oppor-

tunity to lay his religious convictions before the public. His private correspondence of the period, especially in the context of the presidential election of 1800, exhibits his formal political commitments.

In many respects, Dwight was typical of what David H. Fischer has called "Old School Federalists," who adhered to the original and fundamental meaning of the Federalist political philosophy and were horrified at the party politics and popular political organization for which the Democratic-Republicans became notorious. The activities of younger Federalists who began successfully to imitate the tactics of the Jeffersonians only served to exacerbate the anxieties of Old School traditionalists.[119] Dwight made his Old School sensibilities crystal clear in a letter to Ebenezer Huntington, another Old Schooler, just prior to his election to Yale's presidency. Huntington had asked Dwight to preach at a meeting of the Society of the Cincinnati, to which he reluctantly agreed. His hesitation to accept the invitation was not based in any indifference toward the Society itself but stemmed from his disappointment with the nature of the current political climate in Connecticut.

> The politics of this state have lately gone so counter to my judgment and to my wishes, and the present favorite and but too successful measures appear to me fraught with so many evils, that I can scarcely persuade myself to officiate publicly in any instance, out of my weekly round. The reign of democratic clubs and the prevalence of democratic measures, as contradistinguished from our own governmental character, is the reign and prevalence of anarchy, of all despotism the most to be dreaded. Of this evil, I have had the most painful apprehension. I believe the steady and well disposed inhabitants sufficiently numerous, and sufficiently well inclined, to prevent it; but they are so supine, that their enemies generally prevail.[120]

Although he loathed the Jeffersonian tactics, Dwight was a keen political observer and ruefully acknowledged their effectiveness. During the months prior to the presidential election of 1800, Dwight articulated his fears of the Democratic-Republican political machine and its candidates in a letter to his old friend James Hillhouse, United States Senator from Connecticut. Hillhouse was a transitional figure among the Federalists, precariously perched between the conservatism of the Old School and the party savvy of the New School. So deep were Dwight's fears of a Federalist rout that he urged Hillhouse to fight fire with fire and mimic at least some of the organizational dexterity of the Democratic-Republicans:

> The Democratic gentlemen, I have been long aware, intend to make a grand effort against the next election of President. Their industry is immense, committed, and commendable, as an example to the children of light. An organized and systematical effort is everywhere visible, and they boast of certain, or nearly certain, [victory]. . . . You gentlemen at

> Congress ought to imitate these active men in their industry. It seems to me that, unless you make some exertions . . . you will lose perhaps the only and certainly best, opportunity of securing the public safety. The introduction of Mr. Jefferson will ruin the Republic; the postponement of his introduction will . . . save it. This may all be accomplished, if I mistake not, by timely, vigorous, and prudent measures.[121]

After months of intensive negotiation, five presidential candidates stood for the election on 4 November 1800: Thomas Jefferson, as expected, and Aaron Burr, Jr. (Dwight's cousin), for the Democratic-Republicans, and John Adams, Charles Cotesworth Pinckney, and John Jay for the Federalists.[122] Apparently, Dwight believed that his admonitions to Hillhouse and other leaders had some good effect. In a letter to Jedidiah Morse just after the election but before the announcement of the results, he expressed guarded optimism that the Federalists would win the day and that New England would thereby "be saved from ruin."[123] He was to be bitterly disappointed. According to federal law at the time, the candidate who captured the greatest number of electoral votes would become President and the candidate with the second highest electoral tally would become Vice President. To the chagrin of the Federalists, the highest totals fell to Jefferson and Burr. In an ironic twist that lengthened the election process considerably, Jefferson and Burr found themselves locked in a tie, each of them having received seventy-three electoral votes. That the Federalists had lost was granted on all sides, and the question now became which of the victors would become President and which Vice President. As might be expected Dwight was disappointed in the Federalist loss and utterly disconsolate about the duty facing the House of Representatives who would decide the election. As he lamented to Hillhouse prior to the start of the balloting:

> I am doubtful about the election. Mr. Burr is a dangerous man, and all the unpopularity of his measures will fall on the Federalists. They will be responsible for whatever he does. If Mr. Jefferson is elected, the Democrats will take all the responsibility. I have been informed, that Burr has said, that, if he should be President, he will not leave one Federalist bone upon another.[124]

Balloting began in the House on 11 February 1801. Six days and thirty-six ballots later, Jefferson was made President and Burr Vice President. Dwight's final assessment of the election in a letter to Old Federalist Enos Bronson suggests that Dwight and his allies were prepared to accept the loss of the battle of 1800 but would continue their war with the Jeffersonians: "I think that New England Federalists are wholly embarrassed. They are perfectly ready, indeed, to go to all lengths in supporting the Administration, so far as it shall be constitutional and useful to the country, but no further."[125]

In addition to Dwight's homiletic blasts against infidelity and his laments to private correspondents about the Jeffersonians, he engaged in other literary defenses of the Standing Order as well. At the height of the XYZ and Illuminati controversies Morse proposed the publication of a newspaper that would serve as a platform from which orthodox ministers could mount a counterattack. It was christened the *New England Palladium,* and its prospectus declared that it would defend "the government, morals, religion, and state of Society in New England" and "expose Jacobinism in every form both of principle and practice."[126] Morse and the other founders of the enterprise—among them Dwight, his brother Theodore, and the Massachusetts Federalist Fisher Ames—wanted their journal to reach a popular audience but in a manner more refined than that of their Democratic-Republican opponents. As Ames said, "The Palladium should be fastidiously polite and well-bred. It should whip Jacobins as a gentleman would a chimney-sweep, at arm's length, and keeping aloof of his soot."[127]

Dwight published several essays and poems in the early issues of the *Palladium,* some of them anonymously, all of which perfectly modeled the *Palladium's* journalistic outlook. In these pieces Dwight was able to discuss particular planks of the Connecticut Federalist political platform. In "Farmer Johnson's Political Catechism," which ran in March, April, and May 1801, Dwight raised specific political questions and offered party-line answers in catechetical fashion. Though questions about general suffrage and the distribution of land on a fee-simple basis are surveyed in the first installment of the "Farmer Johnson" series, increasingly Dwight's real concern was to defend state support of the Congregational churches.

His defense began with the notion that the general populace was not best educated in schools—a surprising admission from an experienced pedagogue like Dwight—but in public worship where they learned the "two most liberal sciences, theology and morality" (14 April 1801). Having once again placed religion and morality side by side, Dwight compiled reasons why the government ought to support the churches. The churches promoted order and obedience with greater success than the coercive laws and punishments on which the state had to rely (17 April 1801). The state was obligated to do all in its power to promote the greatest good among its citizens, and because the church bore goodness in its very soul, common sense dictated that the churches were the best means to the state's ends (17 April 1801). The demise of the churches would mean the loss of all true happiness (8 May 1801). Lest his readers somehow failed to discern the differences between the traditional platform he was advocating and the more progressive notions of his opponents, Dwight ended "Farmer Johnson" with yet another swipe at the philosophers: "Q: What do you think of the modern principles of philosophy, which confidently promise so much good to mankind? A: They are the shadow which the dog swallowed after he had lost his meat."[128]

In a second series in the *Palladium,* "To the Farmers and Mechanics of New

England," that ran in May and June 1801, Dwight turned from the question of the state support of churches to a long defense against the charge that the clergy were "employed in designs and conduct unfriendly to the public welfare." He was particularly keen to describe the manner in which the clergy were called to their pulpits (i.e., democratically by vote of the church members) and to remind readers that the clergy held no power except in their own congregations. In "Farmers and Mechanics" an early hint of Dwight's thinking on the voluntary character of the system that undergirded the Standing Order emerges. From his perspective, claims that the clergy wielded excessive political power were "assumptions without grounds, false in facts, and advanced without even the appearance of decency." He claimed this was true precisely because Connecticut's citizens were free to exercise their rights of religious freedom. If they chose to worship with Baptists or Episcopalians or to forego public worship altogether, they were free to do so.[129]

Dwight's strong political views received attention from the general public and particularly from Republican opponents. Dwight's students, not all of whom shared Beecher's and Silliman's aweful respect of Yale's president, freely commented on his activities. As one southern student would write to a friend in Virginia,

> [President Dwight] is most grossly infected by this raging political epidemick [sic] & instead of resisting the current of the pestilential malady he is borne willing along. . . . The Revd [sic] old Man occasionally whets his splenitick [sic] appetite in a political Sermon . . . [in which] his prejudices are so irresistible and powerful that they . . . baffle all his powers of ratiocination and change his party hatred and dislike into pitiful individualism and personal animosity—but what of him? [130]

Although this sort of negative student commentary was uncommon and rarely made in public, journalistic attacks on Federalists by the Republican press were routine during the period. As Dwight's prominence grew, he became a favorite target of Republican pundits. Several Republican newspapers served as the opposition press during the period, but two particular publications, *The American Mercury* and *The Philadelphia Aurora,* were unrelenting in their attacks on Dwight and the Standing Order. Every summer a *Mercury* column was devoted to reports of July Fourth celebrations at Republican clubs, nearly all of which included sarcastic (and likely drunken) "toasts" on religious topics: "The Clergy—May they preach the gospel of Jesus Christ—Not their own political gospel"; "Religion—We love it in its purity, but not as an engine of political delusion"; "Federal Religion and Peter Pindar's Razors—"All Cheap"—"Made to Sell"; "Federal Religion—May it soon become Christian."[131] Yale students of Republican sentiment were apparently prohibited from organizing Independence Day celebrations. According to his critics, in place of these genuinely patriotic exhibitions Dwight taught Yale students to "hate our republican government, and rulers, and to despise the promulgation of republican principles."[132] In more sober moods, *The Mercury* attacked one of Dwight's favorite organizations, the Connecticut Missionary Society. *The Mercury* claimed that there was never a greater display "of arrogance than Connecticut puritans shew [sic] in the instance of sending missionaries" to neighboring states. Although missionaries "of peace and heavenly charity deserve respect from all men," *The Mercury* lamented that the Society was controlled by Federalists from Connecticut's leading families. From such "political missionary societies, made up by a junction of the families of Moses and Aaron, we pray God to deliver us."[133] In this tongue-in-cheek swipe at the New England clerical aristocracy the Dwight family pedigree could be easily traced to the lineage of Moses and Aaron.

The Philadelphia Aurora also devoted many anonymous columns to anti-Federalist and anti-Dwight rhetoric. In a clever turn on the public paranoia about the influence of secret societies of the Bavarian Illuminati, *The Aurora* reckoned prominent Federalist leaders "New England Illuminati" who controlled Connecticut behind closed doors. The fact that Dwight, Senator James Hillhouse, Superior Court Judge Tapping Reeve, and several other prominent Federalists were related by marriage made the work of the Republican wags even easier: "Thus are the church and state, and the ties of blood and marriage, united to form an hierarchy and aristocracy in Connecticut, which some fail not to call a monarchy, controlled by Dr. Dwight."[134]

None of the Jeffersonian pundits was more critical of Dwight than the indefatigable John C. Ogden, who lashed both Dwight and the college unmercifully in the press. Ogden, an Episcopal priest whose career is one of the most remarkable of the period, began his assault by impugning Dwight's motives in the Yale revival of 1796–97.[135] Claiming that Yale students were forced to attend chapel and prevented from attending churches of their own choosing, he raised an issue to which he made constant reference—the aristocracy and Dwight's family connection with Edwards:

> This last offense against law, justice, love of truth and order, is persisted in merely to give an opportunity to the President to spread Edwardean [sic] tenets, of which his grandfather and Calvin were teacher, that his family pride may be indulged, and his desire to appear a champion, and leader in divinity and politics—may be gratified.

Dwight's goal from Ogden's perspective was to "direct all public affairs, civil, ecclesiastical, literary, and political," and in this he surpassed even Ezra Stiles:

> Stiles was a bigot, active, obstinate, and persevering; but Dr. Dwight's little finger, will be greater than Dr. Stiles's loins. Dr. Stiles chastised with

the whips of sermons and letters upon politics—But Dr. Dwight will scourge with the scorpions of Calvinism and Edwardeanism [sic], the scorpions of polemic divinity, party politics, poetry, satirical writing, the triumph of Infidelity, and the prejudices circulated by young men taught by him.

Then Ogden introduced what would become one of the favorite cants of the Jeffersonians: "President Dwight . . . is a more formidable character than the Pope of Rome."[136]

Ogden used Dwight and the revival as a foil to air Republican complaints about the state's educational system that was dominated by Federalists and about the public status of the Connecticut's Congregationalist clergy. Irked by the recent financial benefit the college had received from the Legislature's sale of western lands, he complained that "Yale college is too rich already."

> The clergy in the name of the people, petition the almighty with a pathos . . . "to water the school of the prophets, and cause streams to issue annually from thence, which shall make glad the cities of our God, and cause the wilderness to blossom as a rose." The simple meaning of which is, that the people bestow their money, that the college and missionaries may extend the politics, and controverted divinity of the clergy, throughout the nation.

As to the clergy, they were a money-grubbing lot who turned every financial opportunity to their advantage. They "made money as chaplains by purchases made with depreciated money of soldiers" and even used doctrinal squabbles to financial ends, turning profits on the recent predictions of the millennium. They intermarried, and the great clerical families of New England extended their power even further by placing their kin in college presidencies. Burr, Edwards, Finley, and Witherspoon at Princeton, Dwight at Yale—these oligarchs were ravenous wolves in clerical garb. In a classic bit of Jeffersonian rhetoric, Ogden roundly condemned them all with the claim that "the Oppression of the people by great men, the important people of the community, is fostered by the clergy."[137] Though these polemic assaults were very painful Dwight knew better than to allow himself to be drawn into a paper war he could not hope to win. In a letter to Morse just after the publication of one of Ogden's books and in reference to another anti-Federalist newspaper, *The New London Bee,* he wrote "as to Ogden and the *Bee,* I expect that so long as the one is alive and the other published, I shall be their favorite topic of misrepresentation. To this I yield without discomposure, or fear."[138] However slanderous Ogden and his ilk may have been, one thing is certain: by the close of the eighteenth century Dwight had learned a painful lesson: Prominent men, especially those who had sought to gain that pinnacle, were easy targets for critics, pundits, and social revolutionaries.

A Mere Bystander

During the last fifteen years of his life Dwight's stature among New Englanders grew considerably. His labors on behalf of religious and political orthodoxy were well known, he was clearly recognized as a senior statesman among the Congregationalist clergy, he had established himself as one of the nation's most prominent college presidents, and he had secured a place for himself among America's most famous preachers. Notwithstanding these victories Dwight sometimes worried that his major victories had already been won, that he was being pushed to the margins of public life, and that his leadership of the orthodox was merely titular. He mentioned this concern in a private letter to his friend Jedidiah Morse in February, 1802. He began the letter by noting more problems with his eyes: "I have been some days husbanding my eyes in order to write this." He went on to lament that his vision problems were cause for deeper concerns about the extent of his influence in American culture: "My eyes are so poor that I am a mere bystander in the world."[139]

His concerns were well founded. Despite his efforts over more than thirty years to awaken New Englanders to the dangers of progressive thought in church and state, Dwight's grand vision of a godly republic was rapidly losing viability. Thomas Jefferson would serve not one but two terms in the White House. James Madison—whom Dwight disliked only a little less than Jefferson—would soon follow in Jefferson's steps. Although the Congregational churches continued to enjoy the benefits of their status as the established religion in Connecticut, "separatist" bodies were discovering chinks in the armor of the Standing Order. Presumptuous Congregationalist partisans like Dwight recognized the threats but assumed that the populace trained by centuries of ecclesial habit would leave them in power. In this Dwight and his partisans were dead wrong. Armies of revivalists on the frontier were beginning to formulate new Americanized versions of Protestant culture, and Dwight's students, notably Lyman Beecher and Nathaniel W. Taylor, were busy surveying, assessing, and working out the theological implications and ecclesiastical consequences of these new developments. Somewhat unwittingly Dwight helped lay the cornerstones of this new American faith, but he hesitated to allow it to replace the older scheme of traditional Calvinism to which he had adhered for so long.

Battles with skeptics and political opponents over the privileged status of the Standing Order had occupied much of Dwight's energy near the turn of the century. By 1805 he shifted his attention to troubling developments within Congregationalism itself. At the opening of the nineteenth century, New England Congregationalism was fragmented and spread over a wide theological spectrum. Although some clergy moved along the spectrum as their careers developed and others attempted to avoid any sort of theological identification, three major factions emerged.

The broad and somewhat fluid center of the spectrum was made up of ministers who were moderate in their theology. Known variously as Old Calvinists, Moderate Calvinists (or Semi-Calvinists or Arminian Calvinists by more conservative commentators), ministers such as Moses Hemmenway, Moses Mather, and David Tappan honored the main features of the New England theological tradition. Moderate Calvinists professed the doctrine of the Trinity, affirmed the general outlines of the Westminster Confession, operated on the ecclesiology outlined in the Halfway Covenant of the seventeenth century, and adhered in large measure to the traditions of piety set forth by their Puritan forebears.

The left side of the theological spectrum was populated by more liberal Congregationalists who over the final decades of the eighteenth century had moved toward a Unitarian position. These thinkers denied that the God of the Bible existed in three distinct persons, they argued for the oneness and unity of the Godhead, and they lampooned traditional Trinitarians as tri-theists. By the first decades of the nineteenth century, this position was well established, having been championed by the likes of William Ellery Channing and Henry Ware.[140] From the conservative perspective the opinions of the liberals were equated with the dreaded heresies of Pelagianism, Socinianism, and Arianism. In 1803, Harvard's Hollis Professorship of Divinity fell vacant at the death of its incumbent, the traditionalist Trinitarian David Tappan. Seizing the opportunity to place one of their own in what was probably the most prominent professorship in New England, the Unitarians lobbied strenuously for the appointment of liberal Henry Ware. Dwight's friend and colleague Jedidiah Morse led the opposition to Ware. For a time the defense appeared secure. Joseph Willard, Harvard's president, and a majority of the Harvard Corporation supported the orthodox cause. But in 1804, Morse realized that he and his allies were caught unawares. The Harvard Board of Overseers, the group of ministers who advised the Corporation and on which Morse himself sat, recommended Ware's appointment and, in 1805, Ware was elected by the Corporation by a one-vote majority. The Unitarians had captured Harvard. Morse was deeply chagrined by the defeat and began publishing the *Panoplist* magazine in an effort to promote the cause of orthodoxy in the public eye.

The right side of the theological spectrum was populated by stricter "Calvinists" such as Dwight who understood the New England tradition to have reached new heights in the theology of Edwards. The clergy of the right affirmed trinitarianism, defended the sovereignty of God against the encroachments of Arminianism and, in distinction to the Old Calvinists, most of these conservatives rejected the ecclesiology of the Halfway Covenant. Members of their churches were required to make a full, detailed profession of faith before the elders of the church prior to becoming members. Only then were they admitted to the sacraments. There was a good deal of friction among the three major segments of Congregationalism: Liberals and Conservatives fired salvos at one another constantly, and each camp continually sought to woo clergy of the middle to their version of the truth. The right end of the spectrum had itself been ravaged by internecine struggle. Some of Edwards's closest disciples believed that they had "perfected" Edwards's theological system. This group of Edwardseans was itself divided into competing camps. Samuel Hopkins, Nathaniel Emmons, and their followers (sometimes known as the "Consistent Calvinists" or "Hopkinsians") were quite narrow in their interpretation of particular themes within Edwards's theology. Other thinkers, such as Joseph Bellamy, were more moderate and are often gathered under the "New Divinity" rubric. Despite these fractures within the larger Edwardsean movement, by 1802 there was sufficient consensus to allow for the formation of the Massachusetts Missionary Society and the publication of its *Magazine* to promote their views. Another organization shaped by the Edwardseans was the Connecticut Missionary Society, which also thrived in this period.

During the first decade of the century Dwight became increasingly concerned about the fissures within Congregationalism. He temporarily withdrew from the campaigns against infidelity and began working to unite the factions among the Conservatives. After the election of Ware to the Hollis Professorship, an event that "has occasioned very serious sensations in the state and in the western parts of Massachusetts," he perceived two threats to Congregational stability. He worried that the Unitarian campaign would win converts from among the Old Calvinists and thereby weaken the wide middle position. He also feared that the Hopkinsians would react to the Unitarian advances by moving even further to the right. In a letter to Morse five months after Ware's election, he wrote:

> I am disappointed in two things which you mention: the union of the Arminians and the Unitarians, and the separation of the Hopkinsians from the Old Calvinists, i.e., in the present controversy. Both are in my view unwise. The question concerning the Trinity interests them both, equally with the Old Calvinists, so far as they hold their professed doctrines.

Although he realized the havoc that such alliances might create, Dwight was unsure what he and other conservatives could do to prevent a debilitating doctrinal war:

> What assistance can or will be furnished in this State, I cannot determine. There are men enough and talent enough. Had I eyes, you would find one

at least embarking heartily in the design and forwarding it with something beside mere good wishes. You will find occasion for all your prudence and patience, but when the war is fairly begun, I suppose soldiers
will enlist.[141]

In addition to his journalistic efforts, Morse began working toward the
establishment of an independent theological seminary that would train promising ministerial candidates in the canons of orthodoxy. Conversations among
conservatives began in earnest within a year of Ware's election and, after nearly
three years of close negotiations among ministers on the right, plans were laid
for the formation of Andover Theological Seminary. On pedagogic grounds
alone, the start of Andover was an important development in American
theological education. Throughout the colonial period most ministers had
received their classical education in colleges like Harvard, Yale, or Princeton
but had usually studied the theological disciplines as apprentices in the homes
of established clergy. Dwight himself had been trained in this manner by
Jonathan Edwards, Jr. Andover was to be a residential seminary for college
graduates replete with a specialized faculty that would prepare students for the
ministry.[142] Although the historical importance of the founding of Andover
cannot be denied, the political efforts required to establish the school must not
be overlooked. Bickering and recalcitrance among right-wing groups caused
the longest delays. Although the funds for the Andover project had been
pledged early in the process, the equivocations of Samuel Spring and the
Hopkinsian faction impeded progress. Suspicious of the compromises needed
to create a coalition institution, they considered forming a separate Hopkinsian
seminary. The assiduous, conciliatory efforts of Leonard Woods with his
mentor Spring finally won the day. As a token of the new spirit of cooperation
among ministers of the right, Morse's *Panoplist* and the Hopkinsian *Massachusetts Missionary Magazine* merged, and in September 1808 Andover opened its
doors.[143] A triumphant Morse wrote to Dwight in the summer of 1808, "The
camp of the enemy is alarmed, they are awake, and every engine is in requisi-
tion. But we are better fortified and are stronger than they imagine. The union
in Theological Institution and in *Panoplist* and *Magazine* makes us powerful
and enables us to look them in the face boldly."[144]

Dwight worked tirelessly for the establishment of Andover. He lobbied
Massachusetts state officials on behalf of the school, consulted with Morse on
the best manner in which to organize Andover's academic life, discussed
possible faculty appointments, and agreed to serve on the seminary's first
Board of Visitors.[145] It was not surprising that the Andover faculty invited him
to give the inaugural address in September 1808. Although Dwight was quite
aware of the divisions that beset Congregationalism in New England and of the
manner in which these had complicated the Andover enterprise, his inaugural

sermon gave no hint whatever of these difficulties. Instead, he preached an address that focused more on ministers—their training and the effects they could hope to have in their churches and the larger culture—than on the new theological institution.[146]

He opened the address with a series of illustrations that underscored the need for an educated clergy and derided those who denied the importance of formal training in divinity. He believed that these shortsighted folk directly undercut the professional character of the ministry. Though they insisted that "their property [be] managed by skillful agents, their judicial causes directed by learned advocates, and their children, when sick, attended by able physicians; they are satisfied to place their Religion, their souls, and their salvation under the guidance of quackery. Among these people, men become preachers in a moment; and put on the qualifications for the Ministry as they put on a coat." Such ministers lacked the knowledge necessary to defend the faith and were "incapable of the decorum, and dignity which are indispensable in the desk." Dwight extolled the virtues of the new institution—its library, faculty, benefactors, and boards of governance. Of the theological disposition of the school he had little to say except to remind his auditors that the school upheld the faith of the Reformation and adhered to the same orthodox doctrines as those memorable forebears "who converted New England from a desert into a garden." In the center portion of the sermon Dwight turned to the necessity of ministers believing the truth as it is revealed in the scriptures and encouraged student ministers to preach that truth with vigor, reminding them that "a cold preacher naturally makes a frozen audience."[147]

These first sections of the address which contain Dwight's defense of education, his dismissal of untrained ministers, his admonishments to remember New England's great tradition, and his appeal to lively preaching might have been easily anticipated by his auditors. After all he was Yale's renowned president, a prominent conservative minister, and a member of the first Board of Visitors. However, his auditors would surely have been taken aback by the final third of the address. This section began with what might be first mistaken for Dwight's typical jeremiadic lament. Though he describes the political situation in the world in gloomy terms, the spirit suddenly changes to one of cosmic optimism. "Gloomy and dreadful as is the aspect of the political horizon, the Christian world has already roused itself from the slumbers of two centuries, and with a spirit of prayer, zeal, and liberality, scarcely exampled, has wafted the Bible to distant nations, and planted missions in the region of the shadow of death." Indeed, this is one of Dwight's most powerful millennial passages. He argues that the millennial kingdom is at hand and that a universal renovation of humanity is about to begin. Whereas his poetic millennialism of the Revolutionary period focused on the American context and contribution to the establishment of the Kingdom, in this address Dwight avoids such ethnocentrism. The evangelistic enterprise of the church in this version of his millennialism will produce the "great day" and, although no miracles will be employed in its establishment, ministers "will be the instruments by which the Spirit of truth will accomplish this divine transformation."[148] This theme also appeared prominently in his sermon at the fourth annual meeting of the American Board of Commissioners of Foreign Missions in September 1813. What is striking about this feature of his mature preaching is that it represents a distinct shift in his millennial thought. During the Revolutionary era he had interpreted the providential hand of God in the founding of the American nation as a hint of the millennium. After long years of struggle with religious and political heterodoxy, Dwight now viewed the evangelistic enterprise as the quickest means to millennial bliss. Indeed, here Dwight offers a specific prediction: "Almost all judicious commentators have agreed that the Millennium, in the full and perfect sense, will begin at a period not far from the year 2000." As in the Andover sermon, he stressed that the forthcoming conversion of the world would not be brought about by miracles but by the efforts of faithful Christians.[149] These labors on behalf of the global millennium were to be pursued with particular attention to evangelism and missions work in foreign lands. To this end Dwight lent his influence to the founding of the Missionary Society of Connecticut, the American Missionary Society, and the American Board of Commissioners for Foreign Missions.

Dwight celebrated his sixty-second birthday within months of his sermon before the American Board. He had been president of Yale for nineteen years, and both his physical condition and tenure at the college had begun to show signs of aging. Although no specific data of a personal sort survive to verify this claim, the character of Dwight's efforts changed during these years. To be sure, his everyday activities continued much as they had before. He preached regularly, taught his senior students, and produced occasional pieces for publication, though less frequently. Of course, he continued to develop what by now was peculiarly "his" college, though not without occasional resistance.[150] Nonetheless, Dwight's thinking during this period shifted. He began taking measures to insure that his unique understanding of the world would survive him and remain available to future generations.

Assisted by his amanuenses and his sons, Benjamin and Theodore, Dwight began work on the enormous task of transcribing, editing, and compiling what would become the central elements of his literary corpus—*Decisions,* the *Sermons* collection, *Theology Explained and Defended,* and *Travels in New England and New York.* Throughout the final decade of his life, Dwight's participation in the infidelity battles and his diplomatic role in the internecine squabbles within Congregationalism had left him with a sense that his unique

America was fading irretrievably into the past. In the final literary work of his life, Dwight prepared several pieces that would serve to enshrine his vision of America and protect it from critics both within and without the United States. As one commentator noted about the *Travels,* Dwight was making "a final affirmation of what he valued in the world."[151]

Soon after he became president of Yale, Dwight had commenced a series of horseback and carriage tours of New England and New York, often using time between the Yale semesters to visit sections of the country unknown to him. He stayed with friends and acquaintances when possible or at local roadside inns. He took note of the geography of the sites he visited, gathered history from local inhabitants, attended churches in the area, and noted unique architecture he discovered along his way. At the completion of each of these journeys he crafted an account from notes he took while en route, adding letters or excerpts from other reports about the area he had visited. Each travelogue was written in a booklet not unlike the sermon booklets his amanuenses prepared for *Theology.* Dwight had hoped to begin publication of these accounts as early as 1808. In a letter in February of that year he asked Morse to publish the following announcement in the Boston papers:

> Dr. Dwight of New Haven is preparing for the press Observations on a series of Journeys through the States of New England and New York: intended to illustrate the Topography, Agriculture, Commerce, Government, Literature, Manners, Morals and Religion, of those countries. This work, as understood, is considerably advanced.[152]

With the press of other duties the enormous amount of work required to prepare the published version of *Travels* took more time than Dwight had anticipated, and they were not published until some years after his death. The organization of *Travels* and their overall purpose had been in Dwight's mind since he began their composition. Specific elements of the *Travels* will be examined in subsequent chapters of this study, but at present note that Dwight intended *Travels* as an *apologia* for the traditional New England he loved. In some respects, the work serves as an empirical prose account of the idyllic world Dwight had described in the poem *Greenfield Hill.* Throughout the work Dwight shows the reader sturdy yeomen, stable families, moral fiber, order, and, of course, a church as the center of the community.

Time after time in the *Travels* Dwight sought to vindicate the character of New England, especially when it had been besmirched by foreign visitors. In 1814, he was drawn into a war of words during which he would produce his final literary defense of the American character. In 1810, Charles Jared Ingersoll, writing under the pseudonym "Some Unknown Foreigner," had published an essay in vindication of American culture in response to what he took to be its misrepresentation in the British press. Ingersoll's tract bore the title *Inchiquin, The Jesuit's Letters . . . Containing a Favourable View of Manners, Literature, and State of Society, of the United States, and a Refutation of Many of the Aspersions Cast upon this Country, by Former Residents and Tourists.* A very negative review of the work appeared in London's prestigious *Quarterly Review* in 1814. That review drew the attention of the editors of Boston's *North American Review,* who leapt to Ingersoll's defense. On hearing of the squabble Dwight joined the fray with his anonymous *Remarks on the Review of Inchiquin's Letter Published in the Quarterly Review; Addressed to George Channing, Esquire.* He had apparently not read the American reviews of Ingersoll's work but he makes specific references to the *Quarterly Review's* response.

Describing himself as a Federalist, New Englander, and Yankee, Dwight begins by declaring, "There is not, I presume, an Englishman who regards the character and politics of Mr. Jefferson and Mr. Madison with less approbation than myself. The former I consider as a cunning, the latter as a weak, man." Noting that the current war between Britain and the United States "is, in my opinion unnatural, impolitic on our part, causeless, and unjust," he continues correcting the errors of the *Quarterly Review* one by one. While *Remarks* contains some clever turns on British misrepresentations, it is polemical, forced, and predictable. He grants critics a few points, but in the main he responds to British charges with oversimplified or inaccurate countercharges. Typical is his comment on the Methodist revivalists. He is willing to grant the charge that they are untutored and enthusiastic, but reminds his readers that Methodism began in England, not America, and that therefore the British are at least partly responsible for the problems posed by rough-hewn American Methodists.[153] Other interesting questions are raised: the American model of the separation of church and state, the American system of education, the training of American clergy, the moral problems attendant with American slavery. Yet Dwight is never constructive or incisive. He uses the sort of data he gathered for the *Travels* but piecemeal and polemically. In the end, *Remarks* never rises above the din of the fracas into which it was cast. Its appeals to reason and aesthetics are insufficient to hide its anger, its partisan character, and its insecurity. Dwight was stooping low indeed, and had this been his first literary effort instead of his final contribution the history of American literature would have passed him by with little more than a footnote.

Dwight's fulsome descriptions of New England life and letters served as a defense against foreign and domestic critics of traditional New England culture. Sometimes his defense was useful and illustrative, sometimes unhelpful and small. But the genius that lay at the heart of *Travels* and *Remarks* was not merely reactionary. Dwight discovered that it could also function as a prescription for the building of model communities. At a meeting of the General

Association in June of 1816, concerns were raised about the primitive conditions and licentiousness on the western frontier, and Dwight, Beecher, and several other clergymen were asked to draft a publication aimed at encouraging the moral development of recent emigrants to the West. Dwight gladly accepted the assignment to emphasize several of his favorite themes. Published under the title, "An Address to the Emigrants from Connecticut and from New England Generally, in the New Settlements in the United States," and signed "Timothy Dwight, Chairman," the epistle demonstrates the manner in which Dwight could combine his thinking about the ideal community, the missions enterprise, and social reform.

The "Address" is a remarkably patronizing document in which Dwight and his colleagues detail the cultural forms the emigrants should seek to establish in their new lands. It begins with a salute to New England's pious forebears who, the writers assume, were still revered by every citizen in the Republic. But this celebratory tone is short-lived. Within a few paragraphs of the salutation the "Address" becomes little more than a finger-wagging lecture from the moral high ground. The emigrants are reminded of their responsibility to secure the blessings of religion and morality for generations yet unborn. They are warned of the dangers of life in frontier settlements that lack order and institutions for social control. Citizens who are untutored in the laws of society, noted Dwight, are apt to take improper advantage of such circumstances: "No public eye sees them. No moral institutions exist. . . . They can violate the sabbath, if they choose, with impunity. They can drink to excess, or they can swear profanely, or they can cheat, or they can do almost any other wicked thing." In order to avoid these sorts of evil consequences, the settlers are urged to build schools and maintain worship on the sabbath, "the corner stone, the main pillar of virtue and piety and happiness in a community." These institutions and these alone would help to form a "well regulated community, where temperance and peace and truth and justice and industry and charity prevail, and you may there see, what, and how rich, are the temporal blessings of the Gospel." The writers advocate the formation of missionary, bible, and moral societies to help fight "the worst plague of our country, intemperance." The admonition closes with a final exhortation to reverence the Bible: "Shun, as your worst enemies, all who may attempt to weaken your faith in the divine inspiration of the scriptures."[154] Clearly, Dwight viewed the settlement of the West under the larger missions rubric and, therefore, as an occasion not only to save individual souls but also to extend the cultural manifestations that belonged to the New England dominion within the kingdom of God. Given his disposition to equate true religion with moral probity, the connection he made between emigration, evangelism, and social reform is not surprising. In an era when established New Englanders appeared to have grown indifferent to their godly heritage, Dwight appealed to a new generation of vital Americans in the hope that they would honor the wisdom of the past and become a living legacy of the culture he cherished.

The committee deliberations about the need for the "Address" and the labor involved in actually drafting the essay were to be Dwight's last efforts at publication. In the fall and winter of 1816 his health deteriorated markedly. Though the diagnosis would be confirmed only postmortem, he was suffering from a painful form of cancer of the bladder. His friends and colleagues realized that his health was failing, and he seemed to sense that his demise was approaching. In the early months of 1816 he experienced a particularly difficult period of illness that sent him to his sickbed for several weeks. Despite this brush with death, by June he recovered and found he had sufficient strength to preach. The biblical text he chose for the sermon was apt, given his recent sufferings: "Unless the Lord had been my help, My soul had almost dwelt in silence. When I said, 'My foot slippeth'; thy mercy, O Lord, held me up. In the multitude of my thoughts within me, thy comforts delight my soul" (Psalm 94: 17–19). Whatever comfort these verses afforded Dwight during his illness, clearly his physical suffering was not the only thing on his mind. Seeing what he thought would be his demise just over the horizon, Dwight had apparently given a good deal of thought to the character of his life and ministry. According to the *Memoir* published with *Theology*, the focus of his sermon on these verses was the "true character of worldly good." He told his auditors that while on the brink of death he had considered his love of worldly things: "Like others of our race, I have relished several of these things, with at least common attachment. Particularly, I have coveted reputation and influence to a degree I am unable to justify." Beginning with this remarkable confession of his own shortcomings, Dwight warned his young hearers about the evils of vanity, the allure of worldliness, and the need to cleave to the Rock of Ages.[155]

Through the summer and early fall of 1816, Dwight put the best face on things and attended to his duty with resolve. As his health allowed, he preached in the Chapel, celebrated the Lord's Supper with the student body, and met with his seniors for recitation.[156] On 3 November he made his final visit to his beloved "sacred desk" in Yale's college chapel. Though few details of this final event were recorded, Silliman remembered the New Testament text from which his mentor preached his last sermon: "Let your light so shine before men, that they, seeing your good works, may glorify your father which is in heaven."[157]

The choice of this text provided perfect closure to one of the most remarkable careers in early national America. In his final public act Dwight preached on a biblical passage that highlighted two of his favorite religious themes, light and duty. Throughout his life Dwight had believed that genuine Christians had a holy responsibility to shine their light into the dark surroundings in which they found themselves. That meant working hard for things in which one believed and allowing one's gifts and graces to be shaped, guided, and used by the Holy Spirit. The telos of this activity was not self-aggrandizement, fame, or greatness for its own sake. Rather, its end was that others might discern the divine light, accept the love of the Savior, respond to the call of duty, and glorify the God who created, sustained, and redeemed the world.

In the weeks following the sermon, Dwight managed to make a few final public appearances, including a session with the senior class on 27 November. By December, however, he was forced again to his sickbed. This time he would not recover. His physicians did what they could to make him comfortable and in early January they began administering laudanum in the hope of easing his pain. As Dwight lay on his deathbed, Benjamin Silliman asked him if he had any last requests. The only specific comments that were recorded had to do with Dwight's personal papers:

> I do not seem to have any direction except as to publication of books. . . .
> I should like these *Travels* of mine. . . . [and] "Evidence Furnished to St.
> Paul and other Evangelists to the Divine Origin of the Scriptures" [to be
> published] . . . . Any system of sermons, if the public should be willing to
> subscribe for it, I should like to have printed. But whether they will or not
> I do not know. . . . As to sermons which are intended to elucidate some
> doctrine or precept, those who come after will judge better than those
> who [heard them preached.][158]

Dwight did not live to see these requests honored. He died on 11 January 1817. Understandably, Dwight's students and friends lamented his passing publicly with great passion. Lyman Beecher was in the pulpit when he learned of Dwight's death, whereupon he exclaimed, "Dr. Dwight is gone! . . . My father! My father! The chariots of Israel and the horsemen thereof!" Weeks later Gardiner Spring, a Dwight student who would play an important role in the life of American Presbyterianism, exclaimed in his eulogy: "Dwight is gone! The Light of Yale is extinguished. The vital fire is fled. Like some clear planet, it has left behind its lucid track, and darted to eternity." His own son Benjamin gave him perhaps the greatest praise: "He was, indeed, a father to New England—her moral legislator."[159] Just as predictably, little was heard from those who held Dwight in less esteem. Apparently, they were content to rejoice in private at the fall of this pillar of the Standing Order.

Ultimately, Dwight's legacy did not rest in the hands of his prominent friends and enemies but in the affections and habits of ordinary citizens. Despite all his effort, Dwight's vision for America proved impossible to bequeath to subsequent generations of Americans. Instead of honoring Dwight's vision of America, nineteenth-century citizens—both in New England and on the burgeoning frontiers—jettisoned it. Within two years of Dwight's death, the Federalist Standing Order collapsed, Connecticut Congregationalism was disestablished, and "new measures" revivalism strengthened its hold on the religious imagination of America. Godly Federalism died with Timothy Dwight as the Age of Jackson dawned.

II

The Herald of Reconciliation

It was impossible for him to enter the desk but
as the herald of reconciliation.

—Benjamin Dwight

Timothy Dwight could not see the world in all its fullness. As a result he developed a remarkable genius for creating and describing in spoken words worlds whose reality could only be known by imagination and faith. His myopia was problematic in a number of ways—it embarrassed him, it hindered his studies, it impeded his work—but it never prevented him from speaking with power and authority. Because of his inability to see, Dwight became a consummate American preacher. Preaching became his favorite medium, and he published more sermons than any preacher in America's early national period. From the pulpit he addressed political concerns, constructed his unique systematic theology, and proclaimed salvation to generations of Yale students. Whatever else Dwight was, he was first and foremost a preacher, and no portrait of Dwight can be complete without a consideration of his pulpit eloquence.[1]

His preaching career began in Northampton during the Revolution and continued until the final months of his life. From his first published sermon, *A Sermon Preached at Stamford in Connecticut upon the General Thanksgiving, December 18, 1777* until his last, *A Sermon Delivered in Boston, Sept. 16, 1813, Before the American Board of Commissioners for Foreign Missions at Their Fourth Annual Meeting*, publishers expressed keen interest in everything he uttered from the pulpit. In all, nearly two hundred and fifty of Dwight's sermons were printed, some as single, occasional pieces, others as parts of larger collections. One hundred seventy-three are preserved in the four-volume systematic theology, *Theology, Explained and Defended*. Dwight repeatedly preached these sermons on a four-year cycle to his Yale students.[2] The relative sophistication of the sermons and the orderly manner in which they move from natural religion to Christology, soteriology, and social ethics indicate that they were intended for young Protestant scholars. Dwight's habit of carefully formulating his doctrinal terms—covenant, sin, grace, the will, regeneration, repentance, justification, redemption, adoption, perseverance, benevolence, sanctification,

Timothy Dwight (detail), engraving by
Amos Doolittle. The Connecticut Historical
Society, Hartford. Used by permission.

etc.—reinforces the claim that *Theology* had primarily a didactic purpose. He also preached scores of occasional sermons, sixty-one of which were collected to form the two-volume *Sermons by Timothy Dwight.* In addition to the printed sermons, a smaller corpus of manuscript sermons and sermon outlines is extant, and other manuscript evidence suggests that Dwight preached additional sermons that have not survived in any form.[3] Unlike many other preachers, Dwight was not at all averse to repeating his sermons. Some titles of his published occasional sermons including many from the *Sermons* collection noted the original setting and date of the sermon. The addresses in *Theology,* however, are much harder to date. Most originated during his Greenfield pastorate during which, according to Dwight's son Benjamin, he preached more than one thousand sermons.[4]

Dwight's sermons were almost all preached using brief, written outlines or entirely extempore. He is so well known for his warm style of exhortation and his refusal to rely on a written manuscript that some have understood this practice as a tactical move. One auditor noted that his sermons were rich "in powerful appeals to the heart; in vivid pictures of vice and virtue, sketched from the life; in awful denunciation; in solemn remonstrance; in fervent intercession."[5] Some thought that Dwight's free preaching manner resulted from his aversion to the formal style of "metaphysical" preaching that some of the older Edwardsean preachers were said to have habitually employed. Although the effects of Dwight's extempore style did have positive effects on his hearers, he adopted this style for reasons both physical and rhetorical. Dwight's first trial sermon, given when he was seeking a pastoral position, was delivered from a full manuscript. That experience taught him that his eyesight would never again allow him to write his sermons in full or to read them from the pulpit. Hence, he adopted and then perfected the extempore style. His sermons are best thought of as "oral/aural" productions. He was a master orator who designed his sermons to work on the mind and heart via the ear. Both published sermons and extant manuscript addresses demonstrate that Dwight preached, as it were, phrase by phrase, marking off each section by a pause in delivery that is represented by a comma in the written or printed version. By means of this simple device and in conjunction with his almost slavish use of the same form of sermon each time he spoke, Dwight was able to pace his speech and present his arguments in carefully prescribed doses. Not until the Yale Corporation gave him an allowance for a student amanuensis did he begin to have the *Theology* sermons transcribed. In weekly sessions with his amanuenses during the academic year 1809–10, Dwight dictated from memory the sermons he had delivered that week in the college church, thus completing a manuscript version of what would later become *Theology*.[6]

Memorization on the scale that Dwight routinely must have practiced, amazing to modern homileticians and their auditors, was more common in the eighteenth century and was made somewhat easier by the use of standardized devices. The vast majority of Dwight's sermons conformed to a three-part outline. He opened the sermon with a scripture passage, reading it or reciting it from memory. Then, in the sermon's first major section he would introduce the larger biblical context of the passage in question, noting his understanding of its general meaning. For instance, in an extant manuscript sermon on Ecclesiastes 9:10 ("Whatsoever thy hand findeth to do, do it with thy might: for there is not work, nor device, nor knowledge, nor wisdom, in the grave, whither thou goest"), Dwight reduced the meaning of the text to this simple claim: people must work to achieve salvation today because after death they will have no chance to attend to this important matter. This introductory section would lead to the sermon's second section, which began with a pithy statement of doctrine that was easy to say and to recall. After the introduction in "Ecclesiastes 9:10" Dwight declared, "With this explanation of the text I derive from it the following doctrine: The work of Salvation is a great and arduous work." Dwight would then immediately list the observations he intended to draw from the doctrine and proceed to treat each observation at some length. Each observation would be numbered and given a short title. In the case of Ecclesiastes 9:10 he drew the following observations: "First, The Object is Great," and "Secondly, the things actually done for this end are very great and arduous." To give the sermon even further form and as length and complexity required, he would also number major points under each observation. Having completed his expository work, Dwight would then turn to the final section of the sermon entitled "Remarks." Here he sought to apply to his auditors the meaning of the text and as in the case of Ecclesiastes 9:10 would number and entitle each remark: "First, That multitudes fail of success in this arduous undertaking"; "Secondly, From these observations we learn not to wonder that there is [not] more Religion in countries which are called Christian"; and "Thirdly, These observations teach us that if Salvation is to be obtained, or Religion to prevail, very different measures must be pursued for this end."[7] Extant auditors' notes prove the utility of the outlining system. The Doctrine, Observations, and Remarks sections of a sermon were recorded in auditors' jottings exactly as they would later appear in the printed version of the sermon.

More important than the way in which Dwight prepared, delivered, and collected his sermons are the philosophical and rhetorical systems that undergirded them. He learned the art of preaching from established preachers and by trial and error, but Dwight's homiletic efforts were grounded in a rich and historic intellectual tradition. Known under the general rubric of Scottish Enlightenment thought or Common Sense Realism and developed in reference to several important questions of the eighteenth century, this philosophical outlook became fundamental to American evangelical Protestantism. American Protestants from New England to the South, from the French Revolution to the advent of Fundamentalism, and with reference to both theology and science, relied heavily on Common Sense thinking. Although Common Sense Realism was frequently turned against religious skepticism, its influence extended into educational philosophy, literary criticism, scientific inquiry, and rhetoric. Dwight had interests in all these disciplines, and his intellectual world was powerfully yet subtly shaped by Scottish Enlightenment thought. Two categories of the Scottish intellectual milieu are of particular importance to Dwight's homiletics. The first category addresses the problem of religious skepticism and the defensive strategy Common Sense thinkers developed to hold religious infidelity at bay. The second category deals with literary matters; it begins with "the art of criticism" and moves into rhetoric and homiletics.

Scottish Backgrounds: Infidelity, Skepticism, Criticism, and Rhetoric

Although Timothy Dwight would be considered "the most effective vanquisher of infidelity in American religious history" into the twentieth century, he did not fire the first volleys in the war on religious skepticism.[8] The religious tumult was well underway before his birth. Although Dwight dedicated his first assault on the skeptics to Voltaire—significantly, neither a philosophical treatise nor a sermon, but *The Triumph of Infidelity*—Dwight identified David Hume as the archfiend at the head of the infidel host. Just how he came to this estimate of Hume or to his knowledge of other significant figures who would influence him—John Locke, Thomas Reid, James Beattie, and George Campbell—is not entirely clear. He probably encountered their writings or summaries of their work during his undergraduate years at Yale, but the absence of personal diaries or journals, added to the restictions imposed on him by his visual impairment, makes conclusive judgments about sources and influences impossible.[9] In any case, Dwight understood the historical outlines of the philosophical battle between Christian orthodoxy and infidelity as follows.

In 1690, John Locke published *An Essay Concerning Human Understanding*, which became immensely important among philosophers and theologians in Britain and its New England colonies. In Book I of the *Essay*, he denied the notion that the mind was endowed with innate knowledge or principles of any sort. Having cleared the mind of any predisposition or inherent knowledge, in Book II Locke asked if the mind was like "white paper, void of all characters," "how comes it to be furnished" with knowledge? The answer lay in experience, on which "all our knowledge is founded, and from [which] it ultimately derives itself." For Locke, ideas came to the mind in two ways; by sensation, when one's five senses convey information to the mind, and by reflection, when the mind itself operates on ideas it has already formed. Ideas could be classified under two categories. A simple idea is unmixed or uncompounded and contains "nothing but one uniform appearance or conception in the mind and is not distinguishable into different ideas." Alternatively, a complex idea is "made by the mind out of simple ones."[10] Using simple ideas as constituents, the mind creates complex ideas. Despite the fact that this scheme found wide acceptance among philosophers and theologians (Edwards himself used the simple idea notion in his *Treatise on the Religious Affections*), the system was not without its liabilities.[11] The chief difficulty of Lockean epistemology arose when one posed questions about the real existence of things in the world or when one probed for bridges between the idea of a thing in the mind and the thing itself.

David Hume entered the conversation precisely at this point. His *Treatise of*

Human Nature (1739–40) paralleled Locke's work in several respects. Like any other inquiry, moral philosophy is subject to the Newtonian canons of observation and experimentation. All knowledge is based on experience. The perceptions of the mind fall into two classes, ideas and impressions, each of which can be further subdivided into simple and complex and original and secondary, respectively.[12] Hume's extensions of the Lockean system became quite radical with his unique twist on Locke's work on knowledge and in particular on problems of causation and necessity. According to Hume, because the mind cannot conceive of anything except that which has been experienced, so-called "facts" cannot be granted credibility *a priori*. From Hume's perspective, for something to be true it must have been experienced; otherwise, statements about its truth are mere speculation. The traditional notions of cause and effect under this construction were imperiled. As Hume explains, "All our reasonings concerning causes and effects, are derived from nothing but custom." Belief in the traditional cause and effect notion is better understood "as an act of the sensitive, than of the cognitive part of our natures." With one stroke Hume appeared to have seriously threatened a standard epistemological rationale and with it the underpinnings of much of eighteenth-century orthodox theology.[13]

This assault on beliefs about cause and effect led to intellectual skepticism about truth claims of any sort, religious or otherwise. Elsewhere Hume rejected traditional Christianity even more directly. "Of Miracles," a section of *An Enquiry Concerning Human Understanding* (1748), represents a case in point. Hume begins by defining a miracle as "a violation of the laws of nature." Because "firm and unalterable experience has established these laws, the proof against a miracle, from the very nature of the fact, is as entire as any argument from experience can possibly be imagined." Miracles are suspect because they are impossible to prove; they provide testimony insufficient to counter the weight of natural law. Those who testify to the veracity of miracles tend to be ignorant and barbarous. Moreover, regarding miracles, there is abundant testimony to the contrary. Therefore, anyone who accepts Christianity, which itself rests on the miraculous, must do so by faith not by reason. Indeed, to be a Christian one must affirm "what is most contrary to custom and experience."[14]

Hume's skepticism did not go unchallenged. On strictly philosophical grounds and with an eye toward the defense of the Christian religion, several of Scotland's preeminent literati began constructing bulwarks against Hume's skepticism. Chief among this group was Thomas Reid, professor of moral philosophy at Glasgow. Reid's fundamental difficulty with Humean skepticism, as articulated in Reid's *Inquiry into the Human Mind* (1764) and echoed countless times by Dwight, lay in the belief that there was a definite limit to the tools of human logic and discursive reasoning. Although Reid fully affirmed the power of observation and experimentation, he believed that the scientific method could be forced with disastrous results to deal with matters beyond its proper purview. Reason had limits and to expect it to assess data it was incapable of testing would inevitably lead to error. Intellectual skepticism was not, then, the result of faulty logic but of the improper use of logic. For Reid, the reigning "philosophy of mind," the tradition that ran from Descartes through Malbranche to Locke and culminating in the "ideal system" of Berkeley and Hume was flawed. Though these great philosophers were to be honored for their considerable merits, they had led subsequent thinkers down the primrose path to intellectual and religious skepticism.

Reid's counterattack on the "ideal system" that lay at the heart of Humean skepticism was deceptively simple. He claimed that common sense directly and effectively exposed the limits of idealism. He based his argument on the experience of everyday people. No one equipped with a modicum of intelligence really questioned the reality of cause and effect. No reasonable person could deny that objects existed in the real world of mass, volume, shape, and color. Even the vulgar and unsophisticated trusted their senses to discern the physical world. The use of the senses to learn about the world, therefore, required no special work of logic or reason: "To reason against any of these kinds of evidence [i.e., the evidence of the senses] is absurd: nay, to reason for them is absurd. They are first principles; and such fall not within the province of reason, but of common sense." Common sense was superior to complex reasoning and to the abstruse arguments of theologians and philosophers. It helped ordinary people to understand their world, to distinguish between truth and error, and to confirm the authenticity of their deepest religious experiences. It was the means by which people understood the truths of the Bible. As Reid would exclaim in a tongue-in-cheek peroration about the ideal philosophers, "I despise Philosophy, and renounce its guidance—let my soul dwell with Common Sense."[15]

Although there is no direct evidence that Dwight read Reid's work, surely he read one, and perhaps two, scholars who used Reid's common sense strategy to defend Christian orthodoxy. The first was George Campbell, whose *Dissertation on Miracles* was published in 1762. Campbell believed that Hume's *Essay on Miracles* deserved "to be considered, as one of the most dangerous attacks that have been made on our religion. The danger results not solely from the merit of the piece; it results much more from that of the author." Notwithstanding Hume's genius in other areas of inquiry, Campbell believed that his nefarious *Essay* demanded a response from believing Christians. God had left sufficient evidence about miracles "to convince the impartial, to silence the gainsayer, and to render the atheist and the unbeliever without excuse. This evidence it is our duty to attend to, and to candidly examine." Campbell's counterattack on Hume centered on what Campbell took to be Hume's inconsistent and ambiguous use of the term "experience." Whereas Hume had argued that experience must precede belief, Campbell claimed that in many cases belief preceded experience. He argued that here and elsewhere in the *Essay*, Hume's reasoning was grounded on false hypotheses. Hume had fallen prey to the belief that reason was superior to common sense, with the result that he had penned the foolishness of the *Essay*. In response to Hume's charge that Christianity could only be apprehended by faith and not by reason, Campbell would aver: "I say not, on the contrary, that our most holy religion is founded on reason, because this expression, in my opinion, is both ambiguous and inaccurate; but I say, that we have sufficient reason for the belief of our religion."[16]

Dwight knew Campbell's *Dissertation,* and he was most likely familiar with writings of James Beattie as well. Several of the Connecticut Wits studied Beattie's poem *The Minstrel,* and Dwight mentions Beattie in *Travels.* Dwight probably also knew Beattie's most important contribution to the philosophy of Common Sense, his enormously successful *Essay on the Nature and Immutability of Truth* (1770). Whereas Campbell's *Dissertation* was a direct response to Hume's assault on miracles, Beattie's treatise not only sought to counter Hume on miracles but on skepticism in general.[17] Like Campbell, Beattie's chief complaint about Hume's *Essay* had to do with terminology and semantics. The "skeptical system," said Beattie, "would never have made such an alarming progress, if it had been well understood. The ambiguity of its language, and the intricacy and length of some of its fundamental investigations," he continued, have produced "that confusion of ideas, and indistinctness of apprehension" that lead to "error and sophistry." The philosopher believed "that the horse he saw running toward him at full gallop, was an idea in his mind, and nothing else." When this sort of fallacious reasoning "invades the rights of common sense, and presumes to arraign that authority by which she herself acts, nonsense and confusion must of necessity ensue." With other Common Sense thinkers, Beattie insisted that scholars return to a life of disciplined discernment and once again allow "common sense to be the ultimate judge in all disputes," even if this meant that "a great part of ancient and modern philosophy become useless."[18]

Dwight had learned the Common Sense antidote against skepticism, but this was not the only theme he took from the Scottish Enlightenment. In his early career he was as concerned with literary taste as he was with the philosophy of the mind. Here, too, he drew on Reid's disciples. Dwight's collegiate teaching career began with his Yale tutorship in 1771. Although the curricular responsibilities of tutors were carefully prescribed, Dwight and a group of his colleagues attempted to make adjustments to the traditional Yale course of study. Theirs was a modest effort to introduce contemporary *belles lettres* to Yale students. The text from which they took their lead was *Elements of Criticism* by Henry Home, Lord Kames, first published in 1762.[19] On the face of things, Dwight's use of *Elements* seems to have been inspired by strictly literary considerations. Kames and other Scottish literati had much to offer Yale students, and the introduction of these materials, even as ancillary or supplemental readings, promised salutary benefits for the intellectual and literary life of the College. Dwight, however, had other motives for trying to expand Yale's curriculum. Like many of his contemporaries, he coveted both individual and national reputation. Here is perhaps the earliest vision of Dwight seeking to become a great man from a great nation. On the eve of the Revolution, Yale College was considered an outpost, perhaps even a backwater, among Anglo-American literati. Polite literature, Dwight's favorite idiom during his teens and early twenties, issued from London and moved west to the colonies, not the other way around. Hence, to study the most contemporary forms of British literary criticism and to contemplate the development of an indigenous school of American poetry, as Dwight surely was by this time, was to make a political statement. Americans, like their British counterparts, could create and produce polite literature. Ironically, in the very era when colonial sensibilities ran toward independence from Britain, Dwight emulated contemporary British style.

Kames's *Elements* represented more than a pedagogic device or an attempt on Dwight's part to escape the perceived literary provincialism of the colonies. The volume also served as an avenue into the larger, more complex intellectual world of eighteenth-century Scotland. Kames was himself a member of several literary clubs, one of which was the Rankenian Club, which may have served as a model for Dwight's beloved Wits. Kames counted among his friends and correspondents some of the century's keenest minds: David Hume, John Boswell, George Berkeley, Samuel Clark, and Benjamin Franklin. Although *Elements* was chiefly concerned with literary matters, its scope was broad. In some respects, *Elements* may have found its inspiration in Hume's call, in *Treatise of Human Nature,* for a sustained treatment of "criticism." Hume himself never took up that task in any systematic manner, and some believe that *Elements,* claiming to be an examination of the fundamental principles of the fine arts, "drawn from human nature, the true source of criticism," represents Kames's attempt to fill this gap. *Elements* draws on Kames's previous work on moral theory, his familiarity with Scots law, and his deep commitments to Newtonian empiricism.[20] If *Elements* has any particular claim to fame it lay in this latter connection: it was the first volume to propose a full theory of criticism on the "rational" model of analysis, whereby one moves from observation of particulars to the formulation of principles. Dwight's fondness for "facts"—their collection, organization, and use—is a clear echo of this strategy.[21]

Although Kames's work was pathbreaking, its preeminence in the field of criticism was not lasting. In 1776, George Campbell, the author of *A Dissertation on Miracles*, published *The Philosophy of Rhetoric*, which quickly eclipsed Kames and became the cornerstone of what has been termed the "new rhetoric" of eighteenth-century Britain. In turn, Campbell's work was followed in 1783 by Hugh Blair's *Lectures on Rhetoric and Belles Lettres*, which popularized the new rhetoric in scores of universities on both sides of the Atlantic.[22] These two works were remarkably successful. Campbell's *Rhetoric* went through twenty-one editions, and Blair's *Lectures* went through an astounding one hundred and fifteen—twenty-six in Britain, thirty-seven in the United States, and fifty-two miscellaneous abridged editions.

The heart of the new rhetoric lay in its adjustments to the classical rhetorical tradition enshrined in the works of Aristotle and Quintilian. Campbell and Blair, unlike some of their more traditional colleagues, used contemporary critical tools to "modernize" the classical tradition. Although they valued classicism, they worked on several fronts to recast it for enlightened speakers in the eighteenth century. Both authors rejected what they took to be the excesses of the elocutionist movement, preferring a less formal conversational tone in public speech. In a move anticipated by Kames and other critics, Blair placed rhetoric under the larger rubric of *belles lettres*. Most important, both Campbell and Blair allowed contemporary philosophical conversations about empirical method, epistemology, reason, and common sense to shape their views of rhetoric.

Dwight's vocational trajectory swerved violently in 1777 when he resigned his Yale tutorship for a chaplain's appointment in the Revolutionary army. Fortunately the new rhetoric of Campbell and Blair was flexible enough to allow Dwight to rely on it despite his change in circumstances. Whereas Dwight had formerly used Kames, Campbell, and Blair on polite literature in the classroom, he now turned to the latter two Scots for instruction about sacred eloquence in the sanctuary.[23] Both Campbell and Blair were accomplished preachers. Indeed, Campbell's preaching career lasted nearly fifty years, and Blair was the incumbent of the prestigious pulpit in High Church at St. Giles. Both devoted chapter-length sections of their respective volumes to the eloquence of the pulpit, and some years later Campbell published a series of twelve lectures on sacred rhetoric in his *Lectures on Systematic Theology and Pulpit Eloquence* (1807).[24] What is striking about these treatments is their similarities. Both authors address preaching in a larger consideration of the rhetorical skills required by three sorts of speakers in their proper spheres—

the lawyer at the bar, the senator in the legislative chamber, and the preacher in the pulpit. More importantly, on a host of substantive issues regarding the homiletic enterprise itself, the two are in virtual agreement. For Campbell and Blair, the end of preaching is the reformation of humanity. In Blair's words, the task of preaching was "to persuade men to become good."[25] To attain this end, the preacher must be particularly attentive to the affectional disposition and intellectual capacities of his auditors, be they of inferior or superior social status. The art of preaching lay in "placing the truth in the most advantageous light for conviction and persuasion."[26] Hence, every address from the pulpit should enlighten the understanding, please the imagination, move the passions, and influence the will.[27] This noble task required the preacher to be disciplined in the use of language. The sermon should be delivered (but not read) in the idiom of its auditors. It must eschew the language of metaphysics and avoid clever or abstruse points, and it should have a single, unified, and clear theme drawn from the scriptures. Above all, the sermon must be *perspicuous*. The scriptures revealed God's economy of salvation in a straightforward manner, and the preacher must proclaim the good news in similar fashion.

Dwight the Preacher: Revelation, Biblical Authority, Hermeneutics

Dwight's reliance on the Scottish homiletic literature is evident throughout his sermon corpus and particularly in *Theology*. Like Campbell and Blair, Dwight believed that the end of preaching lay in changed behavior; the purpose of preaching was "to persuade men to become virtuous." Preaching had an ethical or moral end, therefore, and it qualified as a genuine means of grace. Indeed, Dwight argued that preaching was the chief mean or instrument by which a sinful person could gain access to divine grace. As a route to divine grace, it was more important even than prayer.[28]

Good preaching was an art that needed to be carefully cultivated and governed by an authority greater than itself. With the Scots, Dwight believed that pulpit eloquence was properly managed by both the language and the limits of the holy scriptures, and he carefully delineated the subject matter fit for the pulpit. The preacher must proclaim the plain message of the Bible and studiously avoid preaching doctrines that can be only inferred from the biblical record or that rest on the dictates of reason alone.[29] Dwight consistently heeded his own advice on this issue. Not only do most of his sermons begin with a scriptural passage that forms the central theme of the address, but throughout sermons he would sprinkle allusions to or direct citations from other relevant passages from the scriptures. Most often he avoided inferences, preferring instead to argue from what he took to be the plain meaning of biblical texts. His convictions about the use of reason in sermons can be readily observed in the first sermons of *Theology,* in which he treats the subject of Natural Religion. Despite his familiarity with the standard philosophical "proofs" for the existence of God, Dwight denied the proposition that naked reason operating on the evidence gathered from general revelation could lead a person to salvation. Only the special revelation contained in the Bible, rightly understood and faithfully applied to life, led to genuine religion. This affirmation of the inspiration and authority of the Bible and the call to obedience to its precepts were foundational to everything Dwight believed and taught. For him, religion, science, ethics, education, statecraft, even literary taste, all were grounded in the scriptures. Though Dwight's lifelong war with skeptics would issue in countless skirmishes over particular issues, the debate about the veracity of the Bible lay at the heart of the conflagration. He would not publish the following words until 1810, but they serve as a dictum that governed every aspect of his ministry: "The Bible has made millions virtuous. Philosophy has not made one."[30] Merely claiming that the biblical message was to govern the homiletic enterprise did not solve all the difficulties that attended preaching. The scriptures themselves needed to be interpreted, and again Dwight's system for handling this task came directly from the Scottish homileticians.

Dwight articulated his scriptural hermeneutics at several places in *Theology,* but his most sustained treatment is to be found in his *Discourse on the Genuineness and Authenticity of the New Testament* (1793). The foundation of Dwight's argument is itself historical. Most of the heresies that have plagued the church arose because lay folk shirked their duty to read the Bible for themselves and, instead, embraced "preconceived doctrines of Philosophy." Urging his auditors to avoid such deadly extra-biblical systems, Dwight argued that the

> faculties necessary to form a competent judge of all these facts are the usual senses of men, and that degree of understanding which we commonly term Common Sense. It will be doubtless understood that I assert these to be the only faculties necessary for this end. . . . A plain man, thus qualified, would as perfectly as Aristotle, or Sir Isaac Newton, know whether Christ lived, preached, wrought miracles, suffered, died, appeared alive after his death, and ascended to Heaven. The testimony of the senses, under Common Sense, is the deciding and the only testimony by which the existence of these facts must be determined. . . . Plain men, accustomed to active life, usually judge of facts with less prejudice and more accuracy than philosophers, whose unfortunate disposition to theory and system commonly and greatly warps their judgment from the truth." [31]

In his *Thoughts on the Mediation of Christ* first preached at Yale in 1815, Dwight offered an illustration of how the sophists and philosophers tended to abuse the canons of common sense. Concentrating on the scriptural passages that record the risen Christ's conversations with disciples, Dwight attacked infidels in general and particularly the Socinians and Unitarians among them. Claiming that the passages were to be understood allegorically or figuratively, these foolish interpreters would conclude that Christ was merely human. In response Dwight replied that his interpretation, unlike theirs, acknowledged "the obvious meaning of the words in which the declarations are made." He then posed a series of questions to any who might oppose his appeal to the plain meaning of the text.

> What reason can be suggested why God should have so written these declarations, as not to have them easily understood? Why, especially, should he have so written them, as that they should regularly be misunderstood by the great body of Christians, both learned and unlearned, in every age, since they were written? Why particularly, would this single subject . . . be singled out from all others . . . as to make the disclosure a mere succession of riddles? Why should the language, in which it is communicated, be attended with the obscurity of allegorical writing, without possessing any of those characteristics of an allegory, which might lead us to an interpretation? Why, in a word, should it have been made figurative in such a manner, that the great body of readers, should never be able to perceive that it is figurative at all, and that those who profess to perceive that it is figurative, have hitherto differed endlessly concerning its meaning? [32]

Dwight did acknowledge that the Bible contained some passages that were difficult to interpret. But these were few in number and, as he argued in *The Manner in Which the Scriptures Are to Be Understood* (1816), the "Obvious Sense" was accessible "to a plain man, reading them with seriousness and integrity." The scriptures were written by common people "who knew no other than plain language and no other meaning but that which was customary or familiar." Holy writ contained revelation "chiefly for plain men" and the plain teachings of scripture "have spread vital religion in the world." If "the obvious meaning of the scriptures be not the true one, the great body of mankind could not reasonably be reproved or threatened for not believing them," and "the provision made in the scriptures for the salvation of men is imperfect and ineffectual."[33] Thus, there existed a fundamental harmony between the scriptural message and the dictates of common sense. God, asserted Dwight, "is the origin of both. . . . Hence, in all cases, so far as the views of common sense extend, they are exactly accordant with the Scriptures. Philosophy has opposed the Scriptures often: common sense never."[34]

Dwight identified two exemplars of homiletic perspicuity and common sense hermeneutics. The first was Jesus himself, who customarily spoke with "perfect plainness and simplicity. . . . [H]e used the plain, common, language of mankind, and on no occasion, the technical language, customarily used by men of science, and extensively used at that period by all the votaries of the fashionable philosophy."[35] If Dwight's Connecticut colleagues needed a more contemporary illustration of how to preach plainly yet with intelligence and power, they need look no farther than the great Edwards of whom Dwight said, "Though [Edwards was] probably the ablest metaphysician who has appeared, he never warped from the path of common sense."[36]

The Battle with Infidelity

In his popular myth of the Yale revivals, Lyman Beecher forever linked Dwight's preaching prowess to the battle between Congregational orthodoxy and religious infidelity. In many respects, this identification is apt because Dwight did fear, even dread, the religious and social affects of skepticism. Dwight's pulpit exertions against religious infidelity should not be viewed as coterminous with the whole of his evangelistic preaching. Though he believed that his stand against skepticism was germane to the task of evangelism, he did not view these two sorts of preaching tasks as identical. In an attempt to describe how Dwight functioned as the "Herald of Reconciliation" and with an eye toward examining his understanding of revivalism we can separate and examine the ways in which Dwight utilized Common Sense themes to combat infidelity and how this task related to the larger question of evangelism.

Dwight published his first assault on Hume, his favorite target among the "infidels," in his 1788 poem *The Triumph of Infidelity*. Satan, the narrator of the poem, reports that after sowing the seeds of unbelief in England he turned to Scotland:

> There, in the cobwebs of a college room
> I found my best Amanuensis, Hume,
> And bosom'd in his breast. On dreams afloat,
> The youth soar'd high, and, as I prompted, wrote.
> Sublimest nonsense there I taught mankind
> Pure, genuine dross, from gold seven times refin'd.
>
> . . .
>
> And thus the sage, and thus his teacher, sung.
> All things roll on, by fix'd eternal laws;
> Yet no effect depends on a cause:
> Hence every law was made by Chance divine,
> Parent most fit of order, and Design! [37]

These verses are telling for they serve as a shorthand summary of Dwight's fundamental objections to Hume in particular and to infidelity in general.

Skepticism denied the common sense understanding of cause and effect. It led to a foolhardy affirmation of a sterile doctrine of chance and it denied the existence and superintending presence of a sovereign God. It was, in the final analysis, nonsense masquerading as sublime thought. However effective this sort of satiric attack on skepticism might have been, Dwight's most sustained assaults on infidelity—and those on which his reliance on Scottish Common Sense strategies were most pronounced—appear in his sermons, not in his verse. With bellicose *ad hominem* attacks, with reasoned arguments, and often parroting the arguments of other defenders of orthodoxy, Dwight lashed the fundamental flaws of skepticism relentlessly from the pulpit.

An auditor or reader of Dwight's *Theology Explained and Defended* would quickly discover his animus toward the Humean rejection of the standard views about cause and effect. In the opening paragraphs of the first sermon of the collection, entitled "Existence of God," Dwight observed that the "foundation of all reasoning, concerning beings and events, and ultimately, concerning attributes and relations also, is a supposed, or acknowledged connexion between cause and effect." Each of the first four Observations of this sermon describes and affirms an argument in support of the traditional understanding. In the fifth Observation, Dwight concludes that "No absurdity can be greater than to argue with a man who denies this connexion." [38]

In the second sermon of *Theology*, "Atheistical Objections and Schemes of Doctrine Considered," Dwight presses his attack onward by claiming that in an atheistical system the "connexion between cause and effect, and the very existence of causation, are denied." Dwight attempts to turn empiricism itself against the skeptics. The rejection of cause and effect as it is commonly understood is mere hypothesis unsupported by evidence. Based in absurdities, it drives its abettors to seek proofs where none can be found. Regardless of how completely one might answer the skeptic, one demonstration would remain, namely, that matter itself existed. To this Dwight says in concert with the Scots, "I myself believe, indeed, that it exists; but I also know, that its existence cannot be proved." [39]

The third sermon of *Theology* is particularly illustrative of Dwight's sermonic treatment of skepticism, infidelity, and atheism. Given his outright rejection of the claims of skepticism on common sense grounds in the first two sermons, Dwight turns in the third sermon to what will most often characterize his analysis of the evils of skepticism. He shifts from the intellectual problems inherent in skepticism to what for him is an issue of far greater consequence, its moral implications. Entitled "The Comparative Influence of Atheism and Christianity," this sermon treats the biblical text Psalm 14:1: "The fool says in his heart, There is no God. They are corrupt, they have done abominable works; there is none that goeth good." In a characteristic move,

Dwight proposes to show that the necessary consequence of the religious problem of atheism is moral and, therefore, ultimately social. Atheism inevitably tends to "corrupt the character, and to deform the life of Man." To demonstrate this point, Dwight devotes one of the sermon's three main sections to an examination of the atheist's views of the moral world. Dwight claims that the atheist feels subject to "no moral government," is "insusceptible of moral obligation," and is "incapable therefore of virtue, excellence, and loveliness." For persons who choose such a life course, there can be "no personal worth, enjoyment, or hope; no common good; no sense of rectitude; and no efforts for the promotion of general happiness." Dwight is not content to leave this subject without offering his auditors some concrete historical illustrations of these assertions. To this end, he cast forth what became his favorite red herring. Only once in history had people with such commitments "possessed the supreme power and government of a country." That was, of course, "in France, since the beginning of the Revolution." The Revolution in France, engineered by a generation of atheistic and immoral leaders, produced what Dwight could only describe as a literal hell on earth. This cultural desolation was for him the natural result of skepticism left unchecked.[40]

The claim that the social consequences of infidelity were as destructive as its strictly religious consequences became for Dwight a homiletic cant, a rhetorical volley he could freely fire at his opponents. Illustrations of Dwight's concern about the social ramifications of skepticism exist throughout his sermon corpus, but perhaps nowhere are they more pointed than in two sermons preached during the frantic days of the infamous Illuminati scare, *The Nature and Danger of Infidel Philosophy* (1797) and *The Duty of Americans at the Present Crisis* (1798).

Nature and Danger is really two sermons that were preached during Yale's 1797 graduation exercises. Unlike most other sermons in the Dwight corpus, this one was published with occasional footnotes that identify Dwight's sources and includes long lists of claims made by dozens of irreligious philosophers. Although this is one of Dwight's most pedestrian sermons (its length and monotonously negative tone must have rendered it one of Dwight's least effective addresses), it does provide an index to Dwight's knowledge of the western philosophical tradition. On close examination this index is hardly impressive. His summaries of important developments in philosophy are hackneyed and oversimplified, and his use of them is unsubtle. Instead of engaging the ideas of his opponents, he ridicules and derides them.[41] The sermon's rhetorical energy, such as it is, aims at rejecting infidelity because of its alleged social consequences rather than at engaging the problems it identifies and offering alternative solutions. The effect is to transform what he must have intended as a *tour de force* of western philosophy into a farce.

If in *Nature and Danger* Dwight pummeled his auditors with example after example of how bad thinking leads to bad living, in the *Duty of Americans at the Present Crisis* he scintillates them with specific visions of what an infidel world must inevitably look like. In what would become one of the most frequently cited passages from his writings, Dwight asked "For what end shall we be connected with [infidels]?"

> Is it that we may assume the same character and pursue the same conduct? Is it that our churches may become temples of reason, our Sabbath a decade, our psalms of praise Marseillois [sic] hymns? Is it that we may change our holy worship into a dance of Jacobin phrenzy[?] . . . Is it that we may see the Bible cast into a bonfire[?] . . . Is it that we may see our wives and daughters the victims of legal prostitution; soberly dishonored; speciously polluted; the outcasts of delicacy of virtue, and the loathing of God and man[?] . . . Shall we, my brethren, become partakers of these sins? Shall we introduce them into our government, our schools, our families? Shall our sons become the disciples of Voltaire, and the dragoons of Marat; our daughters the concubines of the Illuminati? [42]

Such shrieking denunciations have earned Dwight a well-deserved place in the literature describing the "paranoid style" of American politics.[43] More important to the present discussion, they serve as an accurate distillation of his pulpit attacks on skepticism, infidelity, atheism, and "philosophy." Scottish Common Sense thinkers lent Dwight what might be thought of as the secondary means of defending against infidelity. With the Scots, Dwight averred that the "arguments" of the skeptics were not arguments at all but mere assertions. The dictates of Common Sense made that plain to any honest inquirer. Dwight's primary defense had little to do with the heart of the philosophical arguments of his opponents. Rather, it lay in exposing what he took to be the social telos of infidelity. The cultural consequences of unbelief were horrific; they lead straight to cultural hell, and on that ground alone were to be rejected.

The Problem of Evangelism

The social telos of infidelity, the cultural consequences of unbelief, the specter of cultural hell, these themes recur throughout Dwight's preaching. Time and again he offers auditors harrowing verbal pictures of what a world without faith would look like. But this type of Christian proclamation is negative. It functions as an evangelistic argument from silence. One sees what might occur in the absence of faith but little is offered about the positive content of that faith. To put the problem another way, in passages like these we see Dwight trying to drive infidelity off the scene. But where does Dwight—

known to many as the architect and patriarch of Second Great Awakening revivalism—describe what should replace unbelief? What does he say about what it means to become a Christian? Where does he preach about evil, redemption, the atonement, or the work of the Holy Spirit, in the hopes of seeing a sinner converted to Christianity? In short, what does Dwight have to say, in sermons or in other writings, about the classic rubrics of evangelism? For answers to these questions we turn to illustrative evidence contained in his sermons and in two other sources that describe Dwight's views on these matters.

Despite the systematic arrangement of doctrine in *Theology*, admonitions to godliness and appeals to take up the faith are evident throughout the one hundred seventy-three sermons that make up the collection. For instance, while preaching on the subject of the "Omnipotence and Independence of God," Dwight urged his young auditors to consider "How terrible an enemy to obstinate sinners is an omnipotent God!" He continued the sermon with a pastoral application of this truth: "Let me ask, and let each individual answer solemnly in his own mind, Do you love God? Do you desire to please Him? Do you cheerfully obey his commandments?"[44] Such appeals were not limited to texts in which the mention of God's wrath lent itself to pleas for repentance. Dwight made similar applications from less threatening texts. In "The Priesthood of Christ," for example, he attempted to instill religious interest among unconverted listeners by reviewing the benefits of belonging to the Great High Priest: "Those who trust in the expiation of Christ will certainly inherit the favour of God. . . . Let every believer, then, be completely assured that his case is safe in the hands of God."[45] In another sermon, dealing with the character of Christ as King, Dwight focused on the finitude of fallen humanity and its requisite need for a savior of infinite power. He observed that we are "creatures wholly dependent, frail, ignorant, exposed, and unable to protect ourselves or provide for our interests." From this, Dwight concluded, "We may discern how greatly we need such a friend as Christ."[46] A careful reading of *Theology* yields scores of such exhortations to piety and faithfulness, most of which appear under the heading "Remarks," in the final section of each sermon. Nevertheless, *Theology* contains only infrequent direct appeals to the unbeliever. Few of its constituent sermons are evangelistic in purpose. This being the case, it is incorrect to identify the collection as belonging to the revivalist genre. *Theology* was intended for the converted, not the unregenerate; here Dwight was a didactic theologian, not an evangelist.

Unlike the didactic addresses preserved in *Theology*, the *Sermons* collection contains some of Dwight's most celebrated evangelistic addresses. *The Youth of Nain*, a discourse on the miracle story of Luke 7:11–15, began with a consideration of the revelatory value of the miracle. Christ's benevolence, compassion, and power were marvelously revealed in the account. Dwight did not confine his remarks to the pedagogic value of the passage. His larger purpose was "to consider the material in question as a work of Christ, strongly symbolical of one much more interesting which by his spirit he performs on various persons."[47] Dwight next noted parallels that might have existed between the Youth of Nain and any unconverted young men of Yale. Both were suffering the deleterious effects of sin. Death and judgment stood close at hand, and given this gloomy state of affairs, Dwight offered hope to his audience. Christ, he reminded them, still exerted his miraculous efforts on behalf of sinners. Like the Youth of Nain, these young men could be raised to newness of life in Christ. But even here, in a sermon ostensibly devoted to wooing sinners to Christ, Dwight could not resist the temptation to discuss questions of morality. Near the close of the sermon with his focus still on "seekers," Dwight urged those who sought Christ's mercy to reflect on their behavior: "it is indispensable that such as desire to be interested in [salvation] should begin a total change of their behavior."[48] This shift in subject—from the contemplation of Christ's mercy to personal reformation, from grace to law—occurs rapidly. Indeed, one is tempted to conclude that the sudden emphasis upon duty represents an infelicitous error in Dwight's delivery. Such a conclusion overlooks an important element in Dwight's religious system. For him evangelism did not only entail visions of judgment and pleas to seek the mercy of Christ. These were a part of his evangelism and he considered them indispensable parts of the gospel, but he felt that they were in vain without personal reformation. Conversion was nothing unless it brought with it personal sanctification.[49]

Sometimes Dwight reversed this pattern of personal salvation—moral reformation. Lyman Beecher claimed that he was converted when he heard Dwight preach another of the addresses contained in the *Sermons* collection, *The Harvest Past*.[50] Little wonder, for *Harvest* is an unrelenting appeal to students to become Christians. Dwight uses the scriptural text, "The harvest is past, the summer is ended; and we are not saved" (Jeremiah 8:20) as a refrain that haunts the sermon. Time and again he returns to it, lamenting the loss of those who have not taken advantage of salvation while they had the opportunity to do so. The sermon's introduction in which Dwight rehearses Jeremiah's struggles with stiffnecked believers comprises a social lament. Momentarily silent about the eternal, otherworldly consequences of faith or unbelief, Dwight stresses the social consequences of virtue and vice, fidelity and infidelity in the present world. Analyzing the decline of the Jewish nation at the time of Jeremiah, Dwight notes that the Jews of that time tottered

on the eve of destruction. . . . Infidelity and irreligion had taken entire
possession of the nation. Their kings, their nobles, their priests and their
citizens, with one universal declension, had finally turned their backs on
JEHOVAH, and yielded themselves to the abominations of the heathen.
Truth, justice, and benevolence had fallen in the streets; and falsehood,
injustice, and cruelty rioted without control.[51]

Like Jeremiah, Dwight lamented the tragic decline of the original Israel,
God's people of old. Unlike Jeremiah, Dwight's field of prophetic vision en-
compassed declension in the American New Israel as well. Although he was
careful not to draw an explicit parallel between the fall of Israel and the decline
of New England Congregationalism, Dwight's language nonetheless suggested
such an interpretation. For him, Puritan New England had enjoyed many
seasons in which religion had prevailed and the commonwealth had flourished.
By comparison the contemporary church and state were less vital. For Dwight,
not only a sense of individual guilt but also the awareness of the decline of
culture at large could and should drive thinking people to seek redemption.
Because society and religion were inseparable, social ills naturally followed on
the heels of religious decline. Conversely, renewed interest in religion would
bring an increase in public piety and a new level of cultural sanctification.
Dwight made good use of the standard logic of the Puritan jeremiad.

Addressing a different doctrine, Dwight argued similarly in *On Revivals of
Religion*. Adopting a distinctly postmillennial eschatology, Dwight claimed
that great numbers of people—none of whom one would expect to be converted—would adhere to Christianity in the eschatological future. These
unlikely candidates for election would witness a radical conversion of culture
itself. In that day, civic leaders

will rule justly and in the fear of God. . . . They will cease to be a terror,
because none will do evil. . . . In towns and cities also, the Theatre will
cease to entice, corrupt, and destroy. . . . The Brothel will no more hang
out the sign of pollution. . . . The dram shop will no longer solicit the
surrender of reason, duty, and salvation, to drunkenness and brutality.
Night will no more draw her great curtain over those felon sins. . . . In the
family also, no drunken, cruel husband; no false, abandoned wife; no
rebellious, graceless, debauched children.

Dwight's pragmatism would not allow him to believe that such a cultural
conversion was to be realized only in the future. On the contrary, he espoused
an eschatology in which future blessings were to some extent realized in the
present. He concluded, "From these observations it follows also that the same
things are partially true of every Revival of Religion . . . The difference between this [the millennium] and the other [i.e. contemporary revivals of

religion] being only in degree."[52] As in *The Harvest Past*, Dwight again made a fervent appeal to the consciences of his listeners, asking, "Do you claim to be regarded as patriots, and to love your country?"[53] Here, the rhetorical point is obvious. If the young men of Yale were patriotic, they would become Christians, reform their behavior, promote revivals, and thereby sanctify American culture.

What of extant manuscript sermons in this connection? Do they reveal a more aggressive evangelist, a preacher more characteristic of the revivalist tradition that is associated with the Second Great Awakening? On the basis of the small collection of manuscript sermons that have survived in the Dwight Family Papers at Yale University, this question can be answered in the negative. Most of these sermons (e.g., *Ecclesiastes 9:10, Long Life Not Desirable, The Character of Jabez,* and *The Lord's Prayer*) conform to the pedagogic and admonishment patterns found in the published collections, *Theology* and *Sermons.* The exceptions to this larger rule are few. In *Levity with Respect to Sacred Things,* Dwight employed strong warnings to his auditors about the liabilities of damnation and eternal suffering. Taking his text from Matthew 22, "But they made light of it, and went their ways," Dwight enumerated a series of points about "lightness of mind" with respect to divine things. This sort of levity, he noted, "is ultimately exercised against God himself." It is an "effectual preventative of all serious attention to the great business of attaining eternal life" and it "necessarily hardens the heart."[54] Given the dire consequences of levity, he warns "rash adventurers" to beware their fate: "Before you are, ready to be unbarred, the awful gates of eternity." "Will you smile, and sport, and flutter, before the last tribunal?" A holy and angry God, he reminds them, stands ready to judge the wicked and the frivolous.[55] Similarly, in *Thoughts on the Mediation of Christ,* Dwight urged his listeners to consider their own deaths and to view the deathbed as a gateway to either eternal bliss or endless suffering.[56] Despite the subject matter contained in these sermons they are much like the rest of the Dwight corpus. In measured phrases and with stress on reason over emotion, Dwight urged his students toward personal reformation. Righteous behavior and obedience to the laws of God stood at the heart of his "gospel" proclamation.

This pattern within Dwight's sermon corpus is echoed elsewhere in his writings, two illustrations of which show it most pointedly. In the early summer of 1802, the editors of the *Connecticut Evangelical Magazine* asked Dwight to submit a report on the recent "revival" that had taken place in the college in May. Dwight's response, published under the title "Brief Account of the Revival of Religion Now Prevailing in Yale College," served multiple purposes. Dwight wanted to show his support for the conversion of his students, but he also wanted readers to rest assured that no dangerous theological novelties were afoot in the college. Yale's newfound religious fervor conformed to established orthodox patterns, order was maintained, and social deference was observed. The affected students, some fifty in number, he noted, "exhibited a new and very solemn sense of the importance of salvation." However, "nothing enthusiastic, nothing superstitious, nothing gloomy, morose, or violent" occurred. On the contrary, the student body had been "as diligent, orderly, and decorous, so far as is remembered, as at any former period," and the awakened had "become more attentive to their duty, more modest, more respectful to their instructors, and more affectionate to each other. . . . [A]ll of them are greatly desirous to be taught, and none to assume the office of teaching." From Dwight's perspective, then, the effects of the "revival" were perfect: students worked harder, attended to their duties with greater diligence, and more frequently observed the appropriate social protocols with their superiors. In sum, the "doctrines of grace" had done their work—they had produced "propriety of conduct."[57]

A final, telling source of Dwight's views on conversion appears in an extant letter to Benjamin, his second son, dated 8 August 1803. The occasion of the letter was the death of another of Dwight's children, a son named John. After breaking the sad news, Dwight confessed that he had "good hopes that he [the deceased son] is gone to a better world and that his last end is peace," but he added, "I do not know this and cannot know it. . . I would give a million worlds to be assured of it, were they mine." Given the reality of death and the uncertainty of eternal life, Dwight urged Benjamin (a practicing physician who was often confronted with death) to use the occasion of his brother's death to focus his attention on salvation and eternal life. Salvation was the one thing needful: "Seek this above all things and seek it always. Pray to God every morning and evening, with all thy heart, to sanctify, to preserve, to bless, and to save you. Never lose an opportunity to be present at the worship of God." "Read the Bible every day and two chapters at least. Devote the Sabbath to religion only." "Possess yourself by loan or otherwise of religious books, and read them carefully." "If the family in which you live be not a religious family, exchange it, as soon as you can with propriety, for one which is." "In a word, let religion and salvation be always uppermost in your mind." Again, we see Dwight offering advice that is not typical of the urgings and pleadings considered typical of "second awakeners."[58] As in many of his sermons, his counsel is quite straightforward: seekers should not yearn for a distinct, emotional, conversion experience but rather should employ the recognized means of grace—prayer, worship, preaching, conversation with the godly—and that they should seek to be obedient to the standards of Christian conduct as they pursue salvation.

* * *

Lyman Beecher's mythic account of Timothy Dwight's Yale revival has cast a long shadow on the historiography of American religion. Beecher's description of Dwight's homiletic bid to win the souls of Yale's francophile undergraduates has been one of the most commonly used prologues to the story of the Second Great Awakening. Invariably, authors cast Dwight as the champion of New England orthodoxy. He rescues Yale from the maw of French infidelity, he puts an end to student skepticism, he increases the membership in the College Church, and he rallies bright young men under the banner of the Standing Order. All this he does from the pulpit of Yale's chapel. Over time, Beecher's tale has assumed the stature of a "classic text."

Based largely on the Beecher myth, American historians have attached a good deal of significance to Dwight's role in nineteenth-century Protestantism in general and in the so-called Second Great Awakening in particular. Some scholars, notably Charles Roy Keller, Charles Cuningham, William Clebsch, and Perry Miller, have hailed Dwight's preaching campaign as the first event in America's Second Great Awakening. Building on this interpretive foundation, other scholars have argued that Dwight not only began the Second Great Awakening but did so with distinct political motives. Sidney Mead and Stephen Berk observe that Dwight did more than merely draw students into the fold of orthodox Congregational religion. He also attempted to chase off political infidelity (i.e., Jeffersonian Republicanism), to reassert the hegemony of the Federalist party, and to charge his young Yale disciples to convert and reform America and the entire world. Other scholars demur. Edmund Morgan, Richard Birdsall, Richard Shiels, and David Kling reject the Beecher account and its attendant implications. Although they grant that Dwight was important for Yale and for Beecher, these students of the era believe that his pedagogic and homiletic efforts represented only modest contributions to the larger Second Great Awakening.

Each of these interpretations has evidence that recommends it. Dwight was a master preacher who exerted considerable influence in early national New England. In countless sermonic admonitions over the course of a long career he defended Christianity and attacked infidelity. His sermons were collected and republished many times both in the United States and in England. Notwithstanding Beecher's sophomoric enthusiasm and selective memory, Dwight was the most prominent divine in turn-of-the-century New England. Scholars who are attracted to the "political revival" line of thinking can muster suggestive evidence for their interpretation as well. Dwight's *The Conquest of Canaan, The Triumph of Infidelity,* and *Travels in New England and New York* suggest that "the Pope of Federalism" had amalgamated his political and religious commitments. Indeed, Dwight's shrill francophobic sermons against infidelity—particularly his *Duty of Americans at the Present Crisis* and his *Nature and Danger of Infidel Philosophy,* which pit godliness and Federalism against immorality and democracy—seem to clinch their argument. The revisionists, less concerned with Beecher's filiopietism and Dwight's preaching, and more sensitive to the larger social and religious contexts of early national America, can also be quite compelling. Whatever else we may believe about the collection of events gathered under the rubric "the Second Great Awakening," we must recognize the diversity of the religionists who participated in them. Congregationalists, Presbyterians, Baptists, Methodists, and a host of subgroups—Stoneites, Taylorites, Tylerites, Finneyites, and Cumberlanders—all had a stake in the religious events of the day. Dwight was but one player in one theater of the Second Great Awakening.

Ironically, while each of these schools of interpretation has made important contributions to our understanding of Dwight and the Second Great Awakening, none of them focuses attention on the subject that stands at the heart of the Dwight story, namely, his homiletics. If, as Benjamin Dwight believed, "it was impossible for [Dwight] to enter the desk but as the herald of reconciliation," then what is the significance of Dwight's preaching career?[59] On the basis of the foregoing analysis of Dwight's preaching, we are in a position to offer the outlines of an answer to this question.

First and most important, Dwight's homiletic was the product of a keen and active imagination. This is not to suggest that his pulpit oratory was characterized by a reliance on informal or popular structures of communication, that it was undisciplined, that it was disconnected from the dominant American Protestant theological tradition, or that it tended toward religious enthusiasm. On the contrary, Dwight's religious rhetoric was formal, he developed and consistently used a particular style of address, his preaching relied upon and evoked the standard canon of Protestant orthodoxy, and he abhorred unfettered emotion. What is in view here is the extent to which Dwight was able to reflect on his knowledge of the tradition—learned largely from oral sources— and distill, reshape, and convey the nuanced results of his thinking to a generation of New England's citizens. Using information accessible to him about the Bible, Christian theology, the nature of the church, human personality, American politics, and New England culture, Dwight created alternative worlds, new structures of meaning, and creative avenues to what he believed to be the truth. If pulpit discourse had to enlighten the understanding, please the imagination, move the passions, and influence the will, we must recognize Dwight's signal success as a homiletic artist.

Second, though previously unrecognized, Dwight served as the most important gateway though which Scottish Common Sense Realism entered the New England theological milieu. While the influence of this philosophical strategy has been assessed in relation to other American religious groups (notably Presbyterians in the Middle Colonies) and while its importance among later American Reformed theologians has been noted, Dwight's role as an early purveyor of Common Sense in New England has gone largely unnoticed. This is due in large part to the fact that Dwight's adoption of Scottish Realism was not strictly philosophical but literary. Only after he had familiarized himself with the work of Lord Kames did he turn to the ancillary work of Campbell, where he discovered the homiletic potential inherent within the system. His adoption of the Common Sense method did not occur as part of a systematic appraisal of the philosophy of the day or as an element of a developed critical homiletic. Ever the Christian pragmatist, Dwight recognized that this way of thinking could serve as a powerful weapon in his homiletic attack on the incursion of infidelity into America. Thus, despite his prominence as a theological teacher, Dwight adopted the Scots not for formal or academic reasons but for informal and hortatory considerations. Notwithstanding this, his auditors took the point. Yale students—notably Nathaniel William Taylor—would later embellish Dwight's version of Scottish Common Sense Realism and install it as a prominent fixture of the developing New England Theology.

Third, Dwight played a significant role in the development of a distinctly American homiletic. Though previous generations of clergy had preached thousands of learned sermons to America's collegians, Dwight's contribution to this type of preaching was unique. Intellectual and genealogical heir to Edwards, prominently placed in the presidency of Yale, and grappling with the effects of a physical limitation, Dwight became an archetype among American homileticians. Learned without having published formal theological or philosophical treatises, eloquent without the aid of notes in the pulpit, earnest without emotional appeals, Dwight popularized Edwardsean piety for generations of New Englanders. Just as he was unable to refute in detail the infidels whose thought he loathed, so too he was unwilling to preach on the finer, more difficult points of doctrine that he affirmed. Infidelity he held at bay with Holy Scripture and Common Sense. He resisted theological precisionism, which he distrusted as firmly though not as vehemently, as an aberration of revelation and the proper use of the mind. Between these two dangers he crafted a homiletic of the *via media* that could be understood by nearly anyone and that would serve as a wide foundation upon which reasonable, middle-class believers could erect the superstructures of American evangelicalism.

Finally, what of the task of gospel proclamation itself? What of evangelism? This problem suggests Dwight's fourth contribution to American homiletics. Eschewing difficult philosophical preaching, wary of the finespun webs of high Calvinism, and horrified at the prospects of a theology based on raised emotion or ineffable religious feeling, Dwight promulgated from the pulpit what he had struggled with all his life, Christian duty. Whatever else may have characterized Dwight's homiletics, at the heart of his proclamation stood the conviction that Christian faith and Christian duty were inseparable. Evangelistic preaching was nothing more and nothing less than admonishment to outlooks, practices, and behaviors that were approved by God. "Ought" and "should" framed Dwight's homiletics, and the presence of virtue—constructed as it was on the basis of Dwight's peculiar social, political, and religious world views—became the only useful litmus test for faith. In the pulpit Dwight functioned as an American moralist.

III

A Distinguished Divine

Dr. Dwight's reputation as a preacher rapidly
increased, and in literature and theological
knowledge, he ranked among the best scholars
and most distinguished divines of the country.

—EBENEZER BALDWIN

Timothy Dwight's rise to prominence in New England was based on a number
of factors. He came from a famous family, he was very well educated, and he
was blessed with solid, if not brilliant, artistic and intellectual gifts. Any one of
these advantages would have set him apart from the majority of ordinary
citizens, and taken together they elevated him well above his peers. Yet the
national distinction Dwight sought also depended upon other, more personal
characteristics. He was ambitious, compromising, and if the Parnassus intrigue is any indication, rather cunning. While not necessarily duplicitous or
dishonest, when it came to his own advancement Dwight exhibited adroit
maneuvering and a penchant for artful, covert scheming. Dwight was, in the
broadest sense, a thoroughly political being.

Dwight's model of greatness lay in his moral exemplar, Jonathan Edwards.
He longed to follow Edwards's footsteps along the path of greatness, and at
particular moments he even dreamed of surpassing his beloved grandfather.
He patterned his early career on the Edwards archetype, he studied theology
with Edwards's disciples, and his position at Yale College afforded him access
to the best minds and most influential people on the eastern seaboard. Thousands of Americans—elites and common folk, church leaders and parishioners, Congregationalist stalwarts and New England nonconformists, faithful
friends and infidel foes—had read his verse, heard his sermons, acknowledged
his political savvy, and marveled at his administrative genius. Dwight was
destined to become, like his grandfather, America's theologian.

The path to such greatness, daunting in any era, was strewn with particularly difficult obstacles in Dwight's day. By the time he had ascended to the
presidency of Yale, Edwards's theological legacy was uncertain. Forty years of
internecine debates, squabbles, and metaphysical hair-splitting as well as a
host of cultural and political changes in New England had taken an inevitable
toll. To complicate matters further, Dwight was not the only theologian who

sought to replicate Edwards's success. A cadre of Edwards's students and disciples, including Jonathan Edwards, Jr., Samuel Hopkins, Joseph Bellamy, and others competed for the right to wear their teacher's mantle.

By the close of the eighteenth century, Edwardsean theology needed a highly visible champion who had the wit, the will, and the grace to repristinate the tradition and propel it into the nineteenth century. Dwight hoped to become such a leader. Even small steps along this path to greatness would demand of him the most rigorous application of his intellectual gifts. To forge paths to new heights and to become the standard bearer of the Edwardsean theological tradition in America would require additional skills. He would have to reconcile rival factions, soothe tender egos, and, most important, craft thelogical compromises.

Contrary to his hopes and to the surprise of his contemporaries and subsequent observers, Dwight did not emerge as a forward-looking, construc- tive apologist for Edwards's theology. This chapter begins with a description of the emergence of the Edwardsean tradition and of the terminological problems with which modern interpreters of New England Theology must contend. It then compares Dwight's theology to Edwardsean and New Divinity theologies and concludes with an assessment of Dwight's place within the larger move- ment known as New England Theology.

New Lights, Old Lights, Edwardseans, and New Divinity Theologians

During the Great Awakening of the 1730s and 1740s, New Lights (those ministers and layfolk who supported the Awakening) and Old Lights (those who opposed it) publicly debated a number of questions regarding the legiti- macy of the religious events that seemed to be taking the colonies by storm. Was the Awakening a genuine dispensation of divine grace? Or merely the result of enthusiasm? Did its proponents want to revivify the faith of New England's founders? Or were their novelties a radical departure from the faith once delivered to the saints?

While Jonathan Edwards and other theologians recognized the importance of these questions, they also realized that the New Light–Old Light conflict was symptomatic of deeper and more complex doctrinal problems that had long vexed New England Congregationalism: How badly had sin debilitated an individual human being? Was the effect total, leaving the moral agent entirely helpless? Or did sinners have access to some remnant of genuine virtue by which they could leverage themselves into salvation? If the Holy Spirit had somehow to renovate a sinner in order to enable true goodness, how did this occur? Did God act immediately, without the agency of mundane events or means? Or did the divine spirit employ and rely upon this-worldly agents?

How exactly did Christ's life and sacrifice play a role in the salvific process? How could an individual or a church differentiate between genuine piety and mere feeling parading itself as true religion? Discussion of these substantive doctrinal questions took place in ministers' studies and in scores of learned publications as the public events of the Awkening ebbed and flowed across the better part of a decade.

Edwards quickly emerged as the single most important apologist for the New Light way of thinking. In his early works on the Awakening, *A Faithful Narrative of the Surprising Work of God* (1737) and *Some Thoughts Concerning the Present Revival of Religion* (1742), he sought to interpret the meaning of the events which had taken place. Later, in longer and more formal treatises, *A Treatise Concerning Religious Affections* (1746), *A Careful and Strict Enquiry into the Modern Prevailing Notions of the Freedom of the Will* (1754), *The Great Christian Doctrine of Original Sin Defended* (1758), and the posthumously published *Two Dissertations* (1765), he addressed the doctrinal concerns that operated beneath these events and constructed a foundation on which subsequent thinkers could build. Edwards's untimely death in 1758 prevented him from completing his "Rational Account," a work which many thought might have drawn together his several treatises in a more synthetic or systematic manner. His death also created a sudden problem of leadership. Though Edwards had trained several students, it was unclear who, if anyone, could or would replace him as the undisputed leader of the New Lights. As it turned out, no single individual took Edwards's place at the head of the New Light movement. In the absence of a single leader, with fewer and fewer instances of remarkable awakenings to discuss, and with popular attention becoming increasingly fixed on the question of the colonies' relationship with Britain, the New Light–Old Light debate lost energy, and the easy classification of clergy into one or the other of these opposing groups became problematic.

Although remnants of the New Light and Old Light factions remained and although the theological issues that divided these two groups were quite clear, not every Congregationalist minister identified with one or the other of the aging parties. An amorphous collection of clergy occupied a fluid middle position between the old rivals. These "Old Calvinists" represented a mixed group. Some flirted with one or more liberal doctrines; others leaned toward more orthodox traditions of New England. Some had been nurtured in Old Light congregations; others had been awakened in New Light churches. Because they occupied a broad center position on the theological spectrum, the Old Calvinists were often forced to become theological peacemakers. In an era when political tempers were running dangerously short, the Old Calvinists counseled moderation. They believed that the rarefied air of abstract theology was meant to be breathed in the privacy of the study but not broadcast from the pulpit. They were content to keep traditional Calvinist affirmations regarding original sin, predestination, and limited atonement—all of which had been modified and upheld by Edwards—politely hidden under the proverbial bushel.

Not surprisingly, the irenic admonitions issued by theologians of the *via media* rankled the most aggressive among Edwards's disciples. These New Light stalwarts believed that the inherited corpus of Reformed dogmatics contained troubling inconsistencies that demanded correction. Edwards's protégé Samuel Hopkins was adamant about the need for revision. In a letter to Samuel Miller, Hopkins cited a host of Reformed authorities including Calvin and Edwards himself and complained that "most of these did not indeed fully explain some of these doctrines that are asserted or implied in their writings. And they are in some instances inconsistent with themselves, by advancing contrary doctrines."[1] The Preface to Hopkins's *System of Doctrine Contained in Divine Revelation, Explained and Defended* offers additional evidence of his commitment to a more "consistent Calvinism":

> If the Bible be a revelation from heaven, it contains a system of consistent important doctrines; which are so connected, and implied in each other, that one cannot be so well understood if detached from all the rest, and considered by itself; and some must be first known before others can be seen in proper and true light.[2]

Armed with new insights and energized with a zeal born in the heyday of the Awakening, Hopkins and his colleagues scoffed at calls for homiletic moderation and began aggressively preaching their discoveries from the pulpit. The response from vocal Old Calvinists was at first modest and only concerned matters of homiletic style. They chided Hopkins and his ilk about their penchant for "metaphysical preaching." Later the Old Calvinists focused their criticisms on the substance of Hopkins's theology, and their chiding veered closer to invective. They charged Hopkins and other zealous followers of Edwards with promulgating an entirely "new divinity." The moniker stuck.

Just here modern interpreters of New England Theology encounter a vexing terminological problem—one that becomes particularly acute in an attempt to describe Dwight's theological inclinations. Generations of historians have used the descriptive expression "New Divinity" generically or even interchangably with the terms "Edwardsean," "Hopkinsian," or "Consistent Calvinist." Recent scholarship has made it abundantly clear, however, that this heuristic convention leads to confusion and erroneous conclusions. In fact, there were many New Englanders who counted themselves among Edwards's followers and who, at the same time, rejected the more radical departures of Samuel Hopkins, Joseph Bellamy, and Nathaniel Emmons. In other words, the New Divinity theology constituted only one wing—albeit the most visible and controversial—of a larger movement best described as Edwardseanism.[3]

Edwardseans affirmed the broad outlines of their namesake's theology as expressed in his major published treatises. They appropriated Edwards's distinction between natural and moral necessity, his nuanced use of the doctrine of imputation, his stress on the affective appreciation of God as the sole evidence of regeneration, and his rejection of the Halfway Covenant. New Divinity thinkers affirmed these ideas and additional ones as well. They repudiated the doctrine of imputation, placed a high premium on the notion of disinterested benevolence, adopted the governmental theory of the atonement, and questioned the utility and legitimacy of the classical means of grace. They attempted to systematize Edwards's thought (or to make it consistent) by making it conform to the canons of rigorous logic. In this respect, the New Divinity theologians might be thought of as Edwardsean precisionists.

This chapter argues that Timothy Dwight was an Edwardsean but not a New Divinity theologian. Although his appropriation of Edwards's thought was piecemeal and somewhat idiosyncratic, the following analysis of his theology indicates that he was committed to the larger rubrics of Edwardseanism but opposed to many of the more radical doctrines of the New Divinity theologians. This examination is organized around two themes. The first is the logic or "mechanics" of Calvinist soteriology. In traditional Reformed thought, sin and righteousness were taken from one agent and "imputed" to another. Edwards made adjustments to several doctrines—notably original sin, the atonement, and justification—in which imputation traditionally functioned. His New Divinity followers made additional changes and in some respects so did Dwight. Were the analysis to stop here, as it has for many interpreters, one might conclude that Dwight did affirm New Divinity theology. But that conclusion would be premature. This will be made evident in the examination of a second theme, which concerns questions of moral agency and ecclesiology. Edwards's most unique contribution to the Reformed tradition had to do with the subjective or affective appropriation of soteriology. Working with the problems of philosophical necessity, the will, and the affections, he developed a theocentric ethic that suggested new ways of understanding church membership. Using his foundation, the New Divinity theologians erected unique and radical views of moral agency and ecclesiology that became a hallmark of their movement. Here Dwight took leave of the New Divinity quite forthrightly.

The Logic of Soteriology

The Calvinist gospel narrated a story of a sovereign God who superintended the fall of humanity, the work of Christ, and the salvation of the elect.[4] In their attempt to explain the mystery and paradox of the gospel, Calvinist interpreters depended upon the notion of imputation, by which it was thought that moral good or evil—or in theological terms, righteousness or sinfulness—could be transferred from one moral agent to another. Reformed interpreters, and both Edwardseans and New Divinity theologians among them, gave special attention to three doctrines in which imputation functioned: original sin, the atonement, and justification by faith.

Reformed theologians taught that Adam's first sin affected him as well as his descendants. All members of humanity, irrespective of their individual moral performance, were held accountable for Adam's first or original sin. Proponents of this view carefully described how this sin was passed from Adam to his progeny. His sin became theirs by imputation; it was reckoned to their moral accounts. To be sure, Reformed divines taught that every person's actual sins incurred additional guilt, but such a state of moral affairs had its genesis in the spiritual inheritance received from humanity's primeval forebear. Infants and "innocent" young children were not exempted from this indictment. A dying child who was too young to be capable of rationalized moral behavior was bound for perdition. Although the child had incurred no personal guilt (because he or she had not yet sinned actually), Adam's imputed sin was sufficient to warrant damnation.

The doctrine of imputation also functioned under a second Reformed rubric. Just as Adam's guilt was affixed to the individual in original sin, so the sins of the elect were affixed to Christ in the atonement. The individual moral agent, polluted with imputed and actual sin, was freed from that burden by Christ's work on the cross. Christ, the perfect sacrifice, who was sinless, took upon himself the sins of those whom he intended to save. The sinner's sins were imputed to Christ, who paid the ultimate penalty for sin, death.

Reformed theologians used imputation in a third area of soteriology as well. In the Calvinist plan, the simple removal of a sinner's guilt was not sufficient to secure eternal life. To enter the Kingdom of God the sinner had to possess a positive righteousness. In justification, therefore, the righteousness of Jesus Christ was imputed to the sinner who could then claim both innocence (the sinner's sins—both actual and original—had been "removed" and imputed to Christ in the atonement) and positive righteousness (Christ's perfect righteousness had been imputed to the sinner in justification).

Despite the logical symmetry of this series of imputations—and perhaps because of it—Calvinism's critics objected to this scheme on biblical, philosophical, and pragmatic grounds. Not surprisingly, the assault on imputation began during the heady days of the French and Indian War, as British colonists struggled anew with questions of political and individual accountability. Less surprising, the first target of the assault was the doctrine of original sin. Although British theologians had been working on this problem for years, as can be seen in the controversial work of the Arminian divine John Taylor, New Englanders' sensibilities were shaken by a popular tract on the subject. In

1757, Samuel Webster anonymously published a clever essay entitled *A Winter Evening's Conversation upon the Doctrine of Original Sin*, which brought the colonial debate about original sin to a boil.[5]

Webster's polemical treatise is thinly disguised as the report of a "Conversation, upon the Doctrine of Original Sin, between a minister and three of his neighbors accidentally met together."[6] Webster's minister, a warm advocate of Arminian views, begins by charging that "compar'd with the great fundamentals of religion" the doctrine of original sin "'tis a very little thing."[7] Original sin, he assures his inquisitive neighbors, must be rejected because it is not "plainly and indisputably laid down in your bibles."[8] After a summary refutation of several of Calvinism's classic proof-texts in support of the doctrine, two of the neighbors capitulate to the minister's exegetical arguments. Unlike his friends, the third neighbor is reluctant to give up the doctrine so quickly but vows to "take the matter into more serious consideration," confessing "I had never examined it as I ought, nor knew much that could be said on one side or the other."[9]

Webster addressed more than the Calvinist assertion that original sin was taught in the Bible. Arminian critics also refused to accept the notion that a person could be held accountable for another's sin, and here Webster mounted the attack upon the doctrine of imputation. Beginning with the case of infants who die in childbirth and who under the Calvinist interpretation "first open their eyes in [hell's] torments," the minister attacks the doctrine of imputation on two fronts.[10] First, echoing one of the Arminians' favorite complaints, he argues that imputation violates the justice of God by making God the author of sin. Surely, the Arminians argued, if God had actively transferred Adam's guilt to other moral agents, God was in some part responsible for the corruption of those agents. Second, the minister tries to demonstrate the "natural impossibility" of imputation by quizzing his neighbors about their elected representatives. Consider, he says, "our representatives, whom we honestly chose." If they, "unbeknown to us, murder a family . . . should we become thereupon guilty of murder?" On hearing the neighbor's response, "By no means," the minister proceeds: "If we are not chargeable with their sin, whom we have voluntarily chosen to represent us, then surely not with [Adam's], who was not chosen by us."[11] Nothing in human consciousness, he argued, indicated that a person was a co-participant with Adam in anything. To believe that a just and loving God would do what level-headed colonists would never think to do was worse than wrongheaded—it was impious.

Finally, Webster aired what perhaps was the most pragmatic and rhetorically explosive of the Arminian objections. The Calvinist scheme, the Arminians believed, was inimical to moral exhortation. If, on one hand, the Calvinists taught that sin was inevitable and that every human was doomed to a life of sin and then damned because of it, how could they, on the other hand, urge people to live godly lives? If people must first confess that they are inalterably evil, wherein lies the logic of that most Christian of pastoral duties, moral exhortation? How could people in the pew be led to face their actual guilt when according to the Calvinists they were already guilty before they were capable of moral action? With these logical and rhetorical flourishes, the minister claimed that theologians who affirmed original sin

> look upon the doctrine as a natural fountain of sin in them, and so a cloke [sic] for all their wickedness. . . . [T]hey only waste their time in gloomy imaginations, to the great neglect sometimes (it is to be fear'd) of a proper mourning for their daily, and, it may be, heinous transgressions.[12]

Whether or not Webster's *Conversation* merely parroted Taylor's more systematic treatise, one thing was clear. The doctrinal paper war of which Webster's clever polemic was but one Arminian volley required a full Calvinist response. Jonathan Edwards, who had been working on this theological conundrum for years, offered that response in *The Great Christian Doctrine of Original Sin Defended* (1758). As one student of the period noted, "with Edwards's book in the field . . . there remained little reason for the orthodox to continue the pamphlet war."[13] It appeared to the orthodox that a Calvinist champion was about to counter the Arminian threat.

In *Original Sin* Edwards acknowledged the critical role imputation played in Calvinist theology. In his attempt to vindicate original sin, he employed a notion of the unity of humanity that rested on a novel doctrine of "continual creation." With this doctrine, Edwards perhaps unwittingly framed the arguments that would eventuate in the repudiation of the notion of imputation. Edwards claimed that "God, in each step of his proceedings with Adam, in relation to the covenant or constitution established with him, looked on his posterity as being one with him."[14] This federal unity of humanity, Edwards continued, rested upon "the immediate continued creation of God" whereby God created all things "out of nothing at each moment of their existence."[15] Thus, an individual was not constituted a sinner by imputation as such. God did not, as it were, transfer Adam's sin across time and affix it to the soul of each of his progeny. Rather, due to the ontological unity of humanity, Adam's error occasioned the damnation of all humanity. In Edwards's view, Adam's sin did not become humanity's "merely because God imputes it to them; but it is truly and properly theirs" because they are continually one with Adam "and on that ground, God imputes it to them."[16]

In the traditional understanding of imputation, God applied Adam's sin to moral agents who did not participate in Adam's primeval act. But Edwards's theory of continual creation appeared to justify God's imputative action on the basis of humanity's participation in Adam's original offense. Given Edwards's thinking, humanity, like its primeval forebear, only received the just deserts of its co-participation with Adam, its federal head. The effect of this strategy was striking: Edwards's God appeared less arbitrary than the God of traditional covenant theology.[17]

While Edwards's apparent solution to the problems posed by the traditional doctrine of imputation satisfied some of his readers, others found it wanting. To those who demurred, the notion of continual creation added an unduly metaphysical notion to what was already a cumbersome and taxing intellectual defense of original sin. Chief among the dissenters was Samuel Hopkins, who developed his own unique strategy to deal with the problem. Like his mentor, Hopkins modified the traditional scheme of imputation in original sin:

> It is carefully to be observed, that sin does not take place in the posterity of Adam, in consequence of his sin, or that they are constituted sinners by his disobedience. . . . It is not to be supposed that the offense of Adam is imputed to them in their condemnation . . . or that they are guilty of the sin of their first father, antecedent to their own sinfulness.[18]

Hopkins agreed with Edwards's claim that Adam's fall brought condemnation upon everyone as well as with Edwards's belief that the traditional doctrine of imputation failed to explain this state of affairs. However, Hopkins believed that Edwards's proposal did not provide a fully satisfactory account of the fallen state of humanity. Humanity was still held accountable for a sin in which it did not consciously or directly participate.

Hopkins found himself in a difficult position. He grudgingly granted the Arminian rejection of the traditional notion of imputation and he quietly demurred with Edwards's clever notion of continual creation. But he also wanted to affirm the universal corruption of the human race and the sovereignty of God. In order to forward the latter claims without resorting to the former moves, he fled to the logic of cause and effect and to a radicalized notion of the absolute sovereignty of God. Hopkins argued as follows:

> Everything which is properly an effect, has its foundation in God, as its original cause, without which it could not have taken place. And every such effect is fixed and made sure of existence by the divine decree, and infallibly connected with it.[19]

This reasoning about divine cause and effect, he continued, was properly and usefully extended to the problem of evil.

> It is abundantly evident and demonstrably certain from reason, assisted by divine revelation, that all the sin and sufferings which have taken place, or ever will, are necessary for the greatest good of the universe, and to answer the wisest and best ends; and therefore must be included in the best, most wise and perfect plan.[20]

Because nothing else could account for the presence of evil, Hopkins asserted that God, all the while pursuing a divine plan that would deliver the greatest possible good to the universe, actually created depraved people. Adam and Eve, he argued, were the only persons ever created in a state of innocence.[21] Everyone else was created as a sinner. To many a horrified Old Calvinist onlooker, Yale's president Ezra Stiles among them, Hopkins was dangerously close to claiming that Christians should be grateful to a God who was the author of sin. As Stiles put it in his private diary, members of New Divinity congregations "begin to be tired with the incessant Inculcation and unintelligible and shocking new points . . . that we are to give God thanks, that he caused Adam to sin and involve all his posterity in total depravity."[22]

As noted elsewhere, the doctrine of imputation functioned at other places within Calvinist orthodoxy. If Edwardseans or Hopkinsians rejected the use of imputation in the doctrine of original sin, logical consistency—a goal that many Edwardseans sought—required that it be jettisoned anywhere else it played a role.[23] Traditional Calvinism had affirmed a theory of the atonement that operated on a distributive system of justice, wherein an angry and aggrieved God required eye for eye, tooth for tooth, and blood for blood. To obtain forgiveness, sin had to be paid for with the appropriate penalty, death. Therefore Christ acted as a substitute for the elect. The sins of the depraved were imputed to Christ, who bore their penalty. But the Edwardseans eschewed the notion of imputation. Because moral evil and good were not transferable from one moral agent to another, no one—not even the perfect second person of the Trinity—could pay the penalty for another's sin. They argued that the concept of distributive justice did not properly describe the atonement. Christ's sacrifice, they observed, did not meet the strict requirements of distributive justice for he had not suffered eternally as prescribed by God's law.[24]

As the Edwardseans attempted to construct a defensible theory of the atonement without recourse to the notion of imputation, pressure mounted from other quarters to change additional features of the doctrine. Just as the Arminians had challenged the justice of the imputation scheme, so did the Universalists question the equity of the Reformed notion that Christ had died only for the elect. How could God be called just, these critics asked, if God called everyone to repentance and yet provided atonement for only a fraction of humanity? New Divinity thinkers agreed that the limited atonement appeared to strip moral exhortation of some of its power. But they also recognized that widening the extent of the atonement would encourage something worse, the heresy of Universalism. This difficulty was further exacerbated by important developments outside strictly theological circles. In the world of late eighteenth-century Anglo-America, changes in the definition of law and justice, the very notions upon which the doctrine of the atonement ultimately depended, were occurring.

In the face of these considerations, the Edwardseans steered a middle course between the limited atonement of traditional Calvinism and the unlimited, boundless scope of the atonement held by the Universalists. In place of the doctrine of limited atonement and distributive justice, Edwardsean thinkers placed a governmental theory of the atonement that rested upon a notion of general justice. Sin was construed legally, as an infraction of the divine law. The sanctity of that law, defiled as it was by sin, had to be upheld, lest God be shown to be inconsistent.[25] As Hopkins noted,

> The work of the Redeemer therefore has a primary respect to the law of God, to maintain and honour that, so that sinners may be pardoned and saved consistent with that, without setting that aside, or showing the least regard to it, in the requirements and threatenings of it; but that it may be perfectly fulfilled; and especially that the threatening might be properly and completely executed, without which God could not be true or just in pardoning and saving the sinner.[26]

Old Calvinists viewed the atonement as the means of God's forgiveness. Christ's vicarious death on behalf of the elect paid their debt, and God tendered forgiveness to sinners. But under the Edwardsean governmental scheme, grace worked immediately, without means. The atonement was only necessary to uphold the good estate of God's moral government. This vindication of divine law did not necessarily result in the forgiveness of sin. To be sure, forgiveness was available to the elect but not because Christ paid the penalty of their imputed sin. Rather, forgiveness came immediately, outside an imputative scheme; it was a direct act of God. In this respect, the Edwardseans had again succeeded in giving greater visibility to the notion of God's absolute sovereignty.

Imputation was most conspicuous in a third Protestant doctrinal rubric, justification by faith. In both Lutheran and Reformed wings of the Reformation, justification by faith alone, effected by the imputation of Christ's righteousness, had become a soteriological *sine qua non*. Traditional Protestant thinkers were understandably concerned about the New Divinity's eschewal of imputation. This fact may explain why, in their discussion of justification, some New Divinity theologians equivocated in their use of imputation. Once again, Hopkins serves as a case in point. Having denied that the sinner was condemned by Adam's sin, Hopkins affirmed that the sinner was justified by Christ's righteousness. Justifying righteousness, he argued,

> is called "the righteousness of faith," not because there is any righteousness in faith to justify the sinner, or do any thing toward it; but because faith receives the righteousness of Christ, and so unites the believer to the Redeemer, that by divine constitution and promise, the righteousness of Christ is reckoned in his favor, and avails for his justification.[27]

Although much of his language paralleled traditional accounts, Hopkins rarely used the term "impute." When he did revert to the term, he used it with a force different than had traditional Calvinists.[28] At one point in his *System of Doctrine,* for instance, he declared that "It is abundantly declared in scripture that men are justified by faith, or through faith; that faith is counted for righteousness, and imputed to the believer for righteousness." Here Hopkins retains imputation but changes its object. He argues that "believers are justified through Christ's righteousness, yet his righteousness is not transferred to them."[29] The human agent was united to a federal head, be it the first or the second Adam, by divine constitution not by imputation.

Dwight on Soteriology

Twentieth-century scholars affix superlatives to Jonathan Edwards in part because his grandson voiced similar opinions in the eighteenth and nineteenth centuries. In response to the charge that "Federal America has done nothing either to extend, diversify, or embellish the sphere of human knowledge," Dwight claimed that Edwards had "enlarged the science of theology [more] than any divine of whom either England or Scotland can boast."[30] Notwithstanding his high regard for his grandfather and despite his interest in leading the Edwardsean movement into the future, the extent to which Dwight adhered to Edwardsean theology and its several variants remains to be seen.

Like other Calvinists, Dwight began his soteriology with an assessment of the fall of humanity. Though willing to claim that "in consequence of the Apostacy of Adam all men have sinned," he qualified this rather generic formulation with the caveat,

> I do not intend that the posterity of Adam are guilty of his transgression. Moral actions are not, so far as I can see, transferable from one being to another. . . . Neither do I intend, that the descendants of Adam are punished for his transgression.[31]

Without specific reference to the term and in good Edwardsean fashion, Dwight jettisoned the notion of imputation. But where the Hopkinsian radicals ventured new explanations of the source of evil, Dwight refused to offer alternative accounts. He acknowledged this lacuna, confessing that he was

> unable to explain this part of the subject. Many attempts have been made to explain it, but I freely confess myself to have seen none which was satisfactory to me, or which did not leave the difficulties as great, and for aught I know, as numerous, as they were before.[32]

Though Dwight found himself unable fully to explain human depravity, he did offer some observations about the subject.[33] Like Samuel Hopkins and Joseph Bellamy, Dwight examined the question of God's role in the introduction of sin into human culture.[34] Unlike them, he studiously avoided the conclusion that in permitting sin to enter the world God was somehow responsible for the human condition. "Man," Dwight argued, "is the actor of his own sin." The notion that "the volitions of man are immediately produced by omnipotence, are the acts of God himself, and not at all of man," Dwight rejected as illogical.[35]

Although Dwight believed his views satisfied the canons of "perfect justice," he also recognized that "still it will be asked why God suffered a thing, so evil and distressing, as sin, to exist?"[36] Here he somewhat halfheartedly mouthed the Hopkinsian line of argumentation by observing that "if Adam had not fallen, Christ would not have redeemed mankind." Had sin not entered the world, "the mercy of God, therefore, the most perfect of his attributes, and the consummation of his excellence, would have been unknown to the universe."[37] Despite this dalliance with the notion that God brought some good out of the fall, Dwight's account differs significantly from that of his Hopkinsian contemporaries. Dwight's God only permitted sin; the God of the most radical New Divinity theologians actively created it.[38] Hopkins not only required that Christians rejoice in the fact of God's creation of sin but also believed that denying this proposition was "highly impious."[39] Dwight objected. The idea that God created the "sinful volitions of mankind, is a doctrine, not warranted in my view, either by Reason or Revelation."[40]

Here lies one essential difference between Dwight and the most radical Edwardseans. Fearing the challenges of the Arminians, the New Divinity theologians pursued relentlessly the logical implications of a system characterized by paradoxes. Dwight also feared for Calvinism's future, but he was hesitant about the role of inexorable logic. He insisted that the human mind, if left unchecked, could probe too far producing disastrous results. Some mysteries, he said, are "so high, and so vast, that we cannot attain to them."[41] Dwight recognized a "bound . . . beyond which the mind cannot pass, and it is as easily found investigating this subject, as in any course of human inquiry."[42] The truly pious must not pursue logic to its limits, but rather must confess their "inability to judge . . . and take the station of humble learners, at the feet of our Divine Instructor, rather than ascend the chair of philosophical judgment, and haughty decision."[43]

Although Dwight believed that in their doctrine of original sin the Hopkinsian theologians had been overcome by the very reason they sought to employ, he was inclined to agree with their theory of the atonement. He, too, rejected the limited atonement: "If Christ has not made a sufficient atonement for others beside the elect; then his salvation is not offered to them at all; and they are not guilty for not receiving it. But this is contrary to the whole tenor of the gospel."[44]

Analyzing this doctrine, Dwight was particularly troubled by the Universalist claim "that if Christ expiated the sins of mankind, God is obliged by justice to bestow on them salvation." This conclusion, he argued, was based upon a misapprehension. Christ's atonement did not resemble "the satisfaction made for a debtor by paying the debt which he owed."[45] Though scripture sometimes used debt imagery to describe the atonement, Dwight argued that economic idioms did not accurately describe the scheme of divine justice. The language of exchange was only useful in that it helped sinners understand that they were in God's debt. Any extension of this economic analogy failed to describe things as they really were. If Christ had paid such a debt, justice required that God release all debtors from their moral burden. This, reasoned Dwight, inevitably led to Universalism.

In Dwight's view (here again we see his penchant for an ethic of duty) sin was not a moral debt but a "crime, committed against God's government."[46] The sinner "failed of doing his duty, as a subject to a lawful government, and violated laws, which he was bound to obey; he has committed a fault, for which he has merited punishment."[47] Under such circumstances, "the only reparation for the wrong . . . required by strict justice, is this punishment: a reparation necessarily and always required." Punishment for the infraction of divine law was required, and until this legal stipulation was meted out, "the ruler, however benevolently inclined, could not pardon . . . consistently with his own character, the honour of his government, or the public good."[48] Thus, Christ was punished, God's law was vindicated, and in strict justice, God could pardon any sinner. It is important to note that this understanding of the atonement does not rely on any form of imputation. Christ's death merely vindicated the law but it did not change the character of the sinner. To this governmental theory of the atonement, Dwight added a final assertion that echoed Edwardsean thinking on the subject.

> The atonement of Christ in no sense makes it necessary that God should accept the sinner on the ground of justice; but only renders his forgiveness not inconsistent with the divine character. Before the atonement, he could not have been forgiven. After the atonement, this impossibility ceases.

To insure that his readers did not falsely conclude on the basis of a debt model that God was somehow obliged to forgive them, Dwight added, "Forgiveness is an act of grace only," and not the sinner's due.[49]

Timothy Dwight's doctrines of original sin and the atonement did not rely on the notion of imputation nor did his doctrine of justification. Sermons sixty-five through sixty-nine of *Theology*, without a single reference to the term "imputation," form Dwight's lengthy account of how sinful humanity was justified. In eschewing imputation, these sermons resemble Edwardsean pronouncements but a closer examination reveals Dwight's reliance on more traditional rubrics of Reformed theology. Covenantal language as well as an attempt to resolve the differences between the teaching of Paul and James on the role of faith are prominent in Dwight's prose. Moreover, Dwight devoted an entire sermon to the question of the necessity of moral obligation under a gracious *sola fide* dispensation.

Dwight defended the doctrine of justification on two fronts. On one hand, critics charged that the Reformed *sola fide* scheme lessened the believer's obligation to obey the law. This "antinomian" objection, argued Dwight, was overruled by a plain reading of scripture. Christ required obedience of his followers, and no right-thinking Christian could deny this plain requirement of believers. Other critics claimed that justification by faith weakened the motive to obey. Dwight countered this charge (he labeled it "Arminian") by use of his response to the antinomians. The justified Christian, he argued, had been regenerated by the Holy Spirit. Hence, the true Christian loved God and found joy in conforming to the divine will. The Christian's motive to obey, therefore, was itself rooted in a love for God. God's requirement, and nothing more, provided ample motive for action. For Dwight, justification by faith furnished believers with new life, new obligations, and new motives.[50]

Dwight rounded out his defense of justification with another pragmatic, even moralistic, observation. Those who affirmed justification by faith, he declared, were exemplary people. They observed a "stricter morality," they "punctiliously frequented the house of God," and they enjoyed "the duties of the Sabbath" to a far greater degree than those who opposed the *sola fide* doctrine. Dwight's proof of this last point rested on his observations about Roman Catholics.

> The Papists have generally holden the doctrine of justification by works; while the reformers, almost to a man, hold that of justification by faith. The comparative morality of these two classes of men cannot, here, need any illustration.[51]

On the basis of his understanding of Christian soteriology, then, Dwight can be properly identified as an Edwardsean and at times as a hesitant advocate of the New Divinity theology. An analysis of his thinking on moral agency and ecclesiology will show that his modest affirmation of the New Divinity theological trajectory was limited and circumscribed.

Edwards and the New Divinity on Moral Agency and Ecclesiology

The Edwardsean abandonment of imputation may have softened the harsh image projected by Calvinistic determinism. To conclude that this liberalized American Calvinism, however, is inaccurate. Although many Edwardsean theologians rejected imputation due to its apparent inequity, their theological method drove some of them, particularly the Hopkinsians, to ever firmer attachments to God's omnipotent sovereignty. Ironically, what began as a move toward moderation eventuated in a theological position far to the right of traditional Calvinism.

Most eighteenth-century theologians agreed that sin, whether imputed or actual, affected everyone, but increasing disagreement developed about precisely what these effects were. Debate centered upon the issue of individual moral agency. What moral good could human agents do, unaided by the Holy Spirit? Traditional Calvinists feared the implications of any system that identified moral virtue, however limited, in unregenerate people. If moral agents were capable of both willing and doing the good, they reasoned, God's condemnation of them seemed unjust and Christ's death seemed somehow unnecessary. On another front, Arminians argued that the Calvinist doctrine of radical corruption deprived the moral agent of accountability. A just God, the Arminians asserted, could not blame a moral agent for failing to do something of which he or she was incapable.

Jonathan Edwards addressed these issues in his *Freedom of the Will.* Therein Edwards attempted to counter the Arminians by arguing that philosophical necessity was not incompatible with human liberty. His argument rested on relatively simple definitions of necessity and the will. He defined necessity as that which "must be, and cannot be otherwise." A thing is necessary when "it is, or will be, notwithstanding all supposable opposition."[52] He applied this definition to the problem of human sin; for Edwards, it was inevitable or philosophically necessary that human agents would sin, barring the intrusion of some exterior divine power. He defined the will in terms of choice. The will was "that by which the mind chooses anything . . . an act of the will is the same as an act of choosing or choice."[53] These choices were based on human freedom. Moral agents freely chose from among options and did so on the basis of whatever seemed to them to be the greatest perceived good. Moral agents could never act contrary to their will because they always chose what they wanted and never chose what they did not want or prefer. In order to assess the ethical accountability of acts of the will, Edwards distinguished between two types of necessity, natural and moral. He defined natural necessity as that

> necessity as men are under through natural causes. . . . They feel pain when their bodies are wounded . . . they see the objects presented to them in a clear light . . . they assent to the truth of certain propositions, as soon as the terms are understood; as that two and two make four.[54]

In the case of natural necessity, a person's will might be impeded by a physical force. They could want or will something, but some force of nature could impede their willing. In such an instance, the agent would be prevented from acting according to his or her will and therefore not be held accountable for a failure to act.

The situation changed when it came to what Edwards termed moral necessity. Moral necessity was that "necessity of connection and consequence, which arises from such moral causes, as the strength of inclination, or motives, and the connection which there is in many cases between these and such volitions and actions."[55] Accountability was not dismissed as easily in the case of moral necessity. Unlike its natural counterpart, moral necessity was not liable to the intrusion of an outside force. It had to do with the internal life, with inclinations, preferences, and desires. Moral inability, therefore, consisted in "the opposition or want of inclination."[56] In Edwards's view, the sinner's problem was not that he or she lacked freedom but that, having freedom, he or she failed to want or desire the good. Because the sinner did not want the good, he or she was blameworthy. In sum, Edwards's system allowed him to affirm the claim (contra the Arminians) that one sort of philosophical necessity, namely, moral necessity, was not incompatible with human accountability. Necessity was intact; people had to choose what they wanted. So was accountability; God rewarded righteous acts and condemned sinful ones.

These issues were further developed elsewhere in the Edwards corpus, notably in *The Treatise on Religious Affections* and in the posthumously published *Two Dissertations*. In *Affections* Edwards addressed the experiential aspects of the will's renovation with an eye toward the problem of assurance of salvation. He offered two sets of signs or evidences that believers could use to help discern their spiritual condition. His negative signs listed criteria that could not deliver reliable or certain proof that God had acted graciously on a person. Conversely, his positive signs delineated genuine evidences of divine regeneration and could be trusted as such.[57] In the *Two Dissertations*, Edwards, in effect, shifted his subject from the human will to the divine will and probed the motives that stood behind God's actions, salvific or otherwise. In the first essay of the *Two Dissertations*, entitled *The End for Which God Created the World*, he argued that although God was benevolently inclined toward humankind, this human-oriented benevolence was subject to God's benevolence for the divine self. God's self-love, he claimed, always and forever took precedence over God's love for creation.[58] In the second dissertation, *The Nature of True Virtue*, Edwards continued probing, as it were, the mind of God, though this time with an eye to the character of virtue itself. In the course of the essay he ventured a definition of genuine virtue that disquieted his readers. True virtue, he said, "most essentially consists in benevolence to Being in general."[59]

Although Edwards's followers adopted his *Freedom of the Will* strategy for countering the Arminian remonstrances (as one historian put it, his natural/moral distinction quickly became "the shibboleth of their tribe"[60]), they had a more difficult time working out all of the implications of *Affections* and *Two Dissertations*. While *Affections'* signs, both positive and negative, illuminated the problem of assurance, the problem itself remained. Ostensibly good acts might be performed for evil motives. An unregenerate person, for example, could attend the preaching of the gospel only because he or she wished to impress a neighbor. Given this possibility, how could the observer distinguish between genuinely good and evil acts or, more importantly, between *bona fide* and bogus saints? What of Edwards's insistence that God's self-love was paramount? To many of his followers Edwards's claim in *The End*, that God's "goodness and love to created beings is derived from, and subordinate to, his love of himself,"[61] moved too close to the dreaded notion that God was neither interested in human happiness nor obliged to promote it. In the decades when the social conscience of the New England church was becoming tender—Hopkins was himself becoming deeply troubled by the moral problems of slavery in these years—Edwards's move appeared to threaten Christian social action.[62] His use of the expression "Being in general" seemed even more puzzling. Was the expression "Being in general" intended to stand for God? For all sentient beings? What exactly was the implication of this sort of language for the life of the faithful?

Hopkins was among the first of the Edwardseans to break with his teacher. He objected to Edwards's insistence that God's self-love was to be viewed as paramount among the divine attributes on the ground that God was not so self-centered as Edwards had believed. In Hopkins's view, the best way to describe the situation was to describe God's benevolence as merely "disinterested." For Hopkins, God's chief perfection was to be found in the divine benevolence that was extended to the creation. Indeed, benevolence was so integral to God's moral perfection that "he had always to act in accordance with the moral interests of his creatures."[63] Thus, Hopkins reversed Edwards's conclusion: God's self-love was subordinate to God's benevolence toward other beings. Under Hopkins's rendering the Creator's disinterested benevolence became one of God's primary attributes. Because Christians were to emulate their God it followed naturally that disinterested benevolence should be viewed as the chief of the virtues in redeemed believers. This assertion, in turn, affected the New Divinity's attempt to fashion a method of identifying genuine piety.

New England's Old Calvinists believed that one necessary element in the salvific process was conviction of sin and subsequent fear about one's low moral estate. Empirical reasoning led to this conclusion. Sinners "under conviction" prayed fervently, read the Scriptures frequently, and sought counsel regarding the state of their souls. While no Calvinist interpreted these activities to be the cause of salvation, most agreed that activities like these preceded the conversion event. Sinners who participated in these "means of grace" were encouraged to continue doing so.

Hopkins rejected this view of the means of grace, claiming that the originality of his theology lay in the assertion that the

> unregenerate, under the greatest mental light and conviction of conscience, and in all their external reformations and doings, are more criminal and guilty than they were in a state of ignorance and security. . . . This is necessarily implied in the doctrine of total depravity which all Calvinists hold—that all true holiness consists in disinterested benevolence, and those affections that are implied in it—that the self-love that is not implied in disinterested benevolence is sinful, and that in which all sin essentially and radically consists.[64]

In Hopkins's system, until regeneration occurred the moral agent could do nothing but sin. The use of the means of grace—precisely because the means were selfishly employed to save one's soul—only compounded the sinner's guilt.

This new understanding of the means of grace combined with the long-standing church membership controversy to form yet another characteristic mark of the New Divinity movement. Hopkins believed that unregenerate people who participated in the externals of religion, even when motivated by a desire for salvation, were culpable on the ground of self-interest. His list of proscribed acts of the unregenerate included, of course, participation in the sacraments. Like Edwards and Bellamy, Hopkins argued that sacramental participation required a heartfelt experience of grace—something the unregenerate, by definition, could not claim. Only visible saints, he reasoned, should be permitted to present their children for baptism and partake of the Lord's Supper.[65] Edwards's repudiation of the Halfway Covenant cost him his Northampton pulpit. His disciples were prepared to suffer similar fates in pursuit of the pure church ideal.

By the close of the eighteenth century, the religious landscape of New England Protestantism was littered with the remains of a century of religious controversy. New England Congregationalism found itself in a particularly difficult situation. "Dissenter" groups like the Baptists, Methodists, and Episcopalians were gaining sufficient strength to challenge the legal and religious hegemony of the Congregationalists. In addition, interminable, internecine squabbles continued to dog the feet of the Puritans' heirs. Arminians, Universalists, and Unitarians had successfully challenged the Congregationalist status quo, which was itself fragmenting into competing camps. Edwardsean theological novelties, as helpful and creative as they may have appeared at mid-century, were by 1800 regularly contested. As Timothy Dwight came of age as a theologian, he could rightly anticipate a life of polemic controversy. In order to find his distinctive voice and become a great man in his own right, he would have to engage the thought of the man he most admired, Jonathan Edwards. That task required him to rethink a host of complex problems. His fame and fate depended on the extent to which he could think and speak convincingly about the problems that most vexed his beloved Edwardsean tradition.

Dwight on Moral Agency

Like most Edwardseans, Dwight adhered to his grandfather's claim that philosophical necessity did not ring the death knell on human accountability. Though he avoided overly philosophical or metaphysical language, when need arose he echoed Edwards's use of the natural necessity/moral necessity distinction. Similarly, he relied on Edwards's *Freedom of the Will* and *Religious Affections* to develop the affectional character of his theology. When it came to the problem of defining true virtue, however, Dwight was less apt than his grandfather to champion notions of "benevolence to Being in general" that stood at the heart of *The Nature of True Virtue*. Like Hopkins and more moderate Edwardseans, Dwight preferred the language of distinterested benevolence when he discussed the essential characteristics of genuine virtue. As Yale's theologian-in-residence, he was often called upon to address from the pulpit as well as in private counsel with his students the Christian's assurance of salvation. To that end, he developed tests that seekers could use to determine the presence of genuine grace.

In the systematic treatment of this topic in his *Theology*, Dwight began by asserting that some of the traditional tests were not reliable. In a sermon entitled *Evidences of Regeneration—What Are Not Evidences*, he noted that a sense of moral degeneracy, inordinate guilt, or zeal in the cause of religion were not infallible evidences of the presence of genuine piety.[66] Dwight followed this identification of false signs with a triad of sermons that identified genuine evidences of grace. Nowhere else does Dwight's theological prose more clearly resemble Edwards's. Sermons eighty-eight through ninety represent striking parallels to Edwards's closely reasoned masterpiece, *Religious Affections*. At this very point Dwight took exception to the Hopkinsian claims concerning moral agency. This break came not in Dwight's understanding of the character of disinterested benevolence but in his discussion of the proper use of the means of grace.

For Dwight, the means of grace were activities designed to "impress upon the mind the truth of God."[67]

> When we speak of Means of Grace, in the plural, we always intend either
> different modes of applying the gospel or some or other of its Precepts, or

Ordinances, to the human understanding, or Affections; or to the performance of some act, or series of acts, enjoined in the Scriptures.[68]

Under this broad definition Dwight subsumed two categories. First, the means of grace were actions by which "in the usual course of providence, grace is originally obtained." These "ordinary means of grace" included activities that could be practiced by converts as well as "seekers" who had yet to make a confession of faith. The ordinary means included hearing the gospel preached, reading scripture, praying, corresponding with religious men, and examining one's heart.

Were the ordinary means a spiritual liability as the radical Edwardseans taught? Did "sinners grow worse under conviction of conscience and in the use of means?" To this Dwight answered, "I do not know. Neither do my objectors." Dwight avoided further speculation, fleeing to the safety of divine mystery. Such answers were "beyond the power of man, [and] the whole inquiry is idle and vain." Dwight could see "no good reason why this question should be introduced into theological discourse." It only tended to "perplex and distress."[69] To distinguish himself even further from the Hopkinsians, Dwight argued that conversion was not an "act of Divine power, unconnected to everything else." In other words, conversion did not occur immediately. Rather, "God is pleased in the usual course of his scriptural providence, to instruct, to alarm, to invite, to promise, and to persuade" the unregenerate.[70]

Although Dwight opposed the Hopkinsian nuances regarding the proper use of the means of grace, he avoided strident denials of their doctrines from the pulpit. He was more candid and specific in his private correspondence, however. In a letter to Dr. Ryland on 16 March 1805, he was perfectly clear about his favorite "means of grace," preaching:

> I am not a Hopkinsonian [sic]. President Edwards appears to me to have gone as far as the Bible warrants. Those, who have succeeded him seem to me to have philosophized merely, and to have bewildered themselves and their readers. Their systems I know, but I do not believe, and I think some of them in danger of injuring, greviously, the faith once delivered to the saints. There is now a doctrine, rife in Massachusetts, that nothing is to be said to sinners, from the desk. Yet many things are addressed to them in the scriptures. This seems to be complete proof to a Divine, that such things are still to be said to sinners. . . . My own belief is, that Divines are here, as they have done elsewhere, doing mischief to Theology. My own doctrine on this whole subject is, to the Law and the Testimony; if they teach not according to this word, there is no light in them. Let God be true, but every man a lyar [sic]. Our business, after we have determined, that the scriptures are the word of God, is merely to find out what they say.[71]

Though he was keen to dissociate himself from Hopkins, Dwight feared that his "high" view of the means of grace might lead some to think that he believed that "regeneration could not be absolutely attributed to the Spirit of Truth." To this he responded vigorously.

> This opinion is plainly erroneous. The very means themselves are furnished by this Divine Agent. When furnished, all of them, united, would prove wholly insufficient without his creative influence. . . . Whatever means may be employed in bringing a man from sin to holiness, and whatever may be their influence, the creative power of divine influence is absolutely necessary to accomplish this renovation.[72]

To avoid further the charge that he held too high an opinion of the means of grace, Dwight set aside a shorter list of practices that were of special or limited application. These extraordinary means were the special province of church members and Christian ministers and included the baptism of one's children, participation in the Lord's Supper, and the communion of Christians. Here, then, is Dwight's rationale for his repudiation of the Halfway Covenant. The sacraments were not converting ordinances but ordinances for the converted. He repudiated Stoddardeanism, affirmed the martyred Edwards who was ousted from Northampton because of the communion controversy, but resisted the Hopkinsian claim that the application of the means was fundamentally flawed.[73] Dwight's teaching about moral agency is telling. Dividing the means into two categories, Dwight steered a careful course, neither conservative nor progressive, between Old Calvinist and New Divinity systems of theological ethics. His was not a new trail, however, but a well-worn path. Like the American Puritans prior to the triumph of Stoddardeanism, Dwight affirmed the efficacy of the means of grace while simultaneously refusing to offer the sacraments to the unregenerate.

* * *

New Divinity theology was conceived in a highly charged polemical context. Samuel Hopkins and his colleagues proposed to rescue eighteenth-century American Calvinism from the twin threats of logical inconsistency and theological liberalism. Their attempts largely failed. By pressing their views to logical extremes, divine mystery was replaced with ecclesiastical legalism, and Calvinism's paradoxes were rationalized. As America's Revolutionary epoch unfolded into the constitutional and early national eras, the subtle metaphysics of the New Divinity thinkers paled amid the rhetoric of freedom, rights, and social action. The New Divinity placed disinterested benevolence at the center of the New England social conscience. In this, they left an indelible mark on the history of Protestant Christianity in America. But as the "benevolent empire" began to expand, New England's attentions shifted to the heart not the head, to implementation not theory. The language of disinterested benevolence remained, but the New Divinity's unique rationale for it became little more than a footnote in the history of American theology.

Dwight shared the New Divinity's concern for the well-being of Reformed theology. His vocabulary reflected New Divinity notions, and in several instances his conclusions approximated New Divinity assertions. These similarities notwithstanding, Timothy Dwight did not endorse the New Divinity theological system. He believed that human reason had bounds, that the endless application of logic to the things of God ended in futility, and that an appreciation of divine mystery ought to characterize the Christian's heart and mind. Rejecting the subtleties of New Divinity theology, Dwight argued from biblical revelation and common sense. On the path to salvation, the seeker should engage in human activity as the means to grace. After conversion, the Christian's focus was to fall on practice. For Dwight, orthodoxy unconcerned with orthopraxy was useless.

Dwight's shifting appreciation of the New Divinity vision is nicely captured in a bit of personal history recorded by Nathaniel William Taylor. Some years after Dwight's death in 1817, Taylor was asked to give an assessment of his mentor's theology. Commenting on Dwight's relationship to the New Divinity, Taylor wrote:

> Dr. Dwight told me that, when a young man, he was, on the subject of
> Christian resignation, a thorough-going Hopkinsian; that he wrote a long
> Dissertation in support of that doctrine, and read it to Dr. Hopkins, who
> strenuously urged its publication.

But young Dwight was unsure of himself; he found his own best defense of New Divinity theology unconvincing. He decided to withhold the treatise from publication and to "think of the matter longer." As he matured he began to see more clearly the difficulties that beset the theology of Edwards's disciples. On his ascent to Yale's presidency, Dwight affirmed the broadest outlines of the Edwardsean system but not the more radical proposals forwarded by the New Divinity theologians. When Taylor asked Dwight what he had done with his youthful *apologia* for the New Divinity system, Yale's "distinquished divine" confided, "I put it in the fire."[74]

How can one finally interpret Dwight's role as a theologian? On one hand, his rejection of New Divinity innovations can be viewed negatively. New Divinity stalwarts Samuel Hopkins and Nathaniel Emmons, as well as modern interpreters such as David Brand, would judge the matter from this perspective. In their view, Dwight failed to create imaginative theological responses to the problems that attended the use of imputation because he lacked the intelligence to do so; he was simply incapable of such a task. He refused any encroachment on the utility of the means of grace because he tended toward a softer, Arminian view of human freedom and away from the harsh claims of conservative Calvinists. He dismissed the radical Edwardsean demands for logical consistency because he feared the power of theological systems, preferring ambiguity, paradox, and mystery to the canons of reason.

On the other hand, one can interpret Dwight's relationship to New Divinity innovations and his motives for resisting radical innovations positively. Many of Dwight's moderate congregationalist contemporaries, as well as modern evangelical interpreters such as Stephen Berk and Richard Lovelace, would take this position. From this perspective, Dwight did not create alternatives to imputation because, quite simply, the Edwardsean theological conversation had exhausted all such possibilities. Any move was subject to censure from one or another side in the debate, so he settled for lack of precision and a degree of equivocation because they were the only available options. He championed the means of grace not because he failed to appreciate the pitfalls associated with their use, whereby the unsuspecting might be lulled into thinking that simply by applying the means they could receive salvation. Rather he came to believe that the means of grace were the only effective weapon the church had to fight infidelity and unbelief. To remove the means from the church's arsenal would leave it both impotent and defenseless. Without the means of grace pastors and parishioners alike could only ponder the inscrutable will of a transcendent divine being. Dwight refused to adopt New Divinity beliefs about the radical sovereignty of God because he wanted human beings to be accountable for their sins while at the same time allowing them freely to seek grace from an approachable God who wished to save rather than to damn.

Ultimately, the judgment of historians regarding Dwight's role as an Edwardsean theologian depends largely upon the theological and historical inclinations of the interpreter. Whether positive or negative, such an assessment can be helpfully framed by an Edwardsean analysis. Did natural necessity in the form of limited insight, lack of creativity, or the inability to read, write, and study for significant lengths of time impede Dwight's will or desire to forward the Edwardsean cause? Or was Dwight's failure to become America's theologian the result of moral necessity? Faced with challenges of leadership, did Dwight's will to be a theological leader wane? Did his inclinations run counter to what he thought he wanted? Did his theological judgments incline him in other directions?

Although pure logic of the sort Dwight resisted might require one to affirm only one of these two alternatives, prudence requires that we recognize the power of both of them. The liability of natural necessity played its part. Simply put, Dwight did not possess the intellectual brilliance, constructive genius, or scholarly opportunities necessary to comprehend, redirect, or repristinate the

Edwardsean tradition in America. Though he longed to become its leader, ultimately his gifts as well as his disabilities prevented him from doing so. Dwight's hope to lead was also impeded by the vagaries of moral necessity. Though Dwight was an early advocate of New Divinity theology and recognized its most important distinctions, pastoral experience taught him that, if pressed too far, its liabilities outweighed its promise. Refusing to join the New Divinity radicals yet unwilling to abandon the major outlines of his grandfather's theology, Dwight sought the middle ground of compromise. When it suited his larger ends, he echoed Edwards. When he sensed the dangers of inflexible systems, he preached against the New Divinity. Though resort to compromise had previously served his professional ends, in this case it led to middle-of-the road mediocrity. Only after his death and after a generation of nineteenth-century religious activists had blunted the sharp edges of Edwardseanism would his theology be hailed as a model for American evangelical Protestantism.

IV

An American Clio

> There was scarcely any subject, at the mention
> of which his mind more instinctively kindled,
> and rose into the regions of moral sublimity,
> than the privileges and prospects of the
> American nation.
>
> —William Sprague

Timothy Dwight feared that the American nation, like each one of its citizens, was in perpetual danger of moral declension. Just as an individual could fall from virtue into vice, from godliness into infidelity, so too could America fall from blessedness to cursedness, from divine tranquility into hellish tribulation. Dwight's self-appointed calling was to keep America and its citizens vigilant against the day of doom. He plied this vocation throughout his adult life by means of a number of professional activities. One catches glimpses of Dwight addressing issues of national spiritual and moral health from the pulpit, within his doctrinal theological work, and in his poetry. Quite often his work in these activities had a historical character. Dwight plumbed the past for evidence of the divine constitution of the American nation, probing for moral patterns with which he could educate American citizens. Like many of his contemporaries he believed that the providence of God was clearly discernible in historical hindsight. He understood the telos of his historical efforts to be the inculcation of virtue in the present, and, not surprisingly, Dwight was frequently guilty of historical reductionism. He routinely disregarded the ebb and flow of seventeenth- and eighteenth-century American political and religious history and simply ignored events that were difficult to interpret or that provided contrary evidence to the themes and patterns he most wanted to uncover.

Dwight did not ground his researches in divine chronology on a simple linear model of time. He did not view himself as standing at the mid-point of a one-way, past-present-future chronological trajectory. Standing in the present, Dwight believed himself to be situated at the intersection of two independent vectors or streams of information—one emanating from the past, the other discernible as he looked to the future. Employing a series of imaginative eschatological interpretations, he invested the future with as much authority as he did the past. In his *Valedictory Address* of 1776, in which he celebrated the divine providences enjoyed by the newly independent American nation, Dwight articulated his belief that future blessings could be discerned and interpreted as empirical data, as if they had already occurred:

> I have mentioned several things as present, whose existence is in the future. The reason is, that with respect to the end, which I propose in this description, the distinction is immaterial. For our actions ought all to be inspired, and directed by a comprehensive regard to this scene of glory, which is hastening to a completion.[1]

Dwight believed that the divine chronology was seamless. Each of its elements—past, present, and future—was accessible and had revelatory value.

Not surprisingly, Dwight found the task of making interpretive judgments about the future a tricky business. Using eschatological interpretations as a tool to discern the divine diagnosis of New England's spiritual health, Dwight swung between the poles of optimism / divine confirmation and pessimism / divine condemnation. At some points, Dwight was sure that the Kingdom of God was at hand. At other times, he was certain that Revelation's vials were being emptied and that the dreaded Beast had been loosed upon the world. In either case, he judged present circumstances by imaginative interpretations of future events. This device gave Dwight considerable interpretive and rhetorical control of the raw material of current events. If he judged them godly, he christened them with the holy oil of millennial fervor. If he feared them or reckoned them vicious, he lashed them with the whip of apocalyptic judgment. Having distilled the American experience, both past and future, to a relatively simple diagram of God's work in the world and humanity's response to that work, he placed this schematic within a larger cyclic pattern of the rise and strengthening of piety, its decline into heterodoxy, and its wonderful revivification under new dispensations of grace.[2]

To these cycles of national redemption we now turn. Working with a diverse series of Dwight's writings crafted at several points during his career (sometimes in the very midst of the events he describes, sometimes with the benefit of historical hindsight), the present chapter examines two cyclic revolutions of Dwight's "holy history" of America. The treatment begins at the top of the cycle of redemption with Dwight's idyllic history of New England Puritanism. For him, this was a normative era during which the American character and nation were formed. From this normative, historical, noon-hour the initial iteration of the cycle starts with a downward swing to America's first low ebb of piety, which occurred during the French and Indian War. During this period, Dwight believed, infidelity and European skepticism made their first incursions into the moral fabric of American life. This first cycle of redemption is completed with what Dwight viewed to be a swing back to national piety and righteousness. This revivification occurred during the

American Revolution, a time when Dwight's millennial fervor was nearly unbounded. In celebratory prose and verse he declared that America had not only realigned its spiritual fortunes with the positive model of the Puritan past, but actually approximated the millennial Kingdom of God. From this zenith in the divine pattern, the second cycle of devolution-evolution begins. Near the end of the century, amid fears of the Bavarian Illuminati, the intrigue of the XYZ affair, and Jefferson's presidency, Dwight discerned another but more formative threat from infidelity and skepticism. In the most strident tones of his career, fraught with negative apocalyptic imagery, Dwight warned that the day of doom was at hand. Despite this threat, during which he believed that American national prospects were at their absolute nadir, disaster was diverted. Though the danger of infidelity remained, its power waned in the face of the religious awakenings and a return of American virtue. Once again, Dwight discerned movement toward the top of the cycle of redemption. During the first fifteen years of the nineteenth century and toward the end of his life, Dwight wrote about an America that was once again moving confidently toward millennial bliss though to a decidedly different beat.

Three important features of Dwight's cyclic interpretations deserve particular notice. First, his historical reflections and millennial broodings are profoundly subjective. Not only do they defy anything like "objective" history based on "facts," but they are also deeply personal and driven by his hopes and fears. As Dwight moved from periods of confidence and hope to moments of doubt, fear, and dread, so do his interpretive cycles of national redemption move from the brightness of millennial promise to the gloomy, apocalyptic threats of God's horrible judgment. As his vision is blinded by the brightness of national promise, so too is it dimmed by the prospect of the withdrawal of divine favor. Keeping in mind Silverman's observation that Dwight recognized only cheery birthdays and gloomy doomsdays, his millennial interpretations must be traced across the landscape of his personal history. Second, Dwight's cyclic understanding of America's holy history is itself marked by a distinct pattern. With few exceptions, when he describes American faithfulness, historical points at the top of the redemptive cycle, his eschatological language is gentle and relatively generic. He rarely adheres to a particular biblical text and relies on broad categories—peace, prosperity, and progress—to describe what he sees in America. Herein, these sorts of reflections are described using the term "millennial." When Dwight treats the incursion of infidelity his mood, tone, and interpretive strategies change markedly. At the bottom of the redemptive cycle, his language is often harsh, reactionary, and specific. In such moments he focuses on particular biblical texts and stresses specific evils he finds threatening to the well-being of the Republic. Here he interprets scriptural prophecies and their fulfillment in language that is best described as fully "apocalyptic." Finally, Dwight's understanding of the efficacy of human action in relation to divine activity changes over time. In his earliest eschatological reflections he looks for divine action to establish the millennial reign; his focus is the providential activity of God. As his career develops Dwight lays less stress on divine activity and examines more carefully the usefulness of human effort in bringing about the thousand years of peace and prosperity.[3]

The Religion of New England

Timothy Dwight's understanding of the American nation was based on his deep appreciation of the religion of America's forebears. As elsewhere, he routinely viewed systems of doctrine, morality, religion, and politics comprehensively. This habit of mind is strikingly illustrated in his eschatological work. Whether he is dealing with historical events or with visions of the future, Dwight's critical eye fell upon what he took to be an undifferentiated whole. His description of this cultural entity began with the history of religion in the cradle of America, the New England colonies.

Dwight presented his most detailed history of the religion of New England in a series of eleven letters that appeared under the title "Religion of New England" in the fourth volume of *Travels in New England and New York*.[4] He worked toward two objectives in this, his most sustained piece of historical writing. First, he rendered a summary of the doctrine of the American Puritans, and second, he set the bounds of a normative period in the history of American religion.

In Letter X of "Religion of New England," Dwight remarked that anyone who wished to "describe or understand" that religion must first give attention to the doctrine of the "original planters of New England, viz. the Plymouth colonists." With this in mind, Dwight summarized the theological outlook of American Puritanism under twenty heads of doctrine. These included: a high view of the authority of scripture (Head 1); a recognition of the right of private judgment (Head 2); the claim that the doctrinal articles of the "Reformed Churches" of Europe and the British Isles were "agreeable to the holy oracles" (Head 3); a very strong affirmation of congregational polity (Heads 5–9 and 12–16); and an affirmation of the two sacraments—Baptism "without the sign of the cross, or any other invented ceremony," and the Lord's Supper, received "in the table posture" (Heads 17 and 18). Knowing that these descriptions might apply to a whole range of Protestants, Dwight went a step further and identified the doctrinal particularities of the "New England Way." He acknowledged that his forebears formed exclusive churches of visible saints that were to "consist of those only who appear to believe in Christ and obey him" (Head

6); "That any competent number of such persons have a right to embody themselves in a church for their mutual edification" (Head 7); and "That this ought to be done by *express covenant*" (Head 8).[5]

Dwight's enumeration of Puritan doctrine was intended as something more than a lesson in the peculiarities of seventeenth-century theology. Although he claimed that "the first colonists of New Hampshire, Massachusetts, and Connecticut generally agreed" with these tenets, he quickly moved to a more pointed affirmation of their applicability to his day: "The great body of the present inhabitants of New England hold them in substance at the present time."[6] In other words, Dwight claimed that the theological core of New England Congregationalism had remained essentially unchanged for nearly two centuries. For Dwight, nineteenth-century religion was not erected on the crumbling foundations laid by the seventeenth-century forebears; it *was* the religion of the forebears.

Dwight offered an interesting body of evidence to support this claim. In a remarkable passage that directly followed the twenty heads of doctrine, he listed those groups of New England Christians that did not conform to his normative doctrinal pattern. In eastern Massachusetts a "considerable number of Arminians and perhaps a greater number of Unitarians" were present though he confessed not to know of "a single Unitarian clergyman," and perhaps only "half a dozen Arminian" clergymen in Connecticut. New England Episcopalians "appear generally to hold the Arminian doctrines" and were "of the class who are called high churchmen." Among the Baptists, some were Calvinistic. But the non-Calvinistic Baptists, the "Freewillers," were

> as far as my information extends . . . in considerable numbers fast approximating to deism. . . . [T]hey consider religion as consisting chiefly in being plunged, to deny the Sabbath as a divine institution, to contemn [sic] family prayer, to have few settled ministers, and little even of the external appearance of religion. Many of their preachers are itinerants, and the solemnities of public worship are celebrated by them only occasionally. The moral extent of this evil, I need not explain.

To these dissenters Dwight added "a few Universalists," "Methodists . . . almost all followers of Wesley," Friends, Roman Catholics, a society of Moravians, and a synagogue of Jews.[7]

At first glance, this tour of dissent seems to be motivated by a need to cite evidence of religious diversity and, perhaps more importantly, religious toleration in Congregationalist New England. After all, in the very years when Dwight was making journeys and compiling *Travels*, religious dissent was well underway, and Connecticut Congregationalism was a chief target of the reformers. Even the slightest hint of toleration from the "Pope" of the Standing

Order would have been welcomed. This impression is strengthened by a reading of Letter XI, which begins with a state-by-state listing of the number of congregations belonging to each of these nonconformist denominations. This interpretation, however, gives Dwight an enormous benefit of the doubt. More careful scrutiny of Letter X reveals that a far more polemical motive stood behind his report on New England dissent. In the midst of his delineation of the varieties of dissent, he added a brief assessment of the Antinomians:

> These [Antinomians] are found chiefly in a class of men formerly called
> *Separatists,* most of whom for the purpose of avoiding the legal
> obligation of supporting ministers became Baptists. They were gener-
> ally extremely ignorant, and possessed of strong feelings and warm
> imaginations, in the exercise of which they chose to find religion,
> rather than in the faith and obedience of the Gospel. To demand
> obedience to the divine law, not as the means of justification, but as the
> duty of men, was stigmatized as *legalism,* or as an exaltation of the law
> of God against the grace of the gospel; and they appeared to choose to
> "continue in sin that grace might abound."

Several things about this passage are noteworthy. First, in the section of his narrative devoted to theological heterodoxy Dwight might have launched an assault on the traditional bogeys of New England Protestantism—the Friends' illuminationism, the Roman Catholics' understanding of justification, or even non-Christian religions of the world. Instead, Dwight devoted a paragraph to the intransigence of evangelical Protestants who refused to honor New England's only established religion, Congregationalism. Second, Dwight added a double-edged caveat to his observation about the Antinomians. In a rare footnote to his remarks, he noted: "It is often said, with how much truth I have no means of determining, that a considerable number of Baptists are Antinomians. I have stated in the text the number as small because I did not feel myself warranted to say otherwise."[8] To partisans of the establishment, this may have served as an exemplary illustration of President Dwight's sense of equity and fair play. To an observer outside the Standing Order, such comments could only have been interpreted as the worst sort of theological polemic.

In order to give these attacks some semblance of credibility, Dwight presented a fully consensual view of New England's religious history. To that end, he developed two ploys—one historical, the other theological. First, Dwight purposely ignored the diversity within the history of New England Congregationalism. Although the "venerable Hooker" is memorialized, he says little about the warring parties within Congregationalism. The squabbles between eighteenth-century New Lights and Old Lights or between contemporary Hopkinsians and Old Calvinists simply disappear under his interpretative gaze. Second, Dwight developed a religious *sine qua non* by which he could test a group's orthodoxy. His litmus test for orthodoxy, however, had little to do with the classic doctrines of Christian faith. In assessing "outsider" groups such as Anglicans, Quakers, and Baptists, he did not indict them for their distinctive—and to him, wrongheaded—religious beliefs (e.g., episcopal polity, the inner light, or believer's baptism). Instead, he judged a group's faithfulness as Christians on the basis of their fidelity to the Puritan notion of an established church. Apparently, Dwight was content to demonstrate a degree of "tolerance," i.e., dissenters were free to believe and worship as they pleased. But if they failed to acknowledge the validity of the state-established church, if they attempted to cut the traditional links that bound New England's God to New England's Caesar, then he pronounced a severe judgment. Those who opposed a state religious system (in other words, any group that resisted the hegemony of the Federalist Standing Order) thus became more than religious dissenters. Dwight viewed them as political renegades.[9]

Theology was not the only discipline that suffered at the hands of Dwight's oversimplification. Just as he had argued that one particular constellation of doctrines characterized the religious understanding of the entire region (and, by extension, the entire nation), so he also discerned a chronological period that was foundational for the American religious experience taken as a whole. In the opening paragraph of Letter I of "Religion of New England," he observed:

> To give you a correct view of this subject so far as New England is concerned, it will be necessary for me to go back to the war which commenced in 1755 and terminated in 1763. Antecedently to the first of these periods, all changes in the religious state of this country were such as left the principles of its inhabitants essentially the same. They were not changes of the commanding character, but shades of that character, through which it varied toward greater or less degrees of purity. From the first settlement of the country to the commencement of that war, the same reverence for God, the same justice, truth, and benevolence, the same opposition to inordinate indulgences of passion and appetite prevailed without any material exceptions. An universal veneration for the Sabbath, a sacred respect for government, an unbounding belief in divine revelation, and an unconditional acknowledgment and performance of the social duties constituted everywhere a prominent character.

Lest his readers charge him with naiveté, he qualified, though only slightly, his remarkable claim.

> I have said that the exceptions were not material. It is not intended that the whole number was inconsiderable, nor that vice was not found in various and sometimes very painful degrees. Still, vicious men constituted a very small part of the society, were insignificant in their

character, and independently of the power of their character had little
or no influence on the community at large. They were objects of odium
and contempt, of censure and punishment; not the elements of a party,
nor the firebrands of turmoil and confusion.[10]

Like Dwight's footnote to the Baptists-become-Antinomians, this caveat
strains his readers' credulity. Instead of anticipating the objections of his critics
or tempering his overly optimistic assessment, the "ungodly-amounted-to-
nothing" observation merely enlarged an already inflated claim. But this
passage precisely because of its inclusive sweep served Dwight's larger purpose. In order to facilitate the presentation of his consensus theory of New
England's historical development, Dwight leveled the peaks and valleys of the
American religious experience. For Dwight, there were no epochal events until
1755. New England suffered neither discord nor decline nor defeat. The
Antinomian controversy, the laments of the Puritan jeremiads, the adoption of
the Halfway Covenant, the Salem witch trials—events that should have piqued
the interest of Dwight the theologian—were ignored by Dwight the moralist.
Nor did Dwight describe New England's triumphs at any length. He mentions
the First Awakening, for instance, only briefly in *Travels*. Given the perfect
opportunity to describe and embellish the Edwardsean modifications to the
religion of the founders or to tout the theological tradition that had nurtured
him, Dwight remained oddly quiet.[11]

Like the Puritans he revered, Dwight interpreted the New World enterprise
in cosmic terms. In "Religion of New England," he formulated an imaginative
prose account of America's providential religious history. But Dwight's mythic
vision did more than fulfill his apparent need to regularize the past. In
spinning his hagiographic tale, Dwight erected a peculiar foundation, something of an historical justification by which he could promote his version of
the ideal American religious ethos and from which he could begin his cyclic
understanding of the unfolding of history. According to Dwight the first transit
to declension occurred between the years 1755 and 1763.

The Incursion of Infidelity

Dwight's mythic New England, like paradise in the biblical creation narratives, seemed to come into being *ex nihilo*. God blessed the Puritan forebears
with wisdom and placed them in circumstances appropriate to the fulfillment
of the divine master plan. Like Adam and Eve, who yielded to the fatal
flirtations of a wily serpent, the inhabitants of New England allowed themselves to be victimized by a tempter. The primeval couple disobeyed God on
the prospect of becoming like their creator. Similarly, New England's decline
began with the perverted belief that its citizens could reduce the distance

between creature and creator by remaking the creator in their own image. Dwight described the history of America's first moral lapse in two distinct literary genres written in two different periods of his career. In the first, *The Triumph of Infidelity* (1788), Dwight cast New England's fall from grace in poetic form. In the second, the "Religion of New England" letters in *Travels* (completed circa 1816), he offered an exacting prose account of the events that precipitated that fall: the incursion of European skepticism into New England.[12]

Dwight opened *Triumph of Infidelity* with a facetious dedicatory epistle to "Mons. de Voltaire," who, despite having been

> endowed with shining talents . . . devoted them to a single purpose, the elevation of your character above [God's]. For the accomplishment of this purpose, with a diligence and uniformity which would have adorned the most virtuous pursuits, you opposed truth, religion, and their authors, with sophistry, contempt, and obloquy; and taught, as far as your example or sentiments extended their influence, that the chief end of man was, to slander his god, and abuse him forever.[13]

On this vituperative note, Dwight launched his effusive description of Satan's many triumphs over humanity. To capture the imagination of his readers, Dwight cast Satan himself act as the poem's narrator. Beginning in antiquity, "ere Bethlehem's wonder rose," Dwight chronicled Satan's reaction to the whole of biblical and ecclesiastical history. He writes of the "Progress of infidelity after the death of Constantine the Great," and "under the papal hierarchy," as well as the "injuries done to infidelity, by Peter [and] Paul," "Luther [and] Calvin." Despite attempts of the godly to curtail Satan's progress the Devil wins Europe for himself.

The voracious tempter is not yet sated so he crosses the Atlantic. Upon invading New England, Satan meets stiff resistance. Indeed, the inhabitants of America, "a dread race, my sturdiest foes design'd / Patient of toil, of firm and vigorous mind," firmly resist the extension of Satan's wicked empire. This is true in part because the Americans are led by a man of superhuman fidelity, of whom Satan laments:

> But my chief bane, my apostolic foe
> In life, in labours, source of every woe,
> From scenes obscure, did heaven his ******* call,
> That moral Newton, that second Paul.
> He, in clear view, saw sacred systems roll,
> Of reasoning worlds, around their central soul,
> Saw love attractive every system bind,
> The parent linking to each filial mind;
> The end of heaven's high works resistless shew'd
> Creating glory, and created good;
> And, in one little life, the gospel more

Disclosed, than all earth's myriads kenn'd before
Beneath his standard; lo what number rise,
To dare for truth, and combat for the skies![14]

Dwight's contemporaries and his modern interpreters agree that he intended the seven asterisks in the poem to represent the name "Edwards." The couplet "He, in clear view, saw sacred systems roll, / Of reasoning worlds, around their central soul" most likely refers to Edwards's *History of the Work of Redemption;* the lines "Saw love attractive every system bind, / The parent linking to each filial mind" to Edwards's *Religious Affections;* and the reference to "The end of heaven's high work resistless shew'd" to Edwards's *Dissertation on the End for Which God Created the World.* On this interpretation, Dwight praised his grandfather as he would praise no one else. Edwards, a "Moral Newton" and a "Second Paul," did more for the gospel than anyone else in the modern era. Edwards had saved America by rallying the forces of light under the banner of truth. He had foiled the Tempter's designs on the North American continent. Mary Edwards Dwight had taught her son to revere her father, and here was proof that the lesson had been taken to heart.

As Kenneth Silverman has shown, however, there is a critical inconsistency in *The Triumph.* Although Dwight identified Satan's friends and foes, dropping names or using more cryptic devices such as his identification of Edwards, the exact nature of infidelity remained surprisingly amorphous. In Silverman's words, "The poem attacks not only skeptics or liberal Calvinists, but all the forces of social instability." Indeed, the reader never discovers which species of infidelity, the religious or the political, most troubled Dwight. This uncertainty stems from the fact that Dwight's fears had caused him to broaden the parameters of infidelity, making it serve as his "catch-all abomination." In *The Triumph,* then, Dwight merged religion and politics, church and state, Christianity and culture. Readers of *The Triumph* will also note that the poem ends on an uncertain note (Silverman called it "aimless") as though Dwight's cycle of establishment-decline-renewal had stalled somewhere between its second and third phases.[15] Having been surprised by sturdy American resistance, Satan flees, "proud with triumph" yet sorely "vex'd with spleen" into "the pall of endless night."[16] This ambiguity is perhaps the most astonishing aspect of the poem. Having sketched the history of Satanic assaults on European Christendom, having set out the American allies and enemies of evil, and having observed virtuous Americans cast Satan out of their commonwealth, Dwight had the perfect opportunity to describe a triumphant, even a millennial, America. For whatever reason, he declined it.

The troublesome ambiguities of *The Triumph of Infidelity,* however, were excised from Dwight's prose accounts of the spread of skepticism. Whereas *The Triumph* allowed several, even contrary, interpretations, Letter I of "Religion of New England" tried the case of American infidelity in detail and rendered a fully explicated verdict. Dwight believed that armed conflict—specifically the French and Indian War—had ushered infidelity into America. Although he had observed firsthand the horrors of war, he did not believe that the terror of violence or the loss of loved ones had led New Englanders to begin to doubt their God. These tragic events served only as the occasion for the demise of traditional religion. Infidelity came not on the heels of tragic, epochal events but in the wicked hearts and perverse minds of visitors to American shores. As he noted, "During the [French and Indian] war, foreigners for the first time mingled extensively with the inhabitants of New England." These foreign infidels came from England and France, and from one class of people, military officers. Such men were immediately accepted as models by the naive colonials whose "principles had in many instances been imperfectly formed, and whose ardent dispositions qualified them to decide rather than to reason, to act rather than to think."

Though Dwight claimed that "all infidels earnestly wish to make proselytes," he drew fascinating distinctions between the two nationalities involved in the spread of unbelief. The British infidels, whose influence was at its height during the French and Indian War, had something of an unfair advantage over the unsuspecting colonials. They came from the "mother country," a place "renowned for arts and arms, and regarded by the people of New England as the birthplace of science and wisdom." Moreover, British officers were winsome and "possessed of engaging manners." They "practiced all those genteel vices" that fascinated the youth of New England.

But French officers, whose influence was felt during the French and Indian conflict and later, during the American Revolution, were men of another sort altogether. Whereas British skeptics "commonly exhibited, in appearance at least, some degree of reverence for the Creator," French skeptics "only despised him." Englishmen tended to admit "that there may be an existence hereafter," but Frenchmen knew "*a priori* that there is nothing beyond the grave." Englishmen recognized "a distinction between right and wrong, and acknowledge[d] that men are under some obligation to do that which is right," but Frenchmen considered such beliefs pitiable and clownish. This litany against the French infidels continued: They "knew intuitively, if not instinctively" that God exercised no moral government over humanity, that man himself was merely a "brute upon two legs" who was under no moral obligation whatsoever, that right and wrong were to be judged solely on the basis of convenience or inconvenience to oneself.

Because Dwight's portrayal of New England religion functioned as a mythic presentation of the American past on which he could base his moral system, he needed to identify a specific culprit upon whom he could lay blame for the incursion of infidelity into America. As he searched for a scapegoat, three candidates emerged: the Americans themselves, the British, and the French. Of course, blaming the Americans was unacceptable to the patriotic Dwight. Although his analysis found American prudence wanting and American moral fiber slack, Dwight refused to hold his fellow citizens ultimately accountable for their own mistakes. Neither would he impugn the character of the English, despite their having been the pawns of infidelity. Having "been long assailed by the reasonings of Herbert and Chubb, the subtle frauds of Tindal, the pompous insinuations of Shaftesbury, the eloquent, but empty, declamations of Boling-broke, the wire-drawn metaphysics of Hume, and . . . the splendid impositions of Gibbon," the English, by the opening decade of the nineteenth century, had shown their proficiency at "triumphantly refuting the sophistry."[17] During most seasons of his life an unabashed Anglophile, Dwight reasoned that they would continue with their self-correction and, on the prospect of such ongoing reformation, they were shown mercy.

Having acquitted both the Americans and the British, Dwight was left with only one defendant. Where *The Triumph* had been ambiguous in its identification of the source of infidelity, *The Travels* was explicit. Dwight convicted the French of ruining the American character. In this regard, the French became a very useful tool in Dwight's hand. The French language was unknown to most New Englanders and this fact helped foster New England's and Dwight's nascent nativism. The history of French religion also served his larger apologetic needs. If he wanted further proof of France's insidious character, he could always appeal to New England's Protestant pride. After all, France had always been Rome's handmaiden.

In poetry and prose, Timothy Dwight had spun the tale of the tragic demise of America's religious conscience. In keeping with his cyclical understanding of history, and in anticipation of his prescription for the revivification of American righteousness, he offered his explanation of how the fallen American Eden was redeemed.

Columbia, to Glory Arise!

Whatever initial fears Dwight might have harbored about the incursion of infidelity during the French and Indian War evaporated when he spoke and wrote about the American War for Independence. Like many other politically minded patriots, Dwight understood that the American republic rested upon an aggrandized view of the Revolution. Although Dwight had charged the Revolutionary generation with religious naiveté, he nevertheless held it in high esteem. In the face of oppression and infidelity these heroes and heroines had stood fast in their commitment to liberty and independence. As a result of their efforts the American republic was created, an event of great significance within his eschatological reflections. At the opening of the Revolution Dwight was in New Haven studying theology with his uncle, Jonathan Edwards, Jr., and at the same time continuing to work with his Yale students. Military conflicts near New Haven forced him to flee to Wethersfield in the spring or early summer of 1777. He saw his senior students through the completion of their studies, and in October 1777 he began his service as a military chaplain to the patriot army. During this period, Dwight became an ardent patriot, and in sermons and poetry he constructed a glowing millennial interpretation of America's vital role in the unfolding divine drama.

Dwight unveiled this interpretation in his *Valedictory Address,* delivered on 25 July 1776. The address begins with a rather prosaic account of the geography and natural resources of North America. These advantages, he is quick to point out, are the results of divine blessing, which for him confirmed "the superiority of North America over every other country." Not only did the nation find itself blessed with material wealth but its genesis occurred at a particular point in the history of the West. He believed that the new American empire "is commencing, at a period, when every species of knowledge, natural and moral, is arrived to a state of perfection, which the world never before saw." These evidences of divine blessing, he continued, would culminate in the new nation. History showed that the march of empires had moved from East to West, from Assyria and Persia in the ancient world, to Britain in the modern world. This march made its inexorable transit across the Atlantic to the new North American empire that would be penultimate only to the final Kingdom of God. America will see great "progress of temporal things toward perfection. . . . Here will be accomplished that remarkable Jewish tradition that the last thousand years of the reign of time would, in imitation of the conclusion of the first week, become a glorious Sabbath of peace, purity, and felicity." Reason and scripture led Dwight to conclude that the new nation would ultimately become "the principal seat of that new, that peculiar kingdom, which shall be given to the Saints of the Most High. . . . , the last, the greatest, the happiest of all dominions." In a peroration at the close of the address he proclaimed: "We can scarce forbear to address the enraptured hymn of Isaiah to our country and sing, Arise, Shine, for thy light is come and the glory of the Lord is risen Upon thee! Nations shall come to thy light, and kings to the brightness of thy rising."[18]

Dwight often described the nation in language designed to identify America with the Kingdom of God, and he turned to the Bible for evidence that suggested the American situation was akin to that of the biblical people of Israel. Though he did not employ the terms, he relied on a standard typological scheme of type-antitype. Under this construction, biblical Israel served as a type of America and America as an antitype of Israel. Dwight preached his

Sermon at Stamford, in which this strategy was prominent, on 18 December 1777 just after the defeat of the British General Burgoyne. Beginning with a recitation of a prophetic text from Joel 2 and moving to the story of King Hezekiah and the Assyrian ruler Sennacherib in 2 Kings 18, he drew direct parallels between Judah's conflict with Assyria and America's conflict with Britain. He believed that the political scenarios that lead to the two conflicts were identical. "Hezekiah paid a tribute to Sennacherib, and these States to George the Third; but in both instances insatiable tyranny demanded more, than the tributaries were willing or able to pay; this was the cause." Just as the Assyrian general Rab-Shekah had, in his arrogance, misjudged the bravery of his enemy, so too had Burgoyne failed to recognize or appreciate the fortitude of his opponents. These proud but vanquished men at arms, he said, shared similar fates. Rab-Shekah was cast down, and the proud Burgoyne was defeated. As in Joel's prophecy, the threat of Burgoyne's "northern army" was removed; he was driven into Canada, a "land barren and desolate," during which he was forced to "face toward the east sea." No land or nation except the holy land of Palestine, he argued, "hath in the same time experienced more extraordinary interpositions of Providence than this."

Amidst such millennial optimism Dwight maintained his concern for the moral structures of society. While quick to note that the author of American success had been God, he reminded his auditors that they too must do good. "Nothing obstructs the deliverance of America, but the crimes of its inhabitants; sins, and their authors, are its greatest enemies." If its inhabitants continue to obey God and act justly, "our Independence and happiness [will be] fixed on the most lasting foundations; and that kingdom of the Redeemer which consisteth in righteousness, peace, and joy in the Holy Ghost, highly exalted, and durably established, on the ruins of the kingdom of Satan."[19]

Dwight sounded similar sentiments in another sermon occasioned by the defeat of a British general. In 1781, while still living with his extended family in Northampton, Dwight offered *A Sermon Preached at Northampton . . . Occasioned by the Capture of the British Army under the Command of Earl Cornwallis.* Hopeful that this victory might bring the war to a close, he framed the address with two elements of Isaiah 59: 18, 19: "According to their deeds, accordingly he will repay: Fury to his Adversaries, Recompense to his Enemies" and "When the Enemy shall come in like a Flood, the Spirit of the Lord shall lift up a Standard against him." In a classic bit of moralizing, Dwight offers an assessment of the British in which he argues that their moral failings directly led to their military defeat. With an atypical apocalyptic accent, he argues that European and British selfishness and unbelief typify the worldly powers that will be prevalent prior to the onset of the millennium. Here the type-antitype relationship is between the evil nations of the eighteenth century (nearly every nation of the West, save the United States) and the corrupt nations that prophecy declared would emerge near the end of all things.

Dwight was specific about the character of these corrupt moral structures and described them at length. Satan had invented several devilish engines with which to attack the progress of the Kingdom of God. The first of these was a spirit of ridicule by which "he endeavored to exhibit virtue as a contemptible baseness of soul, that he might engage the pride of all, and especially of the youth, to regard it with dread, or reject it with disdain." The second evil engine was sophistry, a virulent moral system that rejected the doctrines of grace and deviated from biblical morality. The devil had surreptitiously infused both of these strategies into the British doctrine of enlightened self-interest. This hellish theory stood at the heart of Britain's relations with her colonies and quickly became a tool of oppression. In opposition to British self-centeredness, American moral integrity stiffened the colonists' resolve and led to victory. In this triumph of the good, Dwight believed, the world had "seen, for the first time, an extensive empire founded on the only just basis, the free and general choice of its inhabitants." American genius inspired a new sort of civil government that did not encroach on "God's prerogative to govern his church, and without any civil establishments of religion." Scientific inquiry and the arts were blossoming, virtue had defeated vice, and benevolence had overcome selfishness. On America's behalf, God had given "Fury" and "Recompense" to the nation's enemies; the Spirit of the Lord had "lifted a Standard" against Britain. At sermon's end, Dwight abjures his auditors to give thanks to God for delivering the new United States from the hands of its enemies and "for using us as instruments of advancing his immortal kingdom of truth and righteousness."[20]

In addition to these sermonic accounts of the new nation's greatness, Dwight published a series of poems in the 1780s that celebrated the discovery of America and its national transformation in glowing millennial terms. The first of these, *America: Or a Poem on the Settlement of the British Colonies*, published in 1780 (though most likely written earlier) is typical of the approach that Dwight took. Addressed to "Friends of Freedom, and their Country," the poem returns to the march of empire theme developed in the *Valedictory Address*. The glory of the British empire is overshadowed by the new American nation. Indeed, America's power would continue to grow across the globe:

> Hail Land of Light and Joy! Thy power shall grow
> Far as the seas, which round thy regions flow;
> Through earth's wide realms thy glory shall extend,
> And savage nations at thy scepter bend.[21]

This same spirit was evident in his *Columbia: A Song,* which was written in 1783 and functioned as an early national anthem. Opening with the effusive lines "Columbia, Columbia, to glory arise, / The Queen of the world, and the child of the skies!" and continuing "Thy reign is the last, and the noblest of time, / Most fruitful thy soil, most inviting thy clime," the song extols America's heavenly qualities. Built on freedom, science, and virtue, the new nation will take a leading role in western civilization. Excelling in trade and politics and adept at bringing peace to a troubled world, Columbia triumphs, with "earth's little kingdoms" bowing before its power and might.[22]

These themes are further developed in *Prospect of America* (1791). Here the nation is cast as "The last retreat for poor, oppress'd mankind, / Form'd with that pomp, which marks the hand divine" and stands resplendent in its natural beauty. Marked with "spacious plains," "cloudy forests," "rich vallies," and "tall mountains brave," the land teems with "useful iron, and lasting gold." Here he managed to celebrate the nation's political system in verse. He followed his standard cant about European decline with

> Unlike all former realms, by war that flood,
> And saw the guilty throne ascend in blood,
> Here union'd Choice shall form a rule divine;
> Here countless lands in one great system join;
> The sway of Law unbroke, unrivall'd grow,
> And bid her blessings every land o'erflow.[23]

In another poem of the era, *Genius of Columbia* (1793), he follows a similar recitation and mentions taxation systems, governmental aid to religion, and states' rights within the federal union.[24]

Dwight's two most famous poems of the Revolutionary period, *Greenfield Hill* and the *Conquest of Canaan,* conform to the patterns established in his shorter poems. *Greenfield Hill,* a massive pastoral poem totalling nearly two hundred pages of verse, details his unique vision of what villages and towns in godly America should look like. It is a localized vision of the Kingdom. This focus is sharpest in Part VII of the poem subtitled "The Vision." Again, he rehearses the failures of European culture as a foil against which to measure American greatness. Following the couplet, "O happy State! the state, by Heaven design'd / To reign, protect, employ, and bless mankind," Dwight turns to the specific glories of the nation. In the new United States, few citizens are vicious, and many are virtuous. The life of the mind is greatly valued, cultural splendor spreads across the land, sloth is made an outcast, business and enterprise thrive, and wages are not purloined by a corrupt state.[25]

Where *Greenfield Hill* was local and specific, *Conquest of Canaan* proves enigmatic. An epic written in heroic couplets, *Conquest* outlines the Israelites' efforts to settle in the promised land. The biblical text with which he begins is Joshua 7, in which the hero Joshua has just suffered a terrible military defeat. The cause of Israel's troubles, Joshua learns, lies in an Israelite of little faith who had violated the command of God regarding the spoils of war. Once this sin has been dealt with (the perpetrator and his family are stoned), Joshua and the Israelites capture the city of Ai in a resounding victory. In succeeding chapters of the biblical narrative, they overrun Gibeon and a series of other cities and in Joshua 11 take over Canaan.

Using these five chapters of the biblical text as a literary backdrop, Dwight invents a group of fictional characters who live, love, fight, and die under the command of Joshua, their divinely appointed leader.[26] The central characters (who Leon Howard claimed were in reality "eighteenth-century Americans with Hebrew names who talked like Milton's angels and fought like pre-historic Greeks") are Irad and Selima, a young man and woman whose tragic romance begins in the midst of trying times, and Joshua and Hanniel, who wrangle at one another about their adventures.[27] Joshua is eager to press on to faithfulness and military action. Hanniel, on the other hand, speaks for the chorus of stiff-necked and hard-hearted Israelites who have tired of the wilderness sojourn. Despite their memories of the slavemaster's lash, they constantly long for the relative comforts of Egypt. Through eleven "books," each containing from eight hundred to one thousand lines of poetry, Dwight's epic wears on, finally concluding with Israel happily settled in a new land.

Interpretations of the *Conquest,* at least as it relates to Dwight's millennial reflections about the Revolution, are made problematic by his own comments about his intentions in writing the poem. In a letter to Noah Webster dated 6 June 1788, Dwight thanked Webster for defending him from his literary critics. In a published response to a review that had appeared in the *European Magazine,* Webster denied the central claim of the reviewer, namely that the *Conquest* was an allegory that equated the victorious American patriots with the Israelites and George Washington with Joshua. In his letter to Webster Dwight claimed: "The idea of those Gentlemen, that the poem is Allegorical, is so far from a foundation, that, untill [sic] I received your letter, it never entered my mind, that such an apprehension could be entertained by a man of common sense." He claimed that he had begun the poem in 1771, well before the start of the Revolution, and that while he had made various emendations and additions prior to its publication in 1785, none were designed to promote the allegory the reviewer claimed to have found. If readers or reviewers interpreted the poem allegorically, so be it. After all, "That General Washington should be supposed to resemble Joshua is not strange."[28]

Notwithstanding Dwight's disingenuous cavilling (he had, it will be recalled, successfully sought Washington's permission to dedicate the *Conquest* to him in 1778, and in other writings compares Washington with Joshua), the *Conquest* did without a doubt embellish the biblical story of the conquest with profuse allusions to the American situation.[29] Each of the *Conquest's* books begins with a brief prose "Argument," in which Dwight sketched the plotline of the ensuing verses. The Argument for the poem's penultimate Book X reads like a virtual American *heilsgeschichte*. Beginning with the general description "Vision of futurity," he synthesizes the history contained in the Bible. He begins with the Israelite experience in Canaan, moves to the "Birth, Baptism, Miracles, Trial, Death, Resurrection, and Ascension" of the Messiah, and then on to the "Preaching of the Gospel by the Apostles." The next entry in the Argument is entitled "Prospect of America," which is followed by the "Glory of the Western Millennium," "Signs which forebode the end of the World," the "Consummation of all things," and the "Prospect of Heaven."

The "Prospect of America" section of Book X, like his other poetic millennial descriptions of America, is filled with allusions to the natural beauties of the continent. Once again, America's role in the divine cosmic drama is unmistakable:

> Far o'er yon azure main thy view extend,
> Where seas, and skies, in blue confusion blend,
> Lo, there a mighty realm, by heaven design'd,
> The last retreat of poor, oppres'd mankind!
> Form'd with that pomp, which marks the hand divine,
> And clothes yon vault, where worlds unnumber'd shine.[30]

In sum, both Dwight's prose and poetic descriptions of the new nation positively shine with millennial luster. During the Revolutionary era he polished the national reputation with divine Providence and sanction at every opportunity. Even though he understood the United States to function prominently in the unfolding of God's cosmic drama he remained wary of declension. Nearly a decade before he would issue his most apocalytic warnings about the threat of infidelity, he harbored nagging suspicions about the staying power of America virtue. In 1787, he published "An Essay on the Judgment of History Concerning America" in the *New-Haven Gazette and Connecticut Magazine*. He began the brief article with what would become for him a standard litany: if American citizens wished to continue within the Providence of God, they must remain virtuous. If their morality failed them, in the place of the blessings of Providence they would receive divine disfavor. With the Revolution complete and national leaders busy working on the Constitution, he increasingly discerned the traces of moral lethargy. To prod moral introspection, Dwight crafted a description of what a future historian might write about America. His hypothetical scholar, having acknowledged American virtue at the time of the Revolution, might be forced to offer the following assessment of Americans in the late 1780s:

> But soon, very soon, by those streaks of human nature which are very common, though unaccountable, all their bright prospects were overcast, and their rising glory tarnished. The danger over and past, all the

little selfish passions, with all their baleful influence, rushed in upon them at once, and with so much the greater force the more they had been restrained before. From hence arose amongst themselves (for they had no foreign controul [sic]) disunited councils and opposing measures, ingratitude to their benefactors, injustice, cruelty and oppression, contempt of government and laws human and divine, disaffection, distrust and jealousy, with a numberless train of follies and vices, and at length the flames of civil war kindled, and ———. What follows let future historians record. What they will record depends upon ourselves. It depends on ourselves, the present living, active generations, whether respecting our nation and ourselves, the title of virtuous sons of liberty in America shall be handed down to future time as a perpetual mark of distinguishing honour and praise, or as a stigma of everlasting shame and reproach.[31]

Having culled the past for prophetic hints about the nation's destiny, Dwight himself prophesied. Notwithstanding all his optimism, the moralist saw potential danger, even civil war, just around the eschatological corner. In this case, Dwight's vision was accurate. Though he would not live to see the American Civil War he did experience what, at the time, was his worst nightmare, a new and more virulent onslaught of infidelity.

The Challenge of the Sixth Vial

In the first years of Dwight's Yale presidency, American interest in the biblical prophecies concerning the last days rose to an all-time high. With revolution convulsing France and wars and rumors of wars shaking Europe, American interpreters tried their best to align mundane political history with the biblical timetable of the future. France threw off the religious yoke of Rome (an event that was a favorite topic among Protestant prophecy-watchers) and sought liberty and political freedom as had the United States just a decade before. Though there were interpretive problems to overcome, American Protestants hailed the onset and early years of the Revolution as a positive sign from heaven. Not surprisingly, the strongest support came from Republicans, many of them from the middle or southern states, who tended to view liberal Christianity and the American Enlightenment as equal partners in the progressive advance of Western civilization. Many New England clerics, Federalists among them, shared in the millennial enthusiasm.

During the final third of the decade American support for the French Revolutionary cause began to wane. The greatest degree of defection came from the New England clergy. Several suspicions about the French situation had held their initial enthusiasm in check. By 1797 and 1798 their fears were to be justified. French Protestantism, which was supposed to have emerged triumphant over Rome, had proven itself a tepid competitor for the hearts of the French people. To American interpreters, Protestantism in France was still playing second fiddle—no longer to Rome but now to deism and skepticism. To make matters worse, these religious diseases had spread to the United States. In addition to religious problems in France, the newly installed French government gave little evidence of being an improvement over the *ancien régime* when it came to civil liberties and repression. Late in the decade, as if to confirm the worst fears of the Federalists, one of the nation's leading "enlightened" Francopiles, Thomas Jefferson, was serving as Vice President of the United States and, some feared, would soon become President. Among New England Federalists and especially among the clerical contingent of the Standing Order, francophobism burst onto the political scene. Not surprisingly, Dwight was in the vanguard.[32]

His first sermonic blast, destined to become one of his most famous addresses, was published under the title *The Duty of Americans in the Present Crisis Illustrated in a Discourse Preached on the Fourth of July, 1798*. Dwight chose for his text a passage from the book of Revelation that was ripe with apocalyptic meaning: "Behold I come as a thief: Blessed is he that watcheth, and keepeth his garments, lest he walk naked, and they see his shame" (Revelation 16:15). Verses thirteen through sixteen of this chapter function as a parenthetical pause within the vision of the seven angels pouring out vials or bowls of wrath upon the earth. These verses appear just after the description of the pouring out of the sixth vial. They end with an allusion to the gathering at Armageddon and immediately precede the pouring of the seventh and final vial.

In order to locate these sixth-vial events on the calendar of mundane history, Dwight rehearsed the standard Protestant eschatological arithmetic. He reasoned that the duration of any single vial was 170 to 180 years. The Reformation, which began near 1520, was believed to have occurred during the pouring of the fifth vial. Hence, the era of the fifth vial would come to a close sometime during the final decade of the seventeenth century. Give or take a few years, then, the era of the sixth vial began about 1700. Dwight believed that the sixth-vial prophecy would consist of two parts, both of which would be fulfilled during the same period. The first element had to do with the weakening of the Antichristian empire as it moved toward its ultimate destruction. The second concerned the emergence of wicked teachers who, in the shrinking shadow of the Antichristian empire, would spread false doctrines and would persecute the true followers of Christ. Having sketched the outlines and historical placement of the prophecies, he moved to interpretation: "What events in the Providence of God," he asked rhetorically, "verify the prediction?"

As to the first element of the prophecy, Dwight offered a long litany of events since 1700 that helped to verify that the Antichristian empire, headed by the Pope and led by the hierarchy of the Roman Catholic church, was in decline. The Jesuits, who provided Rome its "most formidable internal support," had been suppressed. Roman Catholic secular powers, notably in Poland, France, and Belgium, were falling, and were thereby diminishing the strength of the Catholic empire. Most important, papal power had declined. The Pontiff's revenues had been curtailed, "within the present year his person has been seized, his secular government overturned," and "an apparent and at least temporary end put to his dominion." All these developments completely assured Dwight "that [the Antichristian realm's] former strength can never return."

The second element of the prophecy, like the first, could be verified by a review of recent events. In 1728, Voltaire "formed a systematical design to destroy Christianity, and to introduce in its stead a general diffusion of irreligion and atheism." For the purpose of destroying Christianity in Europe, Voltaire aligned himself with the Encyclopaedists, whose principal objectives were to render "Natural as well as Christian Theology . . . absurd and ridiculous." They attacked the Christian elements of society and constituted themselves a sect that "would serve as a rallying point, for all their followers." They developed a canon of insidious literature and working through a network abetted by their secret Academy dispersed it abroad. To further advance their cause, the *philosophes* invaded the Masonic movement and thoroughly corrupted it. Flush with a sense of victory, with Dr. Adam Weishaput they formed the dreaded Illuminati, an organization "professedly a higher order of Masons." Here, "doctrines were taught, which strike at the root of all human happiness and virtue."

> The being of God was denied and ridiculed. Government was asserted to be a curse and authority a mere usurpation. Civil society was declared to be the only apostasy of man. The possession of property was pronounced to be robbery. Chastity and natural affection were declared to be nothing more than groundless prejudices. Adultery, assassination, poisoning, and other crimes of the like infernal nature, were taught as lawful, and even as virtuous actions. To crown such a system of falsehood and horror all means were declared to be lawful, provided the end was good.[33]

Having interpreted the prophecy and described the threat to American virtue and liberty, Dwight, the eschatological historian, outlined the defensive strategies his auditors could use to protect themselves and their nation. "We should be eminently watchful to perform our duty faithfully, in the trying period, in which our lot is cast." He reminded his listeners "that personal obedience and reformation is the foundation, and the sum, of all national worth and prosperity. If each man conducts himself aright, the community cannot be conducted wrong. If the private life is unblamable, the public state must be commendable and happy." Then, he launched a multi-point plan of defense that would insure the public safety. First, citizens must keep the Sabbath, the "bond and union of Christians; the badge by which they know each other; their rallying point; the standard of their host." Second, they must carefully separate themselves from their evil enemies. Dwight could imagine no purpose whatever in associating with infidels and launched his most infamous rhetorical question: "For what end shall we be connected with [infidels]?" His answer, an equally famous diatribe, claimed that social intercourse with skeptics would lead sons to "become the disciples of Voltaire, and the dragoons of Marat," and "daughters the concubines of the Illuminati." The French infidels were polluted beyond belief, their sins so great that "No guilt so deeply died in blood, since the phrenzied malice of Calvary, will probably so amaze the assembly of the final day." He completed his list of defensive measures with two other duties: union among faithful Christians who perceived the threats facing the nation, and an "unshaken firmness in our opposition" to that evil.

If this was not enough to suggest to his audience that Dwight sought always to view American prospects from the perspective of the unfolding divine plan, he concluded the sermon with a recitation of God's direct intervention in the formation of the American nation. Dwight was utterly confident that the same God who had raised Washington to guide American armies, who had destroyed enemy fleets with wind and wave, who had brought victory at Yorktown, and who had roused the present resistance to infidelity would yet again bless the nation. "The advent of Christ," he concluded, "is at least at our doors." This final word, sounding more like a premillennial interpretation than his standard postmillennial scheme, replaced his usual rendition of the advent of the millennial reign of peace and prosperity.[34]

Dwight preached three other sermons that dealt with the significance of late eighteenth-century infidelity. In two of them, the *Nature and Danger of Infidel Philosophy* (preached just nine months prior to *Duty*) and *A Discourse on Some Events of the Last Century* (preached New Year's week in 1801), he gives more attention to the mundane history and social effects of infidelity than to its meaning for the unfolding divine timetable. In both addresses he repudiates "philosophism," which he believes to be the chief threat to American liberty and happiness. In *Nature and Danger* (treated at length in a previous chapter) he attempts to compile a *tour de force* survey of the chief European promoters of infidelity. In *Some Events* he appears more irenic—at least as far as the Catholic menace is concerned. Indeed, in what might have appeared a theological *faux pas* just years earlier, Dwight revealed a new ecumenical spirit. He argued that it was technically improper to identify the hierarchy of the Roman Church as the Antichrist—the dreaded "Beast" perhaps or the "son of perdition" but not evil incarnate! He even manages a backhanded compliment to Catholics, calling them Christians.[35] Apparently, Dwight was sufficiently convinced of the breadth and depth of the infidel threat that he was willing to soften his harsh judgments about Catholics. A Christian united front seemed a more formidable defense against the growing menace of infidelity than did a fractious group of defenders divided into competing Catholic and Protestant groups.

The third of these three sermons deserves further mention. In July and August of 1812, Dwight preached two long fast sermons, both of which were entitled *Discourse in Two Parts*. The occasion of the July sermon was a Connecticut fast service; the August sermon was preached at a national fast service. The political event that triggered these observances was the war upon which the United States had just embarked with Britain. Like his Federalist colleagues, Dwight was entirely opposed to the War of 1812 and he made this plain in both sermons.[36] The political aspects of the sermons aside, what is most striking about the addresses is their return to apocalyptic themes. Though Dwight had not preached on the pouring out of Revelation's vials for nearly fifteen years, he did so with gusto, particularly in the first of the *Two Parts* addresses. The reason one must assume is that the war with Britain was causing some to advocate an alliance with France. This prospect astonished the Federalist community. Dwight responded by revisiting the theme of America's place within God's redemptive plan and by returning to his apocalyptic attacks on France.

The text of the first sermon is from Isaiah and is summarized in a brief question, "Watchman, what of the night?" (Isaiah 21:11). While he is quick to note that his text is "very concise, very figurative, and very obscure," Dwight launches his interpretation with full confidence. Isaiah, he argued, was being asked to declare the future, and the prophet's inspired response was fully applicable to America in 1812:

> A season of prosperity is immediately before you, and will be succeeded by a season of adversity. . . . If ye are really desirous to know your destiny, and to learn the things that belong to your peace, come, and inquire at the mouth of God. Return to him by returning to the religion from which you have departed, ever since the days of your first founder. Come again; and renew your allegiance to God.

With this call to repentance and a return to the faith of the New England's forebears in place, Dwight then retreats to his stock apocalyptic account of the seven vials, with one interesting difference. As before, he argues that the present era was represented by the sixth vial, and that during this period the wicked will attack the faith. Once again, he rehearses his account of the rise of deism, the work of Voltaire, the emergence of the Illuminati, and issues graphic assessments of the character of infidelity. "The spirit of infidelity has the heart of a wolf, the fangs of a tyger [sic], and the talons of a vulture. Blood is its proper nourishment." The miseries it wreaked on the nation of France were horrific. "France became a kind of suburb to the world of perdition," "a charnel house of Atheism," "where the final knell had been tolled at the departure of life, and hope, and salvation."[37]

But here Dwight added a new twist to his interpretive work with the vials. Whereas he had formerly argued along the lines of accepted postmillennial doctrine that the millennium would occur in conjunction with the pouring out of the seventh vial, in the first installment of the *Discourse in Two Parts,* he abandoned the party line. He now predicted that at the close of the sixth-vial age, Armaggedon would occur, which would pit the forces of evil against the legions of the Almighty. Armageddon was not a single battle, he said, but a long series of struggles at the end of which God would vanquish all those who opposed true religion. At this moment of victory, the seventh vial would be poured out, and a number of remarkable events would occur. A voice would cry from heaven, "It is done"; the world would be convulsed in a series of conflicts; Babylon would be divided into three parts; and sinners who had blasphemed God would suffer a plague of hail. Under his former interpretive scheme, Dwight would have argued that the millennium would occur at this point. But instead, he hints that the second advent of Christ might occur next on the divine timetable. Noting that Christ himself said, "Behold, I come as a thief," Dwight implied Jesus would return and set the millennium in place. However interesting this shift away from a postmillennial strategy may be, Dwight used the occasion to incite his auditors' passions for righteousness. Noting that the "end of all these observations is to warn, to rebuke, to reclaim, to persuade to repentance, and to effectuate reformation," Dwight urged Americans to walk with great care, lest they fall from divine favor and find their nation facing the wrath of Jehovah.[38]

The Dawn of the Millennium

The fifth and final era that Dwight treated within his cycles of redemption began soon after the opening of the nineteenth century and continued to the end of his life. During this period he vaunted the significance of the revivals of religion that were sweeping New England and the West and shifted his millennial thinking from negative apocalyptic to a more progressive scheme, the success of which would require human effort, albeit divinely inspired. At points, his confidence is sufficiently high that he actually hints that America is on the very threshold of the millennial age.

Although Dwight is often identified as one of the most significant of the nation's revivalists, the events that historians have called the "Second Great Awakening" played only a modest role in his interpretive schemes. When he did address the significance of the religious revivals that swept across much of the nation during the years following 1795, he tended (not surprisingly) to tie the progress of these revivals to resistance against French infidelity. Dwight praised citizens for being duly suspicious of the intellectual bankruptcy of French philosophy, but he believed that infidelity's ultimate defeat would come from citizens' hearts, not their heads. Accordingly, Dwight interpreted the late eighteenth- and early nineteenth-century revivals as the providential religious solution to the problem of infidelity. Where infidelity had wreaked havoc, the revivals brought order. Where infidelity promoted bloodletting, the Second Great Awakening "has been attended with the happiest circumstances and followed by the best consequences." It is of interest to note that Dwight singled out one particular consequence for special attention. Although he rejoiced that thousands of New Englanders were converted, or perhaps reconverted, to the faith of their American forebears, Dwight was even more pleased to report that many of these converts had emigrated to new frontier settlements where they had "begun to build new churches, settle ministers, and established the public worship of God." In effect, God not only saved New England but in the process also enlarged her boundaries. In retrospect he would say of the period,

> [W]hen I look back upon these events; when I consider their magnitude, their portentous efficacy at times on the morals and the evils which distressed us; when I remember how the wisest men were perplexed, and the firmest trembled; I cannot willingly avoid saying, and I hope my countrymen will say with me "Had not the Lord been on our side when men rose up against us, they had swallowed us up quick, and the proud waters had gone over our soul."[39]

This focus on the work of God on behalf of the nation and Dwight's shifting thinking about the character and timing of the millennium became evident in several of his major sermons of the period. In two of these, *Sermon Preached at the Opening of the Theological Institution in Andover* (1808) and *Sermon Delivered in Boston . . . before the American Board of Commissioners for Foreign Missions* (1813), Dwight promulgated the belief, common among many American eschatologists of the day, that the millennium would begin around the year 2000. In the contexts in which he preached these sermons, he felt a particular obligation to stress the role that ministers would play in the days just prior to the start of the millennial age. In the Andover sermon, Dwight wanted not only to celebrate the opening of a new school but also to call attention to the importance of the clergy in early national America. Similarly, in his remarks before the American Board, he wanted to commend the work of foreign missions and the significance of those men and women who would travel abroad to spread the Gospel. In both cases Dwight argued that the activities of ministers and missionaries had taken on new significance. Whereas God had formerly worked transcendently, shaping and bending mundane events to conform to a providential pattern, now divine activity was fully immanent. The backdrop of the end times was no longer the high drama of great political events but rather the combined efforts of individual Christians. The significance of wars and rumors of wars was replaced with prayer, preaching, Christian unity, and acts of charity; the focus was no longer cosmic but local. Working with a new sort of optimism, Dwight baptized these relatively modest activities and sounded the clarion for inspired voluntarism.[40]

With Dwight's focus on the effort of individuals in bringing about God's reign on earth, his tendency to look for the lasting effects of Christianity in the larger social realm becomes even more pronounced. In other writings of this period Dwight named specific social reforms as evidence of the spread of Christianity and, hence, of the onset of the Kingdom of God. Whereas global political events had formerly interested him, he now scrutinized local social evils that would be eliminated in the coming days—the theater, the pub, and the brothel. In their place, virtue would arise. Civil rulers would lead with justice foremost in mind, husbands would guide families with wisdom and charity, and children would honor their parents. Indeed, Dwight's confidence was so high in this period that he actually entertained notions of human perfection—a remarkably optimistic move given his previous worries about the denigrating influence of France. In an 1814 classroom discussion, Dwight and his senior students debated the question, "Is man advancing to a state of Perfectibility?" Though he was somewhat guarded in his response, Dwight answered in the affirmative. He argued that despotism was sinking in the world and was being replaced by Christianity. The millennium seemed to be taking hold by degrees, and the evils of humanity were being alleviated one by one. The world was moving forward, and this progress, tied as it was to human ingenuity and ultimately governed by God, seemed to be irreversible. "Improvements are making on so large a scale as to outrun everything which has been known before."[41]

These developments hint at Dwight's growing optimism, and in two other texts he makes plain his belief that the dawn of the millennium would soon occur. The first of these texts is the August 1812 installment of the *Discourse in Two Parts*. Continuing his work with the Isaiah passage, "Watchman, what of the night?" Dwight extends his July address, adding further details about the millennial reign and adding a section with practical applications for believers. In a careful retreat from the apocalyptic, premillennial hints contained in his first installment of the *Discourse,* Dwight posits a more traditional postmillennial interpretation of the temporal relationship between the millennium and the sixth vial. Again, he adds a bit of a twist, arguing that the millennium had already begun. From his view, the sixth vial and all its attendant events, particularly the decline of infidelity, was then occurring and, hence, he had grounds to claim that the blessed era had finally dawned.

Having made this remarkable claim, Dwight asked, "What is our immediate duty?" and "What reasons have we to think that God will bless our endeavors?" Answering his first query, Dwight tied his list of stipulations to the forthcoming challenges of the sixth vial event. In these heady days, Christians should abstain from connection with the Romish empire, resist party spirit, and give religion its proper place in their thoughts and conduct. As to the second question, Dwight argued that Christians had many reasons to believe that they were at the doorstep of the millennium. God was advancing the divine plan for Christian America, and the faithful had ample historical data by which to discern the hand of Providence. The American nation had been settled by Christians, who had prospered in the New World. Jews, the ancient people of God, who had been persecuted elsewhere, enjoyed religious freedom and the opportunity to prosper in blessed Columbia. Revivals had occurred in the United States and their influences—among which the nativist Dwight counted the spread of the English language—continued to bring salutary effects.[42] Dwight's belief that the nation was approaching the zenith of blessedness is nowhere more plain than in the final installment of a series of "Observations on the Present State of Religion in the World" that he wrote for the *Religious Intelligencer.* In September 1816, just four months before his death, he offered his final testimony to the triumph of fidelity in America:

> I am constrained to believe a new era in the moral concerns of man to
> have commenced; and anticipate from this period a new order of things
> in the affairs of our world, in which the Religion of the Gospel will rise
> in all its majesty, beneficence, and glory, to the astonished and de-
> lighted view of mankind.[43]

* * *

In his biographical sketch of Timothy Dwight, William Sprague noted that "There was scarcely any subject, at the mention of which his mind more instinctively kindled, and rose into the regions of moral sublimity, than the privileges and prospects of the American nation."[44] This claim nicely summarizes the dynamics that attended Timothy Dwight's activity as an American Clio. The privileges and prospects of the American nation played a leading role in his intellectual world. While this feature of his thinking may be loosely described as historical, its imaginative qualities—and its power among subsequent American thinkers who would embellish these ideas and then craft the popular "Redeemer Nation" ideology—must not be overlooked. He cast his gaze on the past as well as on the future, using the lenses of millennialism and apocalypticism to illumine his subject. Though one may dismiss his forays into historical interpretation as pre-critical and non-technical, or condemn his fixation with the end times as naive and inconsistent, Dwight believed that his ruminations on the outworking of the divine plan were grounded in true stories about the past, the present, and the future. Whatever else may have inspired his swings from optimism to pessimism, clearly Dwight's personal feelings about the nation—his fears and anxieties as well as his moments of elation and triumph—remain the best predictor of the tone of his pronouncements. When the world looked well, Dwight concluded that God was busy blessing and sustaining the nation. When culture revealed its corruptions, Dwight was blinded by images of impending judgment and doom. This unbreakable connection between Dwight's assessment of American faithfulness and his beliefs about God's outlook on the nation—one of Sparks's regions of "moral sublimity"—is evident in Dwight's preaching, in his theology, and in his history. It now remains to demonstrate the manner in which Dwight integrated these features of his life to become "New England's Moral Legislator."

New England's Moral Legislator

> He was, indeed, a father to New England—her
> moral legislator.
>
> —Benjamin Dwight

Preacher, theologian, historian: these activities served as the central foci of
Timothy Dwight's professional life. Clearly, he excelled at each of these activities and each of these aspects of his career deserves careful historical attention
on its own merits. But Dwight's influence and significance transcended these
roles. After all, a life can be greater than the sum of its parts. Vocational
activities do not merely share contexts and thereby mutually interact; they also
intertwine, combine, and tangle to form larger motifs, roles, and identities. In
Dwight, the distinct roles of preacher, theologian, and millennial historian
combined to form a unique amalgam: at the height of his career, Timothy
Dwight became New England's consummate moralist.

In our day the use of the term "moralist" is problematic. It suggests finger-
wagging legalism of the sort that is routinely rejected. Our era, characterized
by a cacophony of moral and religious voices, tolerates very few cultural
visionaries especially when they dare to declare that their vision bears the
marks of divine sanction. Among educated observers, even more profound and
complex problems attend the use of the word. Today's moralists, the intellectuals who function as "moral theologians," "ethicists," or perhaps even "cultural
critics," bear the marks of their particular world views. Fearful that moralists
are nothing more than advocates for a particular group or ideology, contemporaries are inclined to view the "moralist" attribution as nothing more than a
veneer designed to hide the evils of cultural arrogance, backward-looking
provincialism, partisan politics, or naked ambition. Moderns do not suffer
moralists gladly.[1]

In Dwight's era the attribution "moralist" was understood and more generally accepted. Moralists sought to discern general paradigms for the Christian
way of life, they constructed codes of conduct based on these paradigms, and
they continually reexamined and reevaluated these paradigms and codes in
light of larger philosophical questions about right and wrong, good and evil,
the supernatural and the natural. Dwight attended to all three of these phases
of moralism.

He spent most of his career constructing paradigms for a distinctly Christian way of life. In didactic, occasional, and polemic sermons, as well as in the classroom instruction preserved in *Decisions,* Dwight describes what he takes to be the distinctives of the Christian moral outlook. Although his moral perspective was unique, its cultural origins were obvious. Dwight's ethical outlook had a distinctly New England character; it was derived from the theology of his Puritan founders, the ecclesiology of the Congregationalist Standing Order, and the political philosophy of the Old School wing of the Federalist political party.

Moving from these general principles, Dwight constructed specific codes of prescribed and proscribed behavior. He believed that the individual believer's chief duty lay in the transformation of naturally vicious behavior into virtuous, Christ-like behavior. Such transformations were to be sought in every level of culture, be it individual or corporate, and were to be coherent with the paradigmatic ethical foundations he affirmed. Hence, specific directions about personal piety, the relationship of the church to the larger culture, and the character of American politics could be gleaned from the divine guidelines laid down in the inspired scriptures.

Dwight also attended to the third function of moralism—the critical assessment of moral paradigms and codes in light of timely philosophical questions—though with less energy, acumen, and success. In this respect, Dwight's moralism and his theology ran at parallel depths. For good or ill, he refused to examine fully the substance and implications of his moral paradigms in light of contemporary philosophical inquiry. Although he understood the major contours of what in his day was called "moral philosophy" he was hardly a master of the subject. His lack of facility in this area can be explained in part by the nature of the subject in his time; eighteenth-century moral philosophy was a complex and demanding discipline that was undergoing a good deal of change and development. Notwithstanding the force of this caveat, Dwight's facility with the complexities of moral philosophy was at best modest. Instead of training a critical and analytic gaze on contemporary philosophical issues, Dwight summarized positions for his students at a distance. In place of constructive, forward-looking intellectual engagement, he offered simplified critiques. Dwight popularized the more sophisticated thought of others. In the final analysis he was a pedagogue who offered his students bird's eye-views at the expense of close-up analysis.[2]

Notwithstanding his limitations, Dwight's reputation as a moralist is well deserved. During more than three decades of public life, he crafted his unique, idealized vision of what New England ought to be and become. In poetry and prose, from pulpit and podium, Dwight sought to convince right-thinking citizens that his vision of New England and, by extension, his ideal image of the American republic, was authentic, viable, and expressly faithful to God's will. He gave his full energy to the task of insuring that his vision of the nation became a blueprint for the future. If moral suasion was insufficient to this task, he would resort to legal coersion. In either case, he believed that his efforts would be greeted with divine approbation. Dwight's contemporaries, friend and foe alike, acknowledged him to be a powerful moralist and so should interpreters in the present day. Whatever final judgments can be rendered about the validity of his claims, in its own context his moralism was relatively sophisticated and intellectually consistent.

Dwight's stature as an American moralist depended upon more than his ability to engage moral questions. His views about preaching, theology, and history also contributed to his success. As a preacher, Dwight demonstrated a remarkable ability to create alternative worlds. Although his sermons enlightened the mind and inspired the imagination, the telos of his homiletic was obedience to the divine law. At its core, Christianity was about grace but also about duty. He operated under the guidance of Common Sense Realism; truth claims were to be made in plain words spoken directly and without appeal to difficult metaphysics. This approach cohered perfectly with his larger theological views. He honored the limits that divine mystery placed upon theological speculation and urged believers to exert themselves in their quest for individual and corporate salvation. Though wary of Arminian views about the spiritual powers inherent in individual moral agents, he refused to allow his auditors to escape their responsiblity to change their worlds. Even his view of history bolstered his moralism. Although he had studied the complicated varieties of biblical eschatology and although he believed that faithfulness to scripture was of paramount importance, his assessments of American righteousness controlled his pronouncements about the establishment of the Kingdom of God on earth.

Features of Dwight's personality are important in this connection as well. His apparent inability to engage in mutual and open personal relationships and his resultant habit of interpersonal formality had powerful effects on his career. An extremely private person, he was loath to reveal himself to others. Only in rare circumstances, as in the sermon preached in Yale's chapel soon before his death, does he allow his personal feelings about his life to be seen. In this respect, the dearth of "personal sources" about his life represents more than historical accident. Sources do not survive because they were never created. When given political or religious authority, some persons are tempted to hide behind its facade. From the relative safety of this position they find it easy to prescribe behavior. Dwight was such a man.

Dwight's functional blindness also contributed to his inclination toward moralism. His unreliable eyes affected his professional development and lim-

Timothy Dwight, artist unknown. Yale University
Art Gallery. Gift of Mrs. Edward F. Dwight. Used
by permission.

Rev. Timothy Dwight, artist unknown.
Used by permission of The Connecticut Historical Society, Hartford.

ited his impact on the affairs of his day. Engaged in a changing world in which print media was critically important, Dwight was denied the regular opportunity to read and to write. To his credit, he remembered what he read and he spoke better than he wrote. Nonetheless, his disability led to his most painful defeats, it threatened his success, and it put him on the defensive. The problem extended beyond his inability to see, however. Dwight also suffered from cultural myopia. Just as his physical limitations incapacitated him, so his cultural blindness prevented him from fully understanding the social fabric of the culture in which he found himself. Fearful of the dangers that might suddenly loom on the cultural horizon, he became obsessed with his security and the nation's survival. Forced to carry on blindly, as it were, he became preoccupied with moral concerns and with how the world around him ought to be.[3]

Godly Federalism, Dwight's ideal vision of the American republic, provides a window into his unique style of moralism. This vision is best seen in his systematic program for the maintenance of American piety and the various elements of "moral legislation" that he promulgated to that end. Dwight's moral prescriptions fall into three categories. The first deals with individual morality, and the second and third deal with the social institutions that served as the pillars of the godly Republic—the state and the established church.

Individual Piety

Central to Timothy Dwight's vision of godly America was his understanding of the ethical purity of American citizens. In his mind, the social institutions that made up American culture rested on the foundation of individual morality and were entirely dependent on that morality for their well being. Individual morality itself, however, had a foundation; it was grounded on the fundamental doctrines of Christianity. In order to act rightly in the world, the moral agent had first to learn to think and believe rightly. For Dwight, piety and morality were inseparable. Genuine love for God and the truths of God led inevitably to love of neighbor. Hence, the first sections of *Theology, Explained and Defended,* in which Dwight set forth the full array of topics contained in a standard systematic theology, served as a prolegomenon to its middle sections, in which he discussed his ethical outlook. This priority ordering of theological rubrics within *Theology* (the fundamentals of belief, followed by a discussion of how to live), should not be permitted to obscure the overall trajectory of Dwight's system taken as a whole. His ethical reflection leaned decidedly in the direction of moral pragmatism. Though certain beliefs were deemed critical to virtuous behavior, such behavior and not the faith on which they rested was the telos of practical Christianity.

This sort of pragmatism had been the basis on which Dwight had rejected many of the metaphysical doctrines of the New Divinity theologians. In his opinion, they had probed too far into the mysteries of the divine mind, seeking answers to religious paradoxes that were meant to protect the unbridgeable gulf between finite creatures and their infinite creator. Dwight believed that the results of such inordinate probing fell into two categories. First, if inquirers believed they had resolved any of these paradoxes, they immediately fell prey to the sin of vanity. The second consequence of unrestrained inquiry was far worse. Individuals who sought to systematize the divine, Dwight observed, lost their sense of moral balance. In focusing their energies on the rigors of ponderous theological speculation, such people lost sight of their primary purpose—to live in the world as faithful witnesses to Christ.

Given his pragmatic outlook, Dwight devoted large portions of *Theology* to the practical social effects of Christianity. The first ninety sermons of the collection bore the subtitle "System of Divinity." Beginning with Sermon 91 and continuing to Sermon 162, however, Dwight set forth what he called his "System of Duties."[4] This title is itself instructive. Dwight might have referred to these sermons in technical terms, perhaps as a "System of Moral Philosophy," or more generically as a "System of Ethics." But he wanted his students to realize that Christians had responsibilities as well as privileges and entitlements. The word "Duty," with its natural connection to the concepts of law and obligation, perfectly expressed his understanding of the nature of the Christian life. Like the doctrinal portions of *Theology*, the "System of Duties" was straightforward and didactic. Having taught his Yale undergraduates the fundamentals of Christian doctrine, what to believe, he went on to instruct them in Christian morality—how to live.

In the first half of the "System of Duties" Dwight explicated his understanding of the "Duties of Natural Religion." Here he preached eight sermons on Jesus' teaching about the two great commandments, to love God and to love neighbor, and thirty-three additional sermons on the duties required by the Decalogue. In the second half of his "System of Duties" Dwight offered a twenty-nine-sermon analysis of the "Duties of the Christian Religion" that included his views on the means of grace, the sacraments, ecclesiastical polity, and church discipline. In both of these sections his moral analysis refers back to an earlier portion of *Theology* in which Dwight discussed the nature and attributes of God. Given the developments that were afoot in contemporary discussions, Dwight's rendition of the character of God is particularly interesting.

In the first seven sermons of *Theology*, Dwight discussed the eternity, immutability, omnipresence, omniscience, and independence of God. Working forward from the beachhead he had established in these sermons, in Sermon 8, entitled "Benevolence of God Proved from the Works of Creation and Providence," Dwight introduced what was to become the critical element in his doctrine of God and, later, in his ethical system: "Having considered the existence and the natural attributes of God at some length, I shall now proceed to the next subject of theological inquiry, viz. his moral attributes."[5] As was his habit, and again in accordance with the precepts of Common Sense philosophy, Dwight examined facts and evidence drawn from two realms—biblical revelation and human reason.

Two New Testament passages served Dwight's immediate needs. His starting point was a simple but important translation of St. Paul's use of the term *agape* in 1 Corinthians 13.[6] Ignoring the finer points of exegesis, such as the examination of literary context or extended word study, Dwight set out his major premise: "That agape signifies the kind of love, which in English is called Benevolence, will not, I presume, be questioned."[7] Rejecting the traditional translations of *agape* as love or charity, his paraphrase of St. Paul's classic hymn to love might have been rendered: "Three things will last forever: faith, hope, and benevolence. But the greatest of these is benevolence." Benevolence, however, described more than the human experience of the divine *agape*. It also described divinity itself. Here Dwight's proof text became 1 John 4:8, "God is love." Again, Dwight refused to break the cadence of his preaching with exegetical detours. He acknowledged and quickly abandoned the common interpretations of this text (e.g., "God is loving" or "God is benevolently inclined") with the comment, "It is not asserted [in this text], that God is benevolent, but that he is Benevolence."[8]

According to Dwight, reason also taught this doctrine, and here his argument took a different tack. Whereas scripture positively asserted that God was benevolent, reason could merely conclude that God was not malevolent.[9] This could be inferred, for instance, from a consideration of the radicality of divine independence. Because God was dependent on no one and no thing, and because the Godhead was entirely satisfied in itself, Dwight concluded that God would never have recourse to malevolence, nor could God personify malevolence in any manner.[10] Hatred or malevolence in the divine mind, he reasoned, assumed that God needed or wanted something that God could not attain, and this assumption was specious. Dwight grounded a second argument from reason on his beliefs about the makeup of humanity. Human beings, he observed, were so formed that genuine reverence and obedience were elicited in response to love, not hate, and in response to benevolence, not malevolence.[11] Thus, if the Creator were malevolent, creatures would never— indeed, they could never—love and obey the Creator. So, working from his understanding of the moral structure of humanity, Dwight concluded that God was not malevolent.

Satisfied that he had demonstrated that God's chief moral attribute was benevolence, Dwight preached his remaining sermons on the doctrine of God accordingly. In this regard, he subordinated the moral attributes traditionally ascribed to God (justice, truth, mercy, and wisdom) to benevolence. In each of Sermons 10 through 13 Dwight argued that the attribute in question could be proved on the basis of divine benevolence: "As God is benevolent, it is impossible that he should not be just"; "the Truth of God . . . is completely evident from his Benevolence"; "reason naturally leads us to conclude, that God is merciful, because . . . he is Benevolent"; "the Wisdom of God is formed, therefore, of his Omniscience and Benevolence, united in planning and accomplishing all real good."[12]

By subordinating the full range of God's moral attributes to his benevolence, Dwight had taken a small but critically important step away from the theological/ethical system set out by Jonathan Edwards upon which, in other respects, he had depended.[13] In his *Dissertation Concerning the End for Which God Created the World,* Edwards had argued similarly, claiming that the attributes of God, though diverse, were unified. Although God's end in creating the world reflected all the divine perfections, Edwards was careful to note that

> the design of the Spirit of God don't seem to be to represent God's ultimate end as manifold, but as one. For though it be signified by various names, yet they appear not to be names of different things, but various names involving each other in their meaning; either different names of the same thing, or names of several parts of one whole; or of the same whole viewed in various lights, or its different respects or relations. For it appears that all that is ever spoken of in the Scripture as an ultimate end of God's works, is included in that one phrase, "the glory of God."[14]

Dwight agreed with the central idea of Edwards's assertion. He also claimed that when God created the universe, he created it that he might glorify himself. But Edwards immediately followed this affirmation with a peroration on the internal fullness of God's glory and its emanation to the creation at large. In other words, he crafted what might be called a hymn to God; God was its subject, focus, and end. Dwight, on the other hand, followed his affirmation of God's self-glorification with an altogether different hymn—a hymn to benevolence:

> Benevolence is the sum of his [God's] moral character, and the peculiar and distinguishing glory of his nature. This is that which he himself esteems his glory; that for which he chiefly values himself; that which is the prime object of his own complacency. This perfection then, he intended to especially manifest to his Intelligent Creation. . . . [B]enevolence is the moving principle of the divine Mind, whence all its operations spring, and to which they are all conformed.[15]

Edwards's God forever gloried in unified divine fullness, the sum of all of God's equally infinite attributes. Dwight's God raised one peculiar and distinguishing attribute—benevolence—above others. By it, God measured divine glory; for it, God chiefly valued the Godhead; in it, God found a special object of complacency.

Dwight's doctrine of God did more than raise the value of benevolence above the other moral attributes of God. On a number of occasions, Dwight gave divine benevolence a purpose, direction, and focus that would have played only a secondary role in Edwards's understanding of God. Speaking of the glory of God, Dwight wrote: "When God created the universe, it is most evident that he could have no possible view in this great work but to glorify himself in doing good to the creatures which he made."[16] In another place, Dwight referred to the glory of God as "declarative"; it was "manifested in his conduct" toward his creation.[17] Whereas Edwards had reveled in the activity of benevolence within the divine being and independent of any action toward humanity, Dwight gloried in the function of that benevolence on behalf of humanity.[18] Benevolence not only became God's chief attribute; it also became the chief means by which the Godhead communicated good to the creation.

Having argued that benevolence was the chief attribute and wellspring of God's character, Dwight began his consideration of practical social ethics. As he moved from a consideration of God's moral constitution to humanity's moral makeup, Dwight did not shift his gaze away from the attribute of benevolence. Rather, he used the notion of benevolence as a moral bridge or pathway from God to humanity. This critical link between divine benevolence and human benevolence had a special locus in the incarnation. Jesus Christ, the Word made flesh, the divine human,was himself the best illustration of genuine virtue and morality. And Christ, above all human beings, was perfectly benevolent. Here, Dwight faced the theological problem that had riveted the attention of both Edwards and the New Divinity theologians—self-love.

Edwards and his followers had argued that God's benevolence was self-serving; in this sense of the term, it was interested. God, unlike mortal creatures, could perfectly love the divine self in all its perfections, and do so with absolute and perfect righteousness. Indeed, God did not act except from the principle of holy self-interest. As Dwight dealt with this claim, and shifted his focus to the exemplary character of Jesus, he crafted an important qualification to the Edwardsean notion of self-love. Like God the Father, the incarnate Son was perfect in all respects. The Son's perfections, like those of the Father, were chiefly visible in the notion of benevolence. Unlike the Father's benevolence, however, the incarnate Son's benevolence was *disinterested*. Indeed, *disinterested* benevolence was "the crown, the glory, the finishing" of Christ's character.[19] Because the Christian was to emulate Christ, disinterested benevolence became the primary chief virtue of Dwight's ethical system.

But how could one measure or evaluate disinterestedness? How should one deal with the question of genuine virtue?

Eighteenth-century moral philosophy, as Dwight well knew, was fraught with endless debates about subtle definitions of benevolence and virtue. Dwight was not a philosopher, nor was he a particularly original thinker. When he discussed the character of virtue, he merely alluded to larger rubrics other thinkers had established and did little constructive work to forward a particular school of thought. We have observed this habit in Dwight in his battles with skeptical, "infidel" philosophers, and it appears again here in his ethics. The reader of these sermons can discern shadows of Edwards, for instance, but his image is never clearly seen. Whereas Edwards had systematically worked through the relations between the divine perfections, virtue, human morality, and agency, Dwight cobbles together affirmations and corollaries about these problems. His "System of Duties" lacks any systematic treatment of a series of connected moral problems. Instead we find claims that are best described as occasional and that were required, one must suppose, by the homiletic setting in which Dwight crafted his sermonic treatments of these thorny problems. Although Dwight did rely heavily on the major accents of Edwards and other great lights of the New England tradition, he seems in these sermons to be searching for a tangible, simple idiom with which he could illustrate virtue.

This search led him to a series of definitions and corollaries that began with the affirmation: "Virtue, the supreme excellence and glory of Intelligent beings, is merely the love of doing good." Hence, virtue's value was based on its utility within the human community—its tendency to produce good. But this utility itself had a particular effect: "All the worth of Virtue, in my own view, lies in this: that it is the original, or voluntary, and universal source of happiness." Happiness thus became Dwight's measure of human virtue. Having found in happiness his means of measurement, Dwight went on to raise the value of happiness itself: "The only ultimate good is happiness"; there is "nothing valuable but happiness"; "to be blessed is to receive happiness."[20]

Dwight's simplification of the Christian moral life does not end with the move from disinterestedness to happiness. The central spiritual problem to which Christian theologians had to attend was the manner in which the heart became inclined to virtue or, in Dwight's rendition, to genuine happiness. Here his thinking, if not precisely circular, is at least circuitous. In response to the need to describe the theological character and source of happiness, he returns to love or benevolence. The love that is required in the great commandments is "the very same Benevolence formerly described as one of the attendants of regeneration,"[21] and this benevolence "is more productive of happiness than any other."[22]

This train of reasoning, which Dwight began by elevating God's benevolence and ended by elevating humanity's happiness, represents a critical development in the New England Theology. By crafting this theological shortcut from God's attributes to the happiness of created beings, Dwight cut a detour around several knotty theological dilemmas that had dogged the Edwardseans' heels—e.g., the problems of the nature and character of genuine virtue, the problem of self-love, and the problem of determining the presence of true grace. In so doing, Dwight played an important role in the transition that Joseph Haroutunian sought to describe in his *Piety Versus Moralism: The Passing of New England Theology*. Haroutunian believed that the radical New Divinity theologians shifted their attention and commitment from Edwardsean theocentric piety to anthropocentric moralism. Though he played little or no role in Haroutunian's work, Dwight's shortcut had a profound impact on the popular perception of Edwardseanism. Far more popular and widely read than his New Divinity contemporaries, and promulgating a version of New England moralism that was more comprehensive and practical than that of the New Divinity thinkers, Dwight helped to shape the more liberal Edwardsean theological milieu from which Lyman Beecher and Nathaniel William Taylor worked. Haroutunian was looking for someone to blame for what he perceived to be the decline of Edwards's theocentrism, and he believed he had correctly identified the culprits in the New Divinity architects, Samuel Hopkins, Nathaniel Emmons, and Joseph Bellamy. Ironically, he failed to tar Dwight with the same brush he had so aggressively applied to the New Divinity radicals.[23]

Having followed Dwight's path from the attributes of the Creator to the happiness of the creature, and his rapid move from Edwardsean theocentrism to Haroutunian's dreaded anthropocentrism, we can now turn to an examination of the specific duties to which he enjoined his fellow citizens. In his elucidation of the duties of natural religion—that is, duties incumbent on all people, Christian and non-Christian alike—Dwight adopted the scheme of the Decalogue. Given his elevation of the importance of human happiness, it is not surprising that he tried and tested each commandment at the bar of human happiness. Obedience to God's commands required reverence, sabbath-keeping, marital faithfulness, truth-telling, contentment, and the performance of family obligations. These activities pleased God precisely because they promoted human happiness. Conversely, violations of the Decalogue, as evidenced in idolatry, profaneness, murder, drunkenness, lewdness, fraud, slander, avarice, and ambition displeased God because they promoted the opposite of happiness—human misery.

The final section of Dwight's "System of Duties," in which he examined the duties unique to Christians, followed much the same pattern. Dwight began with the observation that everyone had failed to fulfill the duties of natural religion. All of human history had displayed the tragic fact of "the inability of mankind to obey the divine law."[24] Nonetheless, a gracious God had devised a means of restoration. Through "repentance toward God, and faith toward our Lord Jesus Christ," humanity could be redeemed. This redemption carried with it a wide range of spiritual benefits: adoption as sons and daughters, forgiveness, the indwelling Spirit, and—fundamental to the Christian life—a restoration of personal virtue that produced "sincere, exalted, and endearing happiness."[25] In Dwight's view, Christians were people infused with benevolence, governed by benevolence, and committed to the production of happiness in human culture. Working with these plain facts Dwight set out to elucidate the duties and responsibilities of Christian living.

The twenty-nine sermons that make up "The Duties of the Christian Religion" contain few surprises. Despite the remarkable attention to detail that Dwight displayed here, they contain nothing that could not have been predicted by an attentive reader or auditor. The argument of the sermons was invariably patterned on a simple logic: Because Christians were benevolent, and disinterestedly so, they sought the benefits attached to the ordinary means of grace. They attended the preaching of the Word, they prayed fervently, they read scripture, and they inculcated these habits in their children. Christians used the extraordinary means of grace in a similar manner. They worshipped in covenanted congregations; they chose pastors, elders, and deacons; they observed church discipline; and they used the sacraments. The effects of all these activities, of course, were identical—they produced happiness in the individual, in the church, and by extension, in the larger culture.

Two patterns provide symmetry and predictability to the sermons in the "System of Duties." First, Dwight invariably began each treatment with the infusion of benevolence and ends it with human happiness. In other words, his strictly theological ethics frames and determines what might be considered his social ethics or moral prescriptions. Second, Dwight consistently distinguished between what he took to be two classes of people—Christians and non-Christians. He devoted the "Duties of Natural Religion" to both classes and the "Duties of the Christian Religion" to Christians only. In each of these sections, Dwight silently narrowed the broad field of religious ethics in order to address a special concern. Although he appeared to be offering a system of ethics that was universally applicable, he was actually promoting a system of distinctly American ethics. As shall be more fully discussed below, the duties prescribed by Dwight were only intelligible in particular cultural settings. In the case of the "Duties of Natural Religion," where Dwight addressed political ethics, that context was the American republic, viewed through the lens of New England Federalism. Dwight's "Duties of the Christian Religion" had a similarly narrow context—the Congregational church. Though he never explicitly states it, Dwight's System of Duties was his definitive answer to two extremely important questions: Which form of government most promoted American happiness? and Which form of church polity most promoted American happiness?

The State

Dwight recorded his opinions on the political obligations of rulers and subjects in the "Duties of Natural Religion" section of his "System of Duties." Because Dwight believed that the state concerned all people, Christian and non-Christian alike, he was inclined to analyze political obligation under the more extensive and inclusive "Duties of Natural Religion." As has been noted, the biblical text that governed Dwight's consideration of natural duties was the Decalogue. Dwight was forced to choose one of the ten commandments under which to place his theory of the state. He chose the fifth, "Honor thy Father and thy Mother." Just as parents were to govern the family and nurture children in the Christian faith, so rulers, "often styled the fathers of their people,"[26] were to govern the community and inculcate virtue. Despite the Hebrew Bible's relative silence on the issue of the forms of government, the parallels between the family and the state became the justification by which Dwight could place the morality of sound government where he felt it belonged, within the requirements of the Decalogue.[27]

Having placed his political ethics in a particular context, Dwight proceeded to address himself to the problem of defining the moral foundation of government. He began this process with an explicit rejection of two political philosophies, those of Robert Filmer and John Locke. Filmer's defense of the divine right of kings was, in Dwight's view, a "monstrous absurdity." In opposing Filmer, however, Locke suggested something that was "not a whit more rational or defensible." Locke's contention that government is founded in the social compact, opined Dwight, was "groundless . . . The absurdities of this doctrine are endless," In the first place, "such a compact never existed." Moreover, if it be supposed that such a notion "may yet be advantageously employed to illustrate the nature of civil government . . . fatal consequences would follow."[28]

Dwight followed these explicit rejections with the affirmation, "the foundation of all government is undoubtedly the will of God."[29] Having admitted that no particular form of government was prescribed by God, Dwight was forced to devise some means of determining the relative merits of the multitude of forms of government known in the eighteenth and nineteenth centuries. Once again, he turned to the concept of happiness for a solution:

> As God willed the existence of government for the happiness of mankind, it is unanswerably certain that every government is agreeable to his will just so far as it promotes that happiness. . . . [T]hat government which promotes it most is most agreeable to his will . . . [T]hat government that opposes human happiness is equally opposed to his will. From these undeniable principles both rulers and subjects may easily learn most of their own duty.[30]

Although God allowed people the freedom to chose from a variety of political forms, it was God's will that communities adopt some type of political structure. The moral value of such governments was measured by their capacity to produce human happiness. Again, Dwight faced a dilemma: how could one measure this quality in a given political structure? With this problem in mind, Dwight made a predictable Federalist move. Because he believed that the state ought to be led from the top down, not from the bottom up, he shifted his gaze to civic leaders. The good ruler thus became the focus of his critical comments on the moral character of the state.

Dwight's treatment of the good ruler in *Theology* began with a rather pedestrian list of admirable qualities. Good rulers were to lead by personal example; they were to be sincere, just, benevolent, industrious, law-abiding, and careful in the choice of subordinates. To this rather ordinary list of characteristics, Dwight added one other: "A Ruler ought to be a man of piety."[31] Here is something of a sleight-of-hand. Although the obligations of political leadership were best treated under the duties common to all people, non-Christians and Christians alike, Dwight equivocated at this point. In Dwight's mind, the ruler needed "in an eminent degree, the blessing of God to enable him to perform [his duties] aright." This was true because the ruler "has a greater means of doing good put into his hands and needs, in a peculiar degree, the divine assistance to enable him to use them." Moreover, God "usually blesses a nation for the sake of pious rulers, whereas an impious one cannot fail to become a curse."[32] In Dwight's view, of course, nations were best ruled by Christians.

In the "Duty of Rulers" sermon in *Theology*, the requirement that rulers be Christians is present but stark and rather abbreviated. Fortunately, two of Dwight's occasional sermons give this stipulation fuller treatment. In one of these, *A Discourse Occasioned by the Death of His Excellency Jonathan Trumbull, Esquire, Governor of the State of Connecticut,* Dwight took advantage of an opportunity to laud a Christian statesman. The late Trumbull, said Dwight, was a perfect exemplar. Trumbull devoted himself neither to fancy (the province of artists), nor to speculation (the province of philosophers), but to action, the province of heroes and statesmen.[33] The spring of this action was seen particularly in Trumbull's "orthodox," "Reformed," and "Apostolic" piety. Or, to speak historically, "This great and good man was peculiarly attached to the religious system of our ancestors."[34] That Dwight would have so lauded a member of Connecticut's Standing Order is, of course, not surprising.

Dwight preached another eulogy that throws additional light on his prescription that America be ruled by Christians. Needless to say, the subject of Dwight's *A Discourse, Delivered at New Haven, February 22, 1800, on the Character of George Washington* was not a member of Connecticut's Standing Order. Dwight knew this only too well, but it did not daunt him. As was his habit, Dwight began his eulogy historically, with a discourse on great leaders of the past. These people, he argued, fell into two categories: those whose leadership had been supernaturally assisted (here Dwight would only mention biblical characters like Moses and Paul) and those who had become great by "means merely natural." Although Washington fell into this latter category, his success, Dwight argued, stemmed from his virtuous character.[35] But was that character a product of the infusion of divine benevolence? In short, was the man Dwight revered as the father of the American republic a Christian by Dwight's own standards?[36]

Dwight admitted the presence of the problem: "With respect to [Washington's] religious character, there have been differing opinions." Though Dwight reminded his audience that only the divine tribunal could ultimately decide such questions with accuracy, he quickly took advantage of a "providential" opportunity to render a judgment of charity in the case of America's archetypal political ruler:

> For my own part, I have considered [Washington's] numerous uniform and public and most solemn decisions, his veneration for religion, his exemplary and edifying attention to public worship, and his constancy in secret devotion, as proofs, sufficient to satisfy every person willing to be satisfied, that if he was not a Christian, he was more like one than any man of the same description, whose life has been hitherto recorded.[37]

Apparently, it did not matter that Washington's faith was so unlike Trumbull's. Dwight knew he could not claim that Washington was "attached to the religious system of our ancestors" or that his faith was orthodox, Reformed, or apostolic. Therefore, to preserve his prescription that rulers be Christians, Dwight broadened his definition of piety. Secret prayer, public worship, and attention to duty, as opposed to affirmations of the established church, trinitarianism, or moderate Calvinism became Dwight's "distinguishing marks" of conversion. One can only wonder whether it was Washingtons's religious convictions, ambiguous as they may have been, or his presence among the

Federalist pantheon of worthies, that energized Dwight's unusual charity.[38] Thomas Jefferson would never receive such leniency from Dwight nor would any of Dwight's evangelical Baptist brethren who happened to claim allegiance to the Republican party. Here, at least, Federalist political ideology clearly shaped Dwight's vision of the godly republic.

Dwight treated the political obligations of subjects next. Again, the images on which he drew and the political ethos that formed the context of his remarks were designed to resonate with the experience of his auditors. Despite the fact that these remarks fell within the "Duties of Natural Religion" section of his ethical system, Dwight's real goal was to prescribe the political obligations of godly New Englanders. Under this head the reader might expect Dwight to have outlined a plethora of political duties incumbent on virtuous citizens benevolently inclined. But Dwight took another tack altogether. Instead of specifying the duties unique to political subjects, Dwight used this occasion to heighten the importance of political rulers. Indeed, with one notable exception (where Dwight affirmed that "subjects are bound to furnish all necessary supplies for the exigencies of government") the focus of every subject's obligation was the ruler.[39]

The first great duty of subjects became "to elect always, as far as may be, rulers possessing the several characteristics mentioned in the preceding discourse."[40] Though he avoided use of the specific term "democracy" in order to distance himself from Republican rhetoric, Dwight affirmed the basic precept of a republican democracy. Virtuous citizens were obligated to elect virtuous leaders. If they fulfilled this duty, they would be blessed by God. If not, their nation, like Israel under the wicked Ahab, would slide "down the steep slope of declension, and [be] plunged into the gulf at the bottom."[41] This allusion to the Hebrew Bible having served its pietistic purpose, Dwight immediately returned to his controlling idiom, the ruler-oriented nature of political obligation. "Subjects are bound," he wrote, faithfully to obey, honor, defend, and pray for their rulers.[42] By making duty to rulers the primary focus of individual political obligation (as opposed to any number of other practical and necessary activities of political subjects) Dwight revealed one of his central beliefs about the fundamental characterer of the Republic: American virtue had a center of gravity. It lay in the nation's rulers and not in its subjects.[43]

At the outset of *Theology's* two sermons on political obligation, Dwight made the following claim: "I never preached what is commonly called a political sermon on the Sabbath in my life . . . although to preach such sermons is unquestionably the right, and in certain cases the duty, of every minister of the gospel."[44] At first blush, these sermons substantiate that claim. They contain no mention of party, platform, or candidate. Nonetheless, "Duties of Rulers" and "Duties of Subjects" represent more than a record of Dwight's abstract political theory; they are evidence of Dwight's attachment to a particular party. Evidence for this claim is observed in the major image Dwight employed to describe the American ruler. First and foremost, the ruler was a father figure. Like the eighteenth-century New England patriarch, the political leader ruled his family by virtue of experience and wisdom. What Dwight wisely left unsaid, though it was the obvious implication of his remarks, was that in some sense political subjects played the role of children in this analogy. Like children bereft of a superintending father, political subjects would perish without the constant care of their leaders.

This view of the ruler-father presents a striking parallel to the image of leadership held by many New England Federalists and described by David H. Fischer. One of the rival factions, Fischer's "Young Federalists," became convinced that their political survival depended on their adoption of the political techniques successfully employed by the Jeffersonians. Faced with extinction, these progressives would settle for participation in an America in which a speaking multitude was led by an organized and politically active elite. But "Federalists of the Old School," of whom Dwight was certainly one, rejected this strategy entirely. Though it appeared antiquated to others, they would seek to restore the America of their ancestors, the America in which a silent, undeserving multitude was controlled by the only men capable of leadership, a speaking elite. In sum, the Revolution seems to have done little to change Dwight's way of thinking about New England's rulers. This emphasis on the fifth commandment and his particular use of it would have been just as appropriate in 1730.

The Church

Dwight's *Travels in New England and New York* represents an early example of a literary genre that became quite popular in nineteenth-century America. Despite its legitimacy as a New England travelogue, however, *Travels* was composed and published with several purposes in mind. One "was the injustice done to these countries by European travelers. The United States have been regarded by this class of men as fair game to be hunted down at pleasure." Given New England's greatness, Dwight believed that "a wise man, and especially a good man, will, if I am not deceived, be interested to learn the state of these countries."[45] This main purpose aside, the four-volume production accurately mirrors other fixations of its author. Just as Dwight had become entangled in a complex web of diverse professional endeavors—as educator, author, theologian, poet, and political observer—so too, *Travels* divides its attentions. On one page the reader encounters statistics; on another, a discourse on morality; on another, a detailed prose picture of a peaceful pastoral setting; on yet another, harsh polemics. Considered as a whole, *Travels in New England and New York* did have a purpose that unified its internal diversity—it was a complex apologetic apparatus. In *Travels* Dwight was able to offer his most detailed defense of his program for American culture. Deftly employing his descriptive skills and his knack for simplification, Dwight used his tours of New England as evidence of his contention that "fidelity" inevitably played itself out in culture at large.

Nowhere is this claim better illustrated than in the *Travels's* description of New England's established church. Dwight's Preface to the work plainly signals this:

> In New Hampshire, Massachusetts, and Connecticut, the public worship of God has always been established by law, and for a long time without the communication of special privileges to any class of Christians. Here only in the history of man has this experiment been made. The first practical answer, therefore, to the great question, whether such a state of things is consistent with the public peace, good order and safety, has been given in these states. . . . Here the experiment has been extensively made, and, to say the least, has gone far toward proving that Christians of different classes can live together harmoniously under a government which confers on them equal privileges.[46]

This citation serves as a window into Dwight's understanding of the cosmic significance of New England's ecclesiastical structure. For Dwight, New England's greatness stemmed from its willingness to face humanity's greatest challenge—the establishment of the Kingdom of God on earth. This claim was itself historical. One can hardly fail to perceive the importance of the Puritan "errand into the wilderness" here. But to readers more sensitive to the social ethos of Dwight's own day, the claim must have been astonishing in the extreme.

Dwight's assertion that the "public worship of God has always been established by law" had, to most Americans of Dwight's generation, become a political anachronism. Although the "New England Way" had been erected on the basis of such requirements, this system had all but dissolved by 1800, the year of Jefferson's election to the presidency. In Connecticut, one of established Congregationalism's last strongholds, it was politically dead by 1818, a full three years prior to the publication of *Travels*. Dwight's use of statistics, as in the case of the denominational breakdowns he used in the latter sections of *Travels*, may have given some readers the impression that nineteenth-century New Englanders happily complied with laws requiring them to attend worship. But with this appeal to the regular worship of Baptists, Episcopalians, Catholics, or Jews, Dwight merely begged the larger question. The fact of the matter was that, in Dwight's lifetime, a growing percentage of New Englanders did not attend worship because a growing number of states had repealed the laws requiring such behavior.

Once again, we observe Dwight's curious use of the past. Having paid homage to the Puritans who attempted to solve the "great question" of an era long past, he makes a claim even grander than the experiment he lauds. Ignoring America's growing fixation with Jeffersonian democracy and its growth toward the Jacksonian ethos, Dwight claimed that the Puritan way still prevailed in the United States. Moreover, the political rhetoric Dwight employed here was striking. Truly equal privileges for Christians was not the language of Federalism. Indeed, the demand for equal privileges had become the rhetorical battle cry under which Dwight's enemies had rallied. It was the Republicans, and most especially the faithful Christian worshipers in their midst—Baptists and Episcopalians—who fought hardest for the overthrow of the Federalist Standing Order.[47] The Pope of Federalism knew that the hegemony of the Standing Order was threatened. He was ready to employ any means, even the adoption of Republican rhetoric, in order to bolster the faltering establishment. Just as Washington's religion had, in Dwight's hands, become a "historical" justification for his belief that Christians ought to rule the Republic, here he adopts the Republican demand for equal privileges to defend the established church. In both cases, it appears that pragmatic political considerations, and not the concerns of political theory or ecclesiology, motivated Dwight. In the end, Godly Federalism had far more to do with the contemporary struggles of Federalism than with the ancient prescriptions of godliness.

Several interpretations of this apparent inconsistency in the *Travels*—and in its author—are suggested. It might be argued that this equivocation is evidence of Dwight's cunning and duplicity. Interpreters who have adopted negative assessments of Dwight (such as Vernon Parrington and Richard Hofstadter) may argue that Dwight's "Preface" is nothing but deceptive packaging, a sweetener added to offset the bitterness of the Federalism contained elsewhere in *Travels*. Although this view is not unreasonable, it fails to appreciate the complexity of the apologetic task that Dwight faced in promulgating his notion of a Christian republic. Unlike the other aspects of Dwight's program, the construction of a reasonable and viable defense of the established church was a nearly impossible task. Whereas Dwight's opponents may have dissented from the particularities of his prescriptions for individual morality or for Christian leadership, they would surely have concurred that these sociopolitical institutions did merit some philosophical or theological justification. This was not the case with the established church. Although Republicans of any religious persuasion agreed that freedom of religion was a crucial element of American democracy, they rejected entirely the notion that the any single group should receive special privileges.[48] No single religious group could become normative; for them, the very notion of an established church or churches was indefensible.

Dwight acknowledged this indefensibility. Time and again, given the opportunity to formulate a well-reasoned, detailed defense of the established church, he shunned the canons of argumentation and focused instead on his subtly shaded interpretation of the American past. In *Travels,* instead of defending the established church he waxed eloquent on the "grand experiment" of humanity and on the American Puritans who had the courage to attempt that experiment. Even in his "Duties of the Christian Religion," the best place to defend the established church, Dwight merely assumed its presence. In effect, Dwight made the established church dependent upon his other moral prescriptions for America. In his mind, this strategy was entirely reasonable. If New England's populace would honor the founders, if they would become disinterestedly benevolent, if they would elect Christian magistrates, then America would replicate the Kingdom of God. In that grand day, all her citizens, even dissenters, would readily acknowledge the virtues of having an established church. Relying once again on his peculiar penchant for prescriptive millennial history, Dwight gambled the future of the established church on America's willingness to revitalize itself on the basis of its past.

* * *

To what extent did New England's Moral Legislator establish his vision for the nation in concrete political and ecclesial realities? Some argue that Dwight's blueprint for American culture survived him. Despite the fact that Dwight's political party, the Federalists, and his ecclesial party, the established Congregational church, were overthrown just months after his death, these interpreters argue that his broad cultural plan survived him in the hearts and minds of his closest disciples. Once again, Dwight's New Haven protégés Lyman Beecher and Nathaniel William Taylor provide evidence for this interpretation.

In his *Autobiography* Beecher records his reactions to the great fall of the Standing Order. His initial response was extremely negative. On the morning after the defeat of the Connecticut establishment, Beecher fell into a deep depression. When asked what troubled him, he replied "The Church of God." Of that fateful day he would say, "It was as dark a day as ever I saw. The odium thrown upon the ministry was inconceivable. The injury done to the cause of Christ, as we then supposed, was irreparable."[49] For Beecher (and for Dwight, had he lived to see it), disestablishment was the worst thing ever to befall American Christianity.

Yet the indefatigable Beecher, prone as he was to promoting his causes with vigor and optimism, even when the facts ran counter to his judgments, soon changed his mind about the terrible demise of the Standing Order. Within a few weeks, Beecher reversed his judgment. As he put it, though he had initially "suffered what no tongue can tell," he soon discovered that disestablishment was "the best thing that ever happened to the State of Connecticut. It cut the churches loose from dependence on state support. It threw them wholly on their own resources and on God." Though it first seemed that the clergy had lost influence, Beecher soon came to realize that they had gained. "By voluntary efforts, societies, missions, and revivals, they exert a deeper influence than ever they could by queues and shoe-buckles, and cocked hats, and gold-headed canes."[50] Some believe that had Dwight lived long enough to discover what Beecher had—that disestablishment provided positive opportunities for the churches—he too would have rejoiced.[51]

Those who think that Dwight's vision of America survived the great fall of 1818 also appeal to Nathaniel William Taylor's theology to bolster their claim. Taylor, it is argued, promoted a liberalized version of New England Puritanism that served as the theological foundation of New School Presbyterian and Congregational thought. He took the central aspects of Dwight's theology, added his own more progressive views about the nature of sin and evil, and produced the religious impetus for nineteenth-century Protestant evangelism and social reform. Thus the major emphases of Dwight's system—his extempore style of preaching, his hearty opposition to radical Edwardsean theocentrism, his millennial interpretations of the American past—survived him and became central motifs of nineteenth-century American Protestantism.[52]

These positive views of Dwight have considerable merit. His preaching, theology, political reflections, and millennial thinking did influence generations of American Protestants, though in rather modest ways that elude direct cause and effect links. While it may be tempting and convenient to think of him as the critical link between the Puritans and Edwards on one hand and American evangelicalism on the other, such a view is simplistic. It entirely fails to appreciate the fact that Godly Federalism expired with Dwight.

In the closing remarks of "The Duty of Subjects," Dwight noted that people from many countries had foolishly adopted the maxim "Religion has nothing to do with Politics, or, in other words, with Government." Dwight called this thesis "groundless," and termed it sheer "folly."[53] Scripture, reason, and his own mythic re-creation of the American past led New England's Moral Legislator to the opposite conclusion: American religion and American politics were so tightly intertwined as to make them nearly indistinguishable. In Godly Federalism Dwight outlined a thoroughly integrated cultural platform, including social, political, and religious ideals, all of which he deemed essential to its success. In Dwight's mind, Godly Federalism was an all or nothing proposition. Moderate and restrained revivals of religion and the established church, the Standing Order and the political ethos of Federalism, pious subjects and godly rulers, social reform and happy, benevolent people in family, town, state, and nation—all these (to borrow a term from Edwards) "implied" one another. The establishment of one would tend to the establishment of all, and the demise of one would lead to the collapse of the social order. Here, at least, Dwight's vision was extensive and bold. He believed that his America approximated the Kingdom of God on earth.

The constituent elements of this vision of America survived him by only a few months. Connecticut Congregationalism was disestablished, religious dissenters were granted full religious freedom, moribund Federalism took its last breaths, and popular evangelicalism cut its ties to traditional Calvinism by fully embracing an Arminian theological idiom. Dwight's plan to establish a religious, political and social utopia had been repudiated. He was not a vicarious victor, triumphant through descendants who would resurrect his American vision, but a victim of American religious, political, and social change. As one trenchant critic noted, Dwight's cultural vision is significant not because it succeeded, but because it failed: "his ideas are primarily important because they were largely the doctrines America rejected as it entered the nineteenth century."[54] Dwight ought not be considered a cultural hero whose vision subtly extended itself into the future but a tragic figure whose life's goal—the establishment of his beloved Godly Federalism—was summarily dismissed. Connecticut's repudiation of the Standing Order was not a modest challenge to the promotion of Godly Federalism but an unalterable and final rejection of it.

It may appear that Dwight's political savvy increased his chances of insuring the success of Godly Federalism. Republicans, after all, worried about the political power that Pope Dwight wielded. But Dwight's power was far more circumscribed than his opponents feared. The collapse of the Standing Order did not occur suddenly nor did Godly Federalism die accidentally. Like Dwight's own vitality, the vigor of these cultural platforms waned over time. Just as the leaders of Old School Federalism had failed to pass their vision on to subsequent generations, so Dwight failed to provide American citizens sufficient reason to embrace Godly Federalism. In the final analysis, Dwight's penchant for working things to his personal advantage gnawed at the moral fabric of Godly Federalism. Ostensibly based on virtue and guided by genuine piety, Godly Federalism became entangled in political webs that thwarted the promulgation and application of Edwardsean selfless benevolence. Though he liked to think his system issued from the moral high ground, it was forged in the give and take of Connecticut politics. However clever Dwight may have been in protecting his personal interests, his gifts, his cultural vision, and perhaps even his virtue were insufficient to insure the success of an entire program of cultural renovation.

Ironically, Dwight seemed to be unaware of the ways in which nineteenth-century Americans appropriated religious ideas. Although he appears to have recognized the utility of voluntarism for social and religious reform he failed to analyze fully its sociological and intellectual dynamics. He did not realize that the spirit of voluntarism fed on the freedom to choose among several options. It never occurred to him that New England Christians who stood outside the pale of the Standing Order might have an interest in his conclusions but not in the foundational doctrines on which he thought those conclusions were based. Nineteenth-century New Englanders adopted the spirit of voluntarism, many of them precisely because they had become benevolent, compassionate people. To that extent, they acknowledged the potential of Dwight's system. But their use of Godly Federalism ended there. The democratic piety that motivated their voluntarism also led them to reject Dwight's presuppositions. Seeking Dwight's goal of happiness born of benevolence, they discovered means to that end that were more friendly and efficient than those required by Godly Federalism. Their experience taught them that other programs, grounded on the Arminian view of God and of the human will, on the disestablishment of the Congregational church, on the democratic ethos of the Republican political vision, and on the active application of New Measures in revivalism, simply worked better than the opposite notions upon which Dwight had rested his system. Nineteenth-century evangelicals took from Godly Federalism only what they needed and then abandoned its remains. As these Protestant pragmatists marched into the nineteenth century, New England's Moral Legislator and his vision for the American nation faded into history.[55]

Afterword

The notion that Christians ought to expect the arrival of the Kingdom of God on earth is as old as Christianity itself. Members of the earliest Christian churches awaited Jesus' return and from that day to this a dazzling variety of believers in countless cultural settings have held out hope that one day God would transform their worlds. Restrained only by a few richly multivalent biblical passages and the limits of their own imaginations, Christians in every generation have defied the claim that the significance of faith lies only beyond the grave in life eternal. Catholic, Orthodox, and Protestant Christians have all developed traditions that stress present realities. Codes of individual behavior, political structures, economic doctrines, church polities, pieties, eschatological views, all these are framed by the belief that God is moving creation toward a grand denouement that will forever change the world.

The landscape of American Christianity, and especially of American Protestantism, has been a particularly fertile field for these ideas. New England Puritans, Middle Colonies Quakers, African slaves, Shakers, western revivalists, benevolent women, social gospellers, Transcendentalists, Modernists, Fundamentalists, and a host of ethnic churches have all participated, albeit differently, in this mode of Christian belief. Surveying this rich tapestry of faith, one is tempted to seek a golden thread, a single view of the Kingdom of God that runs through the whole. Yet none exists. Just as there is no single way of being Christian in America, so there is no single American vision of the coming reign of God.

Despite this diversity one thing does characterize these visions. Each one is tightly controlled by the culture in which it was born. American visions of the Kingdom of God reflect notions that Christians of other times and cultures would hardly recognize. Freedom and egalitarianism, justice and liberty, the very emblems of American self-understanding, are everywhere present in Kingdom visions that originate in the United States. Even the cataclysmic events that usher in the glorious day reveal provincial origins. The New Jerusalem is modeled on a great American city; the Antichrist bears a striking resemblance to our most feared enemies. Could it be otherwise? Probably not. Christian faith promises perfect solutions to the problems of life, and faithful Christians have nothing but their own images of perfection to project onto the canvas of the future.

Although Timothy Dwight was not the first to craft a distinctly American image of the Kingdom of God, he was one of the nation's most important cultural visionaries. A curious confluence of unique ideas and events allowed Dwight to emerge as the architect of Godly Federalism.

His Puritan forebears provided him with many of the central ideas necessary to construct his ideal America but his vision extended well beyond their horizons. They had placed the church, pure and unalloyed, at the center of their vision. Theirs was largely an ecclesial enterprise controlled by visible saints. Although Dwight placed great value on the church, he refused to allow the boundaries of the church to limit the shape of the Kingdom. In Godly Federalism he replaced the Puritan church with the American nation. Pure and unalloyed, it became the center of his vision. His was a fully cultural enterprise whose governance depended on visibly virtuous citizens.

He passed his life in a revolutionary era during which the Anglo-American world was turned upside down. Great events shaped him: the French and Indian War, the Declaration of Independence, the Revolution, the Constitution, the "didactic enlightenment," and the revolution in France. He celebrated some of these events as tokens of providence and feared others as harbingers of hell. He journeyed in the company of great figures who changed his thinking. Edwards and Washington inspired hope; Jefferson and Hume roused dread. Yet all of them shaped his vision.

Without his natural gifts Godly Federalism would never have been created. His keen imagination, sturdy intelligence, powerful voice, poetic sensibilities, theological understanding, and determination allowed him to create Godly Federalism. Even his limitations helped. His interpersonal formality inclined him toward solitary leadership and his physical and cultural myopia forced him to create new, unseen worlds. All these influences shaped Dwight and helped him lay the foundations of American exceptionalism and manifest destiny.

What is Timothy Dwight's legacy to America? Where can it be found? When Gardiner Spring eulogized Dwight he uttered prophetic words: "Like some clear planet," he said, the Light of Yale "left behind its lucid track, and darted to eternity." Godly Federalism did not have a lasting impact on American culture, but Dwight did. Though his vision ultimately failed, after he passed from the scene other American prophets with markedly different visions followed his luminous track: William Miller and Joseph Smith, Josiah Strong and William Jennings Bryan, Dorothy Day and Martin Luther King, Jr., even Jim Jones and David Koresh. These believers and their visions of the Kingdom of God in America bear the legacy of Timothy Dwight.

NOTES

Introduction: A Problem of Lights and Shades

1. S. G. Goodrich, *Recollections of a Lifetime: Men and Things I Have Seen, in a Series of Letters to a Friend, Historical, Biographical, Anecdotical, and Descriptive*, 2 vols. (New York and Auburn: Miller, Orton, and Mulligan, 1857), 1:338–39, 347–48, 352. There are a number of fascinating similarities between Dwight and Goodrich. Both were staunch Federalists; both published works in the form of series of letters (Goodrich in *Recollections* and Dwight in *Travels in New England and New York*); both labored under the burden of terrible eyesight; and both were forced to rely on the assistance of amanuenses. For biographical details on Goodrich, see *Dictionary of American Biography*, Allen Johnson and Dumas Malone, 22 vols. (New York: Charles Scribner's Sons, 1928–1958), 7:402–3.

2. Timothy Dwight, *America: or a Poem on the Settlement of the British Colonies; Addressed to the Friends of Freedom and their Country* (New Haven: Thomas and Samuel Green, 1780); Dwight, *The Conquest of Canaan: A Poem in Eleven Books* (Hartford: Elisha Babcock, 1785); [Timothy Dwight], *The Triumph of Infidelity* (n.p., 1788); Dwight, *Greenfield Hill: A Poem in Seven Parts* (New York: Child and Swaine, 1794). *The Triumph* was published anonymously, but most scholars agree that Dwight was the author. See Lewis Leary, "The Author of *The Triumph of Infidelity*," *New England Quarterly* 20 (1947):377–85. For an analysis of the textual problems related to the poem, see Jack Stillinger, "Dwight's *Triumph of Infidelity*: Text and Interpretation," *Studies in Bibliography: Papers of the Bibliography Society of the University of Virginia* 15 (1962):259–66. William J. McTaggart and William K. Bottoroff have collected and reprinted Dwight's major poems in *The Major Poems of Timothy Dwight (1752–1817), with a Dissertation on the History, Eloquence, and Poetry of the Bible* (Gainesville, Fla.: Scholars' Facsimiles and Reprints, 1969).

3. Timothy Dwight, *Theology, Explained and Defended, in A Series of Sermons*, 4 vols. (New Haven: S. Converse, 1825). Hereafter, it will be cited as *Theology. Sermons by Timothy Dwight, D.D., LL.D., Late President of Yale College, in Two Volumes*, 2 vols. (New Haven: Hezekiah Howe and Durrie and Peck, 1828). Hereafter, it will be cited as *Sermons. Theology* went through twelve editions in the United States, the last being a Harper and Brothers edition published in 1860. The work was also reprinted in London in 1819 and in Glasgow in 1831.

4. Timothy Dwight, "Farmer Johnson's Political Catechism," *Mercury and New-England Palladium* 17 (31 March 1801 to 8 May 1801); [Timothy Dwight], *Remarks on the Review of Inchiquin's Letters, Published in the Quarterly Review; Addressed to the Right Honourable George Canning, Esquire* (Boston: Samuel T. Armstrong, 1815); Theodore Dwight, Jr., ed., *President Dwight's Decisions of Questions Discussed by the Senior Class in Yale College, in 1813 and 1814* (New York: Jonathan Leavitt, 1833). Hereafter, it will be cited as *Decisions. Remarks on the Review of Inchiquin's Letters* was published under the name "An Inhabitant of New England," but Abe C. Ravitz and others have argued conclusively that Dwight was the author. See the "Foreword" to Abe C. Ravitz, ed., *Remarks on the Review of Inchiquin's Letters by Timothy Dwight*, reprint ed. (New York: Garrett Press, 1970), pp. v–xx.

5. Timothy Dwight, *Travels in New England and New York*, 4 vols. (New Haven: S. Converse, 1821–22). References will be to the modern critical edition, Barbara M. Solomon, ed., *Travels in New England and New York, by Timothy Dwight*, 4 vols.

(Cambridge: The Belknap Press of Harvard University Press, 1969). Hereafter, it will be cited as *Travels*.

6. Nathaniel W. Taylor to William B. Sprague, 20 February 1844, in William B. Sprague, *Annals of the American Pulpit*, 9 vols. (New York: R. Carter and Brothers, 1857–1869), 2:161.

7. Franklin B. Dexter, ed., *The Literary Diary of Ezra Stiles, D.D., LL.D.*, 3 vols. (New York: Charles Scribner's Sons, 1901), 1:364, 274.

8. Ogden quoted in John Wood, *The History of the Administration of John Adams, Esquire, Late President of the United States* (New York, 1802), pp. 373–74.

9. John C. Ogden, *An Appeal to the Candid, upon the Present State of Religion and Politics in Connecticut* (New Haven: n.p., 1798), p. 14.

10. The most detailed and authoritative sources of information on Dwight are housed in the Dwight Family Papers in the Sterling Library at Yale University. Hereafter this collection will be cited as *DFP*. Two of the most important manuscripts in this collection are entitled "Biographical Hints." Hereafter these will be cited as *Hints*. Sympathetic eulogies delivered on the occasion of Dwight's death also contain a good deal of important biographical information. For further details, see the Bibliographic Essay.

11. [Benjamin Dwight], "A Memoir of the Life of the Author," *Theology*, 1:52.

12. Barbara M. Cross, ed., *The Autobiography of Lyman Beecher*, 2 vols. (Cambridge: Harvard University Press, 1961), 1:242. Hereafter, it will be cited as Beecher, *Autobiography*. Taylor to Sprague, 20 February 1844, in Sprague, 2:161.

13. Vernon Louis Parrington, *Main Currents in American Thought*, 2 vols. (New York: Harcourt, Brace, 1927), 1:358–59; Clinton Rossiter, *Conservatism in America* (New York: Alfred A. Knopf, 1955), p. 127; Richard Hofstadter, *The Paranoid Style in American Politics, and Other Essays* (New York: Alfred Knopf, 1965), pp. 13ff.; Charles Cuningham, *Timothy Dwight, 1752–1817, A Biography* (New York: Macmillan, 1942), pp. 348–50; Stephen Berk, *Calvinism Versus Democracy: Timothy Dwight and the Origins of American Evangelical Orthodoxy* (Hamden, Connecticut: Archon Books, 1974), p. 194.

14. *Hints*, *DFP*. See also Sprague, *Annals*, 2:153–54. There is no medical evidence to suggest that smallpox innoculations result in visual difficulties. The author of *Hints*, who was conflating events, was led to an erroneous conclusion.

15. See, for instance, Dwight to Aaron Burr, Jr., 10 March 1772, American Antiquarian Society, *Proceedings* 29 (1919):55; Dwight to Benjamin Silliman, 7 May, 1805, George P. Fisher, *Life of Benjamin Silliman, M.D., LL.D.*, 2 vols. (Philadelphia: Porter and Coates, 1866), 1:199; Dwight to Morse, 17 March 1809, Morse Family Papers, the Sterling Library of Yale University (hereafter this collection will be cited as *MFP*); and Dwight's Preface to *Travels*, 1:2. Two anonymous eulogia published soon after Dwight's death provide additional information about the eyesight problem. The anonymous writer of "Biographical Memoir of the Rev. Timothy Dwight, S.T.D., LL.D.," *Port Folio* 4 (1817) claims that "for the greater part of [Dwight's] life, he was able neither to read nor write" (p. 364). The anonymous writer of "Biographical Notice of the Rev. Timothy Dwight, S.T.D., L.L.D., Late President and Professor of Divinity of Yale College," *Analectic Magazine* IX (1817), claims that soon after he became president of Yale, Dwight wanted to begin "critical review of the Greek poets" but "the weakness of his eyes obliged him to desist from the undertaking" (p. 278). The same author believes that Dwight's eyesight had an interesting effect on his social habits: "From the weakness of his eyes, already mentioned, and his consequent inability to employ himself much in reading, except by the assistance of others—he was led to devote more of his time to the society of friends, than perhaps in other circumstances he would have judged expedient" (p. 280).

16. [Benjamin Dwight], "A Memoir of the Life of the Author," *Theology*, 1:26. The expression *gutta serena* suggests the total loss of sight because of permanent damage to the optic nerve.

17. See Dwight, "Observations on Light," *Memoirs of the Connecticut Academy of Arts and Sciences* 1 (1816):387–91.

18. Dwight, "Observations," p. 389.

19. Noah Porter, Appendix I, "Philosophy in Great Britain and America: A Supplementary Sketch," in Friedrich Ueberweg, *History of Philosophy from Thales to the Present Time*, 2 vols. (New York: Charles Scribner's Sons, 1909), 2:449.

20. The final leaves of *Hints, DFP*, contains a list of books that may have belonged to Dwight. The author of *Hints* makes no comment on the list, which includes works by Locke, Edwards, Milton, and Taylor.

21. Dwight discusses his reliance on amanuenses as well as the manner in which they helped him record his observations during his journeys in the Preface of *Travels*, 1:2. Dwight's correspondence of the period shows evidence of his extensive use of secretaries. The body of a MS letter to Timothy Pickering, for instance, is written in a hand other than Dwight's, but both his customary closing ("I am, sir, your very obedient servant") and the signature are in Dwight's hand. Apparently, an amanuensis prepared correspondence for Dwight's signature. See Dwight to Pickering, 8 November 1805, Timothy Pickering Papers, Massachusetts Historical Society.

22. See Denison Olmstead, "Timothy Dwight as a Teacher," *Journal of American Education* 6 (1858):569–70.

23. Abel Stevens, "Review of Dwight's *Theology, Explained and Defended*," *The Methodist Quarterly Review*, 3d. ser., 7 (1847):336–37; Rufus Wilmot Griswold, *The Prose Writers of America, with a Survey of the Intellectual History, Condition, and Prospects of the Country*, 4th ed. (Philadelphia: A. Hart, 1851), pp. 81–82.

24. Silliman to Sherlock Andrews, n.d., in Fisher, *Life of Benjamin Silliman, M.D., LL.D.*, 1:307. Later in the citation Silliman indicates that he recorded Dwight's "interesting and instructive sermon on the close of the century," undoubtedly a reference to Dwight's *A Discourse on Some Events of the Last Century, Delivered in the Brick Church in New-Haven on Wednesday, January 7, 1801* (New Haven: Ezra Read, 1801).

25. This view of Dwight as a great man is wonderfully captured in the most famous portrait of Dwight. Entitled *Timothy Dwight*, it was painted by John Trumbull in 1817, the year of Dwight's death. The image is not without its ironies. Contemporaries reported that in his final months of life Dwight was worn down by the disease that would eventually claim his life. Evidence of any disease or weariness is entirely missing from Trumbull's image. Moreover, the portrait reveals no hint of Dwight's poor eyesight. The text to which he points was too far away for him to have read. Trumbull's portrait was repainted by Deane Keller in 1935 and is the property of the Yale University Art Gallery. The Keller portrait appears here with permission of the Yale University Art Gallery.

26. Beecher, *Autobiography*, 1:27.

27. The "lights and shades" quotation with which this chapter begins is found in Goodrich, *Recollections of a Lifetime*, 1:355.

I. The Light of Yale

1. Gregory H. Nobles, *Divisions throughout the Whole: Politics and Society in Hampshire County, Massachusetts, 1740–1755* (Cambridge: Cambridge University Press, 1983), pp. 32–33. John Dwight's role in Dedham is recorded in Kenneth Lockridge, *A New England Town, the First One Hundred Years: Dedham, Massachusetts, 1636–1736* (New York: W. W. Norton, 1970), pp. 43, 61–62.

2. There exists some difference of opinion about the exact identity of the "river gods." Though the Dwights are not often included in the group, Robert Zemsky identifies Joseph Dwight as one of the "gods." See Zemsky, *Merchants, Farmers, and River Gods: An*

Essay on Eighteenth-Century American Politics (Boston: Gambit Press, 1971), p. 32. For additional information about Joseph Dwight, see Benjamin W. Dwight, 2:620ff.

3. *Decisions,* p. 344; *Travels,* 1:241ff. According to Benjamin W. Dwight, 1:118, Colonel Dwight's estate was valued at £9000 in 1771. At first glance, Stoddard's estate appears to have been much larger. Perry Miller records it as £35,432 in 1744. Perry Miller, *Jonathan Edwards* (New York: W. Sloane Associates, 1949), p. 217. Though there appears to be a great disparity between these two figures Dwight was actually wealthier than Stoddard. This becomes clear when both 1771 and 1744 Massachusetts currency is converted to pounds sterling. After such conversions, Dwight's estate is valued at about £6700 sterling, while Stoddard's is valued at something less than £4000 sterling. The conversion data for these comparisons are found in John J. McCusker, *Money and Exchange in Europe and America, 1600–1775* (Chapel Hill: University of North Carolina Press, 1978), pp. 141–42. These calculations are verified by information in Gary B. Nash, *The Urban Crucible: Social Change, Political Consciousness, and the Origins of the American Revolution* (Cambridge: Harvard University Press, 1979), pp. 405–6.

4. *Travels,* 1:240. It is very likely that Colonel Dwight's claim was simply a boast. In the year of his death, Hampshire County Inferior Court docketed a total of 487 cases. This statistic suggests that it is very unlikely that the town of Northampton was entirely free of civil litigation during the period in question. See Charles Robert McKirdy, "Lawyers in Crisis: The Massachusetts Legal Profession, 1760–1790" (Ph.D. diss., Northwestern University, 1969), Appendix IV, Table D, p. 230.

5. Edwards's early biographers, notably his protégé Samuel Hopkins in *Life and Character of the Late Reverend, Learned and Pious Mr. Jonathan Edwards* (Boston, 1765) and his great-grandson Sereno E. Dwight in *The Life of President Edwards* (New York: G. and C. and H. Carvill, 1830), looked for theological reasons lurking behind the events that led to Edwards's dismissal. Modern scholars have viewed the matter quite differently. Perry Miller, in *Jonathan Edwards* (New York: William Sloane Associates, 1949; reprint ed., Amherst: University of Massachusetts Press, 1981), considered Edwards's longstanding squabbles with his kinfolk, the Williamses, to be an important feature of the controversy. Ola Winslow, in *Jonathan Edwards, 1703–1758, A Biography* (New York: Macmillan, 1940), argued that Edwards's real enemy was growing democracy in Northampton. More recently, Patricia Tracy, in *Jonathan Edwards, Pastor: Religion and Society in Eighteenth-Century Northampton* (New York: Hill and Wang, 1980), has shown that the causes of the separation were far more complex and interrelated. She carefully assesses both the familial and the political issues as they played themselves out in the larger context of Edwards's successes and failures as a pastor. See particularly Tracy, pp. 193–94. See also Iain H. Murray, *Jonathan Edwards: A New Biography* (Carlisle, Pa.: Banner of Truth Trust, 1987), pp. 333–49.

6. Edwards to Thomas Gillispie, 1 July 1751, in C. C. Goen, ed., *The Great Awakening,* Volume 4 of *The Works of Jonathan Edwards* (New Haven: Yale University Press, 1972), pp. 561–66. Unless otherwise noted, all subsequent citations from Jonathan Edwards will be taken from this Yale Edition of *The Works of Jonathan Edwards* and will be cited as *Works.*

7. Edwards's nephew, Joseph Hawley, subsequently changed his mind on the question of his uncle's removal. In a letter written in 1754, he begged Edwards's forgiveness for his part in the controversy. Two years after Edwards's death he was still troubled by his conscience and had a second apology made public. Sereno E. Dwight, pp. 422–27. This change of opinion proved costly for Hawley. His relationship with others among the gods took an unhappy turn after his recantation. See Robert J. Taylor, *Western Massachusetts in the Revolution* (Providence: Brown University Press, 1954), pp. 23ff., and E. Francis Brown, *Joseph Hawley: Colonial Radical* (New York: Columbia University Press, 1931), pp. 26–38.

8. The "ablest politician" citation comes from Edwards's funeral sermon for Stoddard,

first published as *A Strong Reed Broken and Withered* (Boston: Rogers and Fowle, 1748). The sermon was later republished under the title *God's Awful Judgement in the Breaking and Withering of the Strong Rods of a Community* in Edward Hicks, ed., *The Works of Jonathan Edwards*, 2 vols. (Edinburgh: Banner of Truth Trust, 1974), 2:36ff. For a fascinating interpretation of Edwards's view of Stoddard, see Perry Miller, "Jonathan Edwards and the Great Awakening," ch. 6 in *Errand into the Wilderness* (New York: Harper and Row, 1956), pp. 163ff. Details of the voting and identification of the pro-Edwards parishioners (among whom is listed both Colonel Dwight and his son, Major Timothy Dwight) are recorded in James Russell Trumbull, *The History of Northampton from Its Settlement in 1654*, 2 vols. (Northampton: n.p., 1898), 2:234. See also Winslow, pp. 250ff.

9. Edwards to John Erskine, one of his Scottish correspondents, 15 November 1750, in Benjamin W. Dwight, 1:117, and Sereno E. Dwight, pp. 415–16.

10. It is not clear why Edwards asked Dwight to serve as intermediary in this period, but the MS evidence suggests that Dwight played this role several times. Colonel Timothy Dwight to Foxcroft, 13 October 1750, *DFP*. Dwight further discusses Hobby's role in the dismissal in Dwight to Foxcroft, 25 December 1751, *DFP*. A confidant and defender of George Whitefield during the Great Awakening, Thomas Foxcroft (1696–1769) was pastor of Boston's First Church from 1717 until his death in 1769. Edwards viewed Foxcroft as one of his most faithful New Light allies. He sought unsuccessfully to have Foxcroft participate on the ecclesiastical council that decided his fate in Northampton and after the dismissal Edwards sent the manuscript that would be published as *Misrepresentations Corrected, and Truth Vindicated, in a Reply to the Rev. Mr. Solomon Williams* (Boston: Kneeland, 1752) to Foxcroft, via Colonel Dwight, for publication. See Sprague, 1:308–10, and Winslow, p. 295. William Hobby (1707–1765), pastor of the church at Reading, Massachusetts, was also a New Light ally of Edwards. He sat on the ecclesiastical council that heard Edwards's case and drew up the minority report, entitled *A Protest*. See Winslow, pp. 254–56.

11. See Winslow, pp. 261ff. and Tracy, pp. 186ff. for details of the Colonel's efforts to retain Edwards. *Hints, DFP*, indicates that Colonel Dwight offered half of his personal annual income to Edwards as an incentive to stay in Northampton and form a second church.

12. Dwight to Foxcroft, 6 June 1753, *DFP*.

13. Dwight to Foxcroft, 7 December 1753, *DFP*.

14. Dwight to Foxcroft, 22 February 1754, *DFP*.

15. Dwight to Foxcroft, undated (circa April 1755), *DFP*. The abbreviation "Wmss" is Dwight's shorthand for "Williamses," one of the clans who consistently opposed Edwards at Northampton. Edwards carried on a theological paper war about the ecclesiastical issues that attended his dismissal with Solomon Williams, a member of the extended family. See Jonathan Edwards, *An Humble Inquiry into the Rules of the Word of God, Concerning the Qualifications Requisite to a Compleat [sic] Standing and Full Communion in the Visible Christian Church* (Boston, 1749); Solomon Williams, *The True State of the Question Concerning the Qualifications Necessary to Communion . . .* (Boston, 1751); Jonathan Edwards, *Misrepresentations Corrected, and Truth Vindicated, in a Reply to the Rev. Mr. Solomon Williams* (Boston, 1752). For more on this exchange see Winslow, pp. 293–97, and Tracy, pp. 183–86.

16. Benjamin W. Dwight, 1:118. Though Mary Edwards was Jonathan and Sarah Edwards's fourth daughter in order of birth she is sometimes counted as their third because her older sister, Jerusha, died in February 1747. See Cuningham, p. 7.

17. Two fascinating studies of the marriage of Jonathan and Sarah Edwards have been published. In different ways both point to the amazing success of the Edwardses' children in American professional life. Though Edwards's story is tangential to the subject at hand, one important fact deserves notice here. An impressive segment of the

family genealogy can be traced through Mary Edwards Dwight. See Elizabeth D. Dodds, *Marriage to a Difficult Man: The "Uncommon Union" of Jonathan and Sarah Edwards* (Philadelphia: Westminster Press, 1971), p. 38, and Alfred E. Winship, *Heredity: A History of the Jukes-Edwards Families* (Boston: Journal of Education, 1925), pp. 74ff.

18. Five consecutive generations of Dwight men were named Timothy. Henceforth, an unqualified "Timothy Dwight" will refer to the subject of this study, Timothy Dwight of Yale (1752–1817). His father and grandfather will be identified by means of their military titles, i.e., Major Timothy Dwight (1726–1777) and Colonel Timothy Dwight (1693–1771) respectively. Throughout the existing secondary literature Dwight is most often referred to as "President Dwight," but even this lacks precision. Dwight's grandson, Timothy the fifth (1828–1916), also served as Yale's president (1886–1899). Because this second President Dwight plays no part in the present study, all uses of "President Dwight" refer to Timothy Dwight (1752–1817).

19. Dwight also noted that until approximately 1760 these hill towns were subject to Native American attacks which further complicated their settlement. See *Travels*, 1:239–40. The demographic figures used in this section are from the detailed appendix in Nobles, pp. 189–204. Nobles, p. 112, indicates that between 1760 and 1769 Hampshire county towns issued a total of 585 warnings to transients. Northampton issued an unusually large percentage of these. For a detailed account of this social problem, see Douglas L. Jones, "The Strolling Poor: Transiency in Eighteenth-Century Massachusetts," *Journal of Social History* 8 (1975):28–49.

20. Anne Baxter Webb, "On the Eve of the Revolution: Northampton, Massachusetts, 1750–1775" (Ph.D. diss., University of Minnesota, 1976), pp. 206ff. Also see Taylor, *Western Massachusetts in the Revolution*, pp. 11ff. For an alternative interpretation about the presence of genuine oligarchies in New England towns, see Michael Zuckerman, *Peaceable Kingdoms: New England Towns in the Eighteenth Century* (New York: Knopf, 1970).

21. Governor Caleb Strong to Sereno E. Dwight, 26 March 1817, cited in Benjamin W. Dwight, 1:130.

22. See Benjamin W. Dwight, pp. 130ff., Franklin B. Dexter, *Sketches*, 1:757–58, and Webb, p. 206. The value of Major Dwight's estate at his death is subject to some question. The estate was recorded in the usual manner, but Major Dwight's financial speculation very near the end of his life likely accounted for a great depletion of its value. The tract of western land that he purchased from his brother-in-law, General Phineas Lyman, was paid for in cash. Subsequently, the deed to the southern tract of land was lost, never to be recovered. In effect, Dwight's scheme not only cost him his life but also a large undetermined amount of his fortune. See Benjamin W. Dwight, 1:132ff. The major's western venture is discussed below.

23. Mary Edwards Dwight is said to have been fond of discussing theology with her son to whom she referred deferentially as "Sir." Both were quite talkative and fond of snuff. During discussions of abstruse points, when one of them would take a bit of snuff, the other would take advantage of the lull in conversation to make a point. Benjamin W. Dwight, 1:136ff., and Sprague, *Annals*, 2:152. For details of Dwight's efforts to gain admission to Yale, see Cuningham, pp. 15–16. Enoch Huntingdon (1739–1809), Yale class of 1759, was congregational pastor at Middletown, Connecticut, a patriot during the Revolution, and secretary of the Yale Corporation from 1788–1793. See Dexter, *Sketches*, 2:594–97. The mean age of the twenty-six members of Yale's graduating class of 1769 was twenty-two. Dwight was only seventeen when he took his bachelor's degree. For personal data on the class of 1769, see Dexter, *Sketches*, 3:304–65. During the Stiles and Dwight administrations (1778–1817), the average age of the entering class was sixteen, the lowest in Yale's history. See Kelley, p. 120.

24. For Dwight's own recollections of these days, see *Theology*, 3:462–73. For more on Mitchell, see Dexter, *Sketches*, 3:37–39, and *Dictionary of American Biography*, 13:65–66.

25. See Cuningham, p. 31, and Increase Tarbox, ed., *The Diary of Thomas Robbins, D.D.*, 2 vols. (Boston: Beacon Press, 1886), 1:692.

26. Dwight, *A Dissertation on the History, Eloquence, and Poetry of the Bible, Delivered at the Public Commencement, at New Haven* (New Haven: Thomas and Samuel Green, 1772), pp. 9, 11, 14. Freimarck, in "Timothy Dwight's Dissertation on the Bible," argues that the *Dissertation* is the best example of Dwight's early thinking about literary criticism and, as such, illustrates his connection to the "Connecticut Wits." Freimarck also notes the great extent to which Dwight's *Dissertation* relied on material he had discovered in Yale's library.

27. Prior to his official appointment as a Yale tutor, Dwight had to write out and sign the following oath that is extant in *DFP*: "I, Timothy Dwight, being chosen tutor of Yale College do hereby declare my free and hearty assent to the doctrines contained in the Assembly's Catechism and the Confession of Faith owned and received in the churches of this Colony convened by delegation at Saybrook, and will accordingly instruct the pupils committed to my care. I do also consent to the rules of church discipline agreed upon and established in this colony." It was dated and signed on 6 November 1771.

28. Major Timothy Dwight to Dwight, 30 December 1771, Massachusetts Historical Society, *Proceedings* 13, p. 124.

29. Dwight to Aaron Burr, 10 March 1772, American Antiquarian Society, *Proceedings* 29 (1919):55. The recipient of this letter was Dwight's cousin, Aaron Burr, Jr. (1756–1836). Both Burr and Dwight were grandsons of Edwards. At the time of this writing the two young men were apparently on cordial terms but were not regular correspondents. Indeed, in the letter cited, Dwight encourages Burr to begin corresponding more frequently with him because "the Edwardses have always been remarkable for this fondness for their relations. If you have the least inclination to prove yourself a true descendent of that (to us) respectable stock, you cannot fail of answering me soon" (p. 56). [Parentheses in original.] From Dwight's perspective, the next three decades showed Burr to be anything but a faithful member of the Edwards clan. Burr was elected Vice President of the United States in 1800 (narrowly losing the race for President to Jefferson) as a Democratic-Republican candidate. After the results of the election were published, Dwight, by then an ardent Federalist, referred to his cousin as "a dangerous man." Dwight to Hillhouse, 15 January 1801, Hillhouse Family Papers, Yale University. Dwight's use of the expression "dangerous man" proved oddly ironic and prophetic. In 1804, several newspapers reported that Alexander Hamilton described Burr as a "dangerous man and one who ought not to be trusted with the reins of government." Burr demanded satisfaction from Hamilton who would not yield. Their conflict led to America's most infamous duel on 11 July 1804, in which Burr fatally wounded Hamilton. In the ensuing *cause célèbre*, scores of preachers launched assaults on the horrors of duelling. Dwight himself led the charge in a commencement sermon preached just two months after Hamilton's death. See Dwight, *The Folly, Guilt, and Mischiefs of Duelling: A Sermon Preached in the College Chapel at New Haven, on the Sabbath Preceding the Annual Commencement, September, 1804* (Hartford: Hudson & Goodwin, 1805). For information on Burr, see *Dictionary of American Biography*, 3:316ff.

30. Dwight to Morse, 6 July 1805, *MFP*. The letter is reprinted in Leonard Woods, *History of Andover Theological Seminary* (Boston: James Osgood, 1885), p. 454.

31. Sprague, *Annals*, 2:153–54.

32. The list of Dwight's amanuenses appears in the Introduction to *Travels*, p. xxvii. For a description of the duties of Dwight's amanuenses, see the recollections of Dwight's son William, who served in this capacity in 1813. Benjamin W. Dwight, 1:149.

33. See *Hints, DFP*. Mary Edwards Dwight transferred her membership to the Norwich church on 5 October 1783. Benjamin W. Dwight, 1:137–39.

34. At least one sympathetic interpreter suggested that Mary Edwards Dwight identified Timothy with her father: "The respect which she felt and manifested toward

him, though perhaps not inferior in native powers of mind, resembled the affection of a dutiful child toward her father, rather than the feelings of a mother for a son." See Olmstead, "Timothy Dwight as a Teacher," p. 578.

35. For a history of the founding of Yale's College Church, see Edmund S. and Helen M. Morgan, *The Stamp Act Crisis: Prologue to Revolution*, revised ed. (London: Collier Books, 1963), pp. 282ff.; Richard L. Bushman, *From Puritan to Yankee: Character and Social Order in Connecticut, 1690–1765* (Cambridge: Harvard University Press, 1967), pp. 241ff.; Gabriel, *Religion and Learning at Yale*, passim; and Bainton, *Yale and the Ministry*, pp. 12–14, 33–36. For backgrounds on the forms and dynamics of religious conversions of the period, see Stephen R. Grossbart, "Seeking the Divine Favor: Conversion and Church Admission in Eastern Connecticut, 1711–1832," *William and Mary Quarterly*, 3rd ser., 46 (1989):696–739, and Kenneth Minkema, "The East Windsor Conversion Relations, 1700–1725," *Connecticut Historical Society Bulletin* 51 (1985/1986):7–63.

36. Kelley, p. 84.

37. *The Boston Evening Post* (Supplement), 28 April 1766. See also *The Boston Gazette*, 31 March 1766. For more on Major Dwight's conscience regarding his oath to the King, see Benjamin W. Dwight, 1:132.

38. Trumbull, 2:372–75.

39. See Webb, p. 201, for Major Dwight's refusal to sign. For more details of the Lyman venture, see Anthony Haswell, *Memoirs of Captain Matthew Phelps of New Haven, Vermont* (Bennington, Vt.: n.p., 1802), pp. 56–72; Benjamin W. Dwight, 1:132; Trumbull, pp. 372ff.; and Cuningham, pp. 88ff.

40. Webb, p. 206, argues that the town's willingness to continue electing Major Dwight despite his loyalism is evidence of Northampton's political priorities. Until the Revolution local issues took precedence over proto-national issues.

41. Webb, p. 206. The relationship between the First Awakening and the Revolution, and more particularly between New Lights and Patriots, has generated considerable attention among historians. A positive correlation between the events was suggested by Edmund S. Morgan, "The American Revolution Considered as an Intellectual Movement," in Arthur S. Schlesinger, Jr. and Morton White, eds., *Paths of American Thought* (Boston: Houghton Mifflin, 1963), pp. 11–33, and this theme was explored with more particularity by Harry S. Stout, "Religion, Communications, and the Ideological Origins of the American Revolution," *William and Mary Quarterly*, 3rd ser., 34 (1977):519–41, and by Rhys Isaac, "Evangelical Revolt: The Nature of the Baptists' Challenge to the Traditional Order in Virginia, 1765–1775," *William and Mary Quarterly*, 3rd ser. (1974):345–68. In this connection see also Alan Heimert, *Religion and the American Mind, from the Great Awakening to the Revolution* (Cambridge: Harvard University Press, 1966). These and other studies show that while colonial evangelical New Lights almost universally served the patriot cause, it is not the case that anti-evangelical Old Lights tended toward loyalism (with the possible exception of Anglicans, who opposed both the Awakening and independence). Indeed, research demonstrates that secular anti-evangelicals (e.g., Jefferson and Paine) and not evangelical New Lights served as the most radical and prominent among the patriot leaders. For a stimulating review of this literature, see John M. Murrin, "No Awakening, No Revolution? More Counterfactual Speculations," *Reviews in American History* 11 (1983):161–71.

42. *Travels*, 1:226. Apparently, Dwight's sons (Major Dwight's grandsons) felt similarly. In their memoir of Dwight in *Theology*, they state that Major Dwight's reason for traveling to Natchez was for the "resettlement . . . of his two sons, by whom he was accompanied." See [Benjamin Dwight], "A Memoir of the Life of the Author," *Theology*, 1:13.

43. Robert L. Ferm, *Jonathan Edwards the Younger, 1745–1801: A Colonial Pastor* (Grand Rapids: Eerdmans, 1976), p. 87. Apparently Major Dwight believed that Timothy's voice was not fit for a preacher. See *Hints, DFP,* and Cuningham, p. 55.

44. Benjamin W. Dwight, 1:144 and 1:167ff. For more on Pierpont Edwards, see Edmund B. Thomas, Jr., "Politics in the Land of Steady Habits: Connecticut's First Political Party System, 1789–1820" (Ph.D. diss., Clark University, 1972), p. 306.

45. Leonard Bacon, "The Old Age of Piety," *The American National Preacher* 20 (February 1846):33–34.

46. See Charles S. Hall, *The Life and Letters of General Samuel H. Parsons* (New York: James Pugliese Archives, 1968), p. 163, for the details of Dwight's commission. My interpretation of Dwight's leaving Yale in order to join the Revolution is one among several that might be forwarded. Morgan, *The Gentle Puritan,* pp. 345–59, renders the situation differently. He suggests that Dwight was dismissed by the Corporation for two reasons: first, his introduction of *belles lettres* into the curriculum; second, his disobedience of an order respecting the class exercises in 1777. I find Morgan less than convincing on this point. No record of a formal dismissal is cited, and elsewhere he states that Dwight resigned. His narrative jumps too quickly from Dwight's tutorship in 1777 to the Northampton Academy in 1780. The result is that Dwight's entry into the chaplaincy—which I take to be a genuinely patriotic act— is treated in insufficient detail. See also Kelley, p. 99, and text below.

47. Dwight to Washington, 8 March 1778, MS letter in Beinecke Library, Yale University. For Washington's response to Dwight, see Washington to Dwight, 18 March 1778, DFP. Both letters are reprinted in Hall, pp. 163–64. John Adams later attempted to arrange for the publication of *The Conquest* in England. Adams wrote Dwight on 4 April 1786 and complimented him by saying he knew "of no heroick [sic] Poem superior . . . in any modern Language, excepting always Paradise Lost." See L. H. Butterfield, ed., *Diary and Autobiography of John Adams* (Cambridge: The Belknap Press of Harvard University Press, 1961), 3:189, note 3.

48. Dwight to Noah Webster, 6 June 1788. Excerpts of the letter appeared in the *American Magazine* n.v. (1788):563–64, and parts of the letter are quoted in *Hints, DFP.* For details of Webster's defense of Dwight and for the full text of the letter see Zunder, pp. 200–2.

49. Dwight described a particularly gruesome post-battle scene in Travels, 3:302ff. He discussed the ethics of war with his students in *Decisions,* pp. 333–38. The question under debate on 20 April 1814 was, "Are Wars Beneficial?"

50. See Dwight to Parsons, 23 April 1779, in Hall, p. 237. For other details of the family's financial difficulties, see Cuningham, pp. 92ff. Several early interpreters, following the lead established in *Hints, DFP,* indicate that Dwight yielded his portion of Major Dwight's estate to his mother and two youngest brothers in order better to insure the survival of the family.

51. For details of Erastus Dwight, see Benjamin W. Dwight, 1:218–19. Also see Richard D. Brown, "The Confiscation and Disposition of Loyalists' Estates in Suffolk County, Massachusetts," *William and Mary Quarterly,* 3rd ser., 21 (1964):534–50.

52. Dwight to General Samuel Parsons, 28 February 1781, in Hall, p. 339.

53. On Dwight's service as a legislator see Cuningham, pp. 97–99, and Benjamin W. Dwight, 1:145. Few details of his legislative career survive. The only piece of substantial information, recorded in several early biographies, concerns a speech he delivered in support of a grant for Harvard College. See Olmstead, "Timothy Dwight as a Teacher," p. 579. Dwight announced the opening of the school in the *Connecticut Courant and Weekly Intelligencer,* 30 November 1779.

54. Benjamin W. Dwight, 1:139. Throughout this section I have argued that Dwight's antipathies toward his father and his desires to follow in the footsteps of his mother's father powerfully shaped his vocational development during his adolescence and early adulthood. This theme is explored with reference to Dwight's poetic efforts during the Revolution by Kafer, "The Making of Timothy Dwight," 189–209. Kafer argues that although Dwight never openly acknowledged his sense of embarrassment and shame over his father's loyalism, his feelings did emerge in his poetry, especially in the *Conquest*

of Canaan. For Kafer, *Conquest* functions as something akin to a shadowy, subconscious Dwight autobiography. Through it, Dwight allows his father (in the person of Herzon), as well as both himself and his wife (in the couple Irad and Selima) to emerge. These poetic fictional figures play out Dwight's actual psychic drama in the poem: Irad (Dwight) laments that he did not help defend Herzon (Major Dwight); Irad (Dwight) discovers the body of his dead father (Major Dwight) on the battlefield only to be visited later by Herzon's (Major Dwight's) ghost. These identifications and the underlying assumptions about Dwight's inability to deal openly with his deepest feelings, however imaginative or convincing, help to personalize Dwight the artist.

55. Leonard Bacon, S.W.S. Dutton, E.W. Robinson, eds., *Contributions to the Ecclesiastical History of Connecticut; Prepared under the Direction of the General Association to Commemorate the Completion of One Hundred and Fifty Years since Its First Annual Assembly* (New Haven: William Kingsley, 1861), details Dwight's ecclesiastical activities in these years including pulpit supply at the church in Kensington and service on a committee to consider a plan of union with the Presbyterians.

56. John Eliot to Jeremy Belknap, 13 March 1783, Massachusetts Historical Society, *Collections,* Series 6, 4:248–49. (The Belknap Papers). For a more thorough treatment of the controversies surrounding "the pudding" see Wright, *The Beginnings of Unitarianism in America,* pp. 187ff.

57. Jonathan Edwards, Jr., *The Faithful Manifestation of the Truth, the Proper and Immediate End of Preaching the Gospel. A Sermon Delivered November 5, 1783, at the Ordination of the Reverend Timothy Dwight, to the Pastoral Office over the Church in Greenfield* (New Haven: Thomas and Samuel Green, 1783). For specifics of the financial arrangements between Dwight and the church, see Cuningham, p. 105. Cuningham does not indicate whether these figures have been adjusted for inflation.

58. Cuningham, pp. 106ff., citing Dwight to Society of Greenfield, 20 July 1783. MS, Greenfield Church Records. An undated copy of the "Confession and Covenant" Dwight used when publicly admitting new church members survives in the Helen D. Perkins Collection at the Historical Society of Pennsylvania. It reads as follows:

> You, and each of you, solemnly profess your belief, that there is but one God in three persons, the Father, the Son, and the Holy Spirit; self-existent, independent, eternal, unchangeable; infinite in power, wisdom, holiness, goodness, and truth: that by Him all things were made; and are preserved and governed, according to His most holy and good pleasure; and that you are His creatures, and are under the most righteous and solemn obligations to serve and glorify him with all your powers while you live. You also profess your belief that the scriptures of the Old and New Testament are the Word of god; revealed to mankind by the Spirit of Truth; and containing every rule of Faith and Practice, which is obligatory on the consciences of mankind. This you profess and believe—.
>
> In the presence, etcetera
>
> You and each of you now solemnly vouch the Lord Jehovah to be your God, your Father, Redeemer, and Sanctifier; and do solemnly give up yourselves to Him as His children; purposing, and engaging so far as you know the state of your own minds, to obey through His grace (without which you can do nothing acceptable to Him), all his commandments and ordinances; and denying all ungodliness, and worldly lusts, to live soberly, righteously, and godly in the present world.
>
> Moreover, you covenant with the members of this church to walk with them through the influence and assistance of the same grace in the order of the gospel; to submit as becometh Christians to the discipline prescribed by the Redeemer; to watch over your brethren; to instruct, reprove, admonish, comfort, and strengthen them; and willingly to be instructed,

and nourished and reproved by them with the meekness, and humility of the gospel.

We then the members of this church of Christ do also covenant with you that through the same Divine Assistance we will perform the same Christian duties to you. And May God enable us to be mutually faithful through Jesus Christ to whom be glory forever. Amen.

59. *Theology* is a series of sermons arranged under the formal rubrics of systematic theology. Like other works of this genre, it begins with theology proper and moves to explications of the doctrines of sin, soteriology, and social ethics. During his Yale presidency, Dwight preached the 173 sermons of *Theology* serially so that each class could hear them all during their undergraduate years. Although *Theology* is best known in its Yale context, many of the sermons were composed for use in the Greenfield pulpit and only later modified for use in the Yale chapel. See *Hints, DFP,* and Cuningham, p. 118. For a fuller analysis of the serial use of these sermons at Yale, see below.

60. See Tyler, *Three Men of Letters,* p. 92; Griffith, pp. 235–50; and Elliott, p. 71.

61. Dwight, *Greenfield Hill: A Poem in Seven Parts* (New York: Childs and Swain, 1794), p. 168. Dwight sought to secure the copyright for *Greenfield Hill* in a letter to Simeon Baldwin. See Dwight to Baldwin, 11 November 1794, Yale University, Sterling Library, Baldwin Family Papers.

62. "Naomi's Bond" survives in *DFP.*

63. *The Triumph of Infidelity,* in McTaggart and Bottorff, pp. 369, 329.

64. *The Triumph* is formally anonymous. In place of a publisher's name the title page indicates "Printed in the World" and the dedicatory epistle to Voltaire is signed "Writer of this Poem." Although there has been some discussion of its authorship, most literary scholars conclude that Dwight wrote the poem. Dwight himself, however, refused to acknowledge the poem. In a letter to the editor of the *American Mercury* dated 14 February 1803, Dwight wrote: "A writer in some subsequent numbers of the *Mercury* has charged me with being the author of the *Triumph of Infidelity; . . .The Triumph of Infidelity* I have never acknowledged or denied, nor shall I now do either. Nor will this writer be able to produce the least testimony that I wrote the poem; particularly he will be able to find no person living who will say that he copied this poem from a Ms [sic] in my handwriting. If he could it would not prove me to be the author. I am perfectly willing that he should consider the work as mine, or not mine, as he pleases." See Dwight to *American Mercury,* 14 February 1803, *DFP.* On the question of authorship, see Leary, "The Author of *The Triumph of Infidelity,*" pp. 377–85. Dwight's confidence that no person alive could testify that the poem was written in his handwriting is likely based on his knowledge that he never wrote the poem onto paper but rather dictated it to a secretary.

65. *Hints, DFP.*

66. The advertisement was published in *Connecticut Journal,* 20 December 1783. According to the subsequent newspaper writer, Dwight's school promised to be "one of the best of the kind in America." In addition to its beautiful setting, students had the advantage of "receiving the best education, free from bad examples, which are often dangerous to schools in and near populous cities." *New Haven Gazette and Connecticut Magazine* I (22 June 1786):150. For a brief description of the building that housed the school, see Anon., "Timothy Dwight and the Greenfield Academy," *The American Historical Record* 2 (1873):385–87. Dwight's grammar school included students of both sexes, and he expected similar academic achievement from both groups. See Dexter, *Literary Diary,* 3:247. For Dwight's opinion of the fashionable education of women, wherein the romantic novel was the literary staple, see *Travels,* 4:372–75.

67. Little is known of the circumstances surrounding the granting of this honorary doctorate. Princeton University Archives contain little additional information about the reasons Dwight was granted the degree.

68. Dexter, *Literary Diary of Ezra Stiles,* 1:364.

69. Edmund S. Morgan, "Ezra Stiles and Timothy Dwight," Massachusetts Historical Society, *Proceedings* 72 (1957–1960): 101. Stiles suspected Dwight and his young New Divinity friends of having "a disposition . . . to struggle for preheminence [sic] . . . they all want to be Luthers. But they will none of them be equal to those strong reasoners President Edwards and Mr. Hopkins. Geniuses never imitate. Imitation may reach something above laudable and very useful mediocrity, but can never reach originality." Dexter, *Literary Diary,* 3:274, 275.

At another point in the *Literary Diary,* Stiles makes the only critical comment about Dwight's eyesight that I have found in the literature. In a footnote to his 16 May 1790 entry, Stiles suggests that Dwight's visual difficulty was affected and that he used his alleged handicap as an excuse for his failure to be properly prepared to preach. "Dr. Dwight is Miops and affects to be blind, or unable to use his eyes for writing. Hence he used to dictate his Poem[s] to an amanuensis. . . . At Enfield he employed Rev. Mr. Prudden to write 8 or 9 pages from his mouth, while he sat in Contemplation and wrapt up in Sentiment with his eyes shut absorbed in fictitious Contemplation and Study." Stiles goes on to report that this prolonged session with Prudden resulted in Dwight's late arrival at an important gathering. Dexter, *Literary Diary,* 3:394–95, n.3.

70. Dexter, *Literary Diary,* 2:422, 531. On the rival institution theory, see Dexter, *Literary Diary,* 2:422–23. During this period Dwight was apparently invited to lead several other academies. The David Avery Papers housed at Princeton Theological Seminary contain documents that give the details of a scheme to begin a Presbyterian school to be named "Clio Hall" in Vermont. The plan was endorsed by John Witherspoon, and Dwight served as a member of the board and was at one point invited to become the rector. See David Avery to Dwight, 25 August 1780; David Avery to Dwight, 19 September 1780; David Avery to Dwight, 7 November 1780.

71. Dexter, Literary Diary, 2:529–31; Morgan, *Gentle Puritan,* pp. 470–71.

72. One extant petition that makes such a threat is contained in the Trumbull Papers (Connecticut Historical Society) and is cited in Morgan, *Gentle Puritan,* pp. 355–56.

73. See *Connecticut Courant,* 11 February 1783; 18 March 1783; 11 February 1783.

74. See *Connecticut Courant,* 22 April 1783.

75. Morgan, *Gentle Puritan,* p. 350.

76. See Dexter, *Literary Diary,* 3:116 and 3:121.

77. For Stiles's own suspicions about the identity of Parnassus, see Dexter, *Literary Diary,* 3:59. In *Gentle Puritan,* pp. 345ff., Edmund Morgan notes, "It has proved impossible to discern who Parnassus was." Nonetheless, Morgan believed that Dwight was Parnassus. Although others denied writing the Parnassus articles, Morgan argues, "Timothy Dwight did not [deny writing them], and though no evidence connects him with the letters, he had the ability, the access to inside information, and, if Stiles's estimate of him was correct, the inclination." Ibid., p.xxx. Other scholars have concurred with Morgan's identification of Dwight as Parnassus. See, for instance, Kelley, p. 487, n.28; and Sheldon S. Cohen, "The Parnassus Articles," *History of Education Quarterly* 5 (1965):174–86.

78. *American Mercury,* 30 April 1803. In ancient mythology Mount Parnassus, the highest peak of a mountain range near Delphi, represents the seats of Apollo and the Muses. Efforts to identify ESCHINES have proved fruitless.

79. See *Decisions,* p. 92.

80. Dexter, *Literary Diary,* 3:457.

81. Jonathan Edwards Jr.'s name appeared on the first ballot only. Because he received only one vote (Levi Hart's), his name was withdrawn from subsequent ballots. See Dexter, *Literary Diary,* 3:506. Although he was duly elected by the Corporation, Lathrop chose not to accept the position. The professorship remained vacant until Dwight

became president. Dwight filled it temporarily on a year-to-year basis. Henry Davis, a Yale tutor, was finally chosen as a permanent incumbent. Soon afterwards, Davis fell ill and was thus prevented from assuming the duties of the professorship. In 1805, the Corporation persuaded Dwight to take the post permanently. In addition to his regular presidential salary Dwight was given $500 annually to pay for his amanuenses. For unknown reasons, neither Governor Samuel Huntington nor Lieutenant Governor Oliver Wolcott took part in this election. Stiles's recollections are found in Dexter, *Literary Diary,* 3:451. Stiles was aware of the complaints of the New Divinity ministers, as well as of what he perceived to be their plans to "take" Yale for their own purposes. *Literary Diary,* pp. 3:451, 460ff. For the Stiles letter to Williams, see *Literary Diary,* 3:505–6, n.1.

82. For travelers' accounts of Dwight during this period, see "Journal of a Tour of Connecticut in Autumn of 1789, by Samuel Davis," Massachusetts Historical Society, *Proceedings,* 1st ser., 11 (1869–1870):9–32; and Ashbel Green, *Life of Ashbel Green, V.D.M.* (New York: Robert Carter and Brothers, 1849), pp. 210ff.

83. Dwight, "Address to the Ministers of the Gospel of Every Denomination in the United States," *American Museum* 4 (1788):33.

84. For instance, see Dwight, *The Seasons Moralized, American Museum* 5 (1789):302–3; *A Hymn Sung at the Public Examination of the Scholars, Belonging to the Academy at Greenfield, May 2, 1788, American Museum* 6 (1789):171–72; *A Song; Written in 1771, American Museum* 5 (1789):408–9; "Epistle from Dr. Dwight to Colonel Humphreys. Greenfield, 1785," in *The Miscellaneous Works of Colonel Humphreys* (New York, 1790). Dwight published the following poems in Matthew Carey, ed., *The Beauties of Poetry, British and American* (Philadelphia, 1791); *The Deity and His Dispensations,* pp. 209–11; *Creation,* pp. 211–13; *Original State of Man,* pp. 214–15; *Three Fold State of Man Emblematized,* pp. 215–17; and *Prospect of America,* pp. 217–19. During this period David Rittenhouse recommended Dwight's poetry to Thomas Jefferson, noting that "the northern people have taken the lead in this very entertaining path of polite literature." See Rittenhouse to Jefferson, 8 November 1788, in Julian Boyd, ed., *The Papers of Thomas Jefferson* (Princeton: Princeton University Press, 1950–), 14:51.

85. Dwight, *Virtuous Rulers a National Blessing: A Sermon, Preached at the General Election, May 12, 1791* (Hartford: Hudson and Goodwin, 1791).

86. Dwight to Philip van Rensselaer, 16 March 1795, MS New York Historical Society Library. Cited in Cuningham, p. 166.

87. The comment is recorded in the journal of Ashbel Green, dated 20 June 1791, included in his *Life of Ashbel Green,* p. 211.

88. The poem is recorded in Cuningham, p. 165. He indicates that he heard it from Geraldine Woolsey Carmelt, a descendant of Dwight.

89. The "meridian of his life" citation comes from Anon., "Biographical Memoir of the Rev. Timothy Dwight, S.T.D., LL.D.," *Port Folio* 4 (1817):360. The "useful and honourable" quotation with which this chapter begins is found in Sprague, *Annals,* p. 2:156.

90. Anon., "Biographical Memoir," *Port Folio* 4 (1817):360.

91. Dwight had refused to attend certain ecclesiastical functions due to theological scruples that were at least Edwardsean and perhaps even smacked of the more narrow New Divinity theology. On 4 August 1784 the North Haven church affirmed the Halfway Covenant and for the first time baptized children on this plan. Dwight refused to attend these baptisms. Dexter, *Literary Diary,* 3:132. For Dwight's comment on the Northampton church, see Dexter, 3:286.

92. Dwight to Jonathan Ingersoll, 24 June 1795, in E. E. Beardsley, *The History of the Episcopal Church in Connecticut,* 2 vols. (New York: Hurd and Houghton, 1868), 2:212.

93. Beardsley, 2:212.

94. The Corporation's announcement to Dwight of his election came to him at Greenfield in a letter dated 25 June 1795: "The fellows of Yale College . . . have made choice of you as President . . . . We trust, Sir, that you will attend to this as an important call of Divine Providence: the circumstances of this seminary are such as greatly need a President and require his presence and exertions in office. A favorable answer as soon as may be with conveniency, will be very favorable to this Board. We wish you the direction and guidance of Heaven in this important affair." Yale Corporation to Dwight, 25 June 1795, *DFP.*

95. For details of the congregation's objections and the negotiations with the Consociation, see Cuningham, pp. 167ff.

96. "Dr. John Pierce's Manuscript Journal," Massachusetts Historical Society, *Proceedings,* 2nd ser., 3 (1886–1887):46.

97. Morgan, *Gentle Puritan,* pp. 323–24.

98. "At the commencement of his presidency, the professorship of theology was vacant. The Corporation proposed to appoint him, in form, to the office. For the first ten years, he would consent to none but an annual appointment. In 1805, it was made permanent." [Benjamin Dwight], "A Memoir of the Life of the Author," *Theology,* 1:26.

99. See Brown, *Benjamin Silliman, passim,* for a full treatment of Dwight's efforts to expand the faculty at Yale.

100. See Kelley, pp. 125–27, for details.

101. See Novak, p. 23, for details of student unrest. Dwight wrote New Jersey Governor Joseph Bloomfield to express his support for other college administrators who were put in difficult positions by student unrest. "The cause in which the governors of the College of New Jersey are engaged is the common cause of all colleges." Dwight to Bloomfield, 16 May 1807, John Maclean Papers, Princeton University Archives. Cited in Novak, p. 181, note 77. For a full treatment of student violence at Princeton in this era, see Mark A. Noll, *Princeton and the Republic: The Search for a Christian Enlightenment in the Era of Samuel Stanhope Smith* (Princeton: Princeton University Press, 1989), pp. 157–84.

102. Dwight, *Decisions,* p. 221.

103. Quoted in Brown, *Benjamin Silliman,* p. 22.

104. See Olmstead, "Timothy Dwight as a Teacher," pp. 582–83.

105. For an illustration of Dwight's pastoral work with students, see Bennet Tyler, *Nettleton and His Labours: The Memoir of Dr. Asahel Nettleton, Remodeled in Some Parts by Andrew A. Bonar,* reprint ed. (Edinburgh and Carlisle, Pa.: Banner of Truth Trust, 1975), pp. 45, 47–48. See also Denison Olmsted's comments on this aspect of Dwight's presidency in Sprague, 2:160 and Nathaniel W. Taylor's views in Sprague, 2:162–63. For an example of the manner in which Dwight kept parents updated on the progress of their children at Yale, see Dwight to Morse, 17 March 1809, *MFP,* and Dwight to Morse, 22 April 1809, *MFP.* Three of Jedidiah Morse's sons graduated from Yale during Dwight's presidential tenure: Samuel F. B. Morse in 1810, Sidney Edwards Morse in 1811, and Richard Carey Morse in 1812. Perhaps one of the most informative sympathetic accounts of Dwight's role as minister and educator came from Benjamin Silliman's mother, Mary Dickinson. She knew Dwight for many years—as Yale student, Greenfield pastor, and Yale president. Her reminiscences on Dwight's career are contained in a letter she wrote to her son on learning of Dwight's death in 1817. Among other details, Dickinson provides an account of Dwight's pastoral skills when she was bereaved. See Mary Dickinson to Benjamin Silliman, 20 January 1817, Silliman Family Papers, Sterling Library, Yale University. See also Silliman to Dickinson, 2 April 1817, Silliman Family Papers; Chandros Michael Brown, *Benjamin Silliman: A Life in the Young Republic,* pp. 299–302; and Joy Day Buel and Richard Buel, Jr., *The Way of Duty: A Woman and Her Family in Revolutionary America* (New York: W. W. Norton, 1984), pp. 280ff.

106. Beecher, *Autobiography,* 1:31. Dwight briefly outlined elements of the Yale curriculum in *Travels,* 1:150.

107. The episode is recorded in Ravitz, "Timothy Dwight's Decisions," pp. 515–16. Ravitz discovered evidence of the Calhoun-Dwight encounter in a manuscript entitled "Notes on Disputes," by John Pierpont, Yale class of 1804, housed in the Pierpont Morgan Library. Dwight's nativist views became more prominent in the latter half of his life. In the published version of the immigration question that appears in *Decisions,* he noted John Witherspoon, the Scottish president of Princeton, as an exception to his opposition to immigration. See Dwight, *Decisions,* pp. 227–29.

108. Calhoun Correspondence II, *Annual Report of the American Historical Association for the Year 1899* (Washington: Government Printing Office, 1900), p. 81.

109. Theodore Dwight, Jr., *President Dwight's Decisions of Questions Discussed by the Senior Class in Yale College in 1813 and 1814* (New York: Leavitt, 1833). Several MS versions of student notes survive: "Notes Taken from Observations made by Dr. Dwight in the Seniors' Recitation Room, Yale College, A.D. 1806–1807," *DFP;* "Notes on Disputes in Yale College before President Dwight, 1812–1813," Sterling Library, Yale University; "Notes of Disputes in Yale College before President Dwight, 1812–1816," Beinecke Library, Yale University; "Notes on Disputes," John Pierpont, November 1803, Pierpont Morgan Library, cited in Ravitz, "Timothy Dwight's Decisions." With only a few exceptions, the disputation topics listed in these manuscripts appear in *Decisions.*

110. Beecher, *Autobiography,* 2:293.

111. For a helpful consideration of the power that Beecher and his *Autobiography* have exerted on subsequent religious history, see Douglas H. Sweet, "Church Vitality and the American Revolution: Historiographical Consensus and Thoughts toward a New Perspective," *Church History* 45 (1976):345–47. Also see Roger Finke and Rodney Stark, *The Churching of America, 1776–1990: Winners and Losers in Our Religious Economy* (New Brunswick: Rutgers University Press), p. 57.

112. Benjamin Silliman to his mother, 11 July 1802, in G. P. Fischer, *Life of Benjamin Silliman,* 2 vols. (New York: n.p., 1866), 1:83.

113. For Morse's role in the affair, see Joseph W. Phillips, *Jedidiah Morse and New England Congregationalism* (New Brunswick: Rutgers University Press, 1983), pp. 73–101.

114. For more on the XYZ affair, see William Stinchcombe, *The XYZ Affair* (Westport: Greenwood Press, 1980). For an account of the Bavarian Illuminati, see Phillips, pp. 73–101, and Vernon Stauffer, *New England and the Bavarian Illuminati* (New York: Columbia University Press, 1918). Dwight discussed the threat of the Illuminati in Dwight to Morse, 30 December 1799, *MFP,* and in Dwight to Morse, 4 January 1799, *MFP.* Dwight read or had read to him Robison (John Robison, *Proofs of a Conspiracy Against All the Governments and Religions of Europe* (London: 1798)) and heartily approved of the book. In a letter of appreciation Dwight hailed Robison's "efforts in the cause of truth and righteousness" which had become "an immovable standard against the miserable scheme of profligacy." Dwight to Robison, 20 March 1805, in Fisher, *Life of Benjamin Silliman, M.D., LL.D,* 1:157.

115. Timothy Dwight, *The Nature and Danger of Infidel Philosophy, Exhibited in Two Discourses Addressed to the Candidates for the Baccalaureate, in Yale College, September 9th, 1797* (New Haven: George Bunce, 1798), p. 10.

116. Ezra Stiles objected to Dwight's reliance on "ignorant second hand accounts" in *The Triumph of Infidelity.* See Dexter, *Literary Diary of Ezra Stiles,* 3:326.

117. Dwight borrowed from George Campbell, *A Dissertation of Miracles: Containing an Examination of the Principles Advanced by David Hume, Esq.: In an Essay on Miracles* (Edinburgh: Kincaid and Bell, 1762). On Dwight's use of other scholars' ideas, see Herbert Hovencamp, *Science and Religion in America: 1800–1860,* p. 84; and Tyler, *Three Men of Letters,* p. 116.

118. Timothy Dwight, *The Duty of Americans at the Present Crisis, Illustrated in a Discourse, Preached on the Fourth of July, 1798; at the Request of the Citizens of New-Haven* (New Haven: Thomas and Samuel Green, 1798), p. 11.

119. For more on Federalist uses of Jeffersonian electioneering tactics see Fischer, pp. 91–109.

120. Dwight to Huntington, 31 January 1795, Stokes Autographs Collection, Yale University. For more on Huntington see Fischer, pp. 289–90. Dwight's sermon to the society was published as *The True Means of Establishing Public Happiness: A Sermon delivered on the 7th of July, before the Connecticut Society of Cincinnati, and Published at their Request* (New Haven: T. & S. Green, 1795). The Society of the Cincinnati, formed by officers of the Continental Army for mutual support after the war, was named for the Roman general Cincinnatus (viewed by many as an Enlightenment icon). It named George Washington its first president-general. The large financial endowments of the Society plus its policy of extending membership on a hereditary basis roused suspicion among Democratic-Republicans. For more on the Society and on Washington's role therein, see Garry Wills, *Cincinnatus: George Washington and the Enlightenment* (Garden City: Doubleday, 1984). Federalists also developed Washington Benevolent Societies, similar to the Society of the Cincinnati, which rivaled the democratic secret societies. See Fischer, pp. 110–28.

121. Dwight to Hillhouse, 1 March 1800, Sterling, Hillhouse Family Papers, Yale University. Very few accounts of Dwight's political activities survive. One of the most fascinating is recorded by John Adams. In a letter to James Lloyd, Adams tells a story about a meeting of the Society of Cincinnati held in New York just prior to the presidential election of 1800. According to Adams, the meeting was planned by the scheming Alexander Hamilton in the hopes that Adams's name would be dropped from the ticket. Adams noted that Dwight attended the meeting and participated in the cabal. "The learned and pious Doctors Dwight and Babcock, who having been chaplains in the army, were then attending as two reverend knights of the order, with their blue ribbons and bright eagles at their sable buttonholes, [and] were heard to say repeatedly in the room where the society met, 'We must sacrifice Adams. We must sacrifice Adams.' Of this fact I have such evidence that I should dare to appeal, if it were worth while, to the only survivor, Dr. Dwight of New Haven University." See Adams to Lloyd, 17 February 1815, in *The Works of John Adams, Second President of the United States: With a Life of the Author by His Grandson, Charles Francis Adams* (Boston: Little, Brown, 1856), 10:124–25.

122. On 24 November 1800 just after the national election, the Connecticut Academy met at Dwight's home to discuss the political situation. Among other things Dwight and his guests discussed the infidelity of Jefferson and the rumors that Pinckney was an infidel. Of course Dwight affirmed the former claim but denied the truth of the rumors about the Federalist candidate. The conversation was later reported in the press (he thought inaccurately), and he subsequently prepared a corrected statement for publication. See Dwight to Babcock, 14 February 1803, *DFP.*

123. Dwight to Morse, 21 December 1800, *MFP.*

124. Dwight to Hillhouse, 15 January 1801, Hillhouse Family Papers, Yale University. Burr's chequered political history included former alliances with the Federalists. This helps to account for Dwight's fear that should Burr win the election the Federalists would be held accountable for Burr's actions.

125. Dwight to Enos Bronson, 26 February 1801, *DFP.*

126. Quoted in Phillips, p. 94.

127. For correspondence relating to the founding of the *Palladium,* see Dwight to Morse, 7 November 1800, *MFP;* Theodore Dwight to Morse, 12 December 1800, *MFP;* Theodore Dwight to Morse, 13 December 1800, *MFP.* The Ames quotation appears in

Fischer, p. 135, in a discussion of the tone of the *Palladium* in comparison to that of the Republican press. Although the founders of the *Palladium* agreed to avoid what they took to be the yellow journalism of the Democratic-Republicans, Robert Edson Lee, "Timothy Dwight and the *Boston Palladium*," *New England Quarterly* 35 (1962):229–38, argues that writers in the *Palladium* including Dwight were not beyond scurrilous journalism themselves.

128. Dwight, "Farmer Johnson's Political Catechism," *New England Palladium*, 8 May 1801. This series ran in the *Palladium* from 27 March through 8 May, 1801.

129. Dwight, "To the Farmers and Mechanics of New England," *New England Palladium*, 12 May 1801. This series ran from 12 May through 5 June, 1801. Other Dwight pieces in the *Palladium* include: "An Extract from 'The Retrospect,'" *New England Palladium*, 3 January 1801; and "Morpheus," *New England Palladium*, 24 November–9 March 1802.

130. James McDowell to Samuel McDowell Reid, 23 February 1814, in "Glimpses of Old College Life," *William and Mary Quarterly* 8, ser. 1 (1900):225–26.

131. *The American Mercury*, 9 July 1801; 8 July 1802; 4 August 1803; 19 July 1804.

132. *The American Mercury*, 26 July 1804.

133. *The American Mercury*, 2 July 1801; 10 April 1806.

134. *The Philadelphia Aurora*, 12 February 1800. See also *Aurora* columns on January 5, 7, 11, 15, 19, and 22, 1799; 5 February 1799; 17 January and 12 February 1800; 31 March 1800.

135. Very little work has been done on John Cosens Ogden, one of the period's most fascinating figures and the first critic to hang the nickname "Pope" on Dwight. Raised in New Jersey, Ogden was educated at Princeton and Yale. Initially, he made his living as a merchant. After his conversion to the Protestant Episcopal Church, he served as a missionary, as a chaplain to the New Hampshire General Court, and as a parish priest in Portsmouth, New Hampshire. Ogden published several sermons and a defense of the Book of Common Prayer entitled *A Useful Essay, Being an Account of the excellency of the Common Prayer of the Episcopal Church* (Hanover: Josiah Dunham, 1793). He also wrote several tracts on religion and politics in Connecticut, including *An Appeal to the Candid, upon the Present State of Religion and Politics in Connecticut* (New Haven: n.p., 1798) and *Friendly Remarks to the People of Connecticut, upon their Colleges and Schools* (n.p., 1799). He was a regular but anonymous contributor to the Republican newspaper, *The Philadelphia Aurora*. His involvement in the highly politicized Matthew Lyon affair at the end of the century led to his imprisonment on charges that he had failed to repay personal debts. This perfectly suited his opponents who denounced him in the Federalist press as "The Rev. Gaolbird," "the half crazy, half idiot priest." A brief biography of Ogden appears in Richard A. Harrison, ed., *The Princetonians, 1769–1775, A Biographical Dictionary* (Princeton: Princeton University Press, 1980), pp. 93–97. See also Dexter, *Biographical Sketches*, V:316–17. Two fine articles by Alan V. Briceland provide further details: "John C. Ogden: Messenger and Propagandist for Matthew Lyon, 1798–1799," *Vermont History* 43 (1975):103–21, and "The Philadelphia Aurora, The New England Illuminati, and the Election of 1800," *Pennsylvania Magazine of History and Biography* C (1976):3–36. The "Gaolbird" and "half-crazy" quotes are cited in Briceland, "Messenger and Propagandist," p. 114.

136. John C. Ogden, *An Appeal to the Candid, upon the Present State of Religion and Politics in Connecticut* (New Haven: n.p., 1798), pp. 3–4, 11–12, 14. Ogden's complaints about New England oligarchies, especially when aimed at the Edwards clan, were disingenuous at best. In 1774 (long before his defection to the Episcopalians in the mid-1780s) Ogden married Mary Clap Wooster, daughter of David Wooster, prominent New Haven merchant and New Light. Their marriage ceremony was performed by the New Divinity theologian Jonathan Edwards, Jr. Moreover, Ogden's sister was married to

Pierpont Edwards, another son of Jonathan and Sarah Edwards. Jonathan, Jr. and Pierpont were Dwight's uncles. Hence, by marriage, Ogden's sister was Dwight's aunt, and Ogden himself was distantly related by marriage to Dwight.

137. John Cosens Ogden, *Friendly Remarks to the People of Connecticut, upon their Colleges and Schools* (n.p., 1799), pp. 2, 8, 13, 34, 39, 15.

138. Dwight to Morse, 30 December 1799, *MFP.* Typical of other assaults on Standing Order clergy is David Austin, *The Dance of Herodias through the Streets of Hartford on Election Day to the Tune of the Stars of Heaven in the Dragon's Tail; or, A Gentle Trip at the Heels of the Strumpet of Babylon Playing Tricks in the Attire of the Daughters of Zion* (East Windsor: Luther Pratt, 1799), in which Dwight and his colleagues are referred to as "old croakers." For more on the Republican reaction to the clergy, see Purcell, *Connecticut in Transition: 1755–1818,* pp. 202ff. Of particular interest is the note on pp. 209–10 in which Purcell indicates how some Federalists, notably Dwight's brother Theodore, fought back. A portion of Theodore's satiric poem, *Ye Ragged Throng of Democrats,* reads as follows:

> Behold the motley crew, Come crowding o'er the green
> Of every shape and hue, Complexion, form and mien,
> With deaf'ning noise, Drunkards and whores and rogues in scores
> They all rejoice.

See also William A. Robinson, *Jeffersonian Democracy in New England* (New Haven: Yale University Press, 1916), especially ch. 7, "Religious Liberty," pp. 128ff.

139. Dwight to Morse, 4 February 1802. Gratz collection. Historical Society of Pennsylvania.

140. For the history of the development of the Unitarians, see Conrad Wright, *The Beginnings of Unitarianism in America* (Boston: Starr King Press, 1955); Daniel Walker Howe, *The Unitarian Conscience: Harvard Moral Philosophy, 1805–1861* (Cambridge: Harvard University Press, 1970).

141. Dwight to Morse, 6 July 1805, *MFP.* Given Dwight's clear antipathies toward the Unitarians, it appears rather remarkable that Harvard awarded him an honorary doctorate (an LL.D.) in 1810. Why would Harvard, having only recently established its identity as the center of Unitarian thought, honor Dwight, the staunch political and theological traditionalist? Although the Harvard University archives provide little documentation about why Dwight was so honored, the awarding of the degree was most likely a result of institutional courtesy. It was apparently customary for Harvard to honor the presidents of Yale and Princeton with honorary doctorates. Harvard also awarded Samuel Stanhope Smith, president of Princeton, an LL.D. in 1810.

142. Although many colleges and universities in the early republic offered training in theological studies as a part of their regular curricula, Andover was the nation's first theological seminary intended strictly for college graduates. That status did not last long. Princeton Theological Seminary was formed in 1812. Yale Divinity School, first organized as the Theological Department of the college, was begun in 1822 with the naming of Nathaniel W. Taylor as the first incumbent of the Dwight Professorship of Didactic Theology. Dwight's unqualified support of the founding of Andover—a school that might have been seen as a rival to Yale—may have troubled some of his Yale colleagues. This is suggested by a cryptic line that appears in a letter from Dwight to Morse: "I doubt of any success, at present, to your subscription for your library, here. Our people all feel embarrassed." Dwight to Morse, 1 August 1808, *MFP.* The full letter is reprinted in Woods, pp. 602–3.

143. For a full account of the founding of Andover, see Leonard Woods, *History of Andover Theological Seminary.* Also see Phillips, pp. 136–39; K. Alan Snyder, "Foundations of Liberty: The Christian Republicanism of Timothy Dwight and Jedidiah Morse," *New England Quarterly* 56 (1983):382–97; and Conforti, "Edwardsians, Unitarians, and

the Memory of the Great Awakening, 1800–1840," in Wright, ed., *American Unitarianism*, pp. 31–50.

144. Morse to Dwight, 15 July 1808, in Woods, p. 597.

145. Dwight discussed the appointment of Moses Stuart to the Andover faculty in Dwight to Morse, 2 February 1808, *MFP.* On the whole, Dwight thought it best for a school to educate its own faculty: "If you cannot suit yourselves among those already in another [school]. We have pursued this course with the happiest success. [Such a person] will not answer the end quite so well at first, but he will soon become better than most men whom you would select, will ever be." For Dwight's views on the optimum duration of clerical preparation at Andover (on the basis of his experience at Yale he favored a two-year term), see Dwight to Morse, 14 May 1808, *MFP.* Morse alerted Dwight to the forthcoming invitation to preach the inaugural sermon in Morse to Dwight, 1 August 1808, in Woods, pp. 596–97. For Dwight's questions about the details of the address and on Dwight's efforts to gather books for Andover's library, see Dwight to Morse, 1 August 1808, *MFP.* The full letter is reprinted in Woods, pp. 602–3.

146. Timothy Dwight, *Sermon Preached at the Opening of the Theological Institution in Andover; And at the Ordination of Rev. Eliphalet Pearson, LL.D., September 28th, 1808* (Boston: Farrand, Mallory, 1808).

147. Dwight, *Andover Sermon*, pp. 8, 9, 14, 19.

148. Dwight, *Andover Sermon*, pp. 25, 27.

149. Timothy Dwight, *Sermon Delivered in Boston, Sept. 16, 1813, before the American Board of Commissioners of Foreign Missions, at Their Fourth Annual Meeting* (Boston: S. T. Armstrong, 1813), pp. 25, 19–20.

150. In pursuing Stiles's dream of a Yale medical school, Dwight and the Corporation courted Nathan Smith for their first Professor of Medicine in 1813. But Dwight discovered that Smith had flirted with Republicanism and had "doubted the truth of Divine Revelation." Not until Smith swung to the Federalist persuasion and confessed his faith in the authority of scripture would Dwight allow him to join the faculty. See Dr. Nathan Smith to Dr. Mason Fitch Cogswell, undated, in Emily A. Smith, *Life and Letters of Nathan Smith* (New Haven: Yale University Press, 1914), p. xxx.

151. *Travels*, ix. The allowance for an amanuensis is recorded in *Theology*, 1:27 as follows: "In 1805, when he was appointed Professor of Theology, the Corporation allowed him fifty pounds per annum to employ an amanuensis." Although Dwight was in the habit of lending his unpublished manuscripts to students (far too freely, in the opinion of the author of *Hints*), in the latter years of his life he apparently destroyed several manuscripts that he did not want to circulate or appear in print after his death. When asked about the destruction of these materials, Dwight "replied that he had noticed so many instances in which friends and relations had acted indiscreetly in publishing posthumous works that the authors had not probably intended for publication that he thought it advisable to dispose of some of his in that way. In the course of his remarks he said that he had destroyed a number of sermons which were as popular as any that he ever preached." See *Hints, DFP.*

152. Dwight to Morse, 2 February 1808, *MFP.* The Yale University Library collection houses a few manuscript booklets that formed the basis of parts of the published version of *Travels*. The handwriting in these booklets is identical to that in several of the unpublished sermon booklets that were written out by Dwight's son, Benjamin. Some of the *Travels* booklets contain editorial corrections in Dwight's own hand. On the composition of this work, see "A Note on the Text," in *Travels*, pp. xlix–liv.

153. Dwight, *Remarks*, pp. 15, 52.

154. Dwight, *An Address to the Emigrants from Connecticut and from New England Generally, in the New Settlements in the United States* (Hartford: Peter Gleason, 1817), pp. 5, 9, 11, 13, 16.

155. [Benjamin Dwight], "A Memoir of the Life of the Author," *Theology*, 1:34.

156. For details of Dwight's activities on behalf of Yale in his final days, see Ebenezer Baldwin, *The History of Yale College, from Its Foundation, A.D. 1700, to the Year 1838* (New Haven: Benjamin and William Noyes, 1841), pp. 150ff.

157. Silliman, *A Sketch of the Life and Character of President Dwight*, p. 38. The biblical text is from Matthew 5:16.

158. *Hints, DFP.* In the final months of his life Dwight had apparently been working on a major publication concerning the inspiration and authority of the scripture—the "Evidences" he mentioned on his deathbed. This was perhaps an expansion of his "Lectures on the Evidences of Divine Revelation," which appeared in the *Panoplist and Missionary Magazine United* from June 1810 through December 1813. No manuscript of this description survives.

159. Beecher, *Autobiography*, 1:242; Gardiner Spring, *An Oration on the Evening of the Fifth of February, before the Alumni of Yale College, Resident in the City of New York, in Commemoration of Their Late President, Timothy Dwight, D.D., LL.D.* (New York: Dodge and Sayre, 1817), p. 5; [Benjamin Dwight], "A Memoir of the Life of the Author," *Theology*, 1:52. Beecher's outburst on hearing of Dwight's death represents an apt but self-serving bit of *double entendre*. The reference to the "chariots of Israel" is from 2 Kings 2. In the biblical text, Elisha, protégé to the prophet Elijah, offers the exclamation in praise of his beloved master. Beecher's recitation was obviously intended as a compliment to his mentor Dwight. But in casting himself as Elisha, did Beecher lay claim to his mentor's mantle?

II. The Herald of Reconciliation

1. An extant engraving of Dwight reveals him as he was probably best known to his students, as a preacher—a sober, confident, and energetic cleric wearing a clerical tab collar, the sort of man young students would take quite seriously. The artist of the portrait on which this engraving is based is unknown. The stipple engraving is by Amos Doolittle and is owned by the Connecticut Historical Society, Hartford, Connecticut. It appears here with permission of the Connecticut Historical Society.

2. An extant set of auditor's notes indicates how Dwight preached through his *Theology* at Yale Chapel. On 17 July 1808, Dwight preached the sermon that would become Sermon 104 in *Theology*. With remarkable regularity he continued sequentially, preaching one sermon per week, and reached Sermon 147 on 20 August 1809. In October of 1809, he continued with Sermons 150 and following. During a second Sunday service he began preaching the cycle from the start with Sermon 1. Hence, on 10 December 1809 Dwight preached Sermon 7 in the morning and Sermon 157 in the afternoon. See anonymous MS entitled "Theological Discourses by Dr. Dwight," *DFP.* Using this convention, Dwight was able to devote his first Sunday sermon (usually from the earlier portions of *Theology*) to Christian doctrine and his second Sunday sermon (from the latter portions of *Theology*) to Christian duty. Despite his fame as a preacher, Dwight sometimes failed to hold the attention of his young auditors. An anonymous biographer noted that although his "manner of preaching was distinct, forcible, and free from the appearance of affectation," his voice could be "unusually heavy and sonorous." This sometimes tended to "tire the ear, and to lull the attention." See "Biographical Memoir of the Rev. Timothy Dwight, S.T.D., LL.D.," *Port Folio* 4 (1817):367.

3. For a full list of Dwight's extant manuscript sermons see the Bibliographic Essay. *Hints* contains a long list of Dwight's sermon titles and dates including a brief calendar of Yale commencement sermons that he delivered. *Hints* also notes that Dwight lent his manuscript sermons to students and friends "much more freely than was prudent."

4. See "Biographical Hints," *DFP.* After they had been transcribed and prepared for

publication, Dwight's sermon manuscripts were sewn together into small booklets. An illustration of the extent to which Dwight repeated sermons appears in an MS booklet entitled *Long Life Not Desirable* on the text Job 6:16 in *DFP.* The cover of the booklet indicates that it was preached at Greenfield on 22 November 1788, and at Yale on 14 April 1805, 19 March 1809, and 19 November 1812. The sermon was subsequently published in *Sermons,* 2:273.

5. Memoir of the author in *Theology,* 1:53.

6. *Hints* contains information about Dwight's earliest attempts at extempore preaching and indicates that he and his amanuenses began the formal compilation of *Theology* in 1805 and finished the task in 1810. In an extant letter to Edwards Amasa Park, the historian George Park Fisher remembered Nathaniel William Taylor's comments about his role as an amanuensis: "Dr. Taylor told me that Dr. Dwight referred to Emmons in the sermon on 'The Mind Not a Chain,' etc., and Dr. Taylor, unless my memory deceives me, said that he himself wrote that sermon, as amanuensis." Fisher to Park, 23 April 1879, in the Edwards Amasa Park Papers, Trask Library, Andover-Newton Theological Seminary.

7. *Ecclesiastes 9:10, DFP.* The cover of the MS booklet indicates that this sermon was preached 3 April 1795, 4 December 1812, and 30 June 1816.

8. Martin E. Marty, *The Infidel: Freethought and American Religion* (Cleveland: World Publishing, 1961), p. 47.

9. Perhaps one of the most frustrating problems faced by students of Dwight lies in seeking to determine the authors whose writings he had perused, read, or studied. Yale's curriculum during the tenure of Ezra Stiles, Dwight's predecessor in the Yale presidency, is discussed in Morgan, *Gentle Puritan,* pp. 391ff. Dwight himself discusses the Yale curriculum during his presidency in *Travels,* 1:150; his students used Locke, Blair, and William Paley but apparently not Hume.

10. John Locke, "An Essay Concerning Human Understanding" in *Locke's Essays: An Essay Concerning Human Understanding and A Treatise on the Conduct of the Understanding* (Philadelphia: Kay and Troutman, 1847), pp. 75, 83, 110.

11. Edwards claimed that genuine gracious affections were infused directly into the soul by God. In the process of describing the spiritual renovation that occurs in regeneration, Edwards teased out a philosophical description of the event. He noted: "there is what some metaphysicians call a new simple idea." See Jonathan Edwards, *Religious Affections,* John E. Smith, ed. (New Haven: Yale University Press, 1959), p. 205.

12. David Hume, *The Philosophical Works of David Hume, Including the Essays, and Exhibiting the More Important Alterations and Corrections in the Successive Editions Published by the Author,* 4 vols. (Edinburgh: Black and Tate, 1826). For Hume on these particular questions see *Treatise of Human Nature,* Book I, Parts I and II.

13. Hume, *Human Nature,* Part IV, Section I, 1:240.

14. Hume, *An Inquiry into the Human Understanding,* Section 10, "Of Miracles," 4:133, 135, 137, 141, 154. See also Francis J. Beckwith, *David Hume's Argument against Miracles: A Critical Analysis* (Lanham: University Press of America, 1989), especially pp. 19–69.

15. Thomas Reid, *The Works of Thomas Reid, D.D., Now Fully Collected, with Selections from His Unpublished Letters,* 6th ed. 2 vols., ed. Sir William Hamilton (Edinburgh: Maclachlan and Stewart, 1863), 1:108, 101.

16. George Campbell, *A Dissertation on Miracles: Containing an Examination of the Principles Advanced by David Hume, Esq.; In an Essay on Miracles* (Edinburgh: Kincaid and Bell, 1762; reprint, New York: Garland, 1983), pp. v–vi, 3–4, 238. (Page references are to reprint edition.). Evidence of Dwight's having read Campbell appears in his sermon on the "Miracles of Christ" in *Theology,* 2:257, in which he borrows an analogy

verbatim from page 21 of Campbell's *Dissertation on Miracles*. For details of Campbell's argument and for an analysis of the manner in which evangelicals used it to counter Hume, see Hovencamp, *Science and Religion in America,* pp. 83ff.

17. James Beattie, "An Essay on the Nature and Immutability of Truth; In Opposition to Sophistry and Skepticism." In *The Philosophy of David Hume: Eighteen of the Most Important Books on Hume's Philosophy,* ed. Lewis White Beck (Edinburgh: Kincaid and Bell, 1770; facsimile edition reprinted in 20 vols., New York: Garland, 1983). Dwight mentions Beattie's *Minstrel* in *Travels,* 3:65. Howard, *Connecticut Wits,* pp. 28–29, 49–50, 363, provides a helpful discussion of the Wits' familiarity with Beattie's poetry and philosophy. Dowling, *Poetry and Ideology in Revolutionary Connecticut,* pp. 39ff., discusses how Beattie's *Minstrel* may have served as a model for Dwight's *Greenfield Hill.*

18. Beattie, "An Essay on the Nature and Immutability of Truth," pp. 19, 156, 143.

19. Lord Kames, *Elements of Criticism,* 6th ed., 2 vols. (Edinburgh: Bell and Creech, 1785; reprint edition, New York: Garland, 1972).

20. Some Americans were first introduced to Kames the theologian. In his *Essays on the Principles of Morality and Natural Religion* (Edinburgh 1751), Kames took a deterministic view of human moral agency. Though his thought developed and shifted over the course of several subsequent editions of *Essays,* Kames's work on this problem drew the attention of Jonathan Edwards. During the summer of 1757, Edwards wrote his Scottish correspondent John Erskine twice about Kames's views of the will. Edwards's chief concern was to distinguish his own opinions as developed in his *Strict and Careful Enquiry into the Modern Prevailing Notions of . . . Freedom of the Will* (Boston, 1754) from what he took to be the erroneous ideas of Kames. Edwards's first letter to Erskine was published as "Remarks on the Essay on the Principles of Morality and Natural Religion" beginning with the third edition of Edwards's *Freedom of the Will.* For details see Jonathan Edwards, *The Freedom of the Will,* Paul Ramsey, ed. (New Haven: Yale University Press, 1957), pp. 443ff.

21. Dwight's method of collecting, organizing, and recalling facts is described in the anonymous "Biographical Memoir of the Rev. Timothy Dwight, S.T.D., LL.D." *Port Folio* 4 (1817):364ff.

22. Hugh Blair, *Lectures on Rhetoric and Belles Lettres,* 2nd ed. 3 vols. (London: Stahan, 1885; facsimile edition, New York: Garland, 1970). (The original edition was published in 1783).

23. Abe C. Ravitz, "Timothy Dwight: Professor of Rhetoric," *New England Quarterly* 29 (1956):63–72, provides a helpful analysis of the manner in which Dwight relied on Blair's *Lectures.* Working from auditors' notes taken in his Rhetoric class in 1803, Ravitz concludes that Dwight was "an academic commentator deriving from the Scotch Common Sense school. While he quibbled with Hugh Blair on an occasional point, Dwight's system . . . evolved from the principles set down by the Scotch philosopher" (p. 72).

24. Campbell discusses preaching in Book I, ch. 10 of *The Philosophy of Rhetoric;* Blair's treatment of homiletics appears in Lecture XXIX of his *Lectures on Rhetoric and Belles Lettres.* Campbell's longer treatment of preaching comprises the second half of his *Lectures on Systematic Theology and Pulpit Eloquence* (Boston: Wells, Wait, 1807). Several editions of this latter work were issued, one of which was an American edition: Edwards A. Park, ed., *The Preacher and Pastor, by Fenelon, Herbert, Baxter, and Campbell, Edited and Accompanied with an Introductory Essay,* by Edwards A. Park (Andover: Allen, Morrill, and Wardwell, 1845).

25. On the purpose or telos of preaching, see Blair, *Lectures,* p. 305, and Campbell, *Philosophy of Rhetoric,* p. 107.

26. Blair, *Lectures,* p. 303

27. Campbell, *Pulpit Eloquence,* pp. 214ff.

28. *Theology,* 4:247.

29. Dwight discussed these aspects of the homiletic enterprise in "The Extraordinary Means of Grace: The End, Nature, and Subjects of Preaching," *Theology*, 4:246–58, and in "The Extraordinary Means of Grace: The Manner of Preaching," *Theology*, 4:259–72. Elsewhere Dwight noted his strong disapproval of overly emotional appeals from the pulpit. He believed that Methodist frontier preachers were especially guilty of using this ploy. See Dwight, *Remarks on the Review of Inchiquin's Letters*, p. 52.

30. Dwight, "Lectures on the Evidence of Divine Revelation," *Panoplist and Missionary Magazine United* 3 (August, 1810), p. 111.

31. Dwight, *Discourse on the Genuineness and Authenticity of the New Testament*, pp. 21, 28, 29.

32. Dwight, *Thoughts on the Mediation of Christ*, DFP.

33. Dwight, *The Manner in Which the Scriptures are to be Understood*, pp. 194, 196, 197, 198, 249. Dwight addressed biblical manuscript problems and critical textual matters at several places. See Dwight, "A Historical Account of the Gothic Gospel." *New-Haven Gazette and Connecticut Magazine* 2 (1 March 1787):10; Dwight, "Lectures on the Evidences of Divine Revelation." *Panoplist and Missionary Magazine United* 3 (June 1810–December 1813); and *Theology*, 1:404. For a sustained treatment of Common Sense and scriptural interpretation, see Dwight, *Discourse on the Genuineness and Authenticity of the New Testament*, p. 28.

34. *Theology*, 1:365.

35. *Theology*, 2:99.

36. *Travels*, 4:229.

37. Timothy Dwight, *The Triumph of Infidelity*. In *The Major Poems of Timothy Dwight (1752–1817), with a Dissertation on the History, Eloquence, and Poetry of the Bible*, eds. William J. McTaggart and William K. Bottoroff (Gainesville, Fla.: Scholars' Facsimiles and Reprints, 1969):343.

38. *Theology*, 1:75, 78.

39. *Theology*, 1:92, 99. Elsewhere Dwight fires volleys at the "ideal system" that Reid identified as the taproot of skepticism. In his *Theology* sermon entitled "The Soul Not a Chain of Ideas and Exercises," Dwight targets the notion that "we can form no conception of anything in ourselves, beyond our ideas and exercises." That claim, he observes, amounts to saying "that nothing exists, of which we have no conception." The ramifications: "According to the abovementioned principle, all that which we cannot understand concerning God, has no existence, and must stand for nothing." The work of God is invisible, but we know it is there: "Universally, substance, causation, and the modus operandi, lie wholly beyond our reach. But shall we on this account deny the facts; or assert that there are no causes to produce them? In the former case we shall annihilate the universe at once, in the latter, pronounce every fact to be a mere contingency" (*Theology*, 1:366, 367). Echoing Edwards's assault on the Arminians in *Freedom of the Will*, Dwight claims that the "chain of ideas" theory leads to several conclusions: there is nothing that God can punish or reward; neither guilt nor virtue can exist; and the influence of motives is annihilated. (*Theology*, 1:372.)

40. *Theology*, 1:102, 106, 109, 110.

41. In the text of his *Nature and Danger* Dwight cites pithy summaries from a plethora of ancient and modern philosphers including Aristotle, Socrates, Cicero, Lord Herbert of Cherbury, Hobbes, Blount, Clarke, Tindal, Hume, and Bolingbroke.

42. Dwight, *Duty of Americans*, pp. 20–21. In this passage Dwight excoriates several of the most radical changes proposed during the French Revolution. He gives particular attention to the transformation of parish churches into "temples of reason." He also ridicules the promulgation of the Revolutionary Calendar, based on a ten-day week (the tenth day of which was the "decade"), which was designed in part to eliminate the Sabbath.

43. Hofstadter, *Paranoid Style in American Politics*, p. 13.

44. *Theology*, 1:160.

45. *Theology*, 2:223–24.

46. *Theology*, 2:250.

47. *Sermons*, 2:186.

48. *Sermons*, 2:196.

49. Dwight devotes almost the entire second half of *Theology*, Sermons 91 through 173, to social ethics; he subtitles this section of *Theology* a "System of Duties."

50. It was this sermon, or some version of it, that proved instrumental in Lyman Beecher's conversion. See Beecher, *Autobiography*, 1:29.

51. *Sermons*, 2:401–2.

52. *Sermons*, 1:238. Dwight is elsewhere unabashed in his use of millennial language and forthright in his identification of America as the New Israel. See, for example, *The Conquest of Canaan, The Triumph of Infidelity*, and *Duty of Americans at the Present Crisis*. See Bloch, *Visionary Republic*, for an excellent secondary treatment of the political contexts of millennial rhetoric during this era.

53. *Sermons*, 1:239.

54. Dwight, *On Levity with Respect to Sacred Things*," DFP. The MS pages are unnumbered; quoted selections appear on leaves 2, 6, 12. The cover of the MS booklet notes that this was preached in 1790, 1812, and 1816.

55. Dwight, *On Levity with Respect to Sacred Things*, leaves 31, 39, 43.

56. Dwight, *Thoughts on the Mediation of Christ*, DFP.

57. Dwight, "Brief Account of the Revival of Religion Now Prevailing in Yale College," *Connecticut Evangelical Magazine* 3 (July 1802), pp. 31, 32. Dwight was not the only college president to express deep concern about the behavior of students. See Noll, *Princeton and the Republic* for an analysis of similar problems that troubled Dwight's Princeton counterpart, Samuel Stanhope Smith.

58. Dwight to Benjamin Dwight, 8 August, 1803, DFP. Richard Rabinowitz explores the manner in which personal spirituality changed and shifted in both Timothy Dwight's and Benjamin Dwight's generations. See Rabinowitz, *The Spiritual Self in Everyday Life: The Transformation of Personal Religious Experience in Nineteenth-Century New England* (Boston: Northeastern University Press, 1989).

59. Dwight, *Theology*, 1:51. The "herald of reconciliation" attribution is found in "A Memoir of the Life of the Author" that appears in *Theology*. Though formally anonymous, the memoir was written by Dwight's son Benjamin Dwight.

III. A Distinguished Divine

1. Samuel Hopkins to Rev. Samuel Miller, 23 January 1801, Princeton University Library.

2. Samuel Hopkins, *The System of Doctrine Contained in Divine Revelation, Explained and Defended, Shewing Their Consistence and Connexion with Each Other, To Which Is Added, A Treatise on the Millennium*, 2nd ed., 2 vols. (Boston: Lincoln and Edmands, 1811), 1:3. Henceforth, this work will be cited as "Hopkins, *System*." Contemporaries were well aware of the efforts of the New Divinity's attempts to "perfect" Edwards's system. In 1801, Hannah Adams claimed, "This denomination [the New Divinity] suppose, that this eminent divine [Jonathan Edwards] not only illustrated and confirmed the main doctrines of Calvinism, but brought the whole system to a greater degree of consistency and perfection than any who had gone before him. And they profess only to pursue the same design, of still further perfecting the same system." Hannah Adams, *A View of Religions in Two Parts* (Boston: Manning and Loring, 1801), p. 127. Sidney Mead believed that the New Divinity theologians spent their time "ruminating in their isolated rural parsonages over the published works and manu-

scripts of their idolized leader, Jonathan Edwards. They accepted his words as highest truth, but, in the words of Harriet Beecher Stowe, each was 'cheerfully busy' making his own emendations and improvements." (Mead, *Nathaniel William Taylor,* p. 15.) The citation from Harriet Beecher Stowe comes from her *Oldtown Folks* (Boston, 1869), p. 223.

3. The work treating the Edwardseans and New Divinity theologians is varied and rich. The most engaging elements of this literature include: Haroutunian, *Piety Versus Moralism;* Mead, *Nathaniel William Taylor;* Berk, *Calvinism Versus Democracy;* Conforti, *Samuel Hopkins and the New Divinity Movement;* Guelzo, *Edwards on the Will;* Kling, *A Field of Divine Wonders;* and Valeri, *Law and Providence in Joseph Bellamy's New England.* Nineteenth-century authors argued about the evolution, merits, and legitimacy of the New Divinity for decades. Perhaps the most famous of these debates was between Charles Hodge and Edwards Amasa Park. As the respective champions of Princeton Seminary and Andover Seminary, Hodge and Park fought to establish as orthodox their version of Calvinism. See Charles Hodge, "Professor Park and The Princeton Review," *The Biblical Repertory and Princeton Review* 23 (October, 1851), p. 694, and Edwards Amasa Park, *New England Theology; With Comments on a Third Article in the Princeton Review, Relating to a Convention Sermon* (Andover: Warren Draper, 1852), p. 7, for illustrations of this famous paper war.

4. For primary source illustrations of the Reformed tradition on the following doctrinal points, see Heinrich Heppe, *Reformed Dogmatics Set Out and Illustrated from the Sources,* translated by G. T. Thomson, revised and edited by Ernest Bizer (London: George Allen and Unwin Ltd., 1956). On imputation and original sin, see pp. 314ff.; imputation and the atonement, pp. 464ff.; imputation and justification, pp. 548ff.

5. The tract in question is John Taylor, *The Scripture Doctrine of Original Sin Proposed to Free and Candid Examination* (London, 1740). An excellent discussion of this controversy is found in H. Shelton Smith, *Changing Conceptions of Original Sin: A Study in American Theology since 1750* (New York: Charles Scribner's Sons, 1955).

6. Samuel Webster, *A Winter Evening's Conversation upon the Doctrine of Original Sin* (Boston: Green and Russell, 1757), p. 3.

7. Webster, p. 4.

8. Webster, p. 7.

9. Webster, pp. 29–30.

10. Webster, p. 6.

11. Webster, p. 8.

12. Webster, p. 25.

13. Edwards, *Original Sin, Works,* 3:16.

14. Edwards, *Original Sin, Works,* 3:389.

15. Edwards, *Original Sin, Works,* 3:401.

16. Edwards, *Original Sin, Works,* 3:408. It is important to note that Edwards did not argue that sinners are thereby doubly guilty: "I am humbly of the opinion, that if any have supposed the children of Adam to come into the world with a double guilt, one the guilt of Adam's sin, another the guilt arising from their having a corrupt heart, they have not so well conceived the matter." Edwards, *Original Sin, Works,* 3:390.

17. Edwards's relationship with covenant theology has been the subject of some debate. Perry Miller argued that Edwards had "brushed aside the (by his day) rusty mechanism of the covenant to forge a fresh statement of man's plight in a universe which God created." Miller, "The Marrow of Puritan Divinity," in *Errand into the Wilderness,* p. 50. This statement qualified Miller's earlier assertion in the same essay that Edwards was New England's first "consistent and authentic Calvinist" (p. 98). A fuller treatment of this issue is found in Carl Bogue, *Jonathan Edwards and the Covenant of Grace* (Cherry Hill, N.J.: Mack, 1975).

18. Hopkins, *System,* 1:268. Hopkins even suggested that humanity actually con-

sented to Adam's sin: "It was made certain, and known and declared to be so, that all mankind should sin as Adam had done, and fully consent to his transgression, and join in the rebellion which he began" (1:268). Not all of the New Divinity men agreed with Hopkins's teaching about Adam and his posterity. Jonathan Edwards, Jr., for instance, strongly disagreed. In a letter to Hopkins, Edwards, Jr., claimed that "Mankind no more consent to that sin than they do to the sin of Joseph's brethren or any other sin." Edwards, Jr., to Hopkins, 29 October 1793. Cited in Conforti, *Samuel Hopkins and the New Divinity Movement,* pp. 166–67. Joseph Haroutunian, a twentieth-century critic of Edwards's followers, believed that the great irony of the New Divinity movement was that, despite its desire to overthrow Arminianism, it became "a curious hybrid of Calvinism and Arminianism." (Haroutunian, *Piety Versus Moralism,* p. 62.)

19. Hopkins, *System,* 1:85.

20. Hopkins, *System,* 1:113.

21. At this point theologians often discuss the question, "Is God the author of sin?" In his *System* (1:135, 136) Hopkins pursues this question by referring to Edwards's *Freedom of the Will.* Hopkins also addressed the question in *Sin, Thro' Divine Interposition, an Advantage to the Universe . . . in Three Sermons* (Boston: 1773). See also Joseph Bellamy, *Four Sermons on the Wisdom of God in the Permission of Sin* (Morristown, N.J.: Henry P. Russell, 1804).

22. Dexter, *Literary Diary,* 2:504–5. Stiles also noted that New Divinity theologians asserted "that true repentance implies a willingness to be damned for the glory of God; that we are to give God thanks, that he has caused Adam to sin and involve all his posterity in total depravity; that Judas betrayed and the Jews crucified Christ, etc., etc." Dexter, *Literary Diary,* 2:504–5.

23. Stiles, as well as many other contemporaries, understood the profound impact that the New Divinity denial of imputation had on the Reformed theological system. He confided to his diary, "New Divinity! Denying the imputation of Adam's Sin to his posterity, and the sins of the world to Christ, and of Christ's righteousness to Believers in Justification." Dexter, *Literary Diary,* 3:480–81.

24. For details of Hopkins's view of the suffering of Christ, see his *System,* 1:408ff.

25. Two important works treat New Divinity views of the atonement: Dorus Paul Rudisill, *The Doctrine of the Atonement,* and Edwards Amasa Park, *The Atonement: Discourses and Treatises by Edwards, Smalley, Maxcy, Emmons, Griffin, Burge, and Weeks. With an Introductory Essay by Edwards A. Park* (Boston: Congregational Publishing Society, 1859).

26. Hopkins, *System,* 1:398.

27. Hopkins, *System,* 2:60, 61.

28. Hopkins, *System,* 2:60.

29. This citation from Hopkins appears in Adams, *A View of Religions in Two Parts,* p. 133.

30. Dwight, *Travels,* 4:228.

31. Dwight, *Theology,* 1:478–79.

32. Dwight, *Theology,* 1:480.

33. Fond of reasoning from empirical data, Dwight appealed to a fascinating body of facts as "proof" of the perniciousness and universality of depravity. In *Theology* he recited a litany of statistical data on the crime rate of France, the veritable seat of infidelity. Dwight included data on illegitimate births, prostitution, murders, and poverty. Dwight, *Theology,* 1:474.

34. See, for instance, Bellamy's *The Wisdom of God in the Permission of Sin, Vindicated* (Boston: 1760).

35. Dwight, *Theology,* 1:414.

36. Dwight, *Theology,* 1:414.

37. Dwight, *Theology,* 1:416. To this assertion, Dwight added an interesting interpretation. He argued that if Adam had obeyed and not fallen, the resulting earthly existence

of humanity (a continuation of the Edenic circumstances) would evidence less glory to God than had resulted from the Fall-Redemption situation. "The former legal system, therefore, of which the primitive state of Adam was a part, had comparatively no glory, by reason of the excelling glory of the system of Redemption." Dwight, *Theology,* 1:416. Moreover, Dwight also claimed that if Adam had not fallen, "no human beings would have been admitted to heaven," Dwight, *Theology,* 1:415.

38. For a discussion of God's "authorship of sin," see H. Shelton Smith, *Changing Conceptions of Original Sin,* pp. 63ff. Smith argues that Nathaniel Emmons was the most strident of the New Divinity men on this issue, asserting that only an inconsistent theologian could not believe that God created sin. Smith compares Dwight to Emmons and finds Dwight's doctrine far more moderate.

39. Hopkins, *System,* 1:134.

40. Dwight, *Theology,* 1:254.

41. Dwight, *Theology,* 1:416.

42. Dwight, *Theology,* 1:254.

43. Dwight, *Theology,* 1:416. In another place Dwight noted, "The truth is, the subject of Moral Evil is too extensive and too mysterious to be comprehended by the understanding. Some things the scriptures teach concerning it, and these are usually furnished with important evidence from facts. Many other things pertaining to the subject lie wholly beyond our reach. What we can know it is our duty and our interest to know. Where knowledge is unattainable, it is both our duty and interest to trust humbly and submissively to the instruction of Him, the Only Wise." Dwight, *Theology,* 1:487.

44. Dwight, *Theology,* 2:218.

45. Dwight, *Theology,* 2:222.

46. Dwight, *Theology,* 2:195.

47. Dwight, *Theology,* 2:223.

48. Dwight, *Theology,* 2:223

49. Dwight, *Theology,* 2:223.

50. Dwight, *Theology,* 2:358.

51. Dwight, *Theology,* 2:369.

52. Edwards, *Freedom of the Will, Works,* 1:149.

53. Edwards, *Freedom of the Will, Works,* 1:137.

54. Edwards, *Freedom of the Will, Works,* 1:156–57.

55. Edwards, *Freedom of the Will, Works,* 1:156.

56. Edwards, *Freedom of the Will, Works,* 1:159.

57. Edwards discusses the negative signs in *Religious Affections, Works,* 2:125–90. He describes the positive signs at length in *Religious Affections, Works,* 2:191–461.

58. This argument appears throughout *The End.* See Edwards, *Two Dissertations, Dissertation I: Concerning the End for Which God Created the World, Works,* 8:403–536.

59. Edwards, *Two Dissertations, Dissertation II: The Nature of True Virtue, Works,* 8:540.

60. William Breitenbach, "Unregenerate Doings: Selflessness and Selfishness in New Divinity Theology," *American Quarterly* 34 (Winter 1982):484.

61. Edwards, *Two Dissertations, Dissertation II: The Nature of True Virtue, Works,* 8:557.

62. Conforti argues that Hopkins own concern for social issues played a large part in his rejection of Edwards's "Being in general" definition. Conforti, *Samuel Hopkins and the New Divinity Movement,* pp. 111ff.

63. Conforti, *Samuel Hopkins and the New Divinity Movement,* p. 118.

64. Hopkins to Miller, 23 January 1801, Princeton University Library.

65. For Hopkins on the sacraments, see his *System,* 2:223ff. Conforti, *Samuel Hopkins and the New Divinity Movement,* pp. 80ff., gives a detailed account of the New Divinity's repudiation of the Halfway Covenant.

66. Dwight, *Theology,* 3:15–26.

67. Dwight, *Theology,* 4:50.
68. Dwight, *Theology,* 4:49.
69. Dwight, *Theology,* 4:71.
70. Dwight, *Theology,* 4:71. Dwight acknowledged that God could work immediately as in the case of the Apostle Paul's conversion. This caveat notwithstanding, Dwight argued that God did not usually work immediately. Normally, God employed means in conversion. Dwight discussed the means of grace at some length in one of his unpublished sermons (preached on 20 August 1812 on 2 Kings 5:9–15) in DFP entitled *The Cleansing of Naaman.* For a further illustration of Dwight's views on evangelism as it related to the New Divinity understanding of the means, see his sermon *Ecclesiastes 9:10,* preached in 1795, 1812, and 1816, in *DFP.*
71. Dwight to Dr. Ryland, 16 March 1805. Sterling Library, Yale University. Dwight was free with his negative opinions of the Hopkinsians at other times. James Alexander reported that Dwight made plain his views of Hopkins's system in a conversation with Dr. Nathan Strong. See James W. Alexander, D.D., *The Life of Archibald Alexander, D.D., First Professor in the Theological Seminary at Princeton, New Jersey* (New York: Charles Scribner, 1854), pp. 240–41.
72. Dwight, *Theology,* 4:58. As Dwight wrote elsewhere, "All the efficacy I have attributed to the means of grace, does not, I acknowledge, amount to regeneration nor ensure it. But it amounts to what St. Paul terms planting and watering. The increase must be, and still is, given by God alone." Dwight, *Theology,* 4:59. Throughout his theology, and particularly in the debates about the efficacy of the means, Dwight tried to keep the sovereignty of God in view: "What is it, that we attempt to comprehend, and explain? The thoughts and works of an Infinite mind: plans, filling eternity and immensity: a train of causes and effects, begun here and reaching in a regular chain through endless duration: causes and effects, now existing, to be explained by consequences, situated in the remote regions of being. Who are we, that thus resolutely enter upon this mighty task? Worms of the dust. When were we born? Yesterday. What do we know? Nothing." Dwight, *God's Ways Not as Our Ways, Sermons,* 1:144.
73. Solomon Stoddard, Edwards's grandfather and pastoral predecessor in the Northampton Church, believed that the sacraments should be viewed as "converting ordinances" available to genuine seekers. He opened a rather wide gate in the fence with which most Puritans surrounded the Lord's Table. His progressive view, which drew considerable fire from the Mathers, became a hallmark of the Northampton church. During the communion controversy that led to his ouster from the Northampton church, Edwards held a conservative view that appeared to pit him against his grandfather's views and his congregation's traditions.
74. Nathaniel William Taylor to William Sprague, in Sprague, *Annals,* 2:164. The "distinguished divine" ascription with which this chapter begins can be found in Ebenezer Baldwin, *The History of Yale College, from Its Foundation, A.D. 1700, to the Year 1838* (New Haven: Benjamin and William Noyes, 1841), p. 143.

IV. An American Clio

1. Dwight, *A Valedictory Address to the Young Gentlemen Who Commenced Bachelor of Arts at Yale College, July 25, 1776* (New Haven: Thomas and Samuel Green, 1776), p. 15.
2. For detailed accounts of Dwight's philosophy of history, consult Griffith, "*The Columbiad* and *Greenfield Hill:* History, Poetry, and Ideology in the Late Eighteenth Century;" Dowling, *Poetry and Ideology,* pp. 23, 64ff., and 72ff.; and Dowling, "Joel Barlow and the Anarchiad."
3. Ruth Bloch's *Visionary Republic* is particularly helpful in sorting out shifts in millennial thinking among Federalists of the early national period. Notwithstanding

the clarity she brings to the problem, in Dwight's case it remains difficult to distinquish clearly between millennial reflections that are "religious" and those that are "political." Dwight's moralism lay precisely in his capacity to make religious beliefs, such as millennial doctrines, and faithful behavior, such as a politics based on such beliefs, nearly indistinguishable.

4. The "Religion of New England" section is contained in *Travels*, 4:258–326. Many scholars have observed that Dwight's *Travels* is not merely a piece of "historical" writing. As Emory Elliott noted: "With this work [*Travels*] Dwight takes his place with Cotton Mather in the seventeenth century and George Bancroft in the nineteenth century as a mythic historian of eighteenth-century America. As in the works of Mather and Bancroft, the portrait of America that emerges from Dwight's *Travels*, is a blend of personal opinion, even prejudice, and fact. He admits that he is creating a new kind of work, one that uses narration for religious ends." See Elliott, p. 89.

5. *Travels*, 4:318–20.

6. Dwight added one remarkable caveat to this claim about the doctrinal commitments of nineteenth-century New England Christians: "In a few particulars, the Hopkinsians have superadded to the doctrinal part of this system." *Travels*, 4:320.

7. *Travels*, 4:320–22. On dissent among New England's religious groups, see William G. McLoughlin, *New England Dissent, 1630–1889: The Baptists and the Separation of Church and State*, 2 vols. (Cambridge: Harvard University Press, 1971). While Dwight shared many religious beliefs with New England's evangelical Baptists, he abhorred their Republican politics. He allowed these political differences, which he viewed as fundamentally religious, to sever the bonds of evangelical faith.

8. *Travels*, 4:321.

9. Dwight defended the legal establishment of the Congregational churches at length in Letters IV and V of the "Religion of New England" section in *Travels*, 4:279ff.

10. *Travels*, 4:257.

11. Dwight briefly mentions the Great Awakening in *Travels*, 4:257.

12. Dwight needed a starting point from which to measure the decline of New England's religious fortunes, and his choice of the French and Indian War seems shrewd, but also a bit curious. On the one hand, Dwight's choice reveals his nativism in that he used the advent of French forces to introduce the evils of European skepticism neatly into his account. On the other hand, in connecting the war with the decline of American religion he put himself at odds with the positive interpretation many contemporary pastors had given the war. As Nathan Hatch has shown, optimistic millennialism and American nationalism, not jeremiads about religious decline, characterized the preaching of the day. When the British defeated the French forces, colonial ministers understood the event in cosmic terms. Protestant forces had thwarted the Catholic menace, good had triumphed over evil, and God had slain Antichrist. Ironically, although Dwight was apt to see the hand of Providence everywhere he looked and showed a penchant for postmillennial interpretation, his retrospective account of the effects of the French and Indian War was essentially negative. His triumphant postmillennial interpretations are not employed until he treats the War for Independence, and the most exuberant of these appear in his poetry. In this connection, see Hatch, *The Sacred Cause of Liberty* and Bloch, *Visionary Republic*.

13. Dwight, *The Triumph of Infidelity*, p. 329.

14. Dwight, *The Triumph of Infidelity*, p. 348.

15. Silverman, pp. 87, 83.

16. Dwight, *The Triumph of Infidelity*, p. 366.

17. Dwight, *Travels*, 4:258, 259, 260, 264–65.

18. Dwight, *Valedictory Address*, pp. 8, 12, 13, 14, 22.

19. Dwight, *A Sermon Preached at Stamford in Connecticut upon the General Thanksgiving, December 18, 1777* (Hartford: Watson and Goodwin, 1778), pp. 9, 13, 15, 16.

20. Dwight, *A Sermon Preached at Northampton on the twenty-eighth of November, 1781 Occasioned by the Capture of the British Army under the Command of Earl Cornwallis* (Hartford: Nathaniel Patten, 1781), pp. 3, 7, 8, 18, 33, 34. This sermon is somewhat anomalous in that while it is preached at a high point in Dwight's cycle of redemption, its positive and millennial tone is spiced with touches of apocalypticism. Dwight offers close exegesis of biblical texts, predicts that the millennium will begin in the year 2000, gives unusual attention to the seven vials of Revelation, and discusses the role of the Antichrist. See particularly pp. 27ff.

21. Dwight, *America: or a Poem on the Settlement of the British Colonies; Addressed to the Friends of Freedom and Their Country* (New Haven: Thomas and Samuel Green, 1780), p. 11. Ernest Tuveson has argued that Dwight's *America* became a literary foundation on which subsequent ideas of American millennialism and manifest destiny were erected. See Tuveson, *Redeemer Nation,* p. 103.

22. Dwight, "Columbia; a Song," *The Boston Magazine* (December 1783), p. 71. The song was republished by the Press of Timothy Dwight College at Yale University in 1960. This commemorative edition includes a brief description of the song that notes that it served as a popular anthem prior to the publication of *Star Spangled Banner* in 1814.

23. Dwight, "Prospect of America" in Matthew Carey, ed., *The Beauties of Poetry, British and American* (Philadelphia: M. Carey, 1791), pp. 217, 218.

24. Dwight, *Address of the Genius of Columbia, to the Members of the Continental Convention,* Elihu H. Smith, ed., *American Poems* (Litchfield, Conn.: Collier and Buel, 1793), p. 60.

25. Dwight, *Greenfield Hill,* in McTaggart and Bottoroff, eds. *The Major Poems of Timothy Dwight,* pp. 511ff.

26. Kafer, in "The Making of Timothy Dwight: A Connecticut Morality Tale," argues convincingly that the real backdrop of the *Conquest* is Dwight's own psyche, and particularly his failed relationship with his father during the Revolution. See Kafer, pp. 203ff.

27. Howard, p. 93.

28. Dwight to Webster, 6 June 1788, in Zunder, "Noah Webster and the *Conquest of Canaan,*" *American Literature* I (1929):201.

29. Dwight treats Washington in several connections, notably in his 1791 sermon, *Virtuous Rulers a National Blessing.* He refers to Washington, our "first Magistrate," as a contemporary illustration of a virtuous leader. Dwight lists the biblical exemplars he hopes American leaders will emulate and the list includes Joshua (pp. 28ff.). Later in the sermon, Dwight compares the United States and biblical Israel, though not at great length (pp. 31ff.). This piece reveals his political theory and will be treated in that connection below.

30. Dwight, *Conquest of Canaan,* in McTaggart and Bottoroff, eds. *The Major Poems of Timothy Dwight,* pp. 258, 273.

31. Dwight, "An Essay on the Judgment of History Concerning America," *New-Haven Gazette and Connecticut Magazine* 2 (12 April 1787):60.

32. For more detail, see Bloch, *Visionary Republic,* chapters 7, 8, and 9.

33. Dwight, *Duty of Americans,* pp. 8, 10, 12. It is often difficult to identify Dwight's sources. In *Duty,* however, he makes specific references to philosophical literature on which he based his address. See particularly his footnotes, a device he rarely used, on pp. 10 and 11.

34. Dwight, *Duty of Americans,* pp. 15, 16, 19, 21, 22, 23, 29, 31.

35. Dwight's observation about the Pope is in *Some Events,* p. 36; the passage about Catholic Christians is on p. 55.

36. Dwight gives a fuller account of the reasons the United States entered the War of 1812 in *Remarks on the Review of Inchiquin's Letters,* pp. 163ff. After a fairly standard

series of arguments against the war, Dwight offers this account of how recent American presidents have served as "negative" moral exemplars to America's citizens: "They have been useful instructors to the American people. Mr. Jefferson has taught us that Infidelity is an unprofitable spirit, and cunning an unprofitable guide, in the management of national interests. . . Mr. Madison . . . has strongly exhibited the visionary nature of theoretical speculation in the public concerns of mankind. From both, also, we have learned that far other moral dispositions, than such as are possessed by these gentlemen, are necessary in the Ruler, who is to do good to his country" (p. 171). William Gribben, *The Churches Militant: The War of 1812 and American Religion* (New Haven: Yale University Press, 1973), pp. 56ff., offers a helpful description of the dilemma in which Federalists found themselves during the war. Opposed to the war with Britain and unwilling to deal with France, they were caught on the horns of a dilemma. France's Napoleon Bonaparte began routing Catholic Europe—under normal situations a virtuous act fully deserving Protestant gratitude. Given Napoleon's role as the head of France, polluted as it had been by skepticism and intrigue, praise was hardly apropos. On the other hand, the British, technically "enemies" of the United States but still revered by many a Federalist, had been involved in the active defense of Spanish and Portuguese Catholic monarchs—exactly opposite of what might have been hoped for. Gribben suggests that the dilemma was resolved, at least for Federalist eschatologists, by shifting the identification of the Antichrist from the Pope, who, under the new strategy, would be identified as the Beast or the Whore of Babylon, to Napoleon. Though Dwight never identifies Napoleon as the Antichrist, he makes this interpretive move with relation to the Pope. See text above describing Dwight's *A Discourse on Some Events of the Last Century.*

37. Dwight, *Discourse in Two Parts* (July), pp. 6, 24, 26, 27. Later in the sermon Dwight offers his judgment about a possible American alliance with France: "To ally America to France, is to chain living health and beauty to a corpse dissolving with the plague. The evils, which we have already suffered from this impure and monstrous connexion, are terrible omens of the destruction which we are to expect from a connexion still more intimate. The horrors of war compared with it, are mere amusement. The touch of France is pollution. Her embrace is death" (p. 52).

38. Dwight, *Discourse in Two Parts* (July), pp. 14, 15ff., 32ff., 52.

39. Dwight, *Travels,* 4:274.

40. See Dwight, *A Sermon Preached at the Opening of the Theological Institution in Andover,* pp. 26ff., and *Sermon Delivered in Boston, Sept. 16, 1813, before the American Board of Commissioners for Foreign Missions,* pp. 22ff.

41. Dwight, *Decisions,* pp. 329–32.

42. Dwight, *Discourse in Two Parts* (August), pp. 65–72 and 80–83.

43. Dwight, "Observations on the Present State of Religion in the World." *Religious Intelligencer* 1 (14 September 1816):245–46.

44. William Sprague's life of Dwight in Jared Sparks, ed., *The Library of American Biography,* 2nd ser. (Boston: Charles Little and James Brown, 1846), 4:225–364.

V. New England's Moral Legislator

1. For many historians of American religion, Joseph Haroutunian's *Piety Versus Moralism, the Passing of New England Theology* (New York: Henry Holt, 1932), has bolstered this negative view of the term "moralism." Haroutunian was keenly aware of the richness of the American moral tradition in the eighteenth century. Indeed, his treatise was written to show that Edwards's disciples had tragically replaced his piety and moral theology with wooden and moribund legalism. Unfortunately, he chose to call the Edwardseans' outlook "moralism." The effect among many interpreters was to

stigmatize the sort of moralism, which included some sense of Edwards's piety, that Dwight and others practiced routinely.

2. Interesting parallels exist between Dwight's pedagogy at Yale and Samuel Stanhope Smith's teaching at Princeton. See Smith, *The Lectures, Corrected and Improved, Which Have Been Delivered for a Series of Years, in the College of New Jersey; on the Subjects of Moral and Political Philosophy,* 2 vols. (Trenton: Daniel Fenton, 1812), and Smith, *Sermons of Samuel Stanhope Smith, Late President of Princeton College, New Jersey, To Which Is Prefixed, a Brief Memoir of His Life and Writings,* 2 vols. (Philadelphia: S. Potter, 1821). See also Noll, *Princeton,* pp. 59–76, 185–213.

3. The two images reproduced in the text nicely capture Dwight the moralist. The first is a painting of Dwight, wearing spectacles and seated at his desk, hard at work on a manuscript. Though an unlikely scene—by his own confession he did little reading and was rarely able to write—it portrays an image of the reflective sage busy preparing a sermon or treatise for publication. This painting is entitled *Timothy Dwight* and was a gift to the Yale University Art Gallery by Mrs. Edward F. Dwight. The artist is unknown. Used with permission of the Yale University Art Gallery. The second image is an engraving that served as the frontispiece in some editions of Dwight's *Theology.* In contrast to the stateliness and warmth evident in the other portraits used in this book, this engraving reveals an older, wan, less vibrant-looking man hidden behind the darkened lenses of his horn-rimmed spectacles. To a greater extent than any other extant portrait of Dwight, this piece forcefully suggests the fact that his visual difficulties "colored" his view of the world. The artist of the portrait on which this line and stipple engraving is based is unknown. The engraving is owned by the Connecticut Historical Society, Hartford Connecticut. It appears here with their permission.

4. There is a third major section of *Theology,* containing the collection's final eleven sermons (Sermons 163 through 173). Dwight called this his "System of Dispensations Consequent on the State of Probation," and there he discussed death and the afterlife. It is important to consider the title of Dwight's moral theology. It is not called a system of *ethics* but system of *duties.* Dwight wanted his students to realize that as Christians, they had responsibilities as well as privileges. He believed that American virtue rested on the individual's capacity to act according to a set of moral precepts or laws.

5. *Theology,* 1:166.

6. This is St. Paul's classic hymn to the human capacity to express divine love. It begins with the words "Though I speak with the tongues of men and of angels, and have not charity, I am become as sounding brass, or a tinkling cymbal," and ends with the famous expression, "And now abideth faith, hope, and charity, these three; but the greatest of these is charity" (KJV).

7. *Theology,* 1:166.

8. *Theology,* 1:166.

9. Here is another instance of Dwight's aversion to placing the evidence from reason over the evidence from revelation. Apparently, it did not trouble Dwight in the least that his own arguments from reason could only prove that "God is not Malevolence," a quite different affirmation from what he hoped to demonstrate, i.e., "God is Benevolence." Because scripture under Dwight's interpretation affirmed the thesis, reason only needs to show that the antithesis is false.

10. Apparently Dwight knew that his reasoning might lead to the opposite conclusion, i.e., God would never have recourse to benevolence. He defends himself from this charge, pointing to the presence of "common grace," whereby God kindly superintends creation. Faced with the problem of the presence of evil in the world, Dwight retreated to his doctrine of sin. God was not the author of sin. People sinned voluntarily and had to pay the consequences. Dwight took refuge in the same doctrine when confronted with the problem of explaining natural disasters that kill godly and ungodly alike: "The evils inflicted by God are always less than the subjects of them merit by their sins." See

Theology, 1:176ff. As has been noted above, Dwight was content to live with such paradoxes.

11. Here Dwight's thought paralleled Edwards's *Religious Affections* and *Freedom of the Will.* Only in wanting good does one will it. Wanting the good cannot spring from a heart that is inclined to evil.

12. *Theology,* 1:196, 1:203, 1:216, 1:226.

13. Some interpreters have argued that benevolence played a much larger role in Edwards's thought. See, for instance, George Nye Boardman, *A History of New England Theology* (New York: A. D. F. Randolph, 1899), pp. 132ff.

14. Edwards, *Two Dissertations, Works,* 8:526.

15. *Theology,* 1:384.

16. *Theology,* 3:128.

17. *Theology,* 3:56.

18. Here Dwight evidenced his version of ethical utilitarianism but on the plane of the divine. Indeed, in his consideration of human virtue, he defended the doctrine "Virtue is founded in utility." See *Theology,* 3:151.

19. *Theology,* 2:161.

20. *Theology,* 3:56, 3:125, 3:122.

21. For Dwight's use of benevolence and love to God, see *Theology,* 3:64. For his use of benevolence and love to neighbor, see *Theology,* 3:121. For his understanding of disinterested benevolence as the first fruit, and therefore the first sign, of regeneration, see *Theology,* 2:467.

22. *Theology,* 3:121.

23. For a more recent assault on the Edwardsean understanding of benevolence in general and on Dwight's moralism in particular, see David C. Brand, *Profile of the Last Puritan: Jonathan Edwards, Self-Love, and the Dawn of the Beatific* (Atlanta: Scholars Press, 1991).

24. *Theology,* 4:16ff.

25. *Theology,* 4:30.

26. *Theology,* 3:321.

27. Dwight believed that the only political system ever instituted and required by God was that of the Old Testament Israelites. That required form of government, however, was abolished with the old covenant. *Theology,* 3:326.

28. *Theology,* 3:324–26. Here Dwight launched a broad attack on the social compact. He believed that the theory justified both the polar extremes of political evil: despotism and anarchy.

29. *Theology,* 3:324.

30. *Theology,* 3:327.

31. *Theology,* 3:331. In another sermon, Dwight wrote that it was a duty of rulers to support religion. This was to be accomplished not by the imposition of a single religious system, but by "steadfastly opposing immorality, by employing and honoring the just, by contemning [sic] the vicious." *Virtuous Rulers a National Blessing,* pp. 18, 19. Dwight did not address the objection that would inevitably rise in the mind of a Republican: Is not the very presence of established congregationalism in Connecticut proof that one ecclesiastical system has been imposed throughout the land?

32. *Theology,* 3:332. Dwight also discussed this theme in *The True Means of Establishing Public Happiness: A Sermon delivered on the 7th of July, before the Connecticut Society of Cincinnati, and Published at Their Request* (New Haven: T. & S. Green, 1795). He argued that virtue, the love of doing good, could be taught in religious education and in public worship. In this sermon Dwight looks more like a Thomist or Aristotelean than either a sentimentalist or a rationalist.

33. Here again one observes Dwight's insistence that morality expressed itself in social action. Artists and philosophers, though useful to a culture, were not heroic

figures. "The end of all thought," he argued, "was action." *A Discourse Occasioned by the Death of His Excellency Jonathan Trumbull, Esquire, Governor of the State of Connecticut and Delivered at the Request of the General Assembly in the Brick Church in New Haven* (New Haven: Oliver Steele, 1809), p. 9.

34. Dwight, *Discourse on Trumbull*, p. 21.

35. In his consideration of Washington's character, Dwight again stressed the importance of action and common sense. He said of Washington: "Perhaps there was never a mind on which theoretical speculations had less influence, and the decisions of common sense more." *A Discourse, Delivered at New Haven, February 22, 1800, on the Character of George Washington, at the Request of the Citizens* (New Haven: Thomas and Samuel Green, 1800), pp. 23, 24.

36. This question posed a serious threat to Dwight's theory of leadership. If Washington could be shown to have been a Christian (despite the fact that he was not a Congregationalist, let alone a member of the Standing Order), Dwight's problem was basically solved. If Washington was not a Christian, that theory was jeopardized. How could an impious man have become the father of godly America? To argue that Providence had established America in spite of Washington's impiety would only have weakened Dwight's arguments.

37. *A Discourse on the Character of George Washington*, pp. 27, 28.

38. Dwight's reverence toward Washington reflected a general opinion among Federalists. Although Dwight preached his Washington address at the general request of New Haven's citizens, he delivered at least one address (*True Means of Establishing Public Happiness*) before the Connecticut Society of the Cincinnati. In Linda Kerber's analysis of Federalism, the Cincinnati played an important role in the public reverencing of Washington. Kerber, pp. 4–8, 10.

39. *Theology*, 3:344.

40. *Theology*, 3:336.

41. *Theology*, 3:336.

42. This series of duties represents the only subheads of "The Duties of Subjects." See *Theology*, 3:336ff. Dwight allowed that in some cases (self-preservation, being one example), the subject's obligation to obey the ruler was lifted. See *Theology*, 3:343.

43. Dwight used the words "citizen" and "subject" interchangeably, though he seemed to prefer the latter.

44. *Theology*, 3:323.

45. *Travels*, 1:8, 9.

46. *Travels*, 1:6.

47. Several works offer useful accounts of the religious elements in the struggle between Federalists and Republicans. See Purcell, *Connecticut in Transition: 1755–1818;* McLoughlin, *New England Dissent;* and McLoughlin, "The Role of Religion in the Revolution: Liberty of Conscience and Cultural Cohesion in the New Nation," in Stephen G. Kurtz and James H. Hutson, eds., *Essays on the American Revolution* (Chapel Hill: University of North Carolina Press, 1973), pp. 197–255.

48. The Republican understanding of "equal privileges" was itself changing. Whereas Dwight lobbied for state recognition of all classes of Christians, the Republicans increasingly demanded that the state be entirely neutral. They eschewed the notion that privileges of any sort should be extended to any religious group, Christian or otherwise.

49. Beecher, *Autobiography*, 1:252.

50. Beecher, *Autobiography*, 1:252–53.

51. See Robert Baird, *Religion in America; Or, an Account of the Origin, Relation to the State, and Present Condition of the Evangelical Churches in the United States, with Notices of the Unevangelical Denominations* (New York: Harper and Brothers, 1856), p. 234. This conclusion seems untenable. Given his single-minded commitment to the Standing Order and his life-long devotion to the establishment of Godly Federalism, one must

conclude that Dwight would have had a most difficult time coping with America's evangelical era had he lived to see it.

52. Dwight's significance for the larger evangelical tradition in America is explored at length in Berk, *Calvinism Versus Democracy: Timothy Dwight and the Origins of American Evangelical Orthodoxy,* and Wenzke, *Timothy Dwight (1752–1817).*

53. *Theology,* 3:344.

54. Walter E. Volkmer, "Timothy Dwight and New England Federalism," *Connecticut Review* 3 (April 1970):82.

55. The "New England's moral legislator" attribution with which this chapter begins may be found in "A Memoir of the Life of the Author," which appears in *Theology,* 1:52.

BIBLIOGRAPHIC ESSAY

Timothy Dwight has been the subject of a great deal of scholarly work. Unfortunately the literature that treats him is limited and circumscribed by the disciplinary boundaries that exist in the academic world. The present work seeks to fashion a more wholistic life of Dwight, but this constructive and synthetic enterprise inevitably relies on previous scholarly work. In order to identify the sources that have informed the present interpretation and in an effort to unencumber its text and endnotes, this essay will identify and survey important secondary literatures in the following categories: Biographical Sources, Literary Studies, Homiletics and Scottish Common Sense Realism, The Second Awakening and New England Politics, The Edwardsean Theological Milieu, and Millennialism in the Early National Era.

Biographical Sources

Although countless authors mention Dwight in passing, and many treat him at length, only one book can be properly considered a full biography. Charles Cuningham's *Timothy Dwight, 1752–1817, A Biography* (New York: Macmillan, 1942), is clearly the most inclusive and complete treatment of its subject and has become the authoritative modern source of much of what we know about Dwight. In Cuningham's interpretation, which sometimes runs toward the celebratory, Dwight plays the renaissance man of Revolutionary and early national America. He is poet and educator, evangelist and theologian, political observer and scientist, father and husband, all spun magnificently into one grand Yale man. The anomalies and interesting dynamics of Dwight's life—his tragic relationship with his father; the looming spectre of Jonathan Edwards in the Dwight household; his shift from enthusiastic Revolutionary to suspicious Federalist Francophobe—are largely ignored, and the subtleties of his theological and ethical reflection get lost in the detailed narrative. It is unquestionably the most helpful starting place for a consideration of Dwight, but Cuningham's enthusiasm leads to an overly sympathetic, even hagiographic treatment that requires careful attention.

Cuningham relied on several nineteenth-century authors who compiled biographies of Dwight that are overly sympathetic and of limited value. The best of the nineteenth-century published biographies are William Sprague's entry on Dwight in his *Annals of the American Pulpit*, 9 vols. (New York: R. Carter and Brothers, 1857–1869), 2:152ff., and Sprague's life of Dwight in Jared Sparks, ed., *The Library of American Biography*, 2nd ser. (Boston: Charles Little and James Brown, 1846), 4:225–364. The Dwight Family Papers housed in the Sterling Library at Yale University contain important biographical information as well. Two manuscript booklets, both entitled "Biographical Hints," were almost certainly composed by Timothy Dwight's son Benjamin. The manuscript booklets may be drafts of a biography (the first booklet is a draft version of the larger, second booklet), though neither was published in the form in which they survive. Much of the material contained in *Hints* appears in the anonymous "Memoir of the Author," published in the first volume of Dwight's *Theology, Explained and Defended*. This fact lends credence to the commonly held view that one or more of Dwight's sons wrote the "Memoir." See Franklin B. Dexter, *Biographical Sketches of the Graduates of Yale College with Annals of the College History,* 6 vols. (New York: Henry Holt, 1903), 3:325, for details about the "Memoir."

A good deal of important information about Dwight's life is contained in histories of the Dwight family and of Northampton. Of particular note are Benjamin W. Dwight, *The History of the Descendants of John Dwight of Dedham, Massachusetts,* 2 vols. (New York: John F. Trow and Sons, 1874), and James Russell Trumbull, *The History of Northampton from Its Settlement in 1654,* 2 vols. (Northampton: n.p., 1898). Of lesser value but still of considerable interest are Daniel Dulany Addison, "Timothy Dwight," in his *The Clergy in American Life and Letters* (New York: Macmillan, 1900), pp. 157–90, and Moses Coit Tyler, "The Great College President and What He Wrote," in his *Three Men of Letters* (New York: G. P. Putman's Sons, 1895), pp. 71–127.

Eulogies delivered soon after Dwight's death are also helpful sources of biographical information. In this connection, see Calvin Chapin, *A Sermon Delivered 14th January, 1817, at the Funeral of the Rev. Timothy Dwight, D.D., LL.D., President of Yale College, in New Haven, and Professor of Divinity in the Institution, Who Died January 11th, 1817, in the Sixty-Fifth Year of His Age and Twenty-Second of His Presidency* (New Haven: Maltby and Goldsmith, 1817); Nathaniel Chauncey, *An Address Delivered before the New England Society of Philadelphia, On the Fourth of May, 1818* (Philadelphia: Office of the Union, 1818); Benjamin Silliman, *A Sketch of the Life and Character of President Dwight, Delivered as a Eulogium, in New Haven, February 12, 1817, before the Academic Body of Yale College, Composed of the Senatus Academic, Faculty, and Students* (New Haven: Maltby and Goldsmith, 1817); and Gardiner Spring, *An Oration on the Evening of the Fifth of February, before the Alumni of Yale College, Resident in the City of New York, in Commemoration of Their Late President, Timothy Dwight, D.D., LL.D.* (New York: Dodge and Sayre, 1817). Two anonymous eulogies reveal important information about Dwight's visual problem: Anon., "Biographical Memoir of the Rev. Timothy Dwight, S.T.D., LL.D.," *Port Folio* 4 (1817):355–69; and Anon., "Biographical Notice of the Rev. Timothy Dwight, S.T.D., L.L.D., Late President and Professor of Divinity of Yale College," *Analectic Magazine* 9 (1817):265–81.

A number of articles and books treat Dwight's role as an educator, and these sources have provided very helpful insights into his professional life and his attitudes toward his vocation. Franklin B. Dexter, ed., *The Literary Diary of Ezra Stiles, D.D., LL.D.,* 3 vols. (New York: Charles Scribner's Sons, 1901), provides a wealth of information about Yale, Dwight's relationship with Stiles, and the educational environment in which Dwight was trained. Other treatments of Dwight at Yale, both as a student and as president, include M. A. DeWolfe Howe, *Classic Shades: Five Leaders of Learning and Their Colleges* (Boston: Little, Brown, 1928); Edmund S. Morgan, "Ezra Stiles and Timothy Dwight"; Edmund S. Morgan, *The Gentle Puritan, A Life of Ezra Stiles, 1727–1795* (New Haven: Yale University Press, 1962); Brooks Mather Kelley, *Yale: A History* (New Haven: Yale University Press, 1979); and Chandros Michael Brown, *Benjamin Silliman: A Life in the Young Republic* (Princeton: Princeton University Press, 1989).

Several studies treat Dwight's classroom work, including: Denison Olmstead, "Timothy Dwight as a Teacher," pp. 567–85; Abe C. Ravitz, "Timothy Dwight: Professor of Rhetoric," *New England Quarterly* 29 (1956):63–72; and Ravitz, "Timothy Dwight's Decisions," *New England Quarterly* 31 (1958):514–19. Studies that focus on rhetoric at Yale and Dwight's use of rhetorical strategies include: Vincent Freimarck, "Rhetoric at

Yale in 1807," *Proceedings of the American Philosophical Society,* 110 (1966):235–55; Gregory Clark, "Timothy Dwight's Moral Rhetoric at Yale College, 1795–1817," *Rhetorica* 5 (1987):149–61; Clark, "Timothy Dwight's *Travels in New England and New York* and the Rhetoric of Puritan Public Discourse" (Ph.D. diss., Rensselaer Polytechnic Institute, 1985); and Christopher D. Grasso, "Between Awakenings: Learned Men and the Transformations of Public Discourse in Connecticut, 1740–1800" (Ph.D. diss., Yale University, 1992). Chapter 8, "Reawakening the New England Mind: The Rhetoric of Timothy Dwight," pp. 366–423, is especially helpful.

Dwight's role as a disciplinarian who like other college presidents of the early national era had to deal with repeated outbursts of student violence is treated in Stephen J. Novak, *The Rights of Youth: American Colleges and Student Revolts, 1798–1815* (Cambridge: Harvard University Press, 1977). Dwight's activities as a theological educator are treated by Ralph Henry Gabriel, *Religion and Learning at Yale: The Church of Christ in the College and University, 1757–1957* (New Haven: Yale University Press, 1958); and Roland H. Bainton, *Yale and the Ministry: A History of Education for Christian Ministry at Yale from the Founding in 1701* (New York: Harper and Brothers, 1957). For information about collegiate education among the New Haven theologians after Dwight's death, see Louise L. Stevenson, *Scholarly Means to Evangelical Ends: The New Haven Scholars and the Transformation of Higher Learning in America, 1830–1890* (Baltimore: Johns Hopkins University Press, 1986).

Literary Studies

Dwight's prose efforts, his poetry, and especially his *Travels in New England and New York* have been interpreted differently by several generations of students of American literature. The four most important treatments of Dwight's literary work are by scholars interested in American literature of the Revolutionary period: Leon Howard, Kenneth Silverman, Emory Elliott, and William C. Dowling.

Howard's work, *The Connecticut Wits* (Chicago: University of Chicago Press, 1943), was the first critical and sustained treatment of the Wits and of Dwight as a poet. Its most valuable contribution was to describe Dwight's literary context. While previous interpreters noted that Dwight's early poetry was clearly an attempt to establish a particular style of elegant, entertaining, and sophisticated literature for the colonies, Howard's careful analysis of Dwight's reliance on British poets and his interest in Lord Kames's *Elements of Criticism* provided new insights into the specifics of Dwight's vision of a distinctly American *belles lettres*. Dwight experimented with new styles and approaches to verse but his innovations met with mixed results. From Howard's perspective, Dwight's chief fault was "his determination to be great before he was merely good" (p. 100), a tragic flaw that led to the literary confusion of the *Conquest of Canaan,* a poem "full of eighteenth-century Americans with Hebrew names who talked like Milton's angels and fought like pre-historic Greeks" (p. 93). Despite these neophytish blunders, Howard's appreciation of Dwight was real. He tracks Dwight from his early years with the Wits, through the challenges of infidelity and the Bavarian Illuminati scare, through his *Theology* and *Sermons,* and finally to the *Travels* and *Inchiquin's Letters,* concluding that while Dwight lacked a constructive imagination he did provide a limited literary stability in an era of rapid and disconcerting change.

For additional assessments of the Connecticut Wits see Vernon L. Parrington, ed., *The Connecticut Wits* (New York: Harcourt, Brace, 1926). Parrington provides an introduction and an edited collection of the Wits' work; it contains some of the most vigorous criticisms of Dwight published at any time since his death in 1817 (especially pp. xxxix ff.). Robert D. Arner, "The Connecticut Wits," in Everett Emerson, ed., *American Literature, 1764–1789: The Revolutionary Years* (Madison: University of Wisconsin Press, 1977), pp. 233–52, also provides useful background information on Dwight's coterie of New England literati. In this connection, it is also helpful to consult George Sensabaugh, *Milton in America* (Princeton: Princeton University Press, 1964), pp. 167–76, which provides a comparison of Dwight's *Conquest* to Milton's *Paradise Lost.*

A second literary treatment, technically a more complete literary biography, is Kenneth Silverman, *Timothy Dwight* (New York: Twayne Publishers, 1969). Silverman examines the ways Dwight's work, especially his poetry, became a vehicle to express his changing views of the prospects and problems of America. Silverman's central thesis is that Dwight's cultural vision was limited or manichean; he could only interpret American culture negatively (as a gloomy "doomsday") or positively (as a cheery "birthday"). This thesis is developed and tested across a taxonomy that Silverman develops. He finds four distinct images of the nation in Dwight's writing, each of which advances and recedes over time as they vie for dominance in Dwight's overall vision of the Republic. Dwight reveals his "Ideal America" in *America* and *The Conquest of Canaan,* productions of an ungifted, sometimes inept poet striving to transcend American provincialism. "Possible America" emerges in *Greenfield Hill,* in which Dwight sets the great Revolutionary truths of *The Conquest* into what for him was a classic setting, the stable, virtuous New England village. "Probable America" emerges in a still later poem, *The Triumph of Infidelity,* as a cautious, fearful Dwight rails against the excesses of the Enlightenment, the Bavarian Illuminati, and the plotters of the XYZ affair. On Silverman's account this Dwight is backward-looking, paranoid, and inflexible. Dwight's "Real America" emerges in the era of the Yale revivals, which offered him some hope for the future and in his massive *Travels,* which serve as a giant, complex apologetic for American culture. Here, despite the positive developments recorded in *Travels* and the promise of a redeemed future provided by the awakenings, Silverman pictures Dwight inculcating the cultural and religious patterns of New England Puritanism. Whatever imaginative dynamism may have infused these four competing images, Dwight's capacity to envision America only in terms of "birthday or doomsday" stifled his intellectual, artistic, and political insight. He was, in the end, an anachronism—a seventeenth-century Puritan tragically stranded in the late eighteenth century.

While having the virtue of assaying Dwight's literary development over time and of attempting to make the idea of America the central theme of the interpretation, Silverman's portrait labors under several burdens. It is clear from the outset that Silverman does not respect his subject. At some points Dwight is merely unimaginative, at other points he is postively dull, at still others he appears the reactionary buffoon. Further, Silverman views Dwight primarily through his poetry. Though he makes use of some occasional sermons that serve his larger America motif (e.g., Dwight's *The True Means of Establishing Public Happiness*), Dwight's religious beliefs and his place in the tradition of New England theology receive little treatment. While Silverman's *Timothy Dwight* is a successful literary biography, his portrait of Dwight the Revolutionary literary figure conceals elements of a more complex and interesting thinker. Silverman treats Dwight in a much larger context in *A Cultural History of the American Revolution: Painting, Music, Literature, and the Theatre in the Colonies and the United States from the*

Treaty of Paris to the Inauguration of George Washington, 1763–1789 (New York: Crowell, 1976).

The third book that treats Dwight's literary efforts is Emory Elliott, *Revolutionary Writers: Literature and Authority in the New Republic, 1725–1810* (New York: Oxford University Press, 1983). Elliott examines Dwight in a larger and somewhat different company of American literati: Joel Barlow, Philip Freneau, Hugh Henry Brackenbridge, and Charles Brockden Brown. Elliott's central thesis is that Dwight and his Revolutionary colleagues, keenly aware of the cultural dangers that appeared amid the Revolutionary era, sought to draw older values, especially those of New England Puritanism, into the cultural fabric of the early national era. With *The Conquest of Canaan,* for instance, Dwight attempted an "enormous feat of synthesis: to transport the Puritan experience of the seventeenth century across the chasm of the Revolution, to annex [to it] the new republican vista, and thus to create a vision of the future that would fuse the Calvinist and Enlightenment world views" (p. 60). Like Silverman, Elliott is aware of the ways in which Dwight sought to use his verse to address larger political and social questions of the day. Unlike him, Elliott does not stress Dwight's negative, shrill denunciations of infidelity and the European Enlightenment. On the contrary, Elliott's Dwight is positive; he looks confidently into the future.

William C. Dowling, *Poetry and Ideology in Revolutionary Connecticut* (Athens: University of Georgia Press, 1990), the fourth important literary study, serves as a clear departure from the work of Howard, Silverman, and Elliott. While the latter three provided students of Dwight with a sophisticated literary context, a comprehensive view of Dwight's understanding of the nation, and an understanding of his place in the Revolutionary era, Dowling views Dwight's literary corpus through much more discriminating lenses. His interest is in the several ways in which Revolutionary ideologies, especially the British Country ideology or the Opposition literary tradition, might have influenced Dwight and his fellow Wits. On Dowling's account, the "shared experience of Augustan poetry as a powerful mode of satiric unmasking" (p. 23) held the Wits together. For them, poetry could be used in America as it had been used in England— as a tool of social criticism in the hands of the opponents of tyranny. For instance, in the *Conquest of Canaan* Dwight's Joshua figure speaks the language of civic humanist morality. He is the personification of the heroic republican. In the *Conquest* and later in *Greenfield Hill,* Dwight brings together his Puritan predilections and his millennial thinking with this Country ideology. The result models a perfect community—Heaven in the guise of Connecticut. Whereas Howard could find little of the constructive genius in Dwight the reactionary, Dowling's Dwight is a subtle visionary keenly interested in using poetry as a political device.

Central to Dowling's work is an assessment of the sorts of historical theories with which Dwight may have operated. In Dowling's view—first noted by John Griffith, "*The Columbiad* and *Greenfield Hill*: History, Poetry, and Ideology in the Late Eighteenth Century," *Early American Literature* 10 (1975–1976): 235–50—Dwight and fellow Wit Joel Barlow operated with two distinct views of the historical process. For Barlow, who would become far more radical with the passing of time, history was progressive and linear. Human effort brought change that was essentially positive and helpful. Barlow's philosophy of history had trace elements of orthodox millennialism, but was essentially secular. On the other hand, according to Griffith and Dowling Dwight held a cyclical view of history. The world might improve; but then again, it might not. Indeed, things could actually become worse. Whatever the outcome Dwight placed the ultimate meaning of history outside of the historical process, in divine Providence, a position consistent with his moderate Calvinism. Political differences eventually drove Dwight and Barlow apart; Dwight remained a conservative Federalist, Barlow became a progressive Republican. Below this obvious difference lurked their different views of history and different beliefs about just how far one could go with Augustan "unmasking." For Dowling, the problematic differences between Dwight and Barlow on notions of history were exacerbated once Barlow realized that he could use poetry against the Federalists as he had once used it against corrupt British Court ideologues.

For additonal background on these matters, see William C. Dowling, "Joel Barlow and the Anarchiad," *Early American Literature* 25 (1990):18–33. The Court and Country ideologies are treated in John M. Murrin, "The Great Inversion, or Court Versus Country: A Comparison of the Revolution Settlements in England (1688–1721) and America (1776–1816)," in *Three British Revolutions: 1641, 1688, 1776.* Ed. by J. G. A. Pocock (Princeton: Princeton University Press, 1980). The intersections of Country, republican ideology and Christian millennial theology are explored in Nathan O. Hatch, *The Sacred Cause of Liberty: Republican Thought and the Millennium in Revolutionary New England* (New Haven: Yale University Press, 1977). This theme, with specific reference to Dwight, is also treated in Alan K. Snyder, "Foundations of Liberty: The Christian Republicanism of Timothy Dwight and Jedidiah Morse," *New England Quarterly* 56 (1983):382–97.

A number of authors have written extensively about what is clearly Dwight's most lasting contribution to American letters, his *Travels in New England and New York.* The appearance of a critical edition of the *Travels* in 1969 spurred a good deal of this interest. John F. Sears, "Timothy Dwight and the American Landscape: The Composing Eye in Dwight's *Travels in New England and New York*," *Early American Literature* 11 (1976–1977):311–21, analyzed the manner in which Dwight, most likely influenced by the British artist William Gilpin, sought to give balance to the scenes he describes by seeing things in a structured, often oversimplified or even monolithic manner. Looking for natural harmony to balance the disparate aspects of a scene, for the established village to offset the wilderness, for regions of economic prosperity to serve as a counterpoint to impoverished townships—all these contrasts became the stuff of Dwight's descriptive prose. Dwight's descriptions of the transformation of an area, from the primitive wilds to a virtuous village, have attracted a good deal of attention as well. Cecelia Tichi, *New World, New Earth: Environmental Reform in American Literature from the Puritans through Whitman* (New Haven: Yale University Press, 1979), sees Dwight as part of the quasi-millennial "environmental reform" movement. John R. Stilgoe, "Smiling Scenes," in *Views and Visions: American Landscape before 1830,* ed. Edward J. Nygren (Washington: Corcoran Gallery of Art, 1986) believes that Dwight's literary art aimed at the expression of a moral vision. His distinctly Protestant point of view and the complex moral arguments he explores are treated further in Robert Lawson-Peebles, *Landscape and Written Expression in Revolutionary America: The World Turned Upside Down* (Cambridge: Cambridge University Press, 1988); Peter Briggs, "Timothy Dwight 'Composes' a Landscape for New England," *American Quarterly* 40 (1988):359–77; Timothy B. Spears, "Common Observations: Timothy Dwight's *Travels in New England and New York,*" *American Studies* 30 (1989):35–52; and Jane Kamensky, "'In These Contrasted Climes, How Chang'd the Scene': Progress, Declension, and Balance in the Landscapes of Timothy Dwight," *New England Quarterly* 63 (1990):80–108. Other assessments of *Travels* include Vincent Freimarck, "Timothy Dwight's Brief Lives in Travels in New

England and New York," *Early American Literature* 7 (1973):44–58; Kathryn Whitford, "'The Young Officer Who Rode Beside Me': An Examination of Nineteenth-Century Naming Conventions," *American Studies* 23 (1982):5–22; John Brinckerhoff Jackson, "A Puritan Looks at Scenery," in *Discovering the Vernacular Landscape* (New Haven: Yale University Press, 1984), 57–64; and Albert Von Frank, *The Sacred Game: Provincialism and Frontier Consciousness in American Literature, 1630–1860* (New York: Cambridge University Press, 1985).

Other individual themes and problems within the Dwight corpus—his views on slavery and racial issues, sexual associations and gender issues, his understanding of science, his ethical system, and even some psychobiographical insights into Dwight— have all been examined by scholars whose approaches vary considerably. For comments on Dwight's view of slavery and racial issues, see Mukhtar Ali Isani, "Far from 'Gambia's Golden Shore': The Black in Late Eighteenth-Century American Imaginative Litera-ture," *William and Mary Quarterly,* 3rd ser., 36 (1979):353–72. For interesting com-ments on sexuality and rhetoric in Dwight's writings, see Shirley Samuels, "Infidelity and Contagion: The Rhetoric of Revolution," *Early American Literature* 22 (1987):183– 91. For Dwight and science, see Kathryn and Philip Whitford, "Timothy Dwight's Place in Eighteenth-Century American Science," *Proceedings of the American Philosophical Association* 114 (1970): 60–71. For Dwight's ethics, see Lewis Buchanan, "The Ethical Ideas of Timothy Dwight," *Research Studies, State College of Washington* 13 (September 1945): 185–99. For a fascinating account of the way Dwight's relationship with his father may have played itself out in his literary efforts, see Peter K. Kafer, "The Making of Timothy Dwight: A Connecticut Morality Tale," *William and Mary Quarterly,* 3rd ser., 47 (1990):189–209. Jay Fliegelman, *Prodigals and Pilgrims: The American Revolution against Patriarchal Authority, 1750–1800* (Cambridge: Cambridge University Press, 1982), pp. 314ff. also treats Dwight on the question of authority. Other brief treatments of Dwight's literary efforts include: Theodore Zunder, "Noah Webster and the Conquest of Canaan," *American Literature* 1 (1929):200–2; Vincent Freimarck, "Timothy Dwight's Dissertation on the Bible," *American Literature* 26 (1952):73–77; Walter Harding, "Timothy Dwight and Thoreau," *Boston Public Library Quarterly* 10 (1958):109–15; Robert Edson Lee, "Timothy Dwight and the Boston Palladium," *New England Quarterly* 35 (1962):229–38; Kathryn Whitford, "Excursions in Romanticism: Timothy Dwight's *Travels,*" *Papers on Language and Literature* 2 (1966):225–33; Lawrence Buell, "Litera-ture and Scripture in New England," *Notre Dame English Journal* 15 (1983):1–28, Lewis Leary, "The Author of *The Triumph of Infidelity,*" *New England Quarterly* 20 (1947):377– 85; Rufus Wilmot Griswold, *The Prose Writers of America, With a Survey of The Intellectual History, Condition, and Prospects of the Country,* 4th ed. (Philadelphia: A. Hart, 1851); and Jack Stillinger, "Dwight's *Triumph of Infidelity:* Text and Interpreta-tion," *Studies in Bibliography: Papers of the Bibliography Society of the University of Virginia* 15 (1962):259–66. For a more substantial interpretation of Dwight's place in the larger New England literary tradition, see Lawrence Buell, *New England Literary Culture: From Revolution through Renaissance* (New York: Cambridge University Press, 1986).

Homiletics and Scottish Common Sense Realism

Timothy Dwight's favorite activity was preaching. He began his pulpit ministry soon after he completed his undergraduate work at Yale, and continued to craft and deliver sermons until the last months of his life. His large and diverse sermon corpus covers a wide range of subjects and the sermons in the collection were delivered in a number of different settings. Two series of Dwight's sermons were collected and published: *Theology, Explained and Defended, in a Series of Sermons.* 5 vols. (Middletown, Conn.: Charles Lyman, 1818–1819) and *Sermons by Timothy Dwight, D.D., LL.D., Late President of Yale College,* 2 vols. (New Haven: Howe and Durrie and Peck, 1828). He preached and published a number of other sermons as well. The titles of those that were published may be found in the Bibliography of the present volume. The Dwight Family Papers contain a number of manuscript sermons that were never published. These include *Long Life Not Desirable* (Job 7:16, 22 November 1788); *Levity to Sacred Things* (Matthew 22:5, 25 September 1790); *The Character of David* (Acts 13:22, 26 October 1788); *The Character of Jabez* (1 Chronicles 4, 5 September 1806); *Thanksgiving Sermon* (Psalm 117, 2 July 1810); *Reverencing the Sanctuary* (Leviticus 19:30, 2 July 1810); *The Almost Christian* (Acts 26:23, 12 March 1815); *The Lord's Prayer* (Matthew 6:9–13, 5 November 1811); *The Cleansing of Namaan* (2 Kings 5:9–15, 20 August 1812); and *Thoughts on the Mediation of Christ* (Revelation 1:5–6, 30 October 1815). The Beinecke Library at Yale University holds a bound volume of notes on eight other Dwight sermons in which he preached from scripture texts drawn from Genesis, Exodus, Isaiah, Daniel, Psalms, and Revelation. An extant set of auditor's notes entitled "Theological Discourses by Dr. Dwight" and housed in the Dwight Family Papers indicates how Dwight preached through the sermons in *Theology* during his Yale career. Several of the nineteenth-century biographical sources noted above provide additional information on how Dwight crafted, delivered, and recorded his sermons.

Although Dwight's sermons are frequently quoted, these citations most often serve as proof texts to demonstrate a particular claim. Though he was one of the most prominent preachers in early national America, surprisingly little research has been done on the way Dwight crafted sermons or what he believed about the ultimate purpose of homiletics. Efforts to learn more about the history of American homiletics reveal a rather trim literature. The most illuminating sources include: Harry S. Stout, *The New England Soul: Preaching and Religious Culture in Colonial New England* (New York: Oxford University Press, 1986); Teresa Toulouse, *The Art of Prophesying: New England Sermons and the Shaping of Belief* (Athens, Georgia: University of Georgia Press, 1987); Donald Weber, *Rhetoric and History in Revolutionary New England* (New York: Oxford University Press, 1988); and Grasso, "Between Awakenings: Learned Men and the Transformation of Public Discourse in Connecticut, 1740–1800" (Ph.D. diss., Yale University, 1992).

The interpretation of Dwight's preaching that appears in the present volume rests on substantial research into the origins of religious skepticism in the eighteenth and nineteenth centuries and on the Scottish Enlightenment's response to these developments. This research began with several treatments of Dwight's nemesis David Hume. These include: V. C. Chappell, *Introduction to the Philosophy of David Hume, The Modern Library of the World's Best Books* (New York: Random House, 1963), pp. vii–lxvii; Angus J. Mackay, "David Hume," in Peter Gilmour, ed., *Philosophers of the Enlightenment* (Totowa, N.J.: Barnes and Noble Books, 1990), pp. 63–73; and Francis J. Beckwith, *David Hume's Argument against Miracles: A Critical Analysis* (Lanham: University Press of America, 1989), especially pp. 19–69. Subsequent inquiries moved to the other Scots literati and philosophers known to Dwight who also opposed Hume and played various roles in the Scottish Enlightenment.

Of considerable help in understanding the thought of Thomas Reid is Joel C. Weinsheimer, *Eighteenth-Century Hermeneutics: Philosophy of Interpretation from Locke to Burke* (New Haven: Yale University Press, 1993), especially chapter 5, "Reid on Common Sense," pp. 135–65. For recent secondary treatments of Reid's religious and social thought, see Nicholas J. Griffin, "Possible Theological Perspectives in Thomas Reid's Common Sense Philosophy," *Journal of Ecclesiastical History* 41 (1990), pp. 425–42, and Peter J. Diamond, "Rhetoric and Philosophy in the Social Thought of Thomas Reid," *Eighteenth Century Life* 15 (1991):57–80.

Helpful sources regarding Henry Home, Lord Kames, and the advent of Scottish literary criticism include: Ian Simpson Ross, *Lord Kames and the Scotland of His Day* (Oxford: Clarendon Press, 1972). Of particular value is his chapter "*Elements of Criticism* (1762)," pp. 260–91, in which he discusses Kames's relations with other literati and philosophers of his era. See also William C. Lehmann, "Literary Criticism and the Question of Style in Writing," in *Henry Home, Lord Kames, and the Scottish Enlightenment: A Study in National Character and the History of Ideas* (The Hague: Martinus Nijhoff, 1971), pp. 220–34; and Helen W. Randall, "The Critical Theory of Lord Kames," *Smith College Studies in Modern Languages* 22 (1940–41):1–147. The development of critical literary theory in nineteenth-century America and its connections to Scotland is treated in William Charvat, *The Origins of American Critical Thought: 1810–1835* (Philadelphia: University of Pennsylvania Press, 1936; rpt. ed., New York: Russell and Russell, 1968).

For an analysis of Hugh Blair's place in the development of the new rhetoric, see Wilbur Samuel Howell, *Eighteenth-Century British Logic and Rhetoric* (Princeton: Princeton University Press, 1971), pp. 648–71. Also see Robert M. Schmitz, *Hugh Blair* (New York: King's Crown Press, 1948); James Golden, "Hugh Blair: Minister of St. Giles," *Quarterly Journal of Speech* 38 (April 1952):155–60; Vincent M. Bevilacqua, "Philosophical Assumptions Underlying Hugh Blair's Lectures in Rhetoric and *Belles Lettres,*" *Western Speech* 31 (Summer 1967):150–64; and Thomas P. Miller, "Witherspoon, Blair, and the Rhetoric of Civic Humanism," in Richard B. Sher and Jeffrey R. Smitten, eds., *Scotland and America in the Age of Enlightenment* (Princeton: Princeton University Press, 1990), pp. 100–14.

For a summary of the principal themes of the new rhetoric, see the "Introduction" to James L. Golden and Edward P.J. Corbett, eds., *The Rhetoric of Blair, Campbell, and Whately* (New York: Holt, Rinehart and Winston, 1968), pp. 1–21. Howell, *Eighteenth-Century British Logic and Rhetoric,* examines the historical development of the new rhetoric in detail. See especially chapter 5, "George Campbell and the Philosophical Rhetoric of the New Learning," pp. 577–612. For a secondary account that argues that Campbell's *Lectures* have not received the attention they deserve, see Clarence W. Edney, "Campbell's *Lectures on Pulpit Eloquence,*" *Speech Monographs* 19 (1952), pp. 1–10. See also George A. Kennedy, *Classical Rhetoric and Its Christian and Secular Tradition from Ancient to Modern Times* (Chapel Hill: University of North Carolina Press, 1980), pp. 232ff.

The literature concerning the impact of Scottish Enlightenment thinking on American culture and thought is rich and diverse. A helpful overview is S. A. Grave, *The Scottish Philosophy of Common Sense* (Oxford: Clarendon Press, 1960). For a useful collection of essays on the subject, see Richard B. Sher and Jeffrey R. Smitten, eds., *Scotland and America in the Age of Enlightenment* (Princeton: Princeton University Press, 1990) as well as Henry F. May, *The Enlightenment in America* (New York: Oxford

University Press, 1976). For a helpful analysis of the problems surrounding the exact definition of the "Scottish Enlightenment" and the ways that the literati used Hume, see Richard B. Sher, *Church and University in the Scottish Enlightenment: The Moderate Literati of Edinburgh* (Princeton: Princeton University Press, 1985), pp. 5ff.

Scottish philosophy's influence on American religion is examined in Sydney E. Ahlstrom, "The Scottish Philosophy and American Theology," *Church History* 24 (1955), pp. 257–72; Mark A. Noll, "Common Sense Traditions and American Evangelical Thought," *American Quarterly* 37 (1985), pp. 216–38; E. Brooks Holifield, *The Gentlemen Theologians: American Theology in Southern Culture, 1795–1860* (Durham: Duke University Press, 1978); and Mark A. Noll, *Princeton and the Republic: The Search for a Christian Enlightenment in the Era of Samuel Stanhope Smith* (Princeton: Princeton University Press, 1989). The legacy of Common Sense Philosophy in later eras of American protestant history are treated in George Marsden, *Fundamentalism and American Culture: The Shaping of Twentieth-Century Evangelicalism, 1870–1925* (New York: Oxford University Press, 1980).

The influence of Scottish thinking on education and on American institutions of higher learning is treated in Richard B. Sher, *Church and University in the Scottish Enlightenment: The Moderate Literati of Edinburgh* (Princeton: Princeton University Press, 1985); Douglas Sloane, *The Scottish Enlightenment and the American College Ideal* (New York: Teachers College Press, 1971), and in Noll, *Princeton and the Republic.* For the role of Scottish thought on science, see Theodore Dwight Bozeman, *Protestants in the Age of Science: The Baconian Ideal and Antebellum Religious Thought* (Chapel Hill: University of North Carolina Press, 1977); and Herbert Hovencamp, *Science and Religion in America: 1800–1860* (Philadelphia: University of Pennsylvania Press, 1978).

The Second Awakening and New England Politics

Three older sources provide good starting places to begin study of Dwight's place in the larger tradition of New England theology: George Park Fisher, *Discussions in History and Theology* (New York: Charles Scribner's Sons, 1880), pp. 259–60, 298–302, Frank Hugh Foster, *A Genetic History of the New England Theology* (Chicago: University of Chicago Press, 1907), pp. 361–66, and Joseph Haroutunian, *Piety Versus Moralism: The Passing of New England Theology* (New York: Henry Holt, 1932), pp. 156, 248–49. More recent work on Dwight's theology largely falls into three distinct but related categories: his participation in the Second Great Awakening; his identification with the theology of Jonathan Edwards, and his interest in millennialism.

In his *Autobiography,* compiled decades after his student days at Yale, Lyman Beecher crafts a famous tale about the religious skepticism he discovered at Yale during his sophomore year. According to Beecher, when Dwight arrived as president, the college was in "a most ungodly state." Infidelity and licentiousness reigned, cocky students hailed one another using the names of famous French skeptics, and the most arrogant among the student body believed that the faculty was afraid of open debate about religious questions. Dwight's strategy to cure the college of infidelity was simple. In the classroom he engaged student skepticism by choosing the question "Is the Bible the word of God?" for disputation. In the chapel, he "preached incessantly for six months on the subject" of infidelity. The result, opined Beecher, was stunning: "all infidelity skulked and hid its head." Barbara M. Cross, ed., *The Autobiography of Lyman Beecher,* 2 vols. (Cambridge: Harvard University Press, 1961), 1:27. According to Benjamin

Silliman, who was also present in these heady days, Dwight not only drove off infidelity but also added to the membership of Yale's college church and transformed the college into a "little temple" where "prayer and praise seem to be the delight of the greater part of the students." Benjamin Silliman, in a letter to his mother, 11 July 1802, in Fisher, *Life of Benjamin Silliman, M.D., LL.D,* 1:83.

What began as a tall tale about religion at Yale has developed historically into a formative event with ever-expanding consequences for American religious culture. In 1942, Charles Roy Keller, *The Second Great Awakening in Connecticut* (New Haven: Yale University Press, 1942), argued that Dwight's Yale revival marked "the beginning of a movement" (p. 42) in the religious history of Connecticut. Twenty-five years later, William Clebsch, *From Sacred to Profane in America: The Role of Religion in American History* (New York: Harper and Row, 1968), broadened Keller's assessment, noting that "the Eastern revivals opened with the century at Yale where President Timothy Dwight inveighed against infidelity and lax morals as causally connected" (pp. 31–32). Sidney E. Mead, *The Old Religion in the Brave New World: Reflections on the Relation between Christendom and the Republic* (Berkeley: University of California Press, 1977), went further still in 1977, claiming that the awakenings that began with Dwight's arrival at Yale "rapidly spread through the country in the often spectacular revivals that are known as the Second Great Awakening" (p. 55). In 1989, Annabelle S. Wenzke, *Timothy Dwight (1752–1817),* Studies in American Religion 38 (Lewiston: Edwin Mellen Press, 1989), expressed what is perhaps the most extensive claim about Dwight's significance: "Specifically, Dwight assimilated Reformed theology with Enlightenment theory and values and bound them irrevocably to the New England culture. The consequent theological system formed the basis for the religious movement later known as Evangelical Protestantism" (pp. 3–4). Beecher's mythic account has in the minds of generations of historians become a foundational but misinterpreted event in the history of American religion.

Dwight's alleged rout of the forces of infidelity can be nicely combined with another element of his biography, namely his relationship to Jonathan Edwards. Just as Edwards is recognized as America's first Great Awakener, so his grandson can be conveniently cast as America's second Great Awakener; just as Edwards defended his unique brand of Reformed Christianity against the assaults of Arminianism, so Dwight can be seen as the champion of Congregational orthodoxy who protects the nation from the ravages of infidelity. As another comparison between Edwards and Dwight shows, the interpretive convenience of this genealogical bridge between the two Awakenings is suspect. Just as Edwards's "Sinners in the Hands of an Angry God" has been woefully misinterpreted, so has "Dwight's Yale revival." In the eyes of generations of interpreters, each bears more importance than its context warrants. Edwards's thought is vastly more complex and creative than a casual reading of "Sinners" indicates, and Dwight's religion is far more subtle and complicated than is described in Beecher's *Autobiography.*

While other scholars have touched on Dwight's role in the Beecher myth and his subsequent reputation as America's "Second Great Awakener" (notably Perry Miller, *The Life of the Mind in America: From the Revolution to the Civil War,* Books One through Three (New York: Harcourt, Brace, and World, 1965), p. 4; Richard F. Lovelace, *The Dynamics of Spiritual Life* (Downers Grove, Ill.: Inter Varsity Press, 1979), pp. 47, 59, 179, and 181, and Stephen A. Marini, *Radical Sects of Revolutionary New England* (Cambridge: Harvard University Press, 1982), p. 37), this interpretation labors under serious difficulties. Not least of these is a chronological problem. Dwight's 1795 revival did antedate the Cane Ridge revival (held August 1801) by several years. Nonetheless, the evangelistic experiments of Barton Stone and other western Presbyterians that led to the religious explosion at Cane Ridge began as early as 1796. Hence, the Yale revival did not appreciably antedate the advent of the broader western revival movement.

To complicate matters further, the theological outlooks of the historians who deal with Dwight's religion color their interpretations. Sidney Mead, fond of lionizing theological liberals, and Vernon Parrington, who took particular delight in tilting at American Calvinists, produced negative interpretations of Dwight that were perfectly consistent with their general disdain for conservative theology in America. Historians who are more open to conservative outlooks tend to see Dwight as a heroic figure. Not all evangelical interpreters view Dwight positively, however. In Stephen Berk, *Calvinism Versus Democracy: Timothy Dwight and the Origins of American Evangelical Orthodoxy* (Hamden, Conn.: Archon Books, 1974), and Richard F. Lovelace, *The Dynamics of Spiritual Life* (Downers Grove, Ill.: Inter Varsity Press, 1979), one finds sympathetic treatments of Dwight's role in shaping the evangelical tradition. Other theological conservatives demur on this point. A case in point is David C. Brand, who argues that Dwight's theology represented "a strange convergence of Arminianism and benevolism" and that Dwight despoiled New England theology, which had reached a high watermark in Jonathan Edwards. See Brand, *Profile of the Last Puritan: Jonathan Edwards, Self-Love, and the Dawn of the Beatific* (Atlanta: Scholars Press, 1991), p. 131. For a non-theological appreciation of Dwight that seeks to renovate his reputation, see William Gribbin, "The Legacy of Timothy Dwight: A Reappraisal," *Connecticut Historical Society Bulletin* 37 (1972):33–41.

The relationship between Dwight's religious commitments and his politics—only hinted in Beecher's account of the Yale awakening—has also attracted scholarly attention. Because many New Englanders feared both the political and the religious implications of infidelity, some scholars have tried to use Dwight's campaigns against it as evidence that both politics and religion were central to the Second Great Awakening. Sidney E. Mead, *Nathaniel William Taylor, 1786–1858: A Connecticut Liberal* (Chicago: University of Chicago Press, 1942), was the first scholar to provide a full critical analysis of connections between religion and politics during the era. In Mead's interpretation, "Dwight was never able to dissociate true religion from the state-established Congregational church" and, as a consequence, the boundaries between religious and political institutions became unclear. The implications of this view in abbreviated form are simple: "Christianity, the Standing Order, and Federalism were to be saved from infidelity, Jacobinism, and the Democrats" (pp. 49, 48).

There is, of course, a good deal of evidence to support Mead's claim that Dwight viewed his political and religious commitments as constituents of a single, unified world view. As L. Douglas Good, "The Christian Nation in the Mind of Timothy Dwight," *Fides et Historia* 7 (1974):1–18, and others have noted, *The Conquest of Canaan, Greenfield Hill, The Triumph of Infidelity, Travels,* and scores of sermons— notably Dwight's shrill and francophobic *The Duty of Americans at the Present Crisis*—reveal substantive links between his religious and political convictions. Indeed, Dwight's own students would probably have concurred with Mead. As Stephen F. Jones noted in a letter to Jared Sparks (Jones to Sparks, 30 January and 28 May 1811, in H. D. Adams, *Life and Writings of Jared Sparks* (Boston: 1893); also cited in Cuningham, p. 247), Dwight and his hand-picked Yale faculty appeared to be "perfectly united in their sentiments with regard to Politics and Religion" (1:45–46). The same Yale student noted that these sentiments were "very nearly the same with those of Calvin and Washington" (1:53–54). It appears that President Dwight had somehow amalgamated Reformed theology and American Federalism, and in his day and ours, observers have puzzled over the meaning of the mix.

One of Mead's students explored fully the extent to which political ideology served as an impetus to the Second Great Awakening. Stephen Berk, in *Calvinism Versus Democracy*, argued forthrightly and at length what Mead had only suggested: the Second Great Awakening was contrived for specific political purposes. As "an expiring establishment relinquished its power to maintain social control, the voluntary agencies and militant revivalism of the Second Great Awakening moved into the void" (p. 160). The Awakening, he argued in a chapter-length analysis, was "contrived" (pp. 161–93). Dwight and his Federalist colleagues engineered the Awakening in order to maintain the decaying ecclesiastical hegemony of the Congregational Standing Order. Responding to their loss of status, these theocratic Federalists—a group of clergy further examined in John R. Bodo, *The Protestant Clergy and Public Issues, 1812–1848* (Princeton: Princeton University Press, 1954), pp. vii, 49, 198, 256—offered something larger than a system of doctrine. Theirs was a complete program of political action. Under Berk's interpretation, Connecticut's Congregational clergy, a body that was almost entirely Federalist, invented and implemented the revivals in the hope that their churches might grow in a particular way. The new members they garnered would be added to the Federalist cause and, more importantly, would be snatched from the hands of aggressive Baptist and Methodist pastors, nearly all of whom were Republicans. In short, Berk claimed that in last stand effort the Standing Order employed ecclesiology for political ends.

This sort of argument functions much like the "declension thesis" that long dominated the historiography of New England Puritanism. Like its seventeenth-century counterpart, this nineteenth-century declension thesis maintains that the New England ministerial elite sought to increase their influence through the leverage of congregational renewal. In an era of declining religious vitality while citizens' attentions were fixed on political questions, the ministers' formula for success was simple: Fill the pews, preach aggressively, revive the churches, and, as a matter of course, the Standing Order's power will be consolidated. Yet this reworking of the seventeenth-century declension thesis is plaqued by difficulties. Robert G. Pope, "New England Versus the New England Mind: The Myth of Declension," *Journal of Social History* 3 (1969–70):95–108, clearly demonstrated that the declension model in any era relies on problematic categories. Hatch, *The Sacred Cause of Liberty,* William L. McLoughlin, *New England Dissent, 1630–1883: The Baptists and the Separation of Church and State,* 2 vols. (Cambridge: Harvard University Press, 1971), and Richard W. Pointer, *Protestant Pluralism and the New York Experience: A Study of Eighteenth-Century Religious Diversity* (Bloomington: Indiana University Press, 1988) argue convincingly that the lull in religious sensibilities necessary to the model was simply not present in the revolutionary age.

Beginning in 1963, a smaller revisionist literature challenged the historiographical pattern that was developing around Beecher, Dwight, and the Second Awakening. Edmund S. Morgan, "Ezra Stiles and Timothy Dwight," Massachusetts Historical Society, *Proceedings* 72 (1963):101–17, began this remonstrance by noting that Beecher's *Autobiography* was not a strictly historical account but rather a pastiche of recollections collated by Beecher's children in his declining years. Beecher's story of the Yale revival, like other tales contained in the *Autobiography*, was likely based on a faulty, partisan memory. Whereas Beecher had implied that the Connecticut revivals began at Yale, Morgan found evidence to suggest that other congregations near the college experienced revivals prior to Dwight's evangelistic endeavors at Yale. Contrary to Beecher's claim that membership at the college church increased soon after Dwight's arrival, Morgan discovered that it did not increase until 1802, seven years after Dwight began his presidential tenure. In fact, Dwight's preaching method apparently had little or no effect on church membership during the early years of his presidency. Beecher had implied that Dwight had instituted bold new methods of collegiate education by encouraging open discussion of controversial topics such as "Is the Bible the word of God?" Previous Yale presidents, Morgan argued, had used similar topics as a matter of course. Beecher's adolescent fondness for his mentor notwithstanding, Timothy Dwight was fulfilling his pedagogic duties in a most traditional manner.

Following Morgan's lead, other historians began to challenge the reigning assumptions about the broader New England revivals of the Second Awakening. Richard Birdsall, "The Second Great Awakening and the New England Social Order," *Church History* 39 (1970):345–64, overturned the notion that the Second Awakening became a political tool in Federalist hands by showing that the Second Awakening originated at the popular level. It occurred precisely because traditional Federalist Congregationalism, the very species advocated by Dwight, had lost its capacity to provide New Englanders with a meaningful explanation of their everyday existence. In an age when the passion for individualism and egalitarianism was mounting, Standing Order ministers demanded social, political, and religious deference. Elitist to the core, these Federalist partisans continued to believe that New England's affairs were best managed by a powerful few. The general populace, if they would but come to their senses, would quietly obey.

Richard Shiels, "The Second Great Awakening in Connecticut: Critique of the Traditional Interpretation," *Church History* 49 (1980), extended Birdsall's revisionist critique of the politics of the Awakening to include the issues of preaching and political power among the clergy. Shiels distilled the standard historiography to three central claims and countered that none of them were correct. First, he concluded that preachers did not trigger the Awakening by self-consciously shifting their style of homiletics from the learned, profound discourse to one of warm, lively, personal exhortation. Second, the Awakening did not commence when "ecclesiastical statesmen" like Dwight gained access to the corridors of political power in Connecticut. Not political praxis but a rapid increase in strictly religious activity (notably the formation of the Connecticut Missionary Society and the expanded publication of the *Connecticut Evangelical Magazine*) properly mark the origins of Connecticut's fascination with revival. Third, the leaders of the Second Awakening were not the leaders of the Federalist party in Connecticut. Shiels isolated a group of thirty-three Connecticut clergymen who were active in missions and religious journalism. These men, he concluded, constituted the clerical leadership of the Second Awakening in Connecticut, and none of them were powerful figures in Connecticut politics. Neither Dwight's name nor the names of any of Dwight's Yale students appear on Shiels's list. Dwight's contribution to the movement, Shiels concluded, was unclear.

A host of other scholars treat the interconnections between religion and politics in Dwight's era. Important assessments of the religious contexts of the Second Awakening incude G. A. Rawlyk, *Ravished by the Spirit: Religious Revivals, Baptists, and Henry Alline*

(Kingston: McGill-Queen's University Press, 1984); Stephen A. Marini, "Religious Revolution in the District of Maine, 1780–1820," in *Maine in the Early Republic: From Revolution to Statehood,* ed. Charles E. Clark, James S. Leamon, and Karen Bowden (Hanover: University of New England Press, 1988), pp. 118–45; Paul R. Conkin, *Cane Ridge: America's Pentecost* (Madison: University of Wisconsin Press, 1990); Harry S. Stout, "Rhetoric and Reality in the Early Republic: The Case of the Federalist Clergy," in *Religion and American Politics: From the Colonial Period to the 1980s,* ed. Mark A. Noll (New York: Oxford University Press, 1990), pp. 62–76; and Nathan O. Hatch, *The Democratization of American Christianity* (New Haven: Yale University Press, 1989). Randolph A. Roth, *The Democratic Dilemma: Religion, Reform, and the Social Order in the Connecticut River Valley of Vermont, 1791–1850* (Cambridge, England: Cambridge University Press, 1987), pp. 66ff., argues that Dwight's journeys of 1797, 1803, and 1812 to the Connecticut River Valley were forms of religious diplomacy on behalf of the unity of the Second Awakening. These forays into the north, especially to Vermont, gave Dwight a chance to mediate the differences between Vermont's hard-line Calvinists and Arminianized Baptists. In a recent article that treats a good deal of the literature on this question, Marc Harris has argued that rationalism or, perhaps more accurately, "supernatural rationalism," is the most promising theme by which to assess the connections between Dwight's religious and political commitments. See Marc L. Harris, "Revelation and the American Republic: Timothy Dwight's Civic Participation," *Journal of the History of Ideas* 54 (1993):449–68.

The politics of the era are given in-depth attention in David H. Fischer, *The Revolution of American Conservatism: The Federalist Party in the Era of Jeffersonian Democracy* (New York: Harper and Row, 1965), and Linda K. Kerber, *Federalists in Dissent: Imagery and Ideology in Jeffersonian America* (Ithaca: Cornell University Press, 1970), provide insightful treatments of the Federalist political program. Though now quite dated, Richard Purcell, *Connecticut in Transition: 1755–1818* (Washington, D.C.: American Historical Association, 1918; rpt. ed. Middletown, Conn.: Wesleyan University Press, 1963), remains a fine treatment of Federalist politics in Dwight's beloved Connecticut. Clinton Rossiter, *Conservatism in America* (New York: Alfred A. Knopf, 1955), Richard Hofstadter, *The Paranoid Style in American Politics, and Other Essays* (New York: Alfred Knopf, 1965), and Vernon Louis Parrington, *Main Currents in American Thought,* 2 vols. (New York: Harcourt, Brace, 1927), are also helpful, if sharply pointed, interpretations of Dwight's political outlooks. Walter E. Volkomer, "Timothy Dwight and New England Federalism," *Connecticut Review* 3 (1970):72–82, focuses entirely on Dwight and places him in his political context. Although he lacks the breadth and subtlety of Fischer, Kerber, or Purcell, Volkomer is keen to note the exent to which Dwight's political vision was a failure: "Dwight's ideas are primarily important because they were largely the doctrines America rejected as it entered the nineteenth century" (p. 81).

The Edwardsean Theological Milieu

If historians have been divided in their assessments of Dwight's role in the Second Great Awakening, they have been even further puzzled as to his overall theological identity. Part of the difficulty rests on what appear to be intractable terminological problems. Several different Protestant groups competed for privileged status in the religious world of late eighteenth-century New England, but it is often difficult to distinguish between the various groups. In some cases, of course, the boundaries between theological schools were clear: Old Lights and New Lights disagreed about the Awakening; Unitarians and Trinitarians disagreed about the trinity; Edwardsean theologians disagreed with Arminians about human depravity and so forth. Notwithstanding these oppositional pairings it is quite difficult to invent a single heuristic device that can account for all the groups. In this case resorting to a left/right, liberal/conservative spectrum can become problematic. While it is easy to place the Universalists on the left and the Edwardseans on the right, there are a number of issues, subgroups, and intramural debates that foil any attempt to place all the groups into one grand scheme. In the face of this difficulty, what can be said of Dwight's theology?

Some elements of Dwight's theological makeup can be identified easily because he was so vocal about them. He was at home in a Reformed, Calvinistic theological environment, he affirmed Congregational polity (though he helped to promote various attempts to ally New England Congregationalists and Presbyterians), he was a convinced paedo-baptist, a combative trinitarian, a New Light (though this distinction began to lose its relevance at about the middle of Dwight's career), and he held a traditional view of the authority of the Bible. In the main, Dwight would rest on the right side of an admittedly inaccurate theological spectrum, and those interpreters who see in him the reactionary, "paranoid style" would place him at the right extreme of that spectrum.

Difficulties arise when one begins to probe the ways in which Dwight treated more subtle issues in his theological system. By the time Dwight was refining the sermons that would eventually become *Theology,* many New England theologians were already busily accepting, rejecting, or modifying the theological legacy of Jonathan Edwards. Like most others of his generation, Dwight was working out his own positions in the wake of his grandfather's master works—*Religious Affections, Freedom of the Will, Original Sin,* and *Two Dissertations.* The question that has puzzled scholars for some time has to do with the extent to which Dwight accepted and was guided by Edwards's teachings. Was Dwight generally speaking an "Edwardsean"? Did he conform to one of the narrower, more carefully nuanced "New Divinity," "Hopkinsian, " or "Consistent Calvinist" camps within the larger Edwardsean milieu?

Several descriptions and interpretations of Edwardsean theology have been written in the last several decades. The best starting points are Joseph Conforti, *Samuel Hopkins and the New Divinity Movement* (Grand Rapids: Eerdmans, 1981); William Breitenbach, "Unregenerate Doings: Selflessness and Selfishness in New Divinity Theology," *American Quarterly* 34 (1982):479–502; William Brietenbach, "The Consistent Calvinism of the New Divinity Movement," *William and Mary Quarterly* 41 (1984):241–64; Mark Valeri, *Law and Providence in Joseph Bellamy's New England: The Origins of the New Divinity in Revolutionary America* (New York: Oxford University Press, 1994); and Allen C. Guelzo, *Edwards on the Will: A Century of American Theological Debate* (Middletown: Wesleyan University Press, 1989). These more general, introductory studies have been complemented by a growing body of research that treats Edwardseanism's connections to other events and movements. Joseph Conforti has explored the connections between the First and Second Awakenings with special reference to the Edwardsean theological legacy in several important essays: Joseph Conforti, "Antebellum Evangelicals and the Cultural Revival of Jonathan Edwards," *American Presbyterianism* 64 (1986):227–41; Conforti, "Edwardsians, Unitarians, and the Memory of the Great Awakening," in Conrad Edick Wright, ed., *American Unitarianism, 1805–1865* (Boston: Massachusetts

Historical Society and Northeastern University Press, 1989), pp. 31–50; and Conforti, "The Invention of the Great Awakening, 1795–1842," *Early American Literature* 26 (1991):99–118. For an illuminating examination of revivalism among New Divinity pastors, see David W. Kling, *A Field of Divine Wonders: The New Divinity and Village Revivals in Northwestern Connecticut, 1792–1822* (University Park, Pa.: Pennsylvania State University Press, 1993). James R. Rohrer, *Keepers of the Covenant: Frontier Missions and the Decline of Congregationalism, 1774–1818* (New York: Oxford University Press, 1995), examines the powerful New England missionary impulse and the importance of the Connecticut Missionary Society among congregationalists in general and Edwardseans in particular.

While most scholars agree that Dwight identified with the broad contours of Edwardsean theology, his attachments to its more radical New Divinity or Hopkinsian forms are less clear. Some interpreters have claimed that Dwight was a New Divinity theologian. Such identifications can be found in Stephen Berk, *Calvinism Versus Democracy*; Bruce Kuklick, *Churchmen and Philosophers: From Jonathan Edwards to John Dewey* (New Haven: Yale University Press, 1985); Conrad Wright, *The Beginnings of Unitarianism in America* (Boston: Starr King Press, 1955); Paul T. Shiber, "*The Conquest of Canaan* as a Youthful Expression of Timothy Dwight's New Divinity and Political Thought" (Ph.D. diss., University of Miami, 1972); and Wayne C. Tyner, "The Theology of Timothy Dwight in Historical Perspective" (Ph.D. diss., University of North Carolina at Chapel Hill, 1971). Other interpreters have argued that Dwight was not strictly speaking a New Divinity thinker but that he promoted a milder form of Edwardseanism. These include Sydney Ahlstrom, *A Religious History of the American People* (New Haven: Yale University Press, 1972), p. 419; Joseph Conforti, *Samuel Hopkins and the New Divinity Movement*, pp. 192 and 227ff.; Frank Hugh Foster, *A Genetic History of the New England Theology* (Chicago: University of Chicago Press, 1907), p. 361–62; Mead, *Nathaniel William Taylor*, and John R. Fitzmier, "The Godly Federalism of Timothy Dwight, 1752–1817: Society, Doctrine, and Religion in the Life of New England's 'Moral Legislator'" (Ph.D. diss., Princeton University, 1986), pp. 111–58.

Unfortunately, simply asking what Dwight's theological inclinations were—Was he an Edwardsean? Or was he a more radical New Divinity apologist?—masks deeper and more interesting questions about the character of the New England theological tradition. Douglas Sweeney, "Nathaniel William Taylor and the Edwardsean Tradition: Evolution and Continuity in the Culture of the New England Theology" (Ph.D. diss., Vanderbilt University, 1995), argues convincingly that the Edwardsean theological tradition, which he believes was a fully institutionalized and socialized "theological culture," was both broader and more pervasive than has been recognized. Whereas nearly all previous interpreters have viewed Dwight's protégé Nathaniel William Taylor as the "Arminianizer" who drove the final nail into the coffin of Edwardsean theology, Sweeney argues that Taylor was in many respects faithful to his Edwardsean, and perhaps Dwightian, roots. Although Taylor's alterations of the Edwardsean tradition were condemned by Princetonians in the south and by Tylerites in the north, his innovations are best understood as attempts to extend the Edwardsean tradition and not as Pelagianizing efforts to destroy it. Sweeney demonstrates that as our appreciation of the complexities of a particular tradition develop, the identification of a particular thinker becomes more, not less, complex. This is certainly true of Dwight.

To associate Dwight with the New Divinity movement is not altogether unreasonable. Dwight clearly revered his grandfather, who is universally acknowledged as the movement's progenitor. He obtained his theological training under an established New Divinity pastor, his uncle, Jonathan Edwards, Jr. Some elements of Dwight's theology—especially his teaching on disinterested benevolence and the Halfway Covenant—closely resemble New Divinity ideas. Both Dwight and the New Divinity theologians sensed that their beloved Reformed tradition was under siege. In other respects, however, Dwight's theology differs considerably from the strict New Divinity theology of thinkers like Nathanael Emmons. Conservative thinkers among the Edwardseans attempted to extend the corollaries of Edwards's system in order to perfect it. For his part, Dwight evidenced growing distrust of philosophical and theological systems. He concluded that the cherished "consistency" of the "consistent Calvinists" amounted to nothing but the application of cold and sterile logic. Dwight founded his theology on the conviction that reason, if not held closely in check, inevitably produced theological distortions. While "orthodox" New Divinity preachers put a high premium on divine omnipotence in evangelism, Dwight recognized the utility of human activity and promoted the "means of grace" in the conversion process. Despite these differences, Dwight was powerfully shaped by the intellectual and theological legacy of Edwards and his coterie of would-be disciples. Discerning the elements of Edwardseanism that were operative in Dwight's theology while simultaneously distinguishing his thought from that of the more ardent and rigorous among the Edwardseans remains a challenging and vexing problem.

Millennialism in the Early National Era.

Like many of his contemporaries in the ministry, Timothy Dwight expressed keen interest in eschatology, that branch of systematic theology that seeks to understand the often mysterious biblical promises that foretell the end of the world and the final establishment of the reign of God. He adhered to what scholars call a "postmillennial" scheme, whereby one affirms that the millennium (the thousand-year era of peace and prosperity promised in the New Testament) would precede the final return of Christ in glory. This interest required Dwight to study the relevant portions of the Old and New Testaments, but it also necessitated that he keep a close eye on his cultural surroundings. If God chose to establish the divine reign on earth, that actuality would surely be embodied in the fabric of human culture—religion, economics, politics, and social life would all be renewed and made holy. Hence, Dwight not only looked to the prophecies themselves for signs of the inbreaking divine reign but also to the rapidly changing world in which he found himself.

Ernest L. Tuveson, *Redeemer Nation: The Idea of America's Millennial Role* (Chicago: University of Chicago Press, 1968), was the first scholar to treat Dwight's postmillennial theology seriously. For this and other reasons, his *Redeemer Nation* became an historiographical landmark in what would become an increasingly complex literature on millennialism in American culture. Other scholars would later note that Dwight's views of the nation and its prospects swung from euphoric to depressed. Recall Silverman's claim that Dwight lived either in a "birthday" or "doomsday" mode. Tuveson was the first scholar to account for these shifting views with insights from eschatology proper. When it came to Dwight's optimistic "birthday" celebrations, Tuveson ventured a remarkable claim: "if there can be identified any moment when America's position in the millennialist pattern becomes 'manifest,' it may be the publication in 1771 of Timothy Dwight's *America: or a Poem on the Settlement of the British Colonies. . . .* Here is not merely a grandiose vision of future 'glory' but a developed historical myth, in fact the kernel of the idea of American millennialism" (p. 103). In *Sacred Cause of Liberty,* Nathan Hatch demurs, noting that Dwight was not the first to make American destiny "manifest" and that Dwight's version of millennial theology was not particularly foundational among later thinkers. From Hatch's perspective, Dwight only added his voice to a chorus of New England clerics who had already begun the millennial chant. Whether he was first or among the first, Dwight helped to launch a strictly theological version of American exceptionalism, a theme that would recur again and again in the nation's history.

Tuveson concentrated on Dwight's role in the development of the optimistic millennialism of the Revolutionary era. James West Davidson, *The Logic of Millennial Thought: Eighteenth-Century New England* (New Haven: Yale University Press, 1977), explored the larger intellectual and theological contexts in which Dwight's post-millennial thinking developed and also examined the technical details of Dwight's millennialism more comprehensively. Whereas Tuveson had treated the millennial nationalism in Dwight's poetry, Davidson examined several of Dwight's sermonic treatments of the end times and discovered important distinctions and developments in Dwight's eschatological thinking. The most significant of these had dealt with the manner in which Dwight conceived the onset of the thousand-year reign of God prior to the eschaton. Some interpreters looked for miraculous heavenly evidence that the end times would begin. They expected that miracles or other sorts of divine intrusions would immediately precede the end. Dwight, however, believed that the millennium would commence not by miracles but by the efforts and work of faithful Christians. Just as he stressed human means in evangelism (which lead to the conversion of individuals), so in his eschatology he believed that human effort would help to establish the millennium (which would lead to the conversion of culture at large). This distinction proves useful for it invites us to identify the sorts of efforts—evangelism, missions, social reform, and political action—Dwight might see as appropriate means to blessedness, either individual or corporate.

The complex interaction between millennial views and social reform ideologies has proven to be a suggestive topic for students of late eighteenth and early nineteenth-century religious history. If human means—cast in the form of social reform efforts—were thought to initiate the millennium, would this help us to understand why so many early national Americans joined reform movements? Berk, in *Calvinism Versus Democracy,* suggests that Dwight's motives for evangelism and social reform included a desire to control New England society. Berk's approach, with something of a millennial twist, rests on a far older literature about social reform and social control. Earlier literature on the benevolent movements, such as Dixon Ryan Fox, "The Protestant Counter-Reformation in America," *New York History* 16 (1935):19–35, argued that the reform movements were intended to return Americans to Christian orthodoxy. Beginning in the 1950s, several studies concluded that the social reform movements were thinly veiled campaigns to gain control of the low and middle classes. Illustrations of this interpretation can be found in Bodo, *The Protestant Clergy;* Charles C. Cole, *The Social Ideas of the Northern Evangelists, 1826–1860* (New York: Columbia University Press, 1954); Charles I. Foster, *Errand of Mercy: The Evangelical United Front, 1790–1837* (Chapel Hill: University of North Carolina Press, 1960); and Clifford Griffin, *Their Brothers' Keeper: Moral Stewardship in the United States, 1800–1865* (New Brunswick: Rutgers University Press, 1960). Lois Banner, "Religious Benevolence as Social Control:

A Critique of an Interpretation," *Journal of American History* 60 (1973):23–41, challenged this interpretation, arguing that the reform movements had to do with the
inculcation of civic republican virtues among the populace and not hidden attempts to
control the masses. Berk's development of the social control thesis itself has been
challenged. Dietrich Buss, "The Millennial Vision of Motive for Religious Benevolence
and Reform: Timothy Dwight and the New England Evangelicals Reconsidered," *Fides
et Historia* 16 (1983):18–34, rejects the social control thesis altogether (either on
Griffin's or Berk's terms) and argues that millennialism was the impetus behind Dwight's
social reform efforts.

Tuveson examined Dwight's millennialism with an eye toward politics and American
identity; Davidson, with an eye toward the history of Christian thought in the American
context. Students of American poetry working from a different series of texts altogether
have also pursued Dwight's millennialism. Mason Lowance, *The Language of Canaan:
Metaphor and Symbol in New England from the Puritans to the Transcendentalists* (Cambridge: Harvard University Press, 1980), described more fully the sorts of cultural
productions Dwight identified as harbingers of the long-awaited reign of God in the
world. In the *Conquest of Canaan* and *Greenfield Hill*, Lowance argues, Dwight clarified
his belief that the millennial state would be discerned in an earthly ideal community of
redeemed sinners and not in a heavenly paradise of angels and sinless saints. The peace
and prosperity described in the pastoral scenes in *Greenfield Hill* become metaphors for
Dwight's version of the Kingdom of God. In making human effort and cultural
productions so central to his millennialism, Lowance believed that Dwight unwittingly
secularized eschatology: the eschaton was not to be seen in a miraculous divine
intrusion but in the gradual progress of human beings working in the world.

Notwithstanding the positive contributions of Tuveson, Davidson, and Lowance to
understanding Dwight's apocalyptic millennialism, a serious interpretive problem
remains. During the Revolution, Dwight's optimism for the new nation was unbounded.
With the appearance of religious skepticism and infidelity his enthusiasm for American
prospects cooled considerably. At the height of the French Revolution, he became
positively pessimistic. How can one account for these dramatic shifts in Dwight's
millennial perceptions?

Ruth H. Bloch, *Visionary Republic: Millennial Themes in American Thought, 1756–
1800* (Cambridge: Cambridge University Press, 1985), constructs an interpretive
framework that offers considerable insight into this difficulty. Although she acknowl-
edges that the overlapping boundaries between millennial theology, the ideology of
civic republicanism, and the secular utopianism of the Enlightenment were often
difficult to discern during the Revolutionary era, Bloch's chief interest is in the manner
in which these ideologies interacted and changed over time. Bloch concludes that the
focus of millennial rhetoric altered with the course of political events in the young
nation. During the 1750s, ministers from several denominations and persuasions, both
Old Lights and New Lights, conservatives and liberals, became interested in the
scriptural passages that discussed the apocalypse. This biblicism was undercut during
the period just prior to the Revolution when secular political thought combined with
traditional millennial thinking and produced during the Revolution itself the foundations of what Tuveson called the Redeemer Nation. After the defeat of the British the
millennial euphoria of American ministers waned. Despite the promise and hope of
millennial bliss in America, a host of problems—debilitating political battles over the
Constitution, dismay over the brutality of the French Revolution, and worries over the

fragile national economy—led to disappointment and moderation. As the 1790s progressed, religious leaders moved away from the heady political millennialism of the Revolution to more traditional and steady biblical interpretations of eschatology. Again, the focus of millennialism had changed: instead of seeing the nation itself as a critical participant in the great cosmic drama, the clergy invested missions and social reform with millennial significance.

Bloch's account of these shifts helps us to understand some, but not all, elements of Dwight's eschatology. Although he was too young to have published work in the pre-Revolutionary period, Bloch accurately notes that his earliest poems (*America: or a Poem on the Settlement of the British Colonies*) as well as his early sermons and addresses (e.g., *A Valedictory Address* (1776) and *A Sermon Preached at Northampton* (1781)) fit the millennialism of the Revolution quite nicely. These works are clearly political and enthusiastically celebrate the divine significance of the new nation. His later millennial works, such as *The Nature and Danger of Infidel Philosophy* (1797) and *The Duty of Americans at the Present Crisis* (1798), also conform to the pattern Bloch discerns. In these treatises Dwight concentrates on strictly biblical issues such as the details of the vials of St. John's Revelation. Late in his career, Dwight's thinking about the millennium is quite closely tied to missions activity, as is made evident in his *Sermon Delivered . . . before the American Board of Commissioners for Foreign Missions* (1813). What remains puzzling, however, is the extent to which the "political" and "biblical" categories become mixed in Dwight's eschatological pronouncements. As scholars have noted time and again, Dwight's religion and politics were intertwined, sometimes to the point of being indistinguishable. While Bloch's categories provide context for Dwight's eschatology, these categories do not provide a full or satisfactory explanation for this feature of his theology.

Three other sources provide useful, though diverse, perspectives on the context and meaning of Dwight's millennial thinking. For a helpful historiographical treatment of millennial themes in the Revolutionary era and particularly of the differences between Hatch's *Sacred Cause of Liberty* and Bloch's *Visionary Republic,* see Gerald R. McDermott, "Civil Religion in the American Revolutionary Period: An Historiographic Analysis," *Christian Scholar's Review* 18 (1989):346–62. For a transatlantic perspective on millennial thought, see Stephen J. Stein, "Transatlantic Extensions: Apocalyptic in Early New England," in *The Apocalypse in English and Renaissance Thought and Literature,* ed. C. A. Patrides and Joseph Wittreich (Ithaca: Cornell University Press, 1984), pp. 266–98. Sacvan Bercovitch briefly notes the interesting junctures between Dwight's millennial and political ideologies in *The American Jeremiad* (Madison: University of Wisconsin Press, 1978), pp. 129ff.

BIBLIOGRAPHY

I. Manuscripts

The most comprehensive collection of manuscripts by and about Timothy Dwight is preserved at Yale University. The Manuscript and Archives Division of the Sterling Library holds the largest number of these materials. Collections that are particularly helpful include the Dwight Family Papers, the Morse Family Papers, and the Hillhouse Family Papers. Among these, the Dwight Family Papers is the most useful. It includes manuscript letters written by Dwight, manuscript sermons (not in Dwight's hand, and most likely prepared by an amanuensis for review by a publisher), two manuscript biographies entitled "Biographical Hints," and student notes taken during the senior recitations that Dwight directed. The Beinecke Rare Book Library of Yale University also houses relevant materials. Of particular note are sermons, student recitation notes, a few of Dwight's early poems, and several sets of student notes taken during Dwight's chapel sermons. These latter materials are of special importance because they enable the reconstruction of the preaching calendar that Dwight employed in the chapel, which later determined the structure of *Theology, Explained and Defended*. Dwight's handwriting is sometimes difficult to read and in a few instances I have had to hazard a guess about the identity of a word or a phrase. These interpretations are enclosed in square brackets.

II. Publications of Timothy Dwight

A Dissertation on the History, Eloquence, and Poetry of the Bible, Delivered at the Public Commencement at New Haven. New Haven: Thomas and Samuel Green, 1772.

A Valedictory Address to the Young Gentlemen Who Commenced Bachelor of Arts at Yale College, July 25, 1776. New Haven: Thomas and Samuel Green, 1776.

A Sermon Preached at Stamford in Connecticut upon the General Thanksgiving, December 18, 1777. Hartford: Watson and Goodwin, 1778.

America: or a Poem on the Settlement of the British Colonies; Addressed to the Friends of Freedom and their Country. New Haven: Thomas and Samuel Green, 1780.

A Sermon Preached at Northampton on the twenty-eighth of November, 1781, Occasioned by the Capture of the British Army under the Command of Earl Cornwallis. Hartford: Nathaniel Patten, 1781.

"Columbia; a Song." *Boston Magazine* (December 1783):71.

The Conquest of Canaan: A Poem in Eleven Books. Hartford: Elisha Babcock, 1785.

"The Friend." *New-Haven Gazette and Connecticut Magazine* 1 (23 March 1786):42–43; 1 (30 March 1786):50–51; 1 (6 April 1786):58–60; 1 (20 April 1786):73–74; 1 (27 April 1786): 81–82; 1 (4 May 1786):89–90; 1 (25 May 1786):113–14; 1 (8 June 1786):129–30; 1 (15 June 1786):137–38; 1 (22 June 1786):145–46; 1 (6 July 1786):161–63; 1 (21 September 1786):245–46; 1 (12 October 1786):269–70; 1 (19 October 1786):277–78; and 2 (4 October 1787):257–58.

"A Historical Account of the Gothic Gospel." *New-Haven Gazette and Connecticut Magazine* 2 (1 March 1787):10.

"An Essay on the Judgment of History Concerning America." *New-Haven Gazette and Connecticut Magazine* 2 (12 April 1787):59–60.

"On the Doctrine of Chance: Containing Remarks of Ethan Allen's Oracles of Reason." *American Museum* 2 (October 1787):408–10.

The Triumph of Infidelity: A Poem. n.p.: "PRINTED IN THE WORLD," 1788.

"Address to the Ministers of the Gospel of Every Denomination in the United States." *American Museum* 4 (July 1788):30–33.

"The Seasons Moralized." *American Museum* 5 (March 1789):302–3.

"A Song; Written in 1771." *American Museum* 5 (April 1789):408–9.

"A Hymn Sung at the Public Examination of the Scholars, Belonging to the Academy at Greenfield, May 2, 1788." *American Museum* 6 (August 1789):171–72.

"Epistle from Dr. Dwight to Col. Humphreys. Greenfield, 1785." In *The Miscellaneous Works of Colonel Humphreys*. New York: Hodge, Allen, and Campbell, 1790.

Virtuous Rulers a National Blessing: A Sermon, preached at the General Election, May 12, 1791. Hartford: Hudson and Goodwin, 1791.

"The Critics. A Fable." *Gazette of the United States* 3 (13 July 1791):2.

"The Deity and His Dispensations." In *The Beauties of Poetry, British and American*. Ed. Mathew Carey. Philadelphia: M. Carey, 1791.

"Creation." In *The Beauties of Poetry, British and American*. Ed. Mathew Carey. Philadelphia: M. Carey, 1791.

"Original State of Man." In *The Beauties of Poetry, British and American*. Ed. Mathew Carey. Philadelphia: M. Carey, 1791.

"Three Fold State of Man Emblematized." In *The Beauties of Poetry, British and American*. Ed. Mathew Carey. Philadelphia: M. Carey, 1791.

"Prospect of America." In *The Beauties of Poetry, British and American*. Ed. Mathew Carey. Philadelphia: M. Carey, 1791.

"Address of the Genius of Columbia, to the Members of the Continental Convention." In *American Poems*. Vol. I. Ed. Elihu H. Smith. Litchfield, Conn.: Collier and Buel, 1793.

"Message of Mordecai to Esther." In *American Poems*. Vol. I. Ed. Elihu H. Smith. Litchfield, Conn.: Collier and Buel, 1793.

A Discourse on the Genuineness and Authenticity of the New Testament, Delivered at New-Haven. September 10, 1793. New York: George Bunce, 1794.

Greenfield Hill: A Poem in Seven Parts. New York: Child and Swaine, 1794.

"New-England Described." In *The Columbian Muse: A Selection of American Poetry, from Various Authors of Established Reputation*. New York: J. Carey, 1794.

"Picture of a New-England Village." In *The Columbian Muse: A Selection of American Poetry, from Various Authors of Established Reputation*. New York: J. Carey, 1794.

"The House of Sloth." In *The Columbian Muse: A Selection of American Poetry, from Various Authors of Established Reputation*. New York: J. Carey, 1794.

"A Female Worthy." In *The Columbian Muse: A Selection of American Poetry, from Various Authors of Established Reputation*. New York: J. Carey, 1794.

"The Miseries of War." In *The Columbian Muse: A Selection of American Poetry, from Various Authors of Established Reputation*. New York: J. Carey, 1794.

"Extracts from a Thanksgiving Sermon." *Connecticut Courant* 30 (16, 23, and 30 March 1795).

The True Means of Establishing Public Happiness: A Sermon Delivered on the 7th of July, before the Connecticut Society of Cincinnati, and Published at Their Request. New Haven: T. & S. Green, 1795.

The Nature and Danger of Infidel Philsophy, Exhibited in Two Discourses Addressed to the Candidates for the Bacculaureate, in Yale College, September 9, 1797. New Haven: George Bunce, 1798.

A Discourse Preached at the Funeral of the Reverend Elizur Goodrich, D.D., Pastor of the Church in Durham, and One of the Members of the Corporation of Yale-College, November 25, 1797. New Haven: T. and S. Green, 1797.

The Duty of Americans at the Present Crisis, Illustrated in a Discourse, Preached on the Fourth of July, 1798, at the Request of the Citizens of New-Haven. New Haven: Thomas and Samuel Green, 1798.

A Discourse Delivered at New Haven, February 22, 1800, on the Character of George Washington. New Haven: Thomas and Samuel Green, 1800.

The Psalms of David, imitated in the Language of the New Testament, and applied to the Christian Use and Worship by I. Watts, D.D.: A New Edition, in which the Psalms omitted by Dr. Watts are versified, local passages are altered, and a number of Psalms are versified anew, in proper Metres. Hartford: Hudson and Goodwin, 1801.

Comp. *Hymns selected from Dr. Watts, Dr. Doddridge, and various other writers. According to the recommendation of the joint committee of the General association of Conn., and the General Assembly of the Presbyterian Church in America.* Hartford: Hudson and Goodwin, 1801.

"An Extract from 'The Retrospect.'" *Mercury and New-England Palladium* 17 (2 January 1801):1.

A Discourse on Some Events of the Last Century, Delivered in the Brick Church in New-Haven on Wednesday, January 7, 1801. New Haven: Ezra Read, 1801.

"Farmer Johnson's Political Catechism." *Mercury and New-England Palladium* 17 (31 March 1801):1; 17 (3 April 1801):1; 17 (14 April 1801):1; 17 (17 April 1801):1–2; 17 (8 May 1801):1.

"To the Farmers and Mechanics of New-England." *Mercury and New-England Palladium* 17 (12 May 1801):1; 17 (15 May 1801):1; 17 (26 May 1801):1; 17 (5 June 1801):1.

"Morpheus." *Mercury and New-England Palladium* 18 (24 November 1801):1; 18 (27 November 1801):1; 18 (8 December 1801):1; 18 (11 December 1801):1; 18 (15 December 1801):1; 19 (2 March 1802):1; 19 (5 March 1802):1; 19 (9 March 1802):1.

"Brief Acount of the Revival of Religion Now Prevailing in Yale College." *Connecticut Evangelical Magazine* 3 (July 1802):30–33.

A Sermon on the Death of Mr. Ebenezer Grant Marsh, Senior-Tutor and Professor Elect of Languages and Ecclesiastical History in Yale College, who died November 16, 1803, in the 27th year of his Age. Hartford: Hudson & Goodwin, 1804.

The Folly, Guilt, and Mischiefs of Duelling: A Sermon, Preached in the College Chapel at New Haven, on the Sabbath preceding the Annual Commencement, September, 1804. Hartford: Hudson & Goodwin, 1805.

A Sermon Preached at the Opening of the Theological Institution in Andover; and at the Ordination of Rev. Eliphalet Pearson, LL.D., September 28, 1808. Boston: Farrand, Mallory, 1808.

A Discourse, Occasioned by the Death of His Excellency Jonathan Trumbull, Esq., Governor of the State of Connecticut, and Delivered at the Request of the General Assembly in the Brick Church in New-Haven. New Haven: Oliver Steele, 1809.

The Charitable Blessed. A Sermon Preached in the First Church in New-Haven, August 8, 1810. New Haven: Sidney's Press, 1810.

"Lectures on the Evidences of Divine Revelation." *Panoplist and Missionary Magazine United* 3 (June 1810):14–19; 3 (July 1810):57–64; 3 (August 1810):101–11; 3 (September 1810): 114–21; 3 (October 1810):201–8; 3 (November 1810):245–54; 3 (December 1810):295–300; 3 (January 1811):351–56; 3 (February 1811):389–96; 3 (March 1811):441–46; 4 (June 1811):5–11; 4 (July 1811):56–63; 4 (August 1811):106–12; 4 (September 1811):155–60; 4 (January 1812):345–54; 4 (March 1812):436–44; 4 (May 1812):529–36; 9 (June 1813):4–11; 9 (July 1813):49–56; 9 (August 1813):111–17; 9 (December 1813):529–36.

A Statistical Account of the Towns and Parishes in the State of Connecticut. Vol. 1, No. 1. New Haven: Walter & Steele, 1811 (Dwight provided the statistical account of New Haven only, pp. 1–84).

The Dignity and Excellence of the Gospel, Illustrated in a Discourse, Delivered April 3, 1812 at the Ordination of the Rev. Nathaniel W. Taylor, as Pastor of the First Church and Congregation in New-Haven. New York: J. Seymour, 1812.

A Discourse in two Parts Delivered July 23, 1812; on the Public Fast in the Chapel of Yale College. New Haven: Howe and Deforest, 1812.

A Discourse in Two Parts Delivered August 20, 1812 on the National Fast, in the Chapel of Yale College. New York: J. Seymour, 1812.

Sermon Delivered in Boston, Sept. 16, 1813, before the American Board of Commissioners for Foreign Missions at Their Fourth Annual Meeting. Boston: S. T. Armstrong, 1813.

Remarks on the Review of Inchiquin's Letters, Published in the Quarterly Review, Addressed to the Right Honourable George Canning, Esq., By an Inhabitant of New-England. Boston: Samuel T. Armstrong, 1815; modern reprint, with a new foreword by Abe C. Ravitz. New York: MSS Information Corporation, 1970.

Female Benevolent Society. New Haven, s.n., 28 April 1815.

"On the Manner in Which the Scriptures Are to Be Understood." *Panoplist and Missionary Magazine United* 12 (May 1816):193–203; 12 (June 1816):249–56.

"Observations on Light." *Memoirs of the Connecticut Academy of Arts and Sciences* 1 (1816):387–91.

"Observations on Language." *Memoirs of the Connecticut Academy of Arts and Sciences* 1 (1816):365–86.

"Summary Account of the Church of Christ in Yale College." *Religious Intelligencer* 1 (8 June 1816):30–31.

"Observations on the Present State of Religion in the World." *Religious Intelligencer* 1 (10 August 1816):161–64; 1 (17 August 1816):177–80; 1 (24 August 1816):193–96; 1 (31 August 1816):209–12; 1 (7 September 1816):225–28; 1 (14 September 1816):241–46.

"The Maniac of Gadara, an Irregular Ode." *The Panoplist, and Missionary Magazine* 12 (November 1816):526–28.

An Address to the Emigrants from Connecticut, and from New-England Generally, in the New Settlements in the United States. Hartford: Peter B. Gleason, 1817.

Theology, Explained and Defended, in a Series of Sermons. 5 vols. Middletown, Conn.: Charles Lyman, 1818–1819.

Sermons by Timothy Dwight, D.D., LL.D, Late President of Yale College. 2 vols. New Haven: Howe and Durrie and Peck, 1828.

President Dwight's Decisions of Questions Discussed by the Senior Class in Yale College, in
  1813 and 1814. Edited by Theodore Dwight, Jr. New York: Jonathan Leavitt, 1833.
Travels in New England and New York. 4 vols. New Haven: T. Dwight, 1821–1822;
  modern ed., Barbara Miller Solomon, ed., with the assistance of Patricia M. King.
  Cambridge, Massachusetts: Belknap Press of the Harvard University Press, 1969.

III. Select Secondary Bibliography

Adams, H. D. *Life and Writings of Jared Sparks.* Boston: Houghton, Mifflin, 1893.
Addison, Daniel Dulany. "Timothy Dwight." In *The Clergy in American Life and Letters.*
  New York: Macmillan, 1900.
Ahlstrom, Sydney E. "The Scottish Philosophy and American Theology." *Church History*
  24 (1955):257–72.
———. *A Religious History of the American People.* New Haven: Yale University Press,
  1972.
Andrew, John A., III. *From Revivals to Removal: Jeremiah Evarts, the Cherokee Nation, and
  the Search for the Soul of America.* Athens and London: University of Georgia Press,
  1992.
Anon. "Biographical Memoir of the Rev. Timothy Dwight, S.T.D., LL.D." *Port Folio* 4
  (1817):355–69.
Anon. "Biographical Notice of the Rev. Timothy Dwight, S.T.D., L.L.D., Late President
  and Professor of Divinity of Yale College." *Analectic Magazine* 9 (1817):265–81.
Anon. "Timothy Dwight and the Greenfield Academy." *American Historical Record* 2
  (1873):385–87.
Arner, Robert D. "The Connecticut Wits." In Everett Emerson, ed., *American Literature,
  1764–1789: The Revolutionary Years.* Madison: University of Wisconsin Press, 1977.
Bacon, Leonard. "An Old Age of Piety." *American National Preacher* 20 (1846):25–34.
Bacon, Leonard, S. W. S. Dutton, E. W. Robinson, eds., *Contributions to the Ecclesiastical
  History of Connecticut; Prepared under the Direction of the General Association to
  Commemorate the Completion of One Hundred and Fifty Years since Its First Annual
  Assembly.* New Haven: William Kingsley, 1861.
Bainton, Roland H. *Yale and the Ministry: A History of Education for Christian Ministry at
  Yale from the Founding in 1701.* New York: Harper and Brothers, 1957.
Baldwin, Ebenezer. *The History of Yale College, from Its Foundation, A.D. 1700, to the Year
  1838.* New Haven: Benjamin and William Noyes, 1841.
Banner, Lois W. "Religious Benevolence as Social Control: A Critique of an Interpreta-
  tion." *Journal of American History* 60 (1973):23–41.
Beardsley, E. E. *The History of the Episcopal Church in Connecticut.* 2 vols. New York:
  Hurd and Houghton, 1868.
Beattie, James. *An Essay on the Nature and Immutability of Truth; In Opposition to
  Sophistry and Skepticism.* Edinburgh: A Kincaid and J. Bell, 1770; rpt. New York:
  Garland, 1983.
Beckwith, Francis J. *David Hume's Argument against Miracles: A Critical Analysis.*
  Lanham: University Press of America, 1989.
Bellamy, Joseph. *Four Sermons on the Wisdom of God in the Premission of Sin.* Morristown,
  N.J.: Henry P. Russell, 1804.
Berk, Stephen. *Calvinism Versus Democracy: Timothy Dwight and the Origins of American
  Evangelical Orthodoxy.* Hamden, Conn.: Archon Books, 1974.

Bevilacqua, Vincent M. "Philosophical Assumptions Underlying Hugh Blair's Lectures in Rhetoric and Belles Lettres." *Western Speech* 31 (1967):150–64.

Birdsall, Richard D. "The Second Great Awakening and the New England Social Order." *Church History* 39 (1970):345–64.

Blair, Hugh. *Lectures on Rhetoric and Belles Lettres*. 3 vols. New York: Garland, 1885; 1970.

Bloch, Ruth H. *Visionary Republic: Millennial Themes in American Thought, 1756–1800*. Cambridge: Cambridge University Press, 1985.

Bodo, John R. *The Protestant Clergy and Public Issues,1812–1848*. Princeton: Princeton University Press, 1954.

Bogue, Carl. *Jonathan Edwards and the Covenant of Grace*. Cherry Hill: Mack Publishing, 1975.

Brand, David C. *Profile of the Last Puritan: Jonathan Edwards, Self-Love, and the Dawn of the Beatific*. AAR Academy Series. Atlanta: Scholars Press, 1991.

Brauer, Jerald C. *Protestantism in America: A Narrative History*. Philadelphia: Westminster Press, 1953.

Breitenbach, William. "Unregenerate Doings: Selflessness and Selfishness in New Divinity Theology." *American Quarterly* 34 (1982):479–502.

———. "The Consistent Calvinism of the New Divinity Movement." *William and Mary Quarterly,* 3rd ser., 41 (1984): 241–64.

———. "Piety and Moralism: Edwards and the New Divinity." In *Jonathan Edwards and the American Experience*. Ed. Nathan O. Hatch and Harry S. Stout. New York: Oxford University Press, 1988.

Briceland, Alan V. "John C. Ogden: Messenger and Propagandist for Matthew Lyon, 1798–1799." *Vermont History* 43 (1975): 103–21.

———. "The Phildelphia Aurora, the New England Illuminati, and the Election of 1800." *Pennsylvania Magazine of History and Biography* 100 (1976):3–36.

Briggs, Peter. "Timothy Dwight 'Composes' a Landscape for New England." *American Quarterly* 40 (1988):359–77.

Brown, Chandros Michael. *Benjamin Silliman: A Life in the Young Republic*. Princeton: Princeton University Press, 1989.

Brown, E. Francis. *Joseph Hawley: Colonial Radical*. New York: Columbia University Press, 1931.

Brown, Richard D. "The Confiscation and Disposition of Loyalists' Estates in Suffolk County, Massachusetts." *William and Mary Quarterly,* 3rd ser., 21 (1964):534–50.

Buchanan, Lewis. "The Ethical Ideas of Timothy Dwight." *Research Studies, State College of Washington* 13 (1945):185–99.

Buell, Lawrence. "Literature and Scripture in New England." *Notre Dame English Journal* 15 (1983):1–28.

———. *New England Literary Culture: From Revolution through Renaissance*. New York: Cambridge University Press, 1986.

Bushman, Richard L. *From Puritan to Yankee: Character and Social Order in Connecticut, 1690–1765*. Cambridge: Harvard University Press, 1967.

Buss, Dietrich. "The Millennial Vision of Motive for Religious Benevolence and Reform: Timothy Dwight and the New England Evangelicals Reconsidered." *Fides et Historia* 16 (1983):18–34.

Butler, Jon. "Enthusiasm Described and Decried: The Great Awakening as Interpretive Fiction." *Journal of American History* 69 (1982):305–25.

Campbell, George. *A Dissertation on Miracles: Containing an Examination of the Principles Advanced by David Hume, Esq.; In an Essay on Miracles.* New York: Garland, 1762; 1983.

———. *The Philosophy of Rhetoric.* Ed. Lloyd F. Bitzer. Carbondale: Southern Illinois Press, 1963; 1776.

Chapin, Calvin. *A Sermon Delivered 14th January, 1817, at the Funeral of the Rev. Timothy Dwight, D.D., LL.D., President of Yale College, in New Haven, and Professor of Divinity in the Institution, Who Died January 11th, 1817, in the Sixty-Fifth Year of His Age and Twenty-Second of His Presidency.* New Haven: Maltby and Goldsmith, 1817.

Chappell, V. C. "Introduction." In *The Philosophy of David Hume.* The Modern Library of the World's Best Books. New York: Random House, 1963.

Charvat, William. *The Origins of American Critical Thought: 1810–1835.* New York: Russell and Russell, 1968; 1936.

Chauncey, Nathaniel. *An Address Delivered before the New England Society of Philadelphia, on the Fourth of May, 1818.* Philadelphia: Office of the Union, 1818.

Clark, Gregory. "Timothy Dwight's Moral Rhetoric at Yale College, 1795–1817." *Rhetorica* 5 (1987):149–61.

Clebsch, William A. *From Sacred to Profane in America: The Role of Religion in American Culture.* New York: Harper and Row, 1968.

Cole, Charles C. *The Social Ideas of the Northern Evangelists, 1826–1860.* New York: Columbia University Press, 1954.

Conforti, Joseph. *Samuel Hopkins and the New Divinity Movement: Calvinism, the Congregational Ministry, and Reform in New England between the Great Awakenings.* Grand Rapids: Eerdmans, 1981.

———. "Antebellum Evangelicals and the Cultural Revival of Jonathan Edwards." *American Presbyterianism* 64 (1986):227–41.

———. "Edwardsians, Unitarians, and the Memory of the Great Awakening." In *American Unitarianism, 1805–1865.* Ed. Conrad Edick Wright. Boston: Massachusetts Historical Society and Northeastern University Press, 1989.

———. "The Invention of the Great Awakening, 1795–1842." *Early American Literature* 26 (1991):99–118.

Conkin, Paul R. *Cane Ridge: America's Pentecost.* Madison: University of Wisconsin Press, 1990.

Cross, Barbara M., ed. *The Autobiography of Lyman Beecher.* 2 vols. Cambridge: Harvard University Press, 1961.

Cuningham, Charles. *Timothy Dwight, 1752–1817, A Biography.* New York: Macmillan, 1942.

Davidson, James West. *The Logic of Millennial Thought: Eighteenth-Century New England.* New Haven: Yale University Press, 1977.

Davis, Samuel. "Journal of a Tour of Connecticut in the Autumn of 1789." Massachusetts Historical Society, *Proceedings,* 1st ser. (1869–1870):9–32.

Davis, Matthew L., ed. *Memoirs of Aaron Burr: With Miscellaneous Selections from His Correspondence,* 2 vols. New York: Harper & Brothers, 1836; rpt. New York: DaCapo Press, 1971.

Dexter, Franklin B. *Biographical Sketches of the Graduates of Yale College with Annals of the College History.* 6 vols. New York: Henry Holt, 1903.

———, ed. *The Literary Diary of Ezra Stiles, D.D., LL.D.* 3 vols. New York: Charles Scribner's Sons, 1901.

Diamond, Peter J. "Rhetoric and Philosophy in the Social Thought of Thomas Reid." *Eighteenth Century Life* 15 (1991):57–80.

Dodds, Elizabeth D. *Marriage to a Difficult Man: The "Uncommon Union" of Jonathan and Sarah Edwards.* Philadelphia: Westminster Press, 1971.

Dowling, William C. "Joel Barlow and the Anarchiad." *Early American Literature* 25 (1990):18–33.

———. *Poetry and Ideology in Revolutionary Connecticut.* Athens: University of Georgia Press, 1990.

Dwight, Benjamin W. *The History of the Descendants of John Dwight of Dedham, Massachusetts.* 2 vols. New York: John F. Trow and Sons, 1874.

Dwight, Sereno E. *The Life of President Edwards.* New York: G. and C. and H. Carvill, 1830.

Edney, Clarence W. "Campbell's *Lectures on Pulpit Eloquence.*" *Speech Monographs* 19 (1952):1–10.

Edwards, Jonathan. *Freedom of the Will.* Ed. Paul Ramsey. *The Works of Jonathan Edwards.* Vol. 1. New Haven: Yale University Press, 1957.

———. *The Great Doctrine of Original Sin Defended.* Ed. Clyde Holbrook. *The Works of Jonathan Edwards.* Vol. 3. New Haven: Yale University Press, 1970.

———. *The Great Awakening.* Ed. C. C. Goen. *The Works of Jonathan Edwards.* Vol. 6. New Haven: Yale University Press, 1972.

———. "God's Awful Judgement in the Breaking and Withering of the Strong Rods of a Community." In *The Works of Jonathan Edwards.* 2 vols. Ed. Edward Hicks. Edinburgh and Carlisle, Pa.: Banner of Truth Trust, 1974.

———. *Dissertation on the End for Which God Created the World.* In *The Works of Jonathan Edwards.* 2 vols. Ed. Edward Hicks. Edinburgh and Carlisle, Pa.: Banner of Truth Trust, 1974.

———. *Dissertation on the Nature of True Virtue.* In *The Works of Jonathan Edwards.* 2 vols. Ed. Edward Hicks. Edinburgh and Carlisle, Pa.: Banner of Truth Trust, 1974.

———. *Scientific and Philosophical Writings.* Ed. Wallace E. Anderson. *The Works of Jonathan Edwards.* Vol 6. New Haven: Yale University Press, 1980.

Edwards, Jonathan, Jr. *The Faithful Manifestation of the Truth, the Proper and Immediate End of Preaching the Gospel. A Sermon Delivered November 5, 1783, at the Ordination of the Reverend Timothy Dwight, to the Pastoral Office over the Church in Greenfield.* New Haven: Thomas and Samuel Green, 1783.

Elliott, Emory. *Revolutionary Writers: Literature and Authority in the New Republic, 1725–1810.* New York: Oxford University Press, 1983.

Fain, William M. "A Study of the Preaching of Timothy Dwight." Th.D. diss., New Orleans Baptist Theological Seminary, 1970.

Faust, Clarence and Johnson, Thomas H., eds. *Jonathan Edwards: Representative Selections.* New York: Hill and Wang, 1935.

Ferm, Robert L. *Jonathan Edwards the Younger, 1745–1801: A Colonial Pastor.* Grand Rapids: Eerdmans, 1976.

Finke, Roger and Rodney Stark. *The Churching of America, 1776–1990: Winners and Losers in Our Religious Economy.* New Brunswick: Rutgers University Press, 1992.

Fischer, David H. *The Revolution of American Conservatism: The Federalist Party in the Era of Jeffersonian Democracy.* New York: Harper and Row, 1965.

Fisher, George Park. *Life of Benjamin Silliman, M.D., LL.D.* 2 vols. Philadelphia: Porter and Coates, 1866.

———. *Discussions in History and Theology.* New York: Charles Scribner's Sons, 1880.

Fitzmier, John R. "The Godly Federalism of Timothy Dwight, 1752–1817: Society, Doctrine, and Religion in the Life of New England's 'Moral Legislator.'" Ph.D. diss., Princeton University, 1986.

Foster, Charles I. *Errand of Mercy: The Evangelical United Front, 1790–1837.* Chapel Hill: University of North Carolina Press, 1960.

Foster, Frank Hugh. *A Genetic History of the New England Theology.* Chicago: University of Chicago Press, 1907.

Fox, Dixon Ryan. "The Protestant Counter-Reformation in America." *New York History* 16 (1935):19–35.

Frank, Von. *The Sacred Game: Provincialism and Frontier Consciousness in American Literature, 1630–1860.* New York: Cambridge University Press, 1985.

Freimarck, Vincent. "Timothy Dwight's Dissertation on the Bible." *American Literature* 26 (1952):73–77.

———. "Rhetoric at Yale in 1807." *Proceedings of the American Philosophical Society,* 110 (1966):235–55.

Gabriel, Ralph Henry. *Religion and Learning at Yale: The Church of Christ in the College and University, 1757–1957.* New Haven: Yale University Press, 1958.

Gaustad, Edwin S. *George Berkeley in America.* New Haven: Yale University Press, 1979.

Gibbs, George, ed. *Memoirs of the Administrations of Washington and John Adams, Edited from the Papers of Oliver Wolcott, Secretary of the Treasury.* Vol. 1. New York: William Van Norden, 1846.

Golden, James. "Hugh Blair: Minister of St. Giles." *Quarterly Journal of Speech* 38 (1952):155–60.

Good, L. Douglas. "The Christian Nation in the Mind of Timothy Dwight." *Fides et Historia* 7 (1974):1–18.

Goodrich, S. G. *Recollections of a Lifetime: Men and Things I Have Seen, in a Series of Letters to a Friend, Historical, Biographical, Anecdotical, and Descriptive.* 2 vols. New York: Auburn, Miller, Orton, and Mulligan, 1857.

Grasso, Christopher D. "Between Awakenings: Learned Men and the Transformations of Public Discourse in Connecticut, 1740–1800." Ph.D. diss., Yale University, 1992.

Grave, S. A. *The Scottish Philosophy of Common Sense.* Oxford: Clarendon Press, 1960.

Green, Ashbel. *Life of Ashbel Green, V.D.M.* New York: Robert Carter and Brothers, 1849.

Greene, Evarts. "A Puritan Counter-Reformation." American Antiquarian Society, *Proceedings* 42 (1932):17–46.

Gribbin, William. "The Legacy of Timothy Dwight: A Reappraisal." *Connecticut Historical Society Bulletin* 37 (1972):33–41.

Griffin, Clifford. *Their Brothers' Keeper: Moral Stewardship in the United States, 1800–1865.* New Brunswick: Rutgers University Press, 1960.

Griffin, Nicholas J. "Possible Theological Perspectives in Thomas Reid's Common Sense Philosophy." *Journal of Ecclesiastical History* 41 (1990):425–42.

Griffith, John. "*The Columbiad* and *Greenfield Hill*: History, Poetry, and Ideology in the Late Eighteenth Century." *Early American Literature* 10 (1975–1976):235–50.

Griswold, Rufus Wilmot. *The Prose Writers of America, with a Survey of the Intellectual History, Condition, and Prospects of the Country.* 4th ed., rev. Philadelphia: A. Hart, 1851.

Guelzo, Allen C. *Edwards on the Will: A Century of American Theological Debate.* Middletown: Wesleyan University Press, 1989.

Hall, Charles S. *The Life and Letters of General Samuel H. Parsons.* New York: James Pugliese Archives, 1968.

Harding, Walter. "Timothy Dwight and Thoreau." *Boston Public Library Quarterly* 10 (1958):109–15.

Haroutunian, Joseph. *Piety Versus Moralism, the Passing of New England Theology.* New York: Henry Holt, 1932.

Harris, Marc L. "Revelation and the American Republic: Timothy Dwight's Civic Participation." *Journal of the History of Ideas* 54 (1993):449–68.

Haswell, Anthony. *Memoirs of Captain Matthew Phelps of New Haven.* Bennington, Vt.: n.p., 1802.

Hatch, Nathan O. *The Sacred Cause of Liberty: Republican Thought and the Millennium in Revolutionary New England.* New Haven: Yale University Press, 1977.

———. *The Democratization of American Christianity.* New Haven: Yale University Press, 1989.

Heppe, Heinrich. *Reformed Dogmatics Set Out and Illustrated from the Sources.* Trans. G. T. Thomson. Rev. and ed. Ernest Bizer. London: George Allen and Unwin Ltd., 1956.

Hoffelt, R. David. "Pragmatics of Persuasion and Disciplines of Piety: The Influence of Timothy Dwight in American Preaching." Ph.D. diss., Princeton Theological Seminary, 1983.

Hofstadter, Richard. *The Paranoid Style in American Politics, and Other Essays.* New York: Alfred Knopf, 1965.

Hopkins, Samuel. *Sin, thro' Divine Interposition, an Advantage to the Universe . . . In Three Sermons.* Boston: n.p., 1773.

———. *The System of Doctrine Contained in Divine Revelation, Explained and Defended, Shewing Their Consistence and Connexion with Each Other, to Which is Added, a Treatise on the Millennium.* 2 vols. 2nd ed. Boston: Lincoln and Edmands, 1811.

Howard, Leon. *The Connecticut Wits.* Chicago: University of Chicago Press, 1943.

Howe, Daniel Walker. *The Unitarian Conscience: Harvard Moral Philosophy, 1805–1861.* Cambridge: Harvard University Press, 1970.

Howell, Wilbur Samuel. *Eighteenth-Century British Logic and Rhetoric.* Princeton: Princeton University Press, 1971.

Hume, David. *The Philosophical Works of David Hume, Including the Essays, and Exhibiting the More Important Alterations and Corrections in the Successive Editions Published by the Author.* 4 vols. Edinburgh: Black and Tate, 1826.

Hume, David. *A Treatise of Human Nature.* Rpt. New York: Clarendon Press, 1978.

Isani, Mukhtar Ali. "Far from 'Gambia's Golden Shore': The Black in Late Eighteenth-Century American Imaginative Literature." *William and Mary Quarterly,* 3rd ser., 36 (1979):353–72.

Jackson, John Brinckerhoff. "A Puritan Looks at Scenery." In *Discovering the Vernacular Landscape.* New Haven: Yale University Press, 1984.

Jones, Douglas L. "The Strolling Poor: Transiency in Eighteenth-Century Massachusetts." *Journal of Social History* 8 (1975): 28–49.

Julian, John. *A Dictionary of Hymnology, Setting Forth the Origin and History of Christian Hymns of All Ages and Nations.* 2nd ed. London: John Murray, 1908.

Kafer, Peter K. "The Making of Timothy Dwight: A Connecticut Morality Tale." *William and Mary Quarterly,* 3rd ser., 47 (1990):189–209.

Kamensky, Jane. "'In These Contrasted Climes, How Chang'd the Scene': Progress,

Declension, and Balance in the Landscapes of Timothy Dwight." *New England Quarterly* 63 (1990):80–108.

Keller, Charles Roy. *The Second Great Awakening in Connecticut.* New Haven: Yale University Press, 1942.

Kelley, Brooks Mather. *Yale: A History.* New Haven: Yale University Press, 1979.

Kennedy, George A. *Classical Rhetoric and Its Christian and Secular Tradition from Ancient to Modern Times.* Chapel Hill: University of North Carolina Press, 1980.

Kerber, Linda K. *Federalists in Dissent: Imagery and Ideology in Jeffersonian America.* Ithaca: Cornell University Press, 1970.

Kling, David W. *A Field of Divine Wonders: The New Divinity and Village Revivals in Northwestern Connecticut, 1792–1822.* University Park, Pa: Pennsylvania State University Press, 1993.

Kuklick, Bruce. *Churchmen and Philosophers: From Jonathan Edwards to John Dewey.* New Haven: Yale University Press, 1985.

Lawson-Peebles, Robert. *Landscape and Written Expression in Revolutionary America: The World Turned Upside Down.* Cambridge: Cambridge University Press, 1988.

Leary, Lewis. "The Author of the Triumph of Infidelity." *New England Quarterly* 20 (1947):377–85.

Lee, Robert Edson. "Timothy Dwight and the Boston Palladium." *New England Quarterly* 35 (1962):229–38.

Lehmann, William C. *Henry Home, Lord Kames, and the Scottish Enlightenment: A Study in National Character and the History of Ideas.* The Hague: Martinus Nijhoff, 1971.

Lockridge, Kenneth. *A New England Town, the First One Hundred Years: Dedham, Massachusetts, 1636–1736.* New York: W. W. Norton, 1970.

Lothers, William T. "The Concept and Rhetorical Treatment of Sin in Selected Sermons of Timothy Dwight." M.A. thesis, University of Oklahoma, 1957.

Lovelace, Richard F. *The Dynamics of Spiritual Life.* Downers Grove, Ill.: Inter Varsity Press, 1979.

Lowance, Mason. *The Language of Canaan: Metaphor and Symbol in New England from the Puritans to the Transcendentalists.* Cambridge: Harvard University Press, 1980.

MacIntyre, Alasdair. *After Virtue, A Study in Moral Theory.* Notre Dame: University of Notre Dame Press, 1981.

Mackay, Angus J. "David Hume." In *Philosophers of the Enlightenment.* Ed. Peter Gilmour. Totowa, N.J.: Barnes and Noble Books, 1990.

Marini, Stephen A. *Radical Sects of Revolutionary New England.* Cambridge: Harvard University Press, 1982.

———. "Religious Revolution in the District of Maine, 1780–1820." In *Maine in the Early Republic: From Revolution to Statehood.* Ed. Charles E. Clark, James S. Leamon, and Karen Bowden. Hanover: University of New England Press, 1988.

Marsden, George M. *The Evangelical Mind and the New School Presbyterian Experience: A Case Study of Thought and Theology in Nineteenth-Century America.* New Haven: Yale University Press, 1970.

Marty, Martin E. *The Infidel: Freethought and American Religion.* Cleveland: World Publishing, 1961.

Mather, Cotton. *Magnalia Christi Americana, Books I and II.* Ed. Kenneth B. Murdock with the assistance of Elizabeth Miller. Cambridge: Belknap Press of Harvard University Press, 1977.

May, Henry F. *The Enlightenment in America.* New York: Oxford University Press, 1976.

McCusker, John J. *Money and Exchange in Europe and America, 1600–1775.* Chapel Hill: University of North Carolina Press, 1978.

McDermott, Gerald R. "Civil Religion in the American Revolutionary Period: An Historiographic Analysis." *Christian Scholar's Review* 18 (1989):346–62.

McGuinness, Arthur E. *Henry Home, Lord Kames.* New York: Twayne, 1970.

McKirdy, Charles Robert. "Lawyers in Crisis: The Massachusetts Legal Profession, 1760–1790." Ph.D. diss., Northwestern University, 1969.

McLoughlin, William G. *New England Dissent, 1630–1889: The Baptists and the Separation of Church and State.* 2 vols. Cambridge: Harvard University Press, 1971.

———. "The Role of Religion in the Revolution: Liberty of Conscience and Cultural Cohesion in the New Nation." *Essays on the American Revolution.* Ed. Stephen G. Kurtz and James H. Hutson. Chapel Hill: University of North Carolina Press, 1973.

McTaggart, William J. and William K. Bottoroff, eds. *The Major Poems of Timothy Dwight (1752–1817), with a Dissertation on the History, Eloquence, and Poetry of the Bible.* Gainesville, Fla.: Scholars' Facsimiles and Reprints, 1969.

Mead, Sidney E. *Nathaniel William Taylor, 1786–1858, a Connecticut Liberal.* Chicago: University of Chicago Press, 1942.

———. *The Old Religion in the Brave New World: Reflections on the Relation between Christendom and the Republic.* Berkeley: University of California Press, 1977.

Miller, Perry. *Jonathan Edwards.* New York: William Sloane Associates, 1949.

———. *Errand into the Wilderness.* New York: Harper and Row, 1956.

———. *The Life of the Mind in America: From the Revolution to the Civil War, Books One through Three.* New York: Harcourt, Brace, and World, 1965.

Miller, Thomas P. "Witherspoon, Blair, and the Rhetoric of Civic Humanism." In *Scotland and America in the Age of Enlightenment.* Ed. Richard B. Sher and Jeffrey R. Smitten. Princeton: Princeton University Press, 1990.

Morgan, Edmund S. *The Gentle Puritan: A Life of Ezra Stiles, 1727–1795.* New Haven: Yale University Press, 1962.

———. "Ezra Stiles and Timothy Dwight." Massachusetts Historical Society, *Proceedings* 72 (1963):101–17.

Morgan, Edmund S. and Morgan, Helen M. *The Stamp Act Crisis: Prologue to Revolution.* Rev. ed. London: Collier Books, 1963.

Murray, Iain H. *Jonathan Edwards: A New Biography.* Carlisle, Pa.: Banner of Truth Trust, 1987.

Murrin, John M. "The Great Inversion, or Court Versus Country: A Comparison of the Revolution Settlements in England (1688–1721) and America (1776–1816)." In *Three British Revolutions: 1641, 1688, 1776.* Ed. J. G. A. Pocock. Princeton: Princeton University Press, 1980.

Nash, Gary B. *The Urban Crucible: Social Change, Political Consciousness, and the Origins of the American Revolution.* Cambridge: Harvard University Press, 1979.

Nobles, Gregory H. *Divisions throughout the Whole: Politics and Society in Hampshire County, Massachusetts, 1740–1755.* Cambridge: Cambridge University Press, 1983.

Noll, Mark A. "Common Sense Traditions and American Evangelical Thought." *American Quarterly* 37 (1985):216–38.

———. *Princeton and the Republic, 1768–1822: The Search for a Christian Enlightenment in the Era of Samuel Stanhope Smith.* Princeton: Princeton University Press, 1989.

———, ed. *The Princeton Theology, 1821–1921: Scripture, Science, and Theological Method from Archibald Alexander to Benjamin Breckinridge Warfield.* Grand Rapids: Baker Book House, 1983.

Novak, Stephen J. *The Rights of Youth: American Colleges and Student Revolts, 1798–1815.* Cambridge: Harvard University Press, 1977.

Ogden, John C. *A Useful Essay, Being an Account of the Excellency of the Common Prayer of the Episcopal Church.* Hanover: Josiah Dunham, 1793.

———. *An Appeal to the Candid, upon the Present State of Religion and Politics in Connecticut.* New Haven: n.p., 1798.

———. *Friendly Remarks to the People of Connecticut, upon Their Colleges and Schools.* N.p.: 1799.

Olmstead, Denison. "Timothy Dwight as a Teacher." *Journal of American Education* 6 (1858):567–85.

Park, Edwards Amasa. *New England Theology; With Comments on a Third Article in the Princeton Review, Relating to a Convention Sermon.* Andover: Warren Draper, 1852.

———. *The Atonement: Discourses and Treatises by Edwards, Smalley, Maxcy, Emmons, Griffin, Burge, and Weeks. With an Introductory Essay by Edwards A. Park.* Boston: Congregational Publishing Society, 1859.

Parrington, Vernon L. *Main Currents in American Thought.* 2 vols. New York: Harcourt, Brace, 1927.

———, ed. *The Connecticut Wits.* New York: Harcourt, Brace, 1926.

Phillips, Joseph W. *Jedidiah Morse and New England Congregationalism.* New Brunswick: Rutgers University Press, 1983.

Pierce, John. "Dr. John Pierce's Manuscript Journal." Massachusetts Historical Society *Proceedings* 3 (1886–1887):46.

Pointer, Richard W. *Protestant Pluralism and the New York Experience: A Study of Eighteenth-Century Religious Diversity.* Bloomington: Indiana University Press, 1988.

Pope, Robert G. "New England Versus the New England Mind: The Myth of Declension." *Journal of Social History* 3 (1969–70):95–108.

Porter, Noah. "Philosophy in Great Britain and America: A Supplementary Sketch." In *History of Philosophy from Thales to the Present Time.* 2 vols. By Friedrich Ueberweg. New York: Charles Scribner's Sons, 1909.

Purcell, Richard. *Connecticut in Transition: 1755–1818.* Middletown, Conn.: Wesleyan University Press, 1963; 1918.

Rabinowitz, Richard. *The Spiritual Self in Everyday Life: The Transformation of Personal Religious Experience in Nineteenth-Century New England.* Boston: Northeastern University Press, 1989.

Randall, Helen W. "The Critical Theory of Lord Kames." *Smith College Studies in Modern Languages* 22 (1940–41):1–147.

Ravitz, Abe C. "Timothy Dwight: Professor of Rhetoric." *New England Quarterly* 39 (1956):63–72.

———. "Timothy Dwight's Decisions." *New England Quarterly* 31 (1958):514–19.

———, ed. *Remarks on the Review of Inchiquin's Letters by Timothy Dwight.* New York: Garrett Press, 1970.

Rawlyk, G. A. *Ravished by the Spirit: Religious Revivals, Baptists, and Henry Alline.* Kingston: McGill-Queen's University Press, 1984.

Reid, Thomas. *The Works of Thomas Reid, D.D., Now Fully Collected, with Selections from His Unpublished Letters.* 6th ed. 2 vols. Ed. Sir William Hamilton. Edinburgh: Maclachlan and Stewart, 1863.

Robinson, William A. *Jeffersonian Democracy in New England.* New Haven: Yale University Press, 1916.

Rogal, Samuel J. *A General Introduction to Hymnody and Congregational Song.* Metuchen.

N.J.: American Theological Library Association and Scarecrow Press, 1991.

Rohrer, James R. *Keepers of the Covenant: Frontier Missions and the Decline of Congregationalism, 1774–1818.* New York: Oxford University Press, 1995.

Ross, Simpson. *Lord Kames and the Scotland of His Day.* Oxford: Clarendon Press, 1972.

Rossiter, Clinton. *Conservatism in America.* New York: Alfred A. Knopf, 1955.

Rudisill, Dorus Paul. *The Doctrine of the Atonement in Jonathan Edwards and His Succesors.* New York: Poseidon Books, 1971.

Samuels, Shirley. "Infidelity and Contagion: The Rhetoric of Revolution." *Early American Literature* 22 (1987):183–91.

Schmitz, Robert M. *Hugh Blair.* New York: King's Crown Press, 1948.

Sears, John F. "Timothy Dwight and the American Landscape: The Composing Eye in Dwight's *Travels in New England and New York.*" *Early American Literature* 11 (1976–1977):311–21.

Sher, Richard B. *Church and University in the Scottish Enlightenment: The Moderate Literati of Edinburgh.* Princeton: Princeton University Press, 1985.

Shiber, Paul T. "The Conquest of Canaan as a Youthful Expression of Timothy Dwight's New Divinity and Political Thought." Ph.D. diss., University of Miami, 1972.

Shiels, Richard D. "The Connecticut Clergy in the Second Great Awakening." Ph.D. diss., Brown University, 1976.

———. "The Second Great Awakening in Connecticut: Critique of the Traditional Interpretation." *Church History* 49 (1980):401–15.

Silliman, Benjamin. *A Sketch of the Life and Character of President Dwight, Delivered as a Eulogium, in New Haven, February 12, 1817, before the Academic Body of Yale College, Composed of the Senatus Academic, Faculty, and Students.* New Haven: Maltby and Goldsmith, 1817.

Silverman, Kenneth. *Timothy Dwight.* New York: Twayne Publishers, 1969.

———. *A Cultural History of the American Revolution: Painting, Music, Literature, and the Theatre in the Colonies and the United States from the Treaty of Paris to the Inauguration of George Washington, 1763–1789.* New York: Crowell, 1976.

Smith, Emily A. *Life and Letters of Nathan Smith.* New Haven: Yale University Press, 1914.

Smith, H. Shelton. *Changing Conceptions of Original Sin: A Study in American Theology since 1750.* New York: Charles Scribner's Sons, 1955.

Snyder, K. Alan. "Foundations of Liberty: The Christian Republicanism of Timothy Dwight and Jedidiah Morse." *New England Quarterly* 56 (1983):382–97.

Spears, Timothy B. "Common Observations: Timothy Dwight's *Travels in New England and New York.*" *American Studies* 30 (1989):35–52.

Sprague, William. *Annals of the American Pulpit.* 9 vols. New York: R. Carter and Brothers, 1857–1869.

Spring, Gardiner. *An Oration on the Evening of the Fifth of February, before the Alumni of Yale College, Resident in the City of New York, in Commemoration of Their Late President, Timothy Dwight, D.D., LL.D.* New York: Dodge and Sayre, 1817.

Stalley, R. F. "Common Sense and Enlightenment: The Philosophy of Thomas Reid." In *Philosophers of the Enlightenment.* Ed. Peter Gilmour. Totowa, N.J.: Barnes and Noble Books, 1990.

Stein, Stephen J. "Transatlantic Extensions: Apocalyptic in Early New England." In *The Apocalypse in English and Renaissance Thought and Literature.* Ed. C. A. Patrides and Joseph Witttreich. Ithaca: Cornell University Press, 1984.

Stevens, Abel. "Review of Dwight's *Theology, Explained and Defended.*" *Methodist Quarterly Review,* 3rd ser., 7 (1847):336–37.

Stilgoe, John R. "Smiling Scenes." In *Views and Visions: American Landscape before 1830.* Ed. Edward J. Nygren. Washington: Corcoran Gallery of Art, 1986.

Stillinger, Jack. "Dwight's *Triumph of Infidelity*: Text and Interpretation." *Studies in Bibliography: Papers of the Bibliography Society of the University of Virginia* 15 (1962): 259–66.

Stinchcombe, William. *The XYZ Affair.* Westport: Greenwood Press, 1980.

Stout, Harry S. "Rhetoric and Reality in the Early Republic: The Case of the Federalist Clergy." In *Religion and American Politics: From the Colonial Period to the 1980s.* Ed. Mark A. Noll. New York: Oxford University Press, 1990.

Sweeney, Douglas. "Nathaniel William Taylor and the Edwardsean Tradition: Evolution and Continuity in the Culture of the New England Theology." Ph.D. diss., Vanderbilt University, 1995.

Sweet, Douglas H. "Church Vitality and the American Revolution: Historiographical Consensus and Thoughts Toward a New Perspective." *Church History* 45 (1976):341–57.

Tarbox, Increase, ed. *The Diary of Thomas Robbins, D.D.* 2 vols. Boston: Beacon Press, 1886.

Taylor, John. *The Scripture Doctrine of Original Sin Proposed to Free and Candid Examination.* London, n.p., 1740.

Taylor, Robert J. *Western Massachusetts in the Revolution.* Providence: Brown University Press, 1954.

Thomas, Edmund B., Jr. "Politics in the Land of Steady Habits: Connecticut's First Political Party System, 1789–1820." Ph.D. diss., Clark University, 1972.

Tichi, Cecelia. *New World, New Earth: Environmental Reform in American Literature from the Puritans through Whitman.* New Haven: Yale University Press, 1979.

Toulouse, Teresa. *The Art of Prophesying: New England Sermons and the Shaping of Belief.* Athens, Georgia: University of Georgia Press, 1987.

Tracy, Patricia. *Jonathan Edwards, Pastor: Religion and Society in Eighteenth-Century Northampton.* New York: Hill and Wang, 1980.

Trumbull, James Russell. *The History of Northampton from Its Settlement in 1654.* 2 vols. Northampton, n.p., 1898.

Tuveson, Ernest L. *Redeemer Nation: The Idea of America's Millennial Role.* Chicago: University of Chicago Press, 1968.

Tyler, Moses Coit. *Three Men of Letters.* New York: G. P. Putnam's Sons, 1895.

Tyner, Wayne C. "The Theology of Timothy Dwight in Historical Perspective." Ph.D. diss., University of North Carolina at Chapel Hill, 1971.

Valeri, Mark. *Law and Providence in Joseph Bellamy's New England: The Origins of the New Divinity in Revolutionary America.* New York: Oxford University Press, 1994.

Volkomer, Walter E. "Timothy Dwight and New England Federalism." *Connecticut Review* 3 (1970):72–82.

Webb, Anne Baxter. "On the Eve of the Revolution: Northampton, Massachusetts, 1750–1775." Ph.D. diss., University of Minnesota, 1976.

Webster, Samuel. *A Winter Evenings Conversation upon the Doctrine of Original Sin.* Boston: Green and Russell, 1757.

Weinsheimer, Joel C. *Eighteenth-Century Hermeneutics: Philosophy of Interpretation from Locke to Burke.* New Haven: Yale University Press, 1993.

Wenzke, Annabelle S. *Timothy Dwight (1752–1817)*. Lewiston, N.Y.: Edwin Mellen Press, 1989.

Whitford, Kathryn. "'The Young Officer Who Rode Beside Me': An Examination of Nineteenth-Century Naming Conventions." *American Studies* 23 (1982):5–22.

———. "Excursions in Romanticism: Timothy Dwight's Travels." *Papers on Language and Literature* 2 (1966):225–33.

Whitford, Kathryn and Philip Whitford. "Timothy Dwight's Place in Eighteenth-Century American Science." *Proceedings of the American Philosophical Association* 114 (1970):60–71.

Winship, Alfred E. *Heredity: A History of the Jukes-Edwards Families*. Boston: Journal of Education, 1925.

Winslow, Ola. *Jonathan Edwards, 1703–1758, A Biography*. New York: Macmillan, 1940.

Wood, John. *The History of the Administration of John Adams, Esquire, Late President of the United States*. New York, n.p., 1802.

Woods, Leonard. *History of Andover Theological Seminary*. Boston: James Osgood and Co., 1885.

Wright, Conrad. *The Beginnings of Unitarianism in America*. Boston: Starr King Press, 1955.

Zemsky, Robert. *Merchants, Farmers, and River Gods: An Essay on Eighteenth-Century American Politics*. Boston: Gambit Press, 1971.

Zuckerman, Michael. *Peaceable Kingdoms: New England Towns in the Eighteenth Century*. New York: Knopf, 1970.

Zunder, Theodore. "Noah Webster and the Conquest of Canaan." *American Literature* I (1929):200–2.

Index

Index

John R. Fitzmier is Associate Dean of the Divinity School and assistant professor of American religious history at Vanderbilt University. He was educated at the University of Pittsburgh, Gordon Conwell Theological Seminary, and Princeton University. He has published *The Presbyterians*, with Randall Balmer, as well as several articles about American religious history.